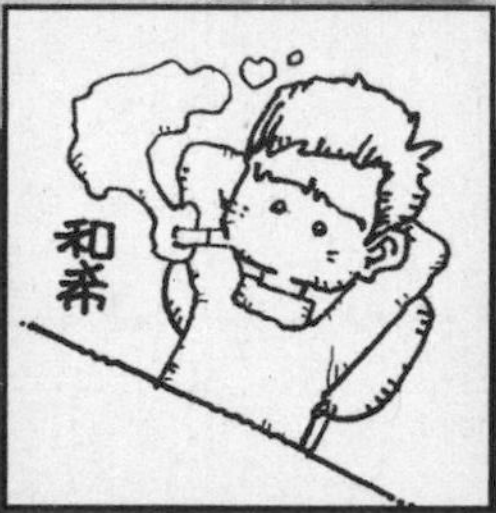
和希

KAZUKI TAKAHASHI

ZEXAL was a concentration of Miyoshi-kun's and Yoshida-san's enthusiasm—and this is the last volume! Great job, guys! And...huh?! You're teaming up again on *ARC-V*?! The fun starts now!

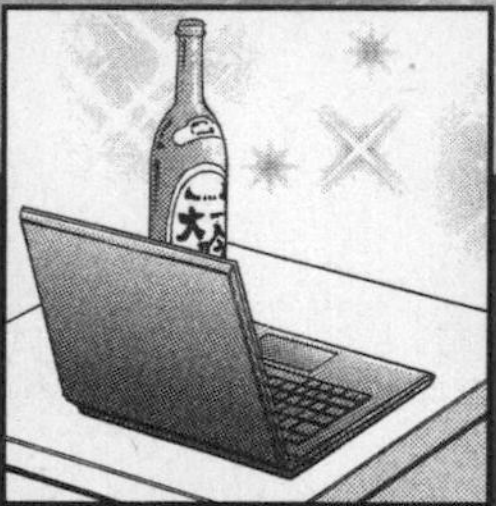

SHIN YOSHIDA

This is it for *ZEXAL*. Yuma and Astral walked alongside me for a long time, in both the anime and the manga. I hope you enjoy the end of their story!

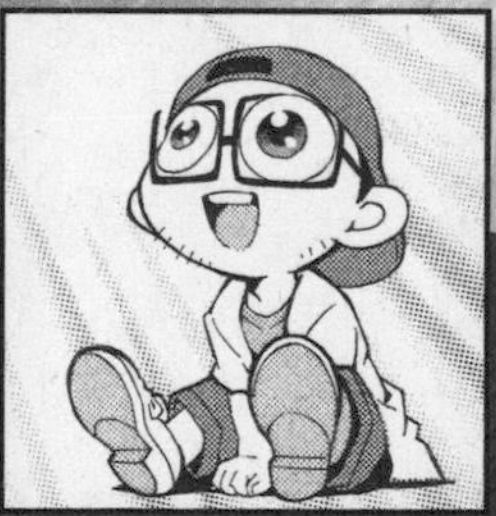

NAOHITO MIYOSHI

Thank you so much to all the readers who cheered us on and lent us their support. I'm lucky to have been involved with *ZEXAL*!

Volume 9
SHONEN JUMP Manga Edition

Original Concept by **KAZUKI TAKAHASHI**
Production Support: **STUDIO DICE**
Story by **SHIN YOSHIDA**
Art by **NAOHITO MIYOSHI**

Translation & English Adaptation **TAYLOR ENGEL AND IAN REID, HC LANGUAGE SOLUTIONS**
Touch-up Art & Lettering **JOHN HUNT**
Designer **STACIE YAMAKI**
Editor **MIKE MONTESA**

YU-GI-OH! ZEXAL © 2010 by Kazuki Takahashi, Shin Yoshida, Naohito Miyoshi
All rights reserved.
First published in Japan in 2010 by SHUEISHA Inc., Tokyo.
English translation rights arranged by SHUEISHA Inc.

Based on Animation TV series YU-GI-OH! ZEXAL
© 1996 Kazuki Takahashi
© 2011 NAS • TV TOKYO

Printed in the U.S.A.

Published by VIZ Media, LLC
P.O. Box 77010
San Francisco, CA 94107

10 9 8 7 6 5 4 3 2 1
First printing, September 2016

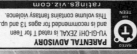
www.shonenjump.com

www.viz.com

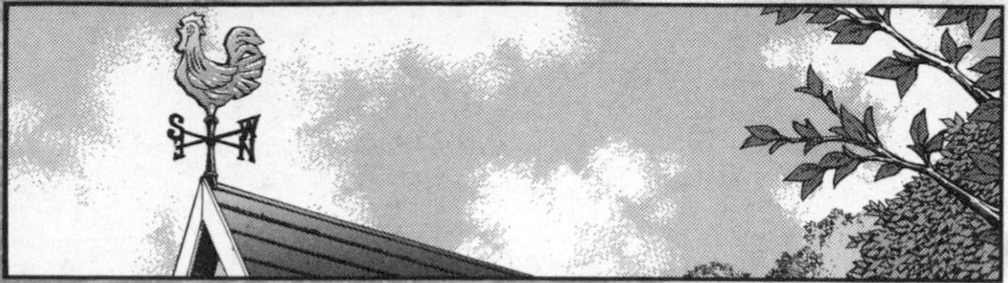

Yu-Gi-Oh! ZEXAL

VOLUME 9: Yuma Jets!!

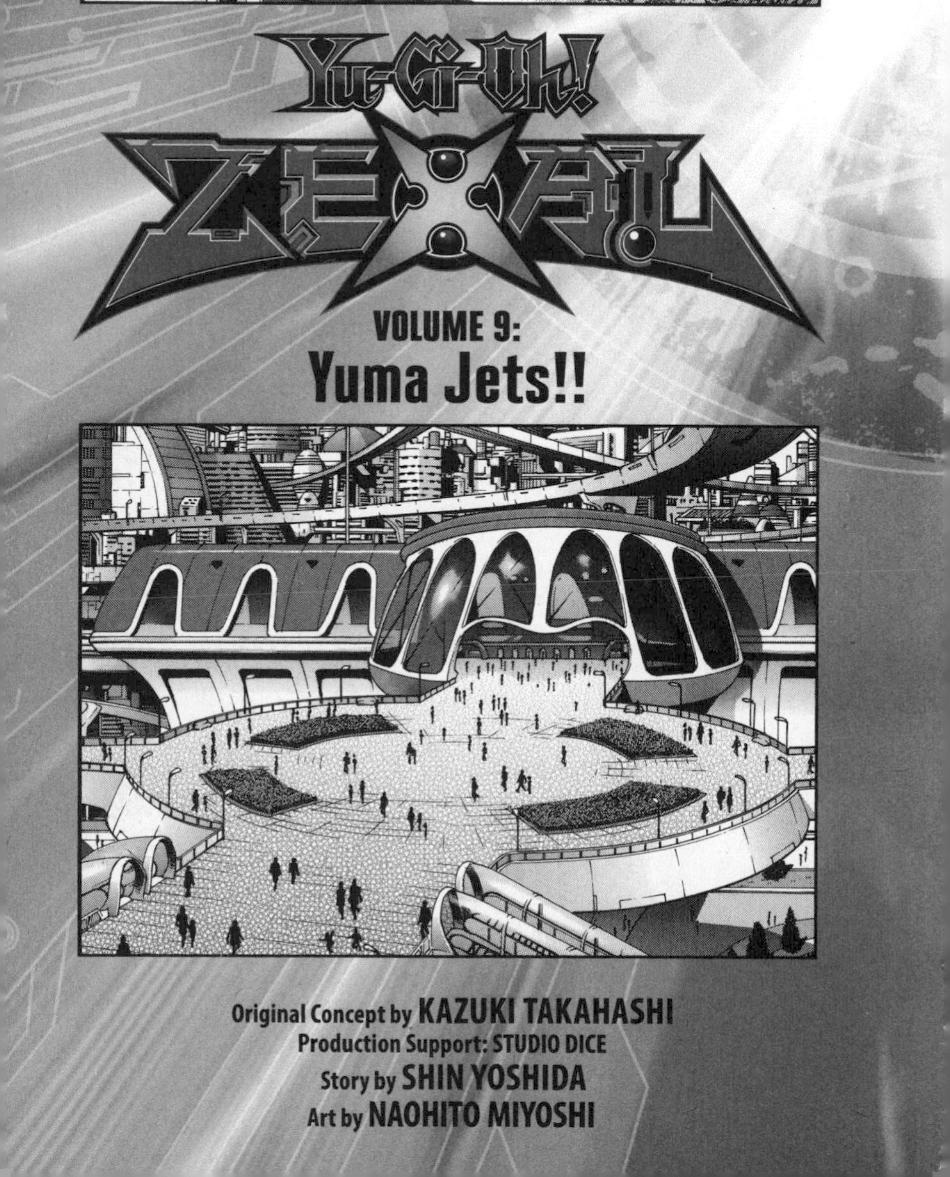

Original Concept by KAZUKI TAKAHASHI
Production Support: STUDIO DICE
Story by SHIN YOSHIDA
Art by NAOHITO MIYOSHI

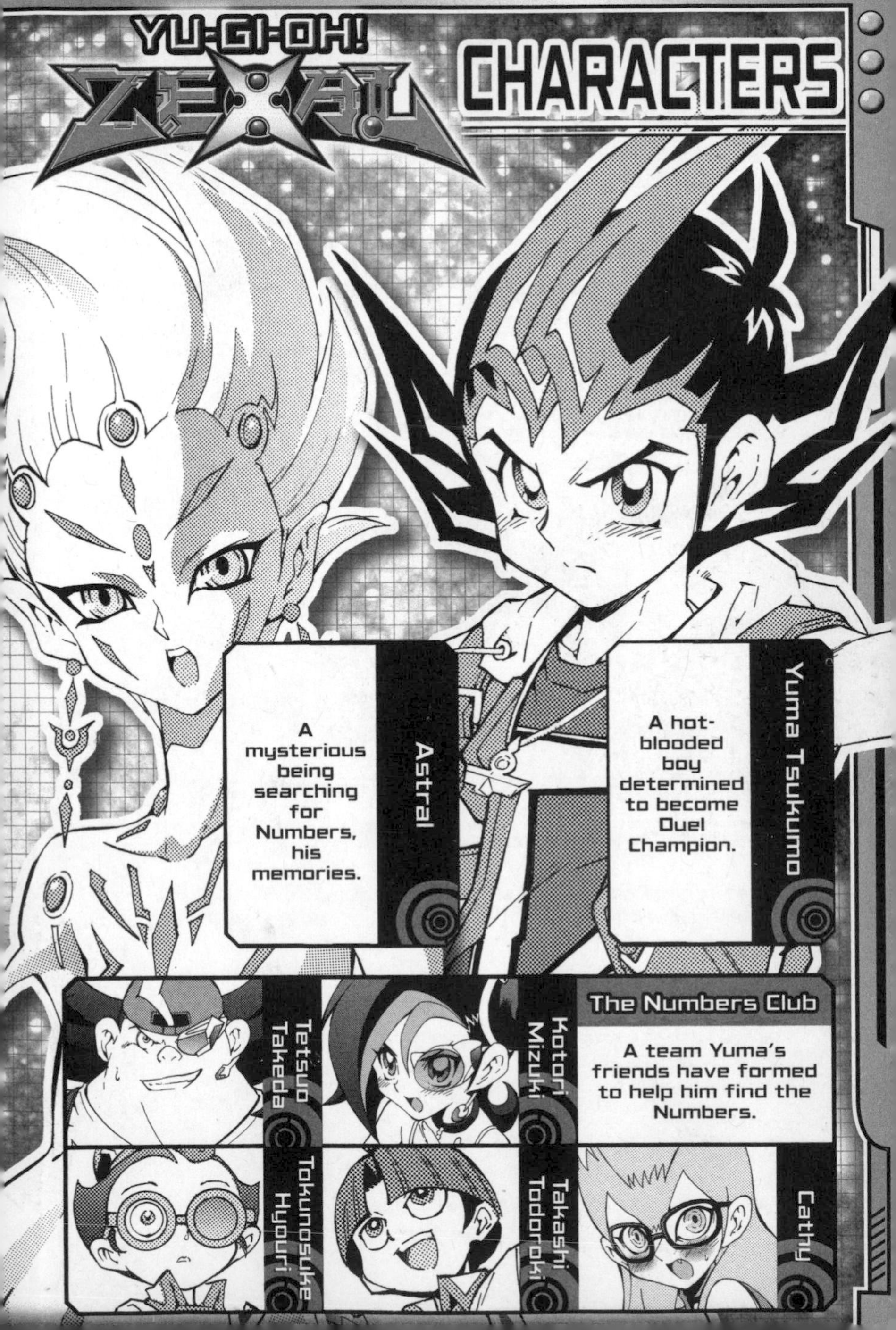
YU-GI-OH! ZEXAL
CHARACTERS
Yuma Tsukumo
A hot-blooded boy determined to become Duel Champion.
Astral
A mysterious being searching for Numbers, his memories.
The Numbers Club
A team Yuma's friends have formed to help him find the Numbers.
Kotori Mizuki
Tetsuo Takeda
Cathy
Takashi Todoroki
Tokunosuke Hyouri

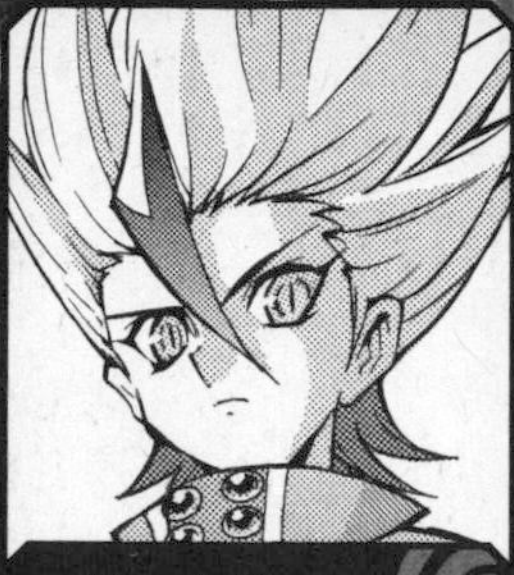

Kyoji Yagumo

He has lured Ryoga and the others into duels to destroy the world.

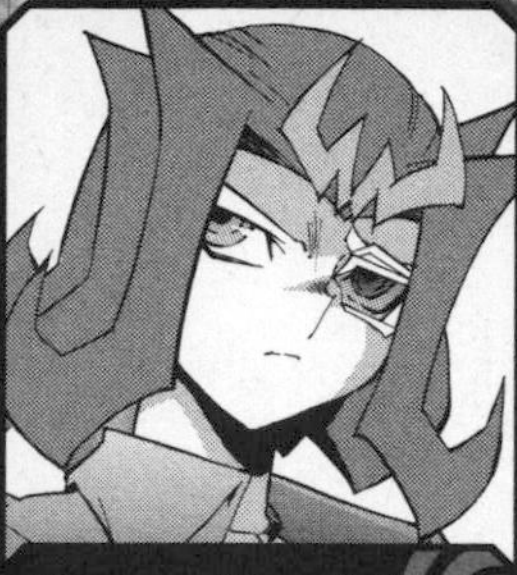

Ryoga Kamishiro

Goes by the nickname "Shark." His fate is tied to Yagumo's.

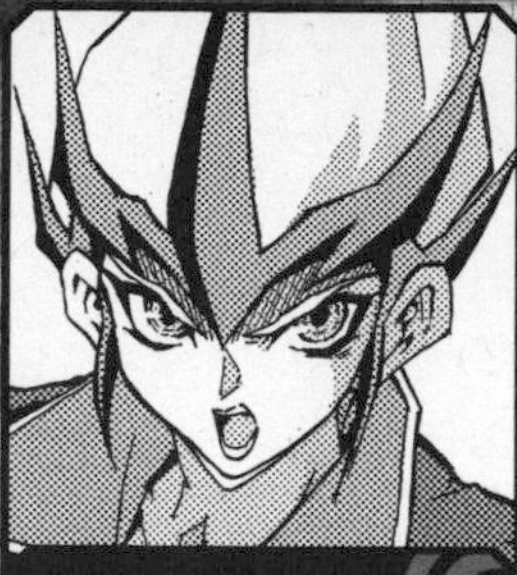

Kaito Tenjo

He's dueling Yuma to save his little brother Haruto.

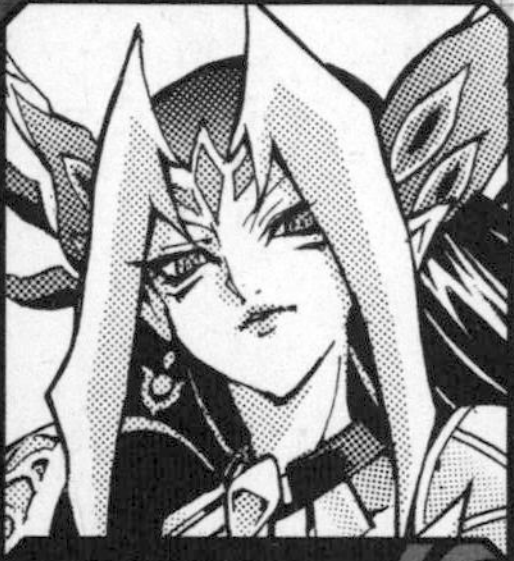

E'Rah

A god of despair who is trying to destroy both worlds.

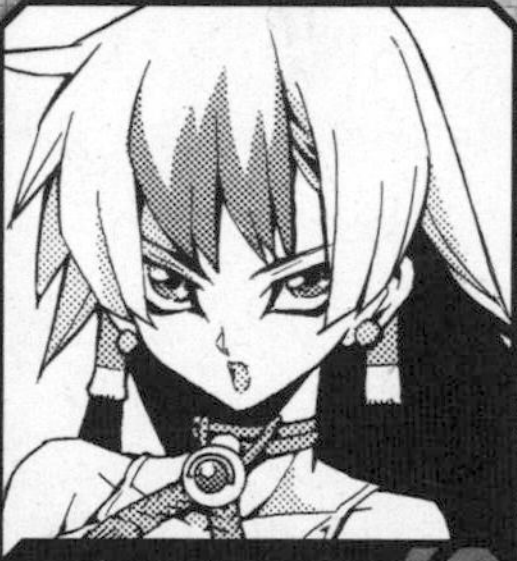

Luna

She's working with the Numbers Club to stop Yagumo's plan.

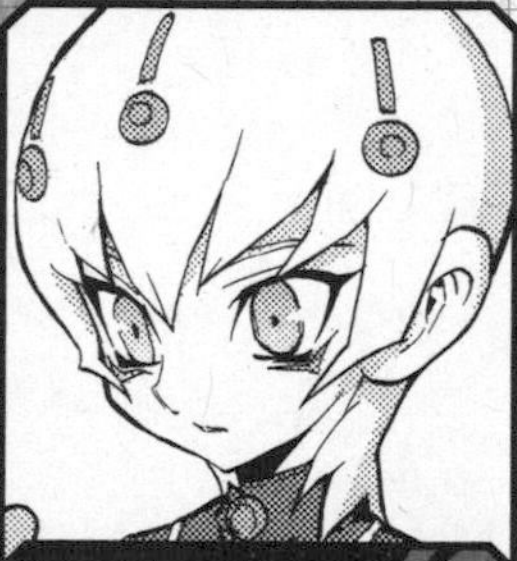

Haruto

He possesses the power to destroy the Astral world.

Previously...

Yuma Tsukumo is crazy about dueling. One day, during a duel, the charm his parents had left him—"the Emperor's Key"—triggered an encounter with a strange being who called himself Astral. Astral was a genius duelist, but his memories had turned into special cards called "Numbers" and were lost. Yuma began working with Astral to find them!

However, three individuals stand in their way: Kaito is hunting the Numbers to help his little brother, Ryoga is trying to wipe them out entirely and Yagumo wants to destroy the world. The Numbers War begins!!

Yuma's power of believing in people saves Kaito and Ryoga, and a bond begins to form between them. However, Yagumo's plot opens the door to another world. In that world, Yuma, Kaito and Ryoga team up to duel Yagumo. As the duel unfolds, E'Rah, the mastermind who has been controlling Yagumo, finally appears. Confronted by her vast power, what will Yuma and the others do?!

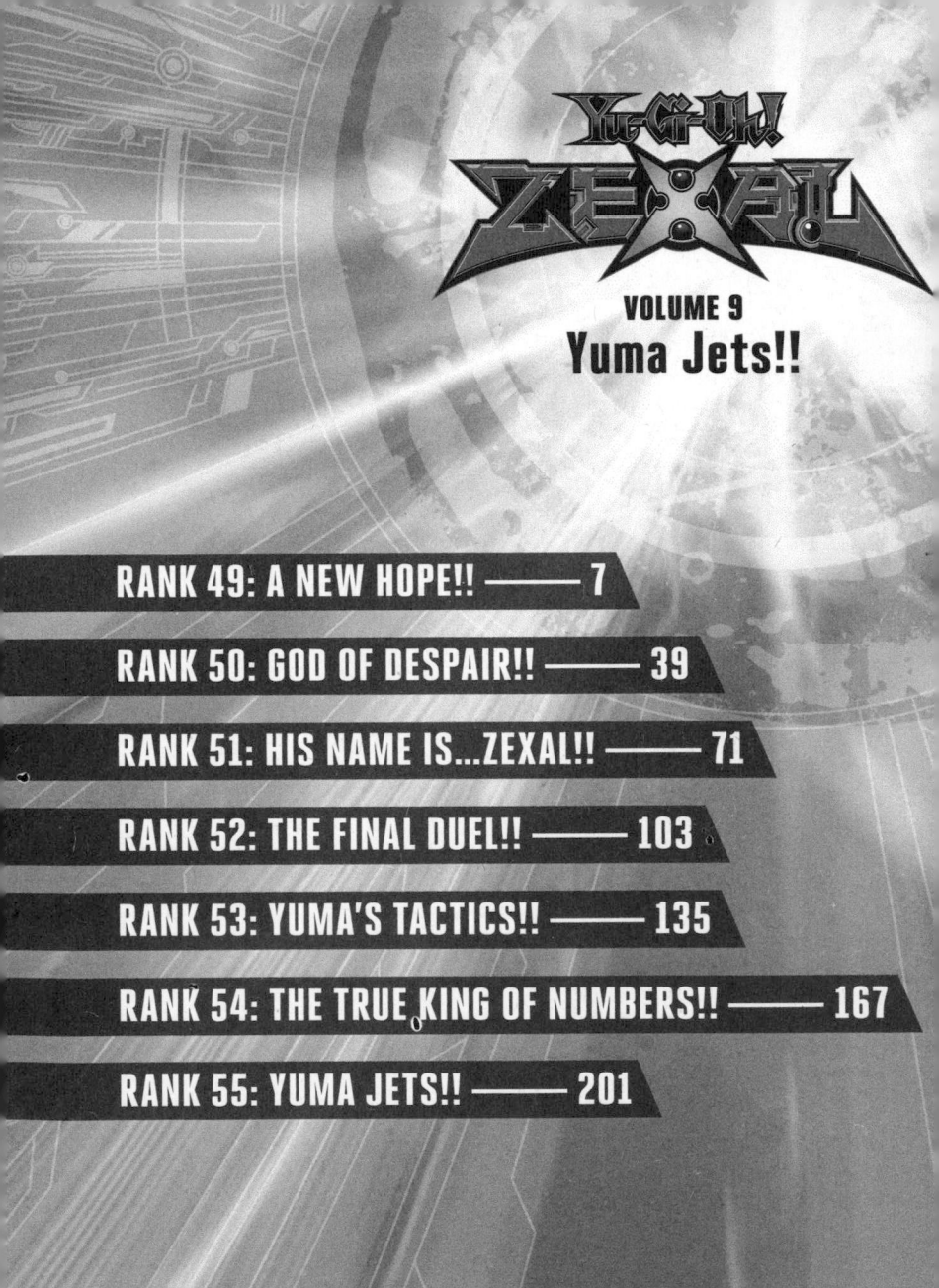

YU-GI-OH! ZEXAL

VOLUME 9
Yuma Jets!!

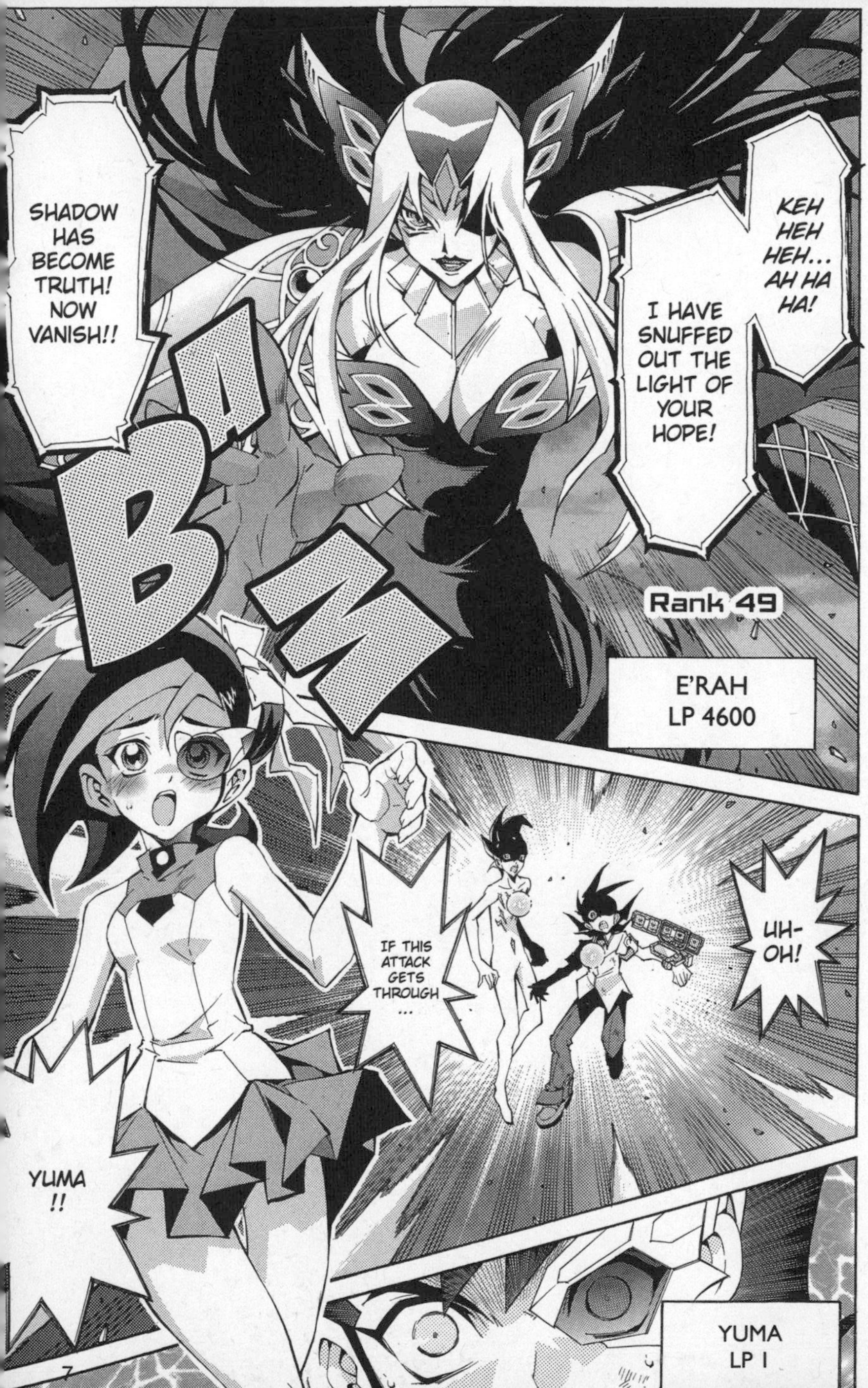
KEH HEH HEH... AH HA HA!
I HAVE SNUFFED OUT THE LIGHT OF YOUR HOPE!
SHADOW HAS BECOME TRUTH! NOW VANISH!!
BAM
Rank 49
E'RAH
LP 4600
UH-OH!
IF THIS ATTACK GETS THROUGH...
YUMA!!
YUMA
LP 1

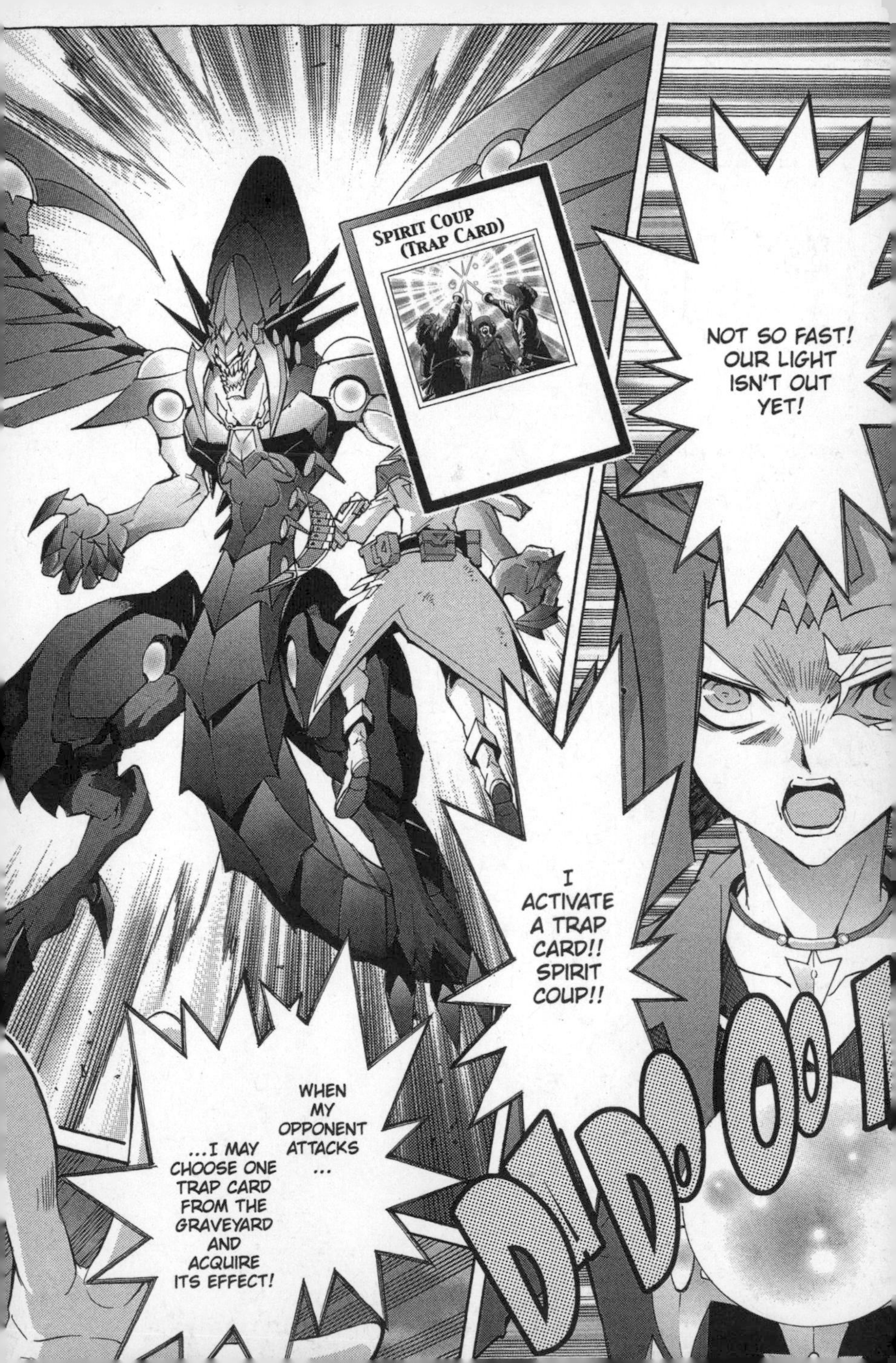
NOT SO FAST! OUR LIGHT ISN'T OUT YET!
SPIRIT COUP (TRAP CARD)
I ACTIVATE A TRAP CARD!! SPIRIT COUP!!
WHEN MY OPPONENT ATTACKS ...
...I MAY CHOOSE ONE TRAP CARD FROM THE GRAVEYARD AND ACQUIRE ITS EFFECT!

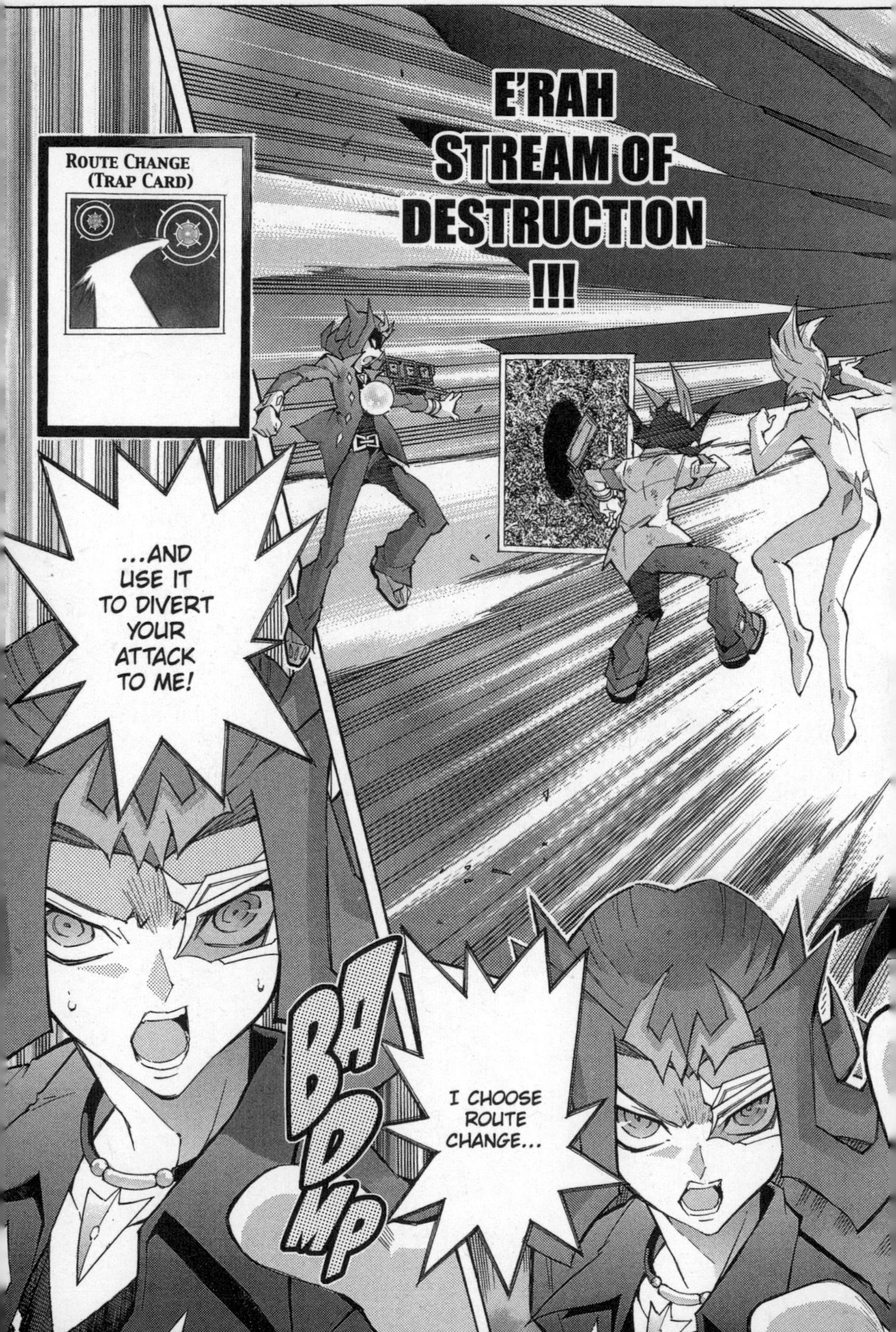
E'RAH STREAM OF DESTRUCTION !!!
ROUTE CHANGE (TRAP CARD)
I CHOOSE ROUTE CHANGE...
BA DUMP
...AND USE IT TO DIVERT YOUR ATTACK TO ME!

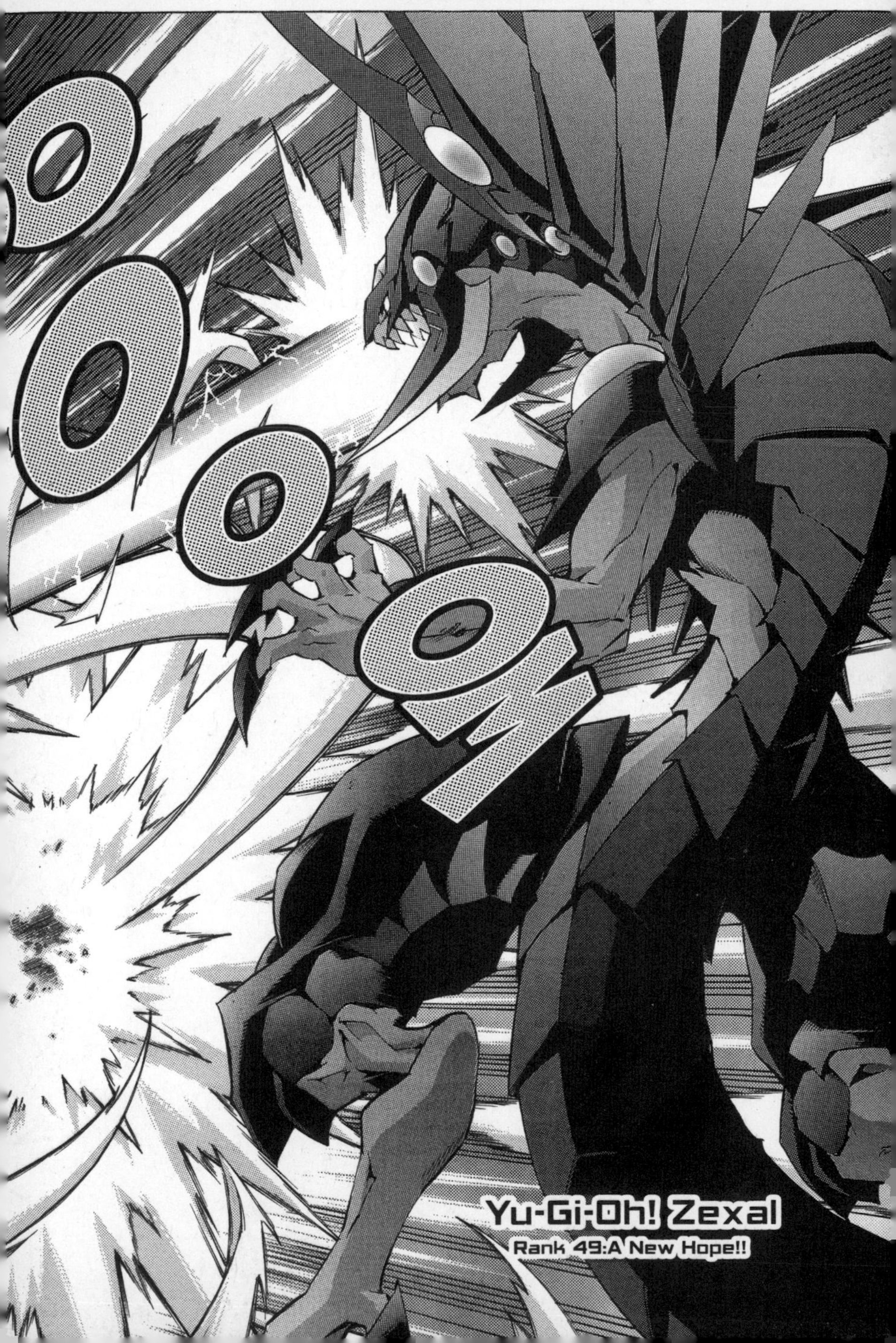
WOOOO
Yu-Gi-Oh! Zexal
Rank 49:A New Hope!!

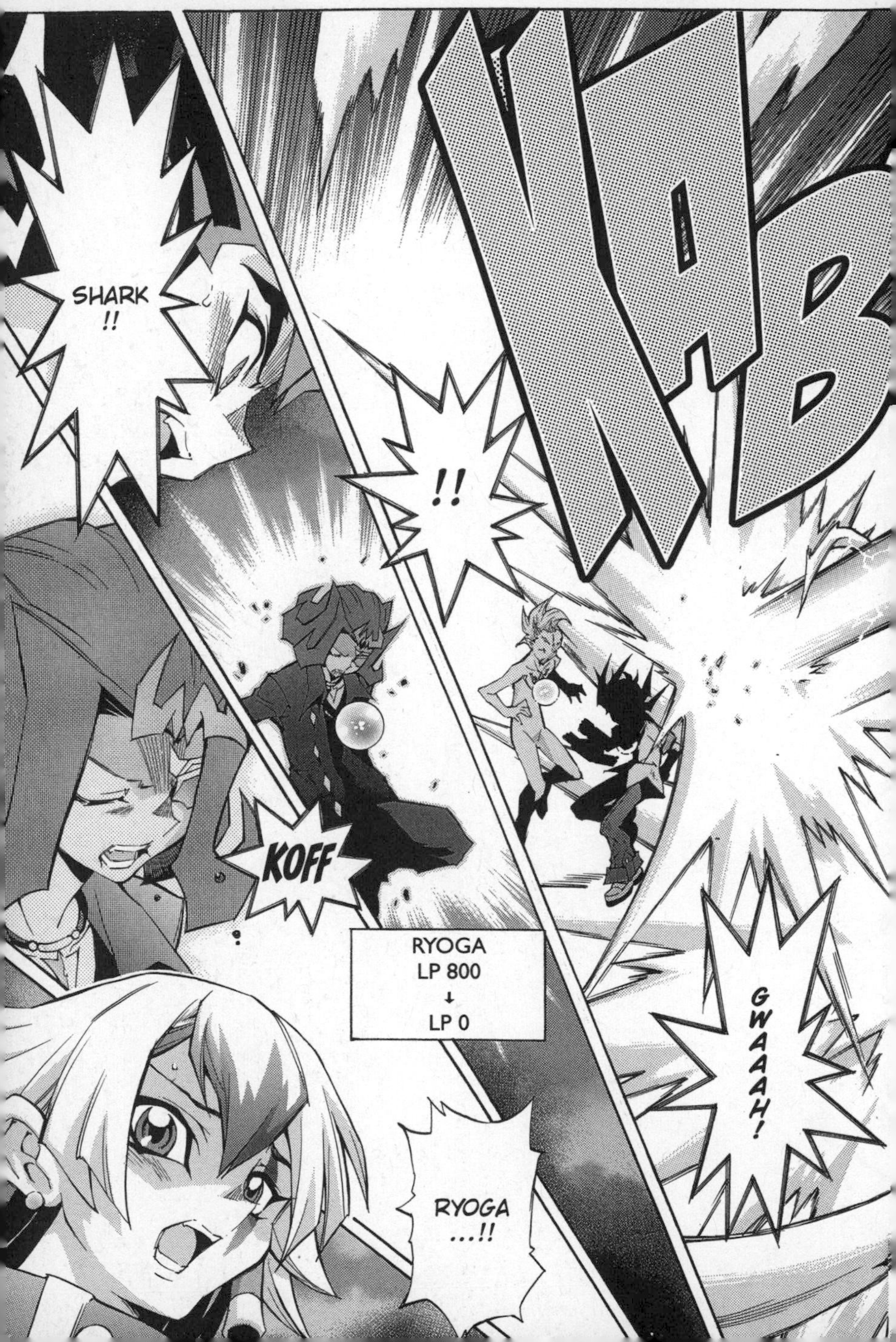
!!
SHARK !!
GWAAAH!
KOFF
RYOGA
LP 800
↓
LP 0
RYOGA ...!!

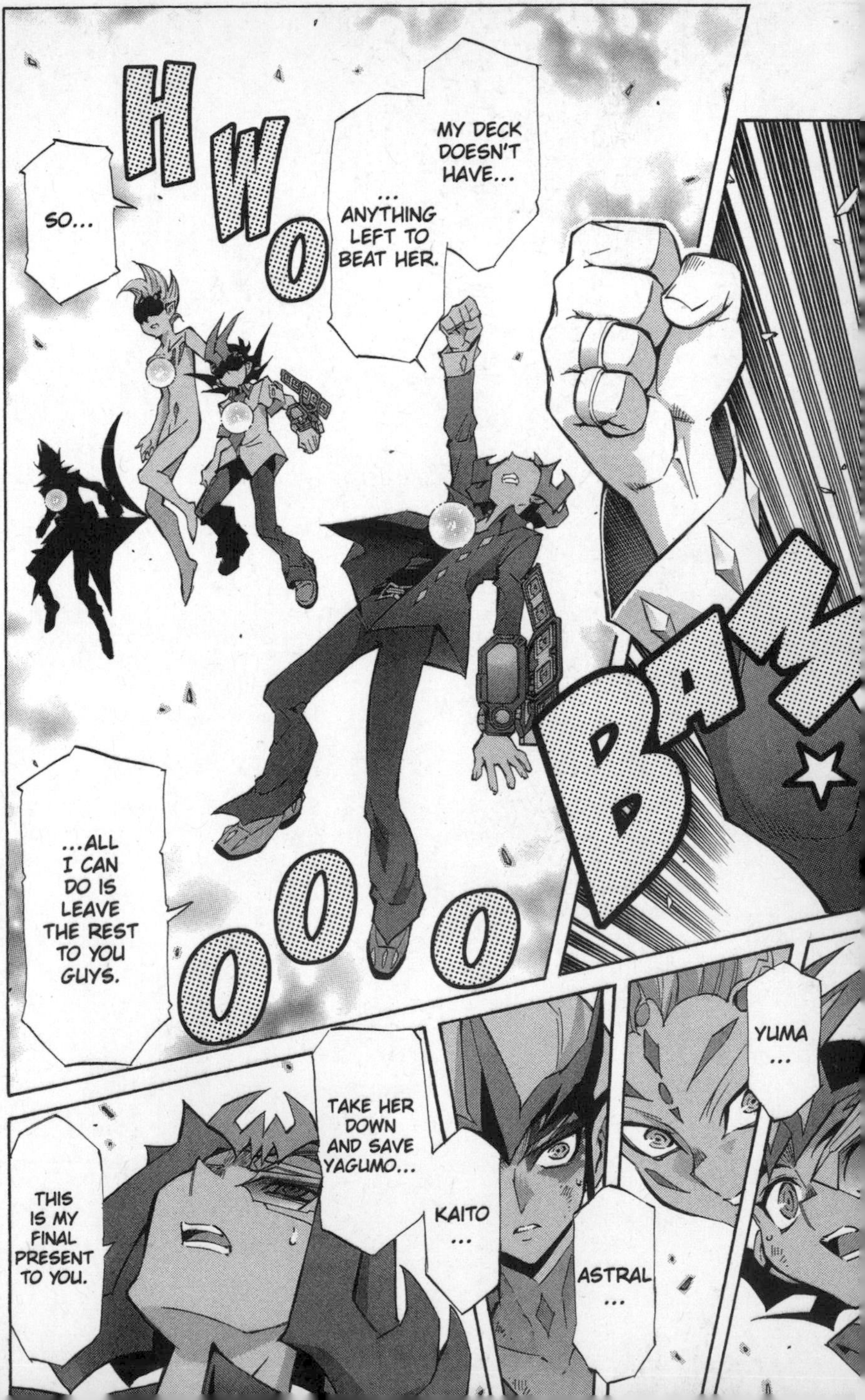
BAM
MY DECK DOESN'T HAVE...
...ANYTHING LEFT TO BEAT HER.
SO...
HWOOOO
...ALL I CAN DO IS LEAVE THE REST TO YOU GUYS.
YUMA...
ASTRAL...
KAITO...
TAKE HER DOWN AND SAVE YAGUMO...
THIS IS MY FINAL PRESENT TO YOU.

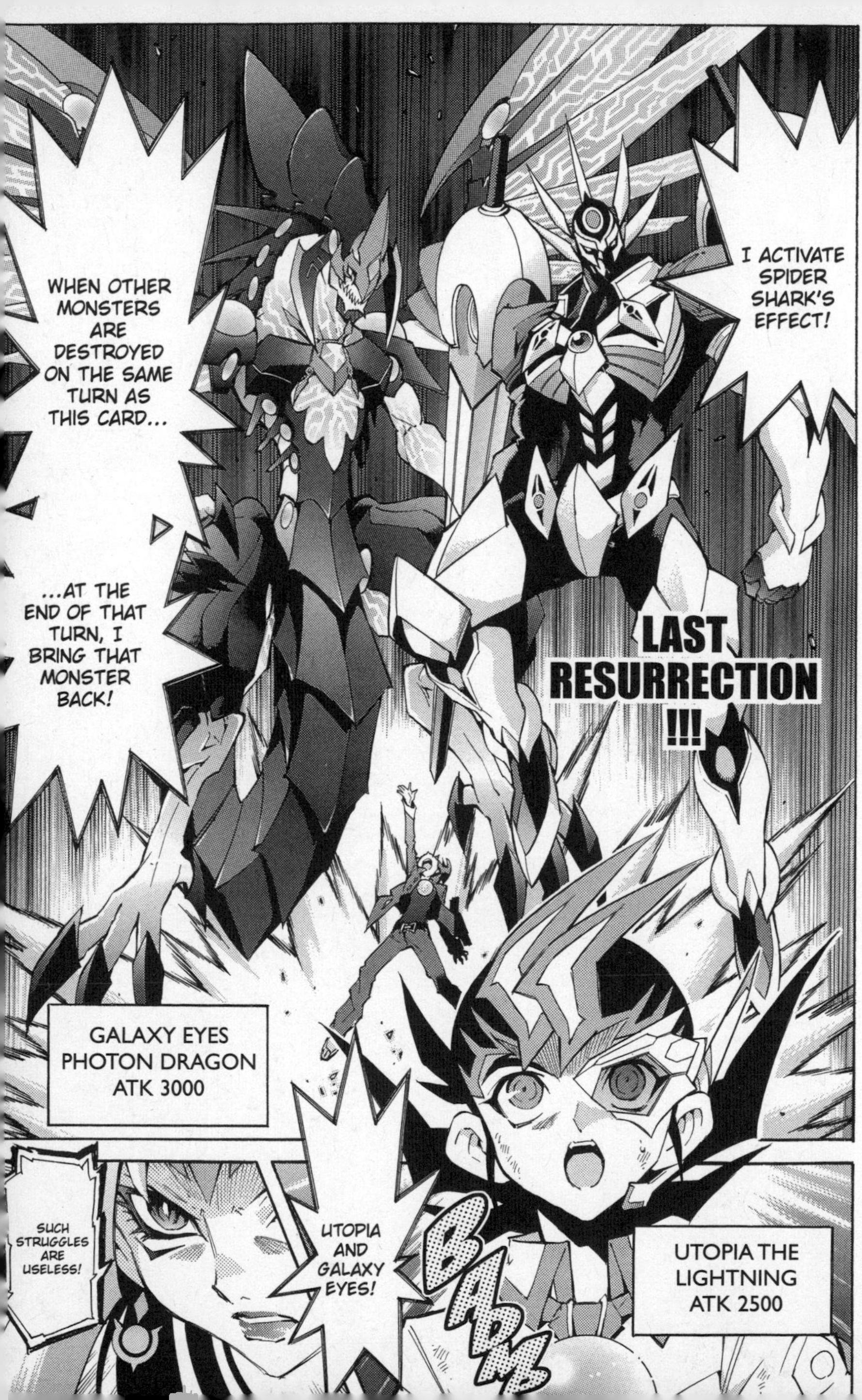
I ACTIVATE SPIDER SHARK'S EFFECT!
LAST RESURRECTION !!!
WHEN OTHER MONSTERS ARE DESTROYED ON THE SAME TURN AS THIS CARD...
...AT THE END OF THAT TURN, I BRING THAT MONSTER BACK!
GALAXY EYES PHOTON DRAGON ATK 3000
UTOPIA THE LIGHTNING ATK 2500
BADUM
UTOPIA AND GALAXY EYES!
SUCH STRUGGLES ARE USELESS!

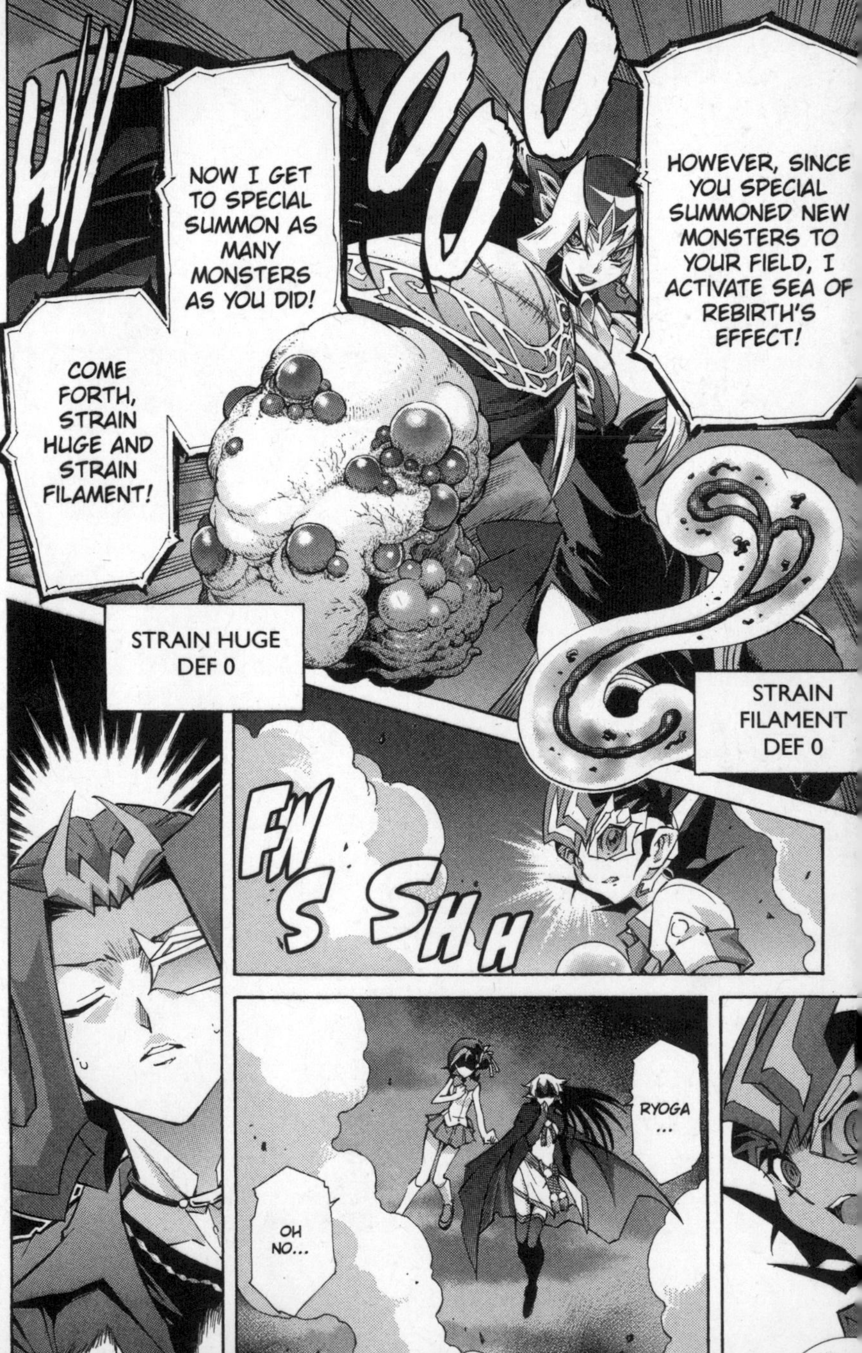
HOWEVER, SINCE YOU SPECIAL SUMMONED NEW MONSTERS TO YOUR FIELD, I ACTIVATE SEA OF REBIRTH'S EFFECT!
OOOO
NOW I GET TO SPECIAL SUMMON AS MANY MONSTERS AS YOU DID!
HH
COME FORTH, STRAIN HUGE AND STRAIN FILAMENT!
STRAIN FILAMENT DEF 0
STRAIN HUGE DEF 0
FWSSSHH
RYOGA...
OH NO...

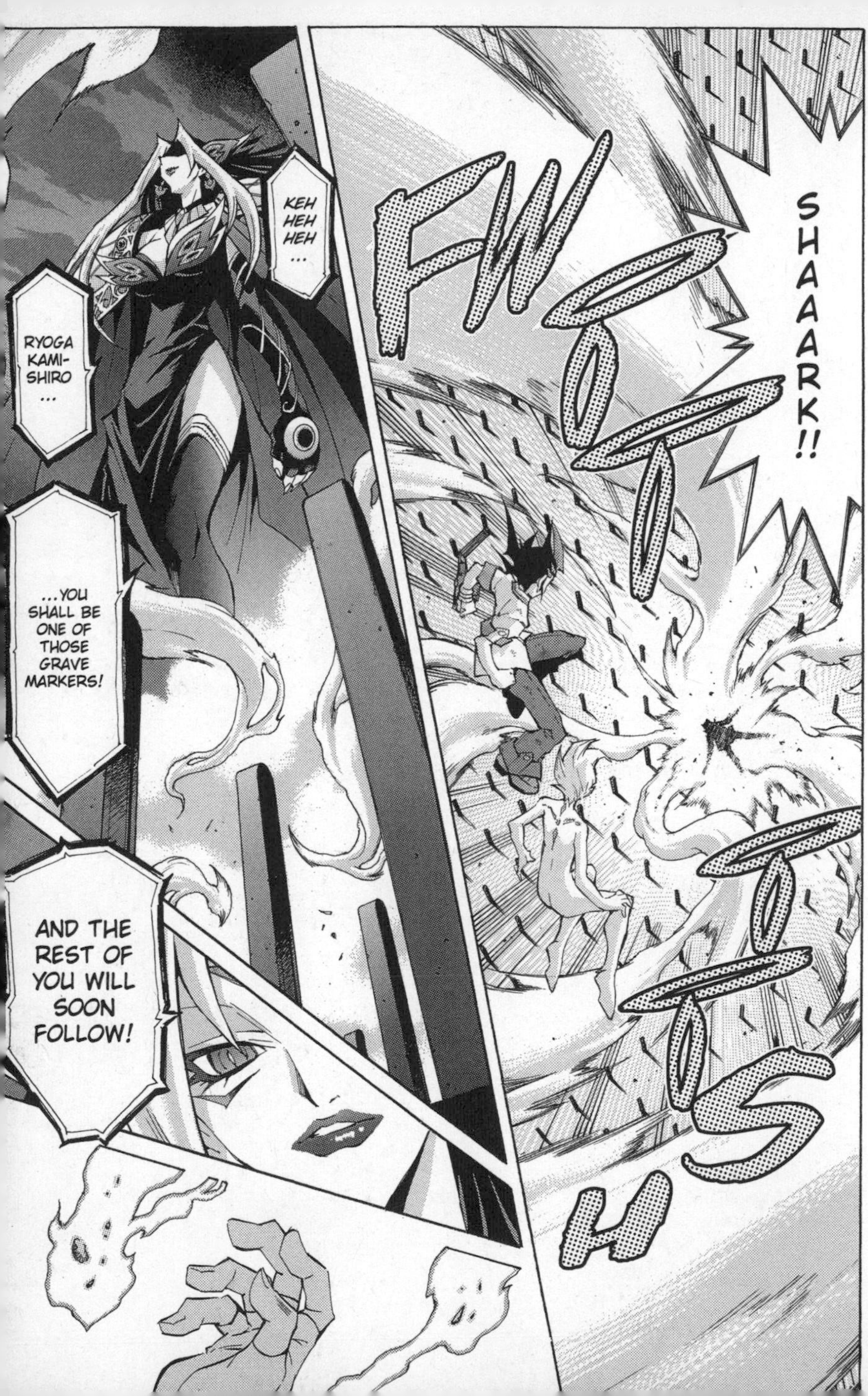
SHAAAARK!!
FWOOOOOOOOSH
KEH HEH HEH...
RYOGA KAMI-SHIRO...
...YOU SHALL BE ONE OF THOSE GRAVE MARKERS!
AND THE REST OF YOU WILL SOON FOLLOW!

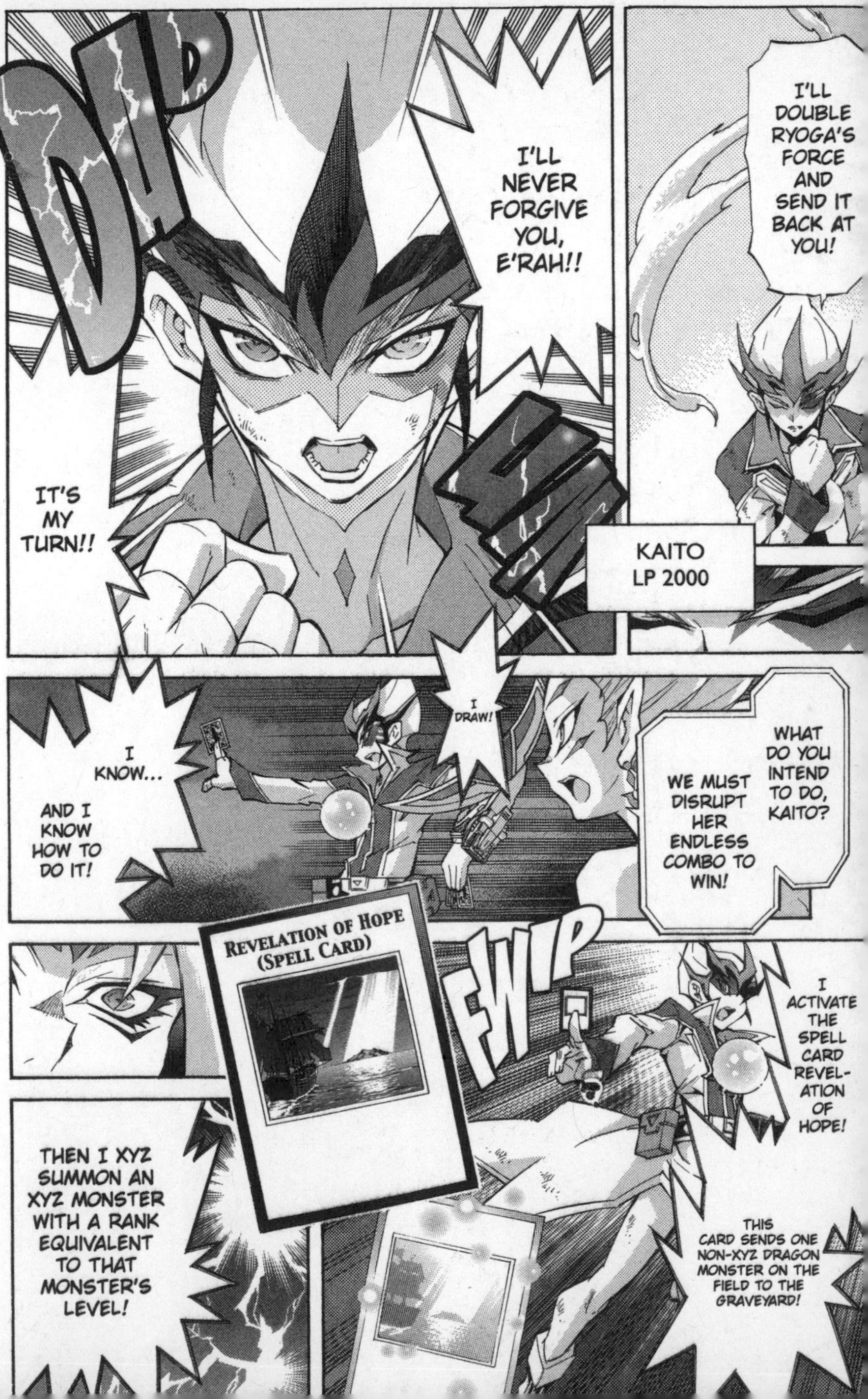
I'LL DOUBLE RYOGA'S FORCE AND SEND IT BACK AT YOU!
KAITO LP 2000
I'LL NEVER FORGIVE YOU, E'RAH!!
DAP
IT'S MY TURN!!
WHAT DO YOU INTEND TO DO, KAITO?
WE MUST DISRUPT HER ENDLESS COMBO TO WIN!
I DRAW!
I KNOW...
AND I KNOW HOW TO DO IT!
I ACTIVATE THE SPELL CARD REVEL-ATION OF HOPE!
FWIP
REVELATION OF HOPE (SPELL CARD)
THIS CARD SENDS ONE NON-XYZ DRAGON MONSTER ON THE FIELD TO THE GRAVEYARD!
THEN I XYZ SUMMON AN XYZ MONSTER WITH A RANK EQUIVALENT TO THAT MONSTER'S LEVEL!

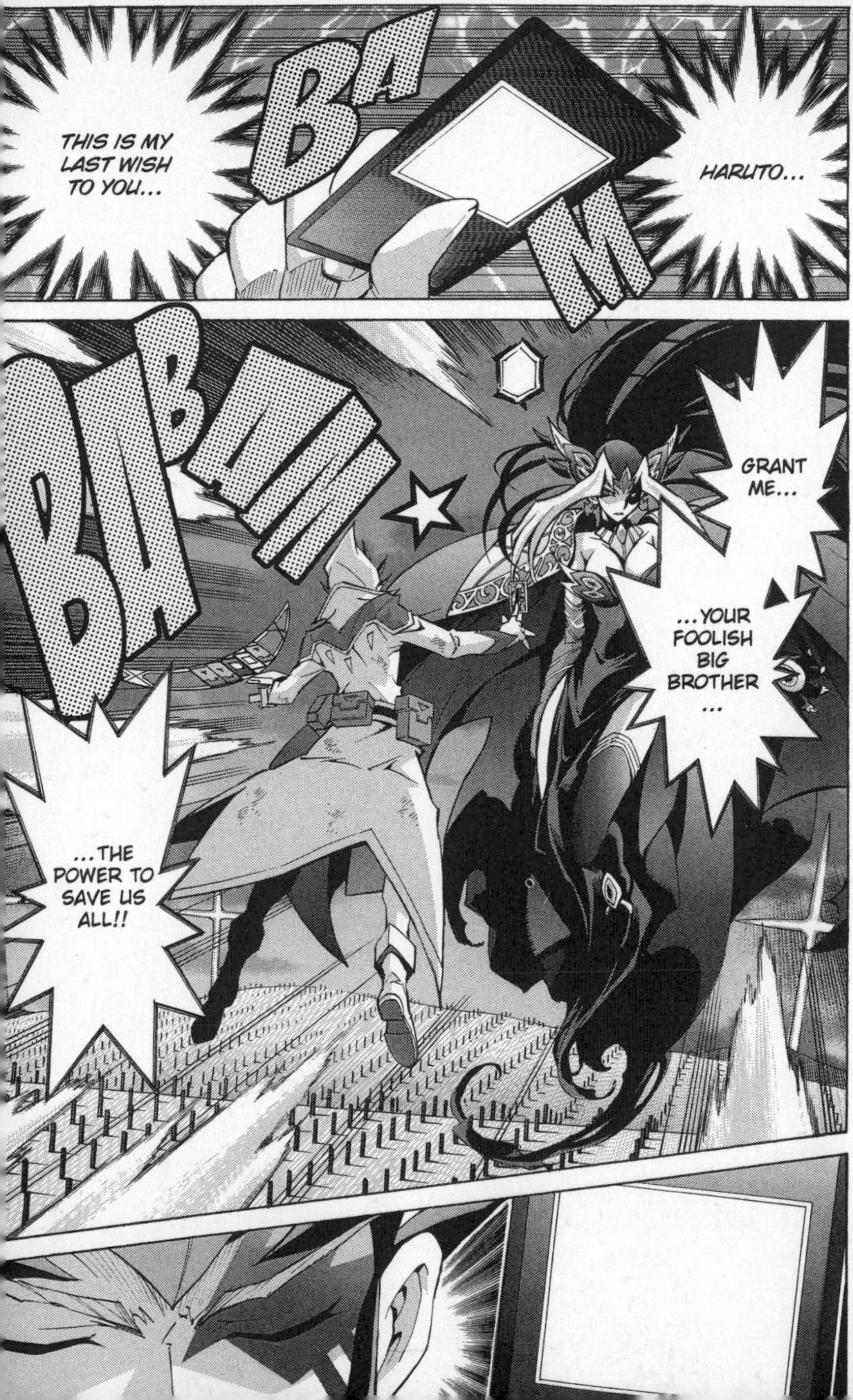
HARUTO...
BAM
THIS IS MY LAST WISH TO YOU...
GRANT ME...
...YOUR FOOLISH BIG BROTHER...
BABAM
...THE POWER TO SAVE US ALL!!

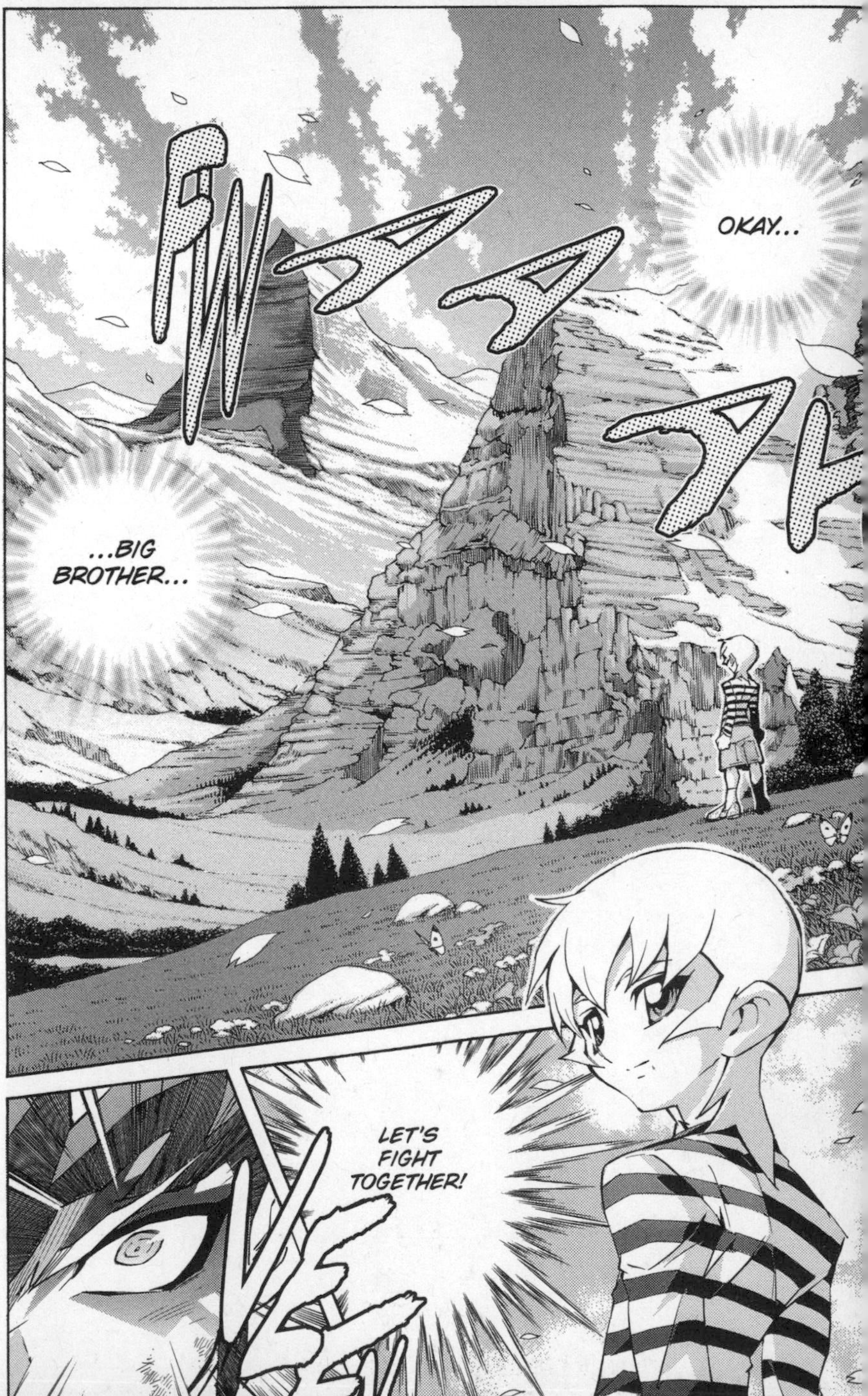
OKAY...
FWAAAH
...BIG BROTHER...
LET'S FIGHT TOGETHER!

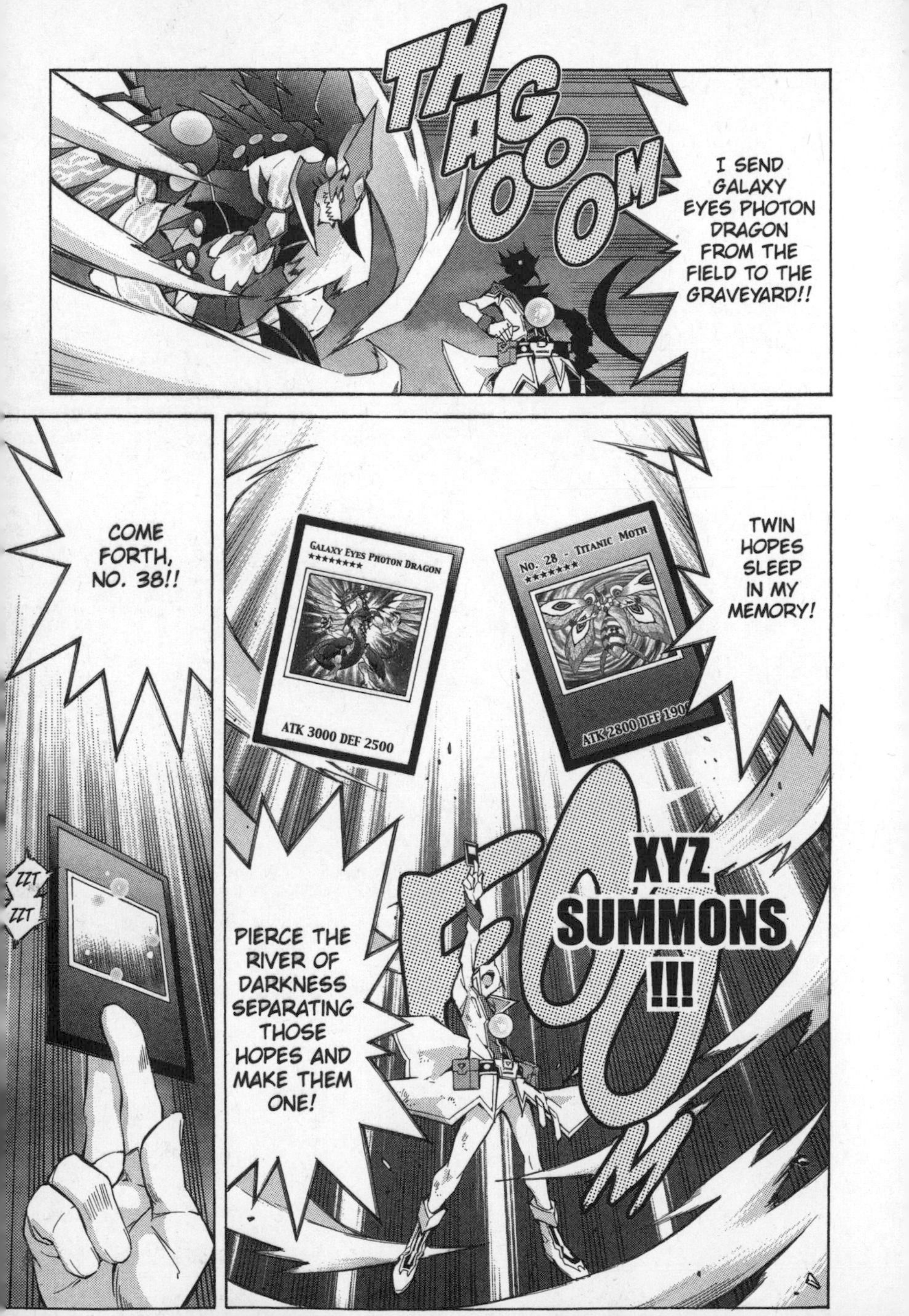
I SEND GALAXY EYES PHOTON DRAGON FROM THE FIELD TO THE GRAVEYARD!!
THAGOOOM
TWIN HOPES SLEEP IN MY MEMORY!
No. 28 - Titanic Moth
ATK 2800 DEF 190
Galaxy Eyes Photon Dragon
ATK 3000 DEF 2500
XYZ SUMMONS!!!
PIERCE THE RIVER OF DARKNESS SEPARATING THOSE HOPES AND MAKE THEM ONE!
COME FORTH, NO. 38!!
ZZT
ZZT

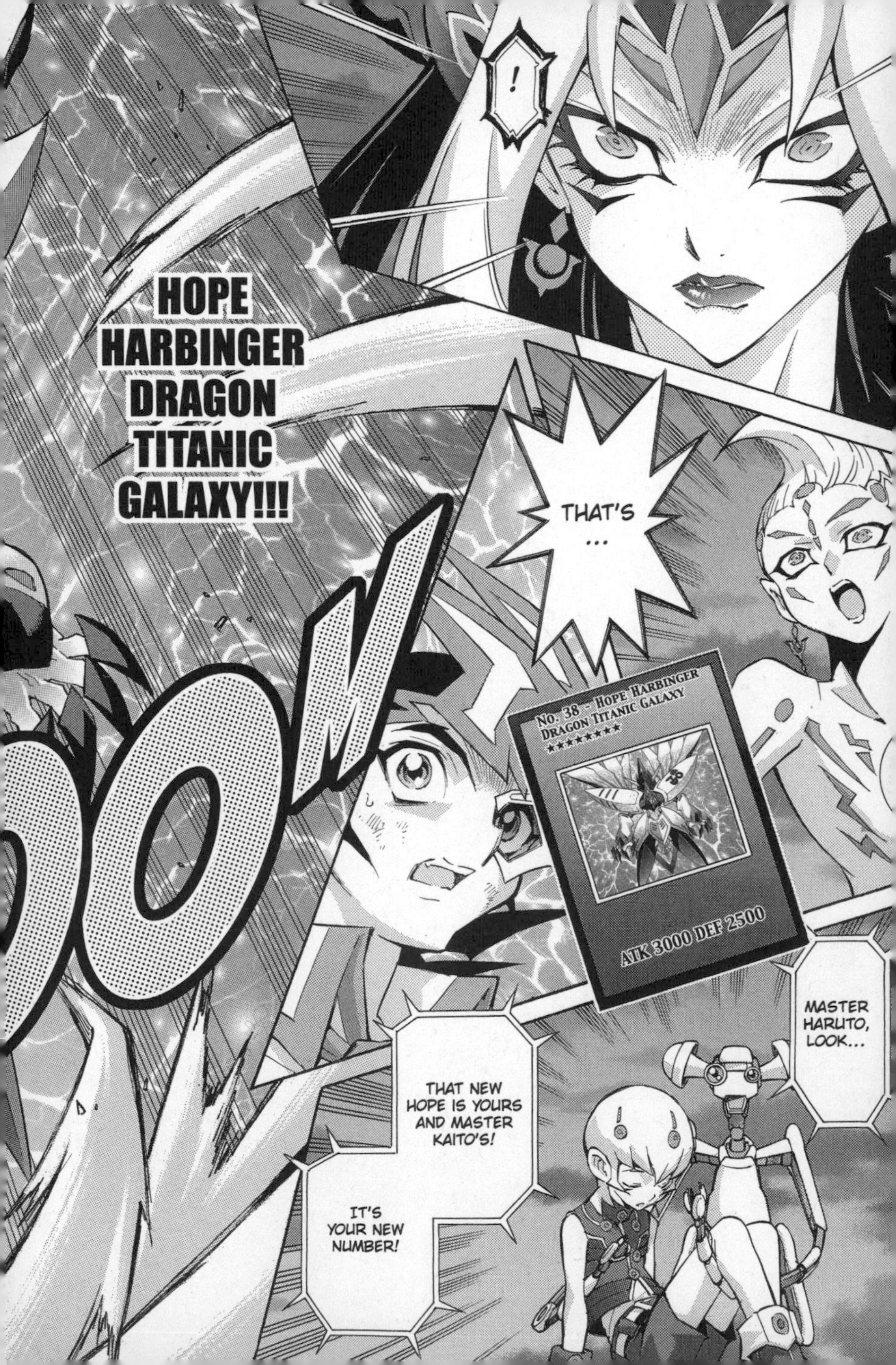
!
THAT'S ...
No. 38 - Hope Harbinger Dragon Titanic Galaxy
★★★★★★★★
ATK 3000 DEF 2500
MASTER HARUTO, LOOK...
THAT NEW HOPE IS YOURS AND MASTER KAITO'S!
IT'S YOUR NEW NUMBER!
HOPE HARBINGER DRAGON TITANIC GALAXY!!!

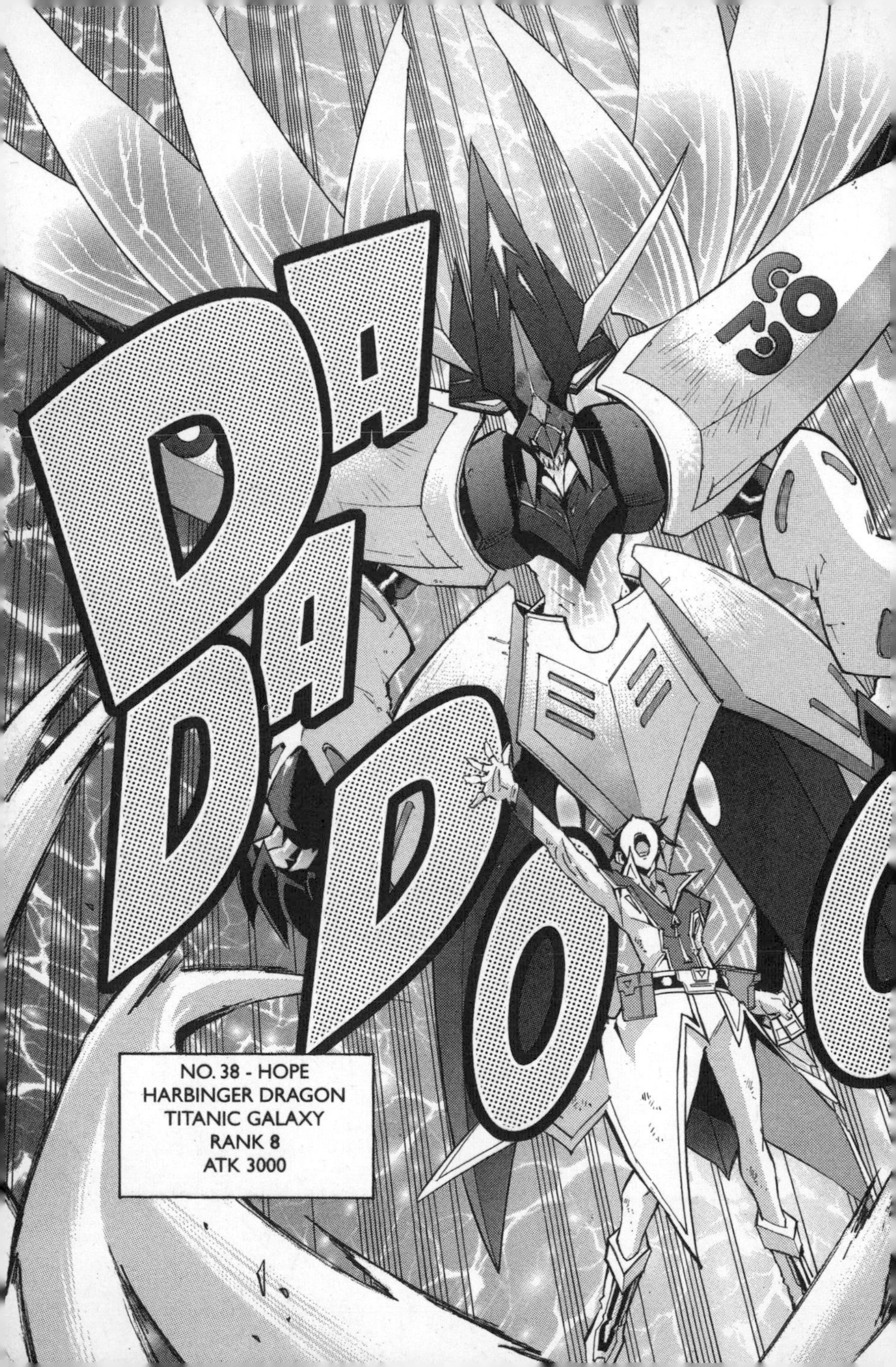
DADADOOO
NO. 38 - HOPE
HARBINGER DRAGON
TITANIC GALAXY
RANK 8
ATK 3000

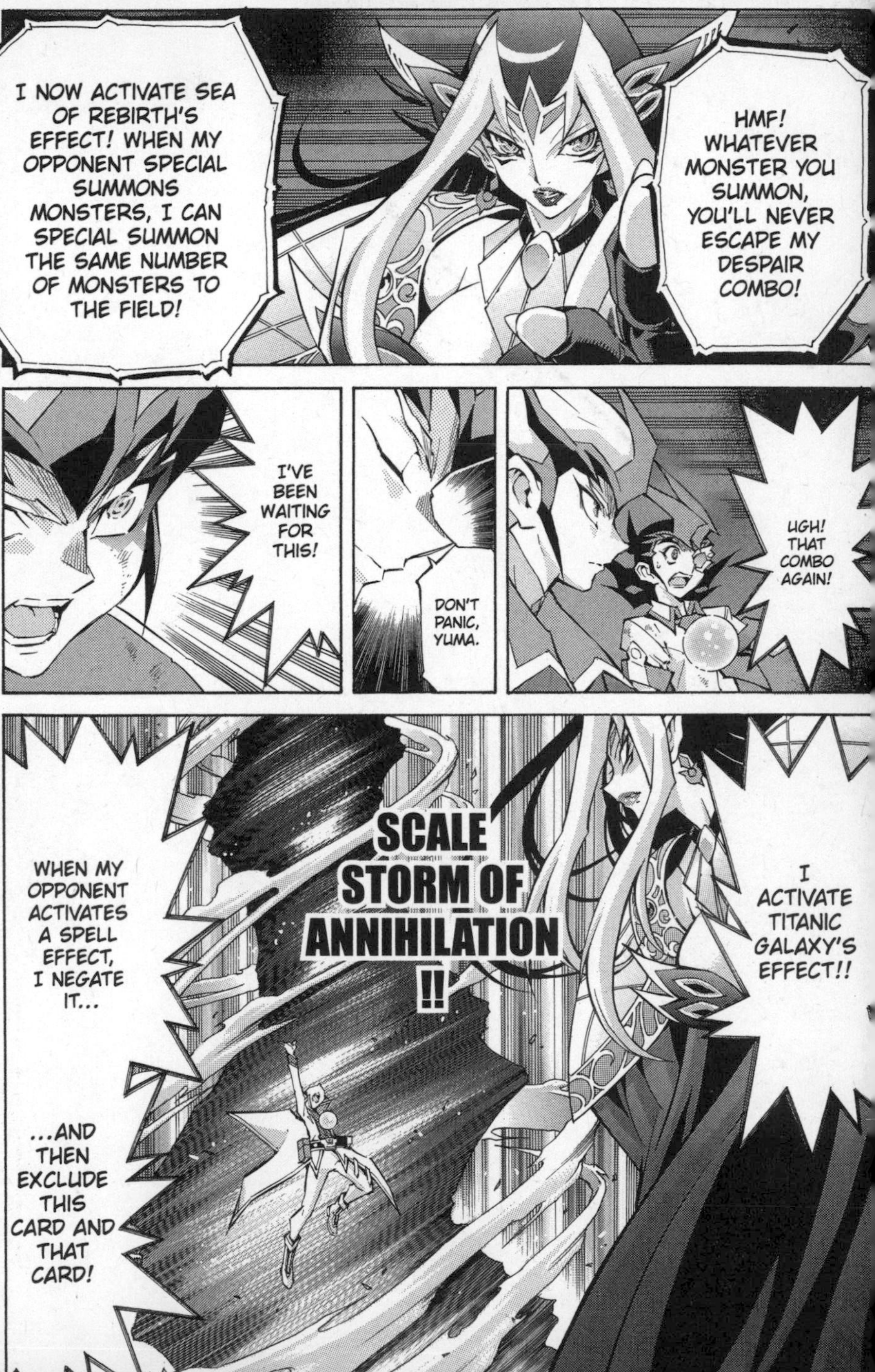
HMF! WHATEVER MONSTER YOU SUMMON, YOU'LL NEVER ESCAPE MY DESPAIR COMBO!
I NOW ACTIVATE SEA OF REBIRTH'S EFFECT! WHEN MY OPPONENT SPECIAL SUMMONS MONSTERS, I CAN SPECIAL SUMMON THE SAME NUMBER OF MONSTERS TO THE FIELD!
UGH! THAT COMBO AGAIN!
DON'T PANIC, YUMA.
I'VE BEEN WAITING FOR THIS!
I ACTIVATE TITANIC GALAXY'S EFFECT!!
SCALE STORM OF ANNIHILATION!!
WHEN MY OPPONENT ACTIVATES A SPELL EFFECT, I NEGATE IT...
...AND THEN EXCLUDE THIS CARD AND THAT CARD!

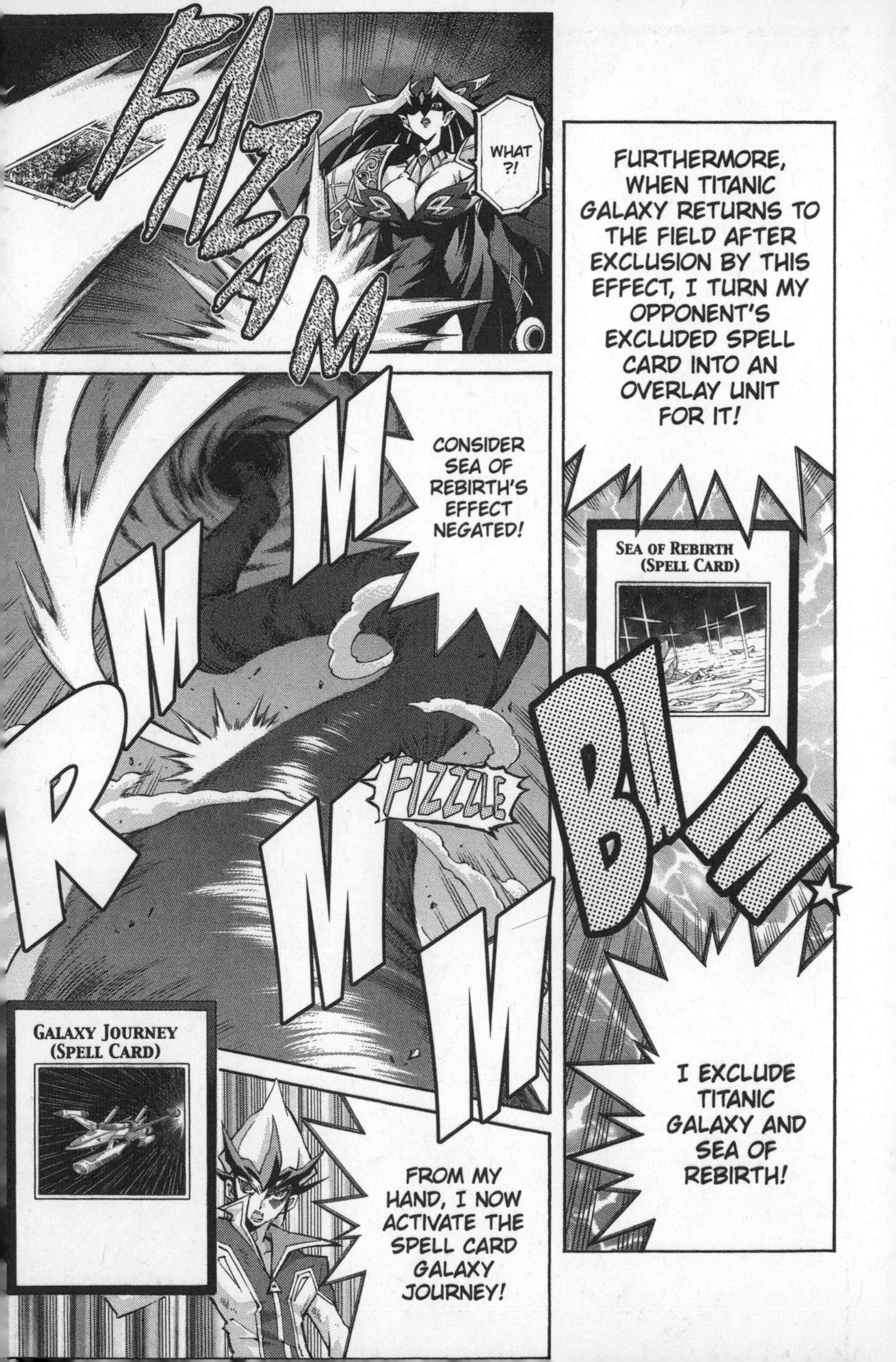
FURTHERMORE, WHEN TITANIC GALAXY RETURNS TO THE FIELD AFTER EXCLUSION BY THIS EFFECT, I TURN MY OPPONENT'S EXCLUDED SPELL CARD INTO AN OVERLAY UNIT FOR IT!
SEA OF REBIRTH (SPELL CARD)
I EXCLUDE TITANIC GALAXY AND SEA OF REBIRTH!
WHAT ?!
FAZAM
CONSIDER SEA OF REBIRTH'S EFFECT NEGATED!
FIZZZLE
GALAXY JOURNEY (SPELL CARD)
FROM MY HAND, I NOW ACTIVATE THE SPELL CARD GALAXY JOURNEY!

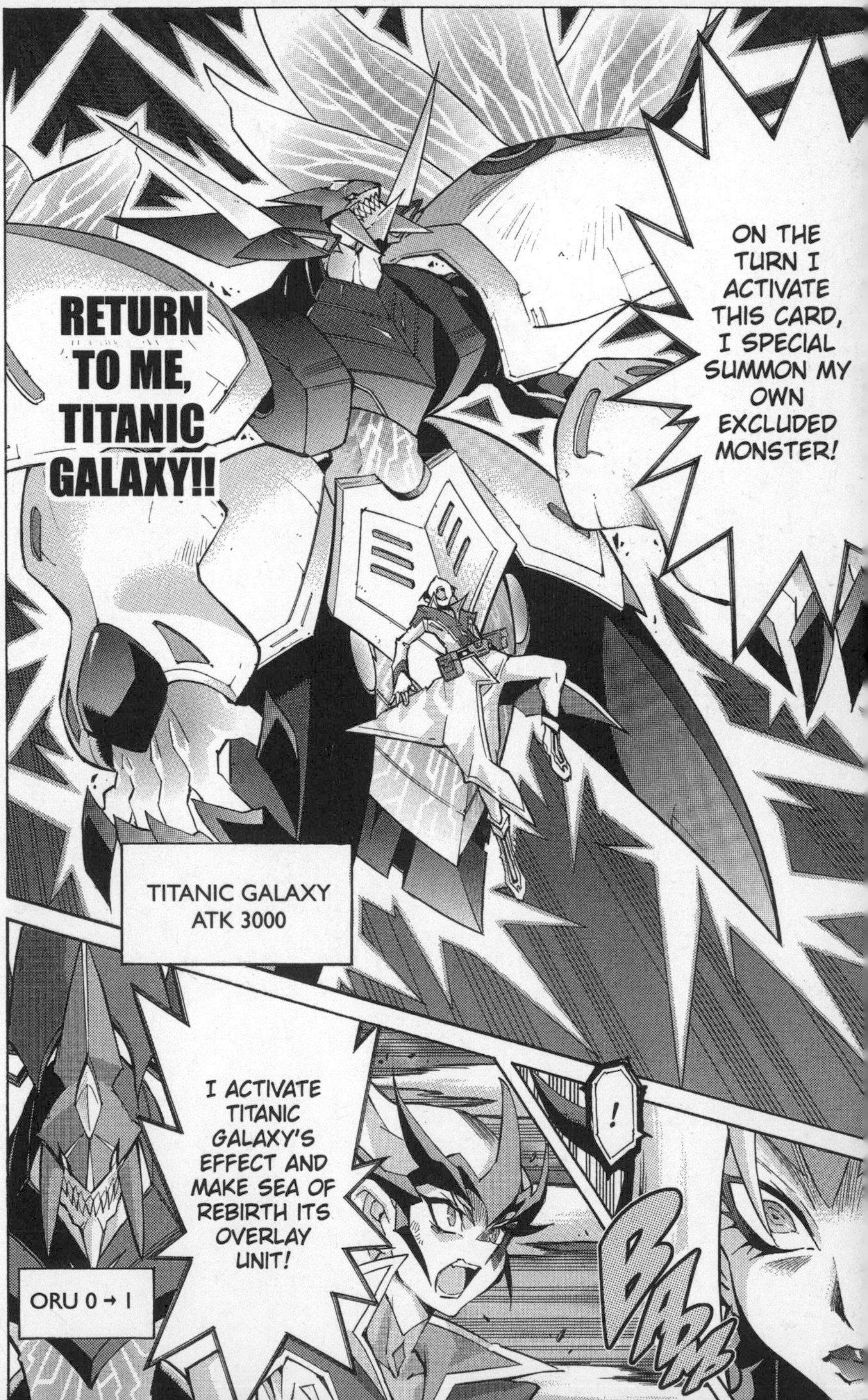
ON THE TURN I ACTIVATE THIS CARD, I SPECIAL SUMMON MY OWN EXCLUDED MONSTER!
RETURN TO ME, TITANIC GALAXY!!
TITANIC GALAXY
ATK 3000
!
I ACTIVATE TITANIC GALAXY'S EFFECT AND MAKE SEA OF REBIRTH ITS OVERLAY UNIT!
ORU 0 → 1

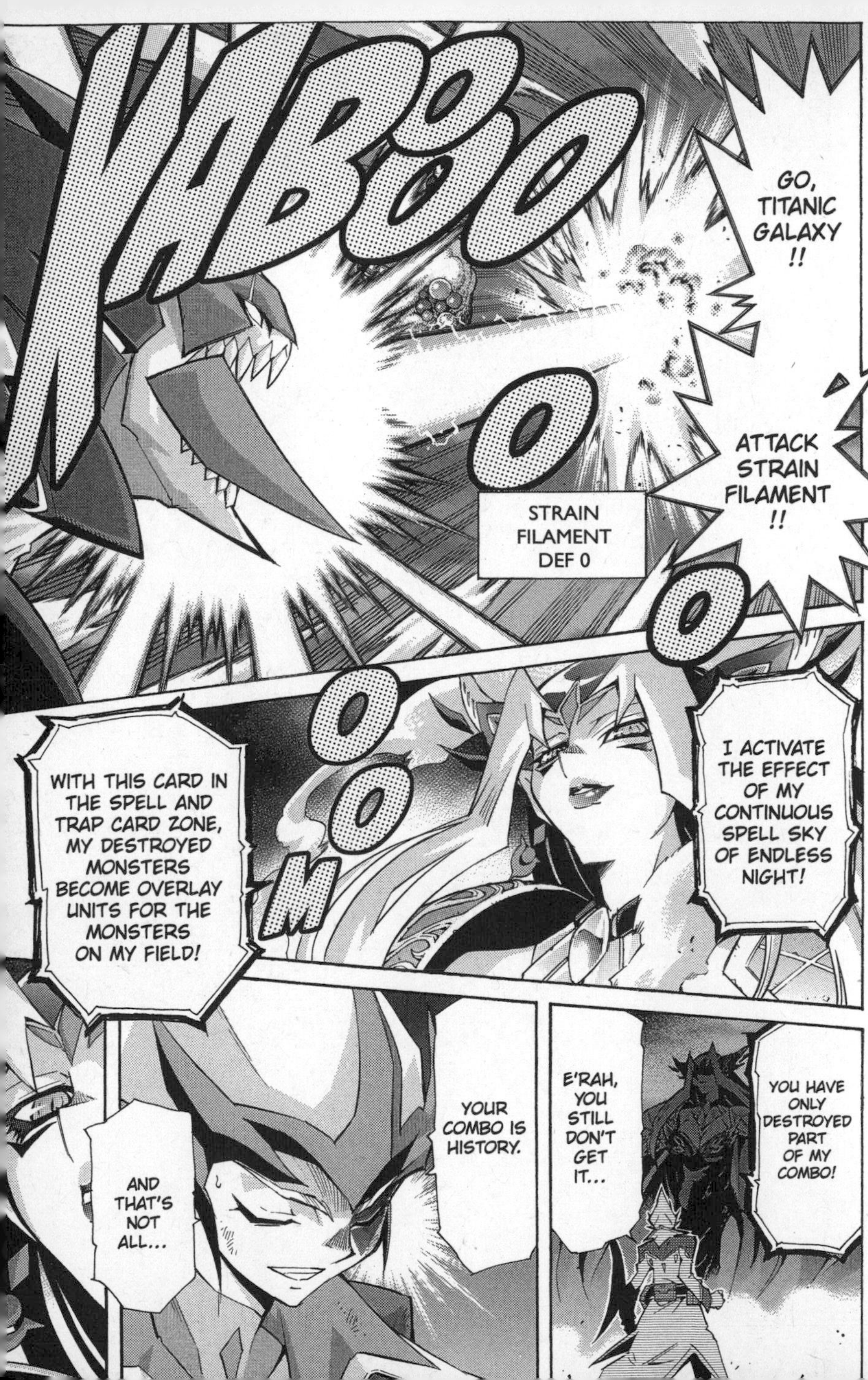
GO, TITANIC GALAXY !!
ATTACK STRAIN FILAMENT !!
STRAIN FILAMENT DEF 0
KABOOOOOOM
I ACTIVATE THE EFFECT OF MY CONTINUOUS SPELL SKY OF ENDLESS NIGHT!
WITH THIS CARD IN THE SPELL AND TRAP CARD ZONE, MY DESTROYED MONSTERS BECOME OVERLAY UNITS FOR THE MONSTERS ON MY FIELD!
YOU HAVE ONLY DESTROYED PART OF MY COMBO!
E'RAH, YOU STILL DON'T GET IT...
YOUR COMBO IS HISTORY.
AND THAT'S NOT ALL...

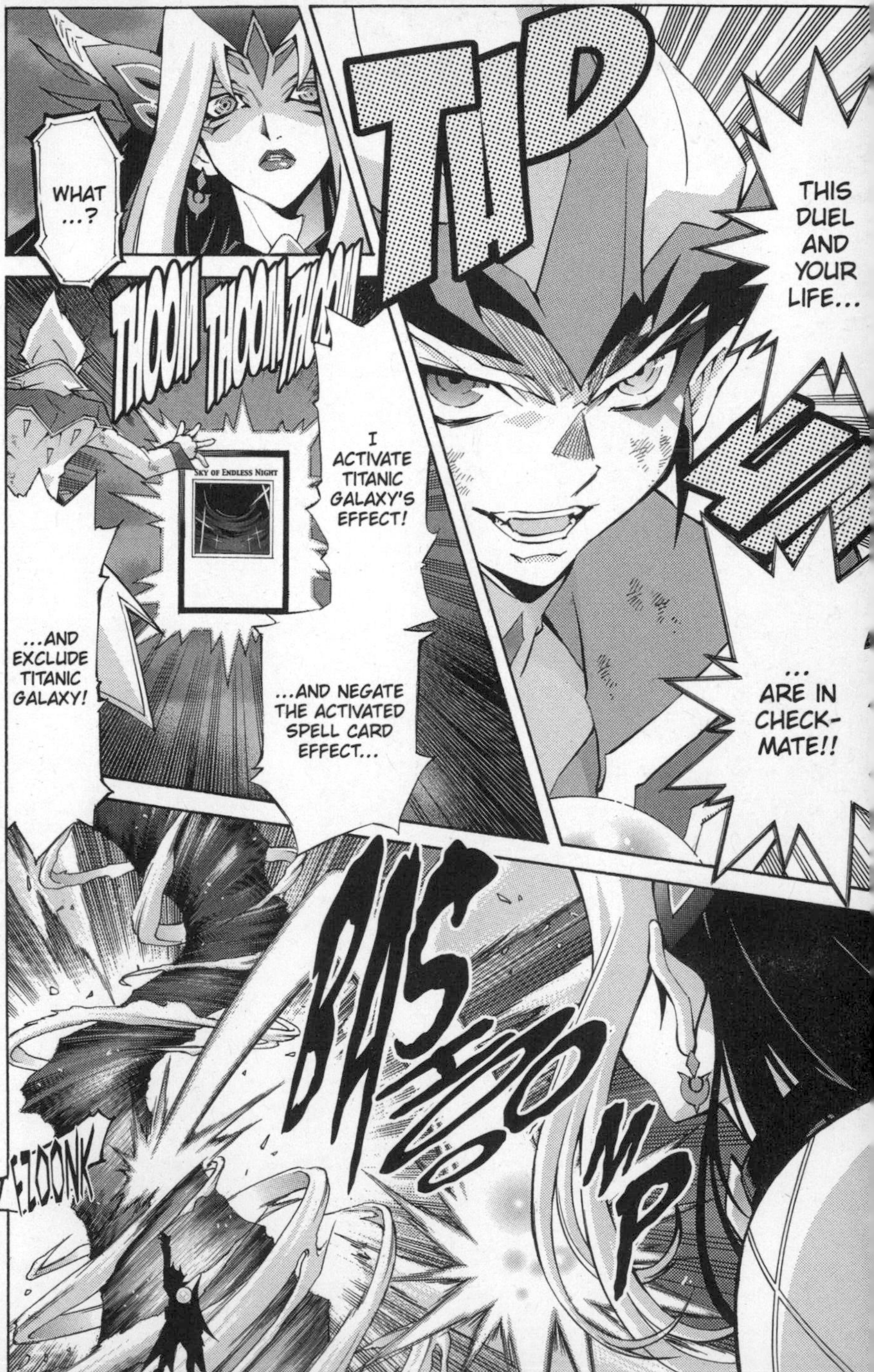
TAP
THIS DUEL AND YOUR LIFE...
...ARE IN CHECK-MATE!!
WHAT ...?
I ACTIVATE TITANIC GALAXY'S EFFECT!
...AND NEGATE THE ACTIVATED SPELL CARD EFFECT...
THOOM THOOM THOOM
SKY OF ENDLESS NIGHT
...AND EXCLUDE TITANIC GALAXY!
BASHOOOMP
FZOONK

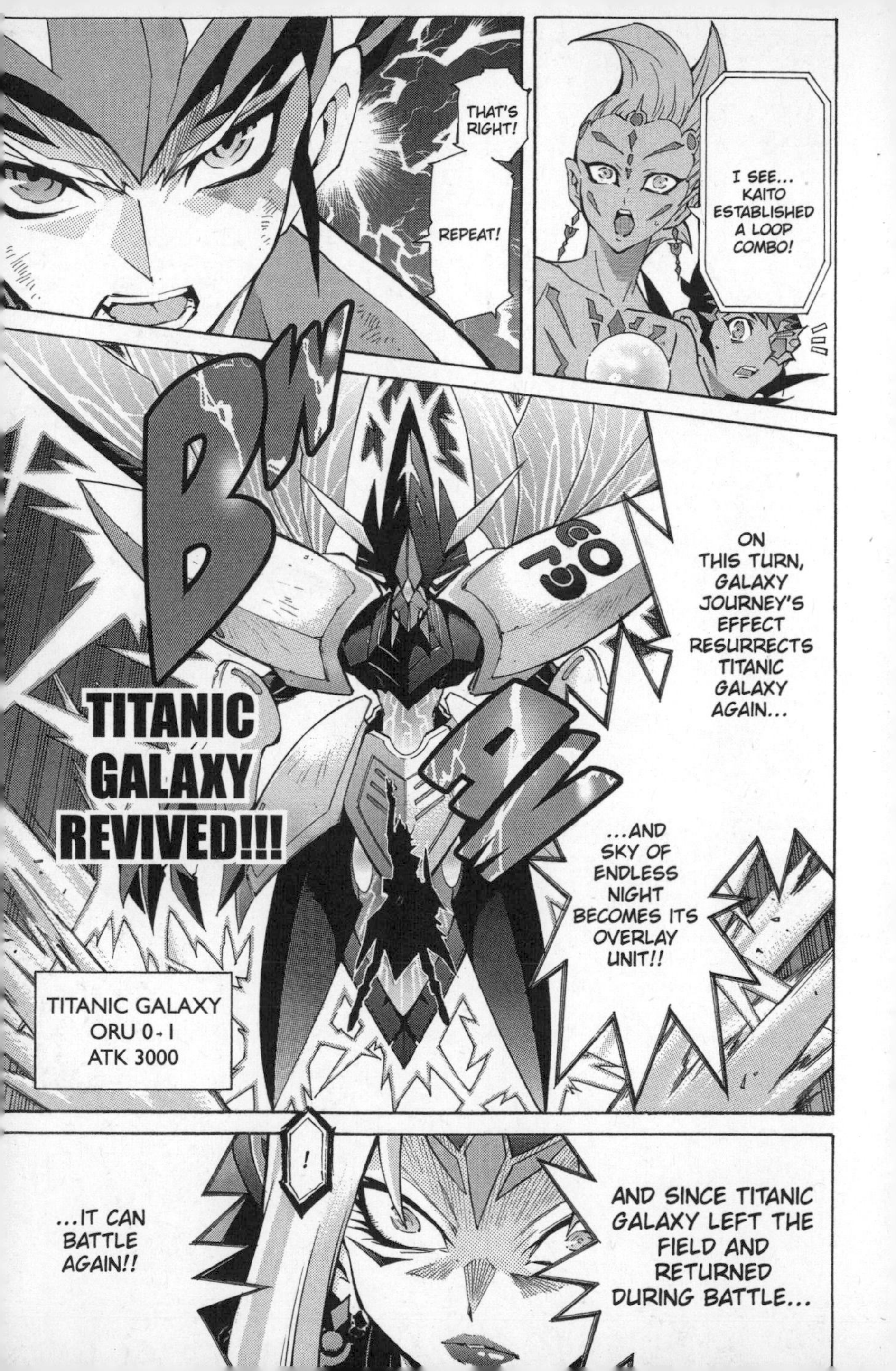
I SEE... KAITO ESTABLISHED A LOOP COMBO!
THAT'S RIGHT!
REPEAT!
ON THIS TURN, GALAXY JOURNEY'S EFFECT RESURRECTS TITANIC GALAXY AGAIN...
...AND SKY OF ENDLESS NIGHT BECOMES ITS OVERLAY UNIT!!
TITANIC GALAXY REVIVED!!!
TITANIC GALAXY
ORU 0→1
ATK 3000
AND SINCE TITANIC GALAXY LEFT THE FIELD AND RETURNED DURING BATTLE...
...IT CAN BATTLE AGAIN!!
!

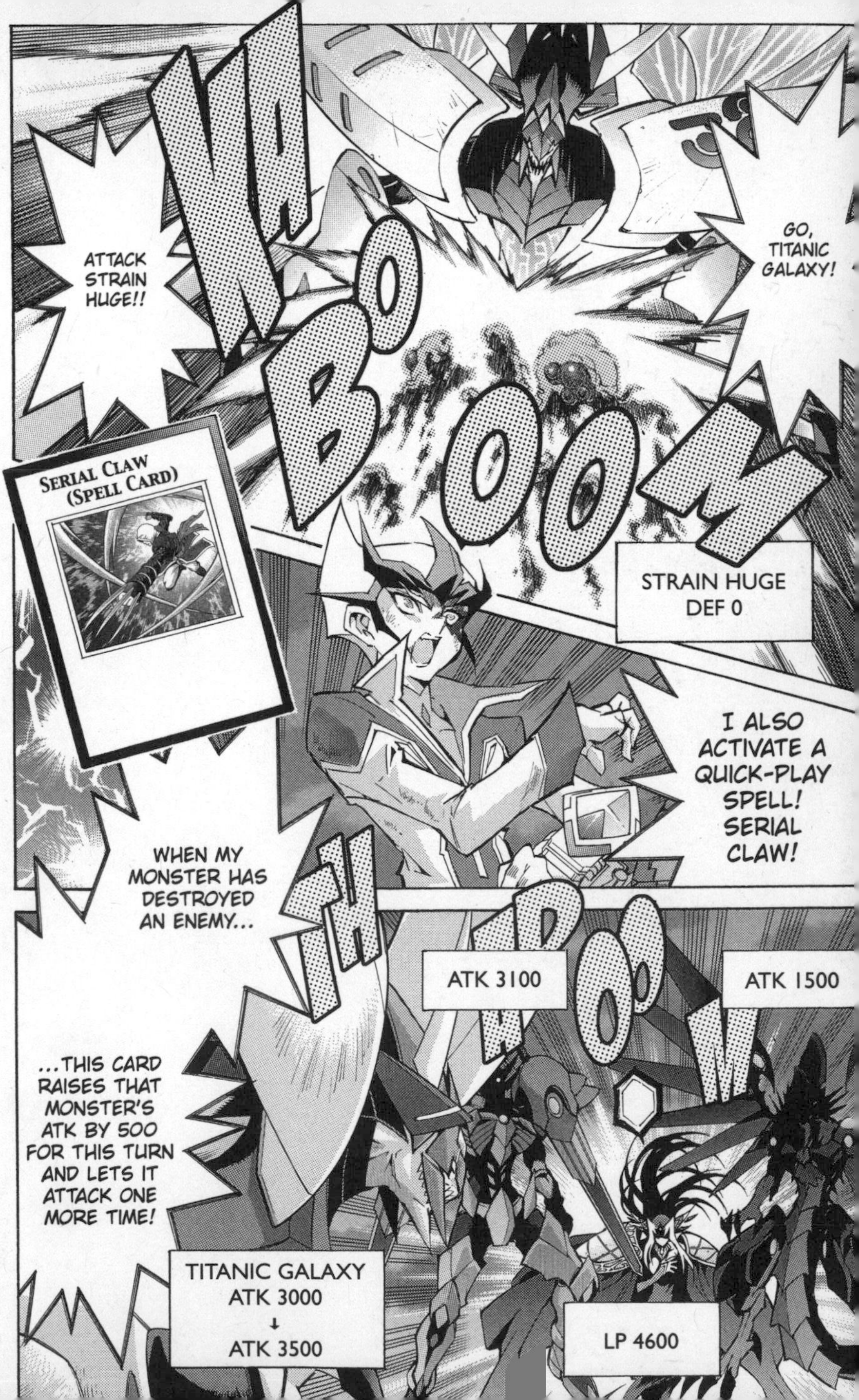
GO, TITANIC GALAXY!
ATTACK STRAIN HUGE!!
WABOOOM
STRAIN HUGE
DEF 0
I ALSO ACTIVATE A QUICK-PLAY SPELL! SERIAL CLAW!
SERIAL CLAW
(SPELL CARD)
WHEN MY MONSTER HAS DESTROYED AN ENEMY...
ATK 1500
ATK 3100
THWOOOM
...THIS CARD RAISES THAT MONSTER'S ATK BY 500 FOR THIS TURN AND LETS IT ATTACK ONE MORE TIME!
LP 4600
TITANIC GALAXY
ATK 3000
↓
ATK 3500

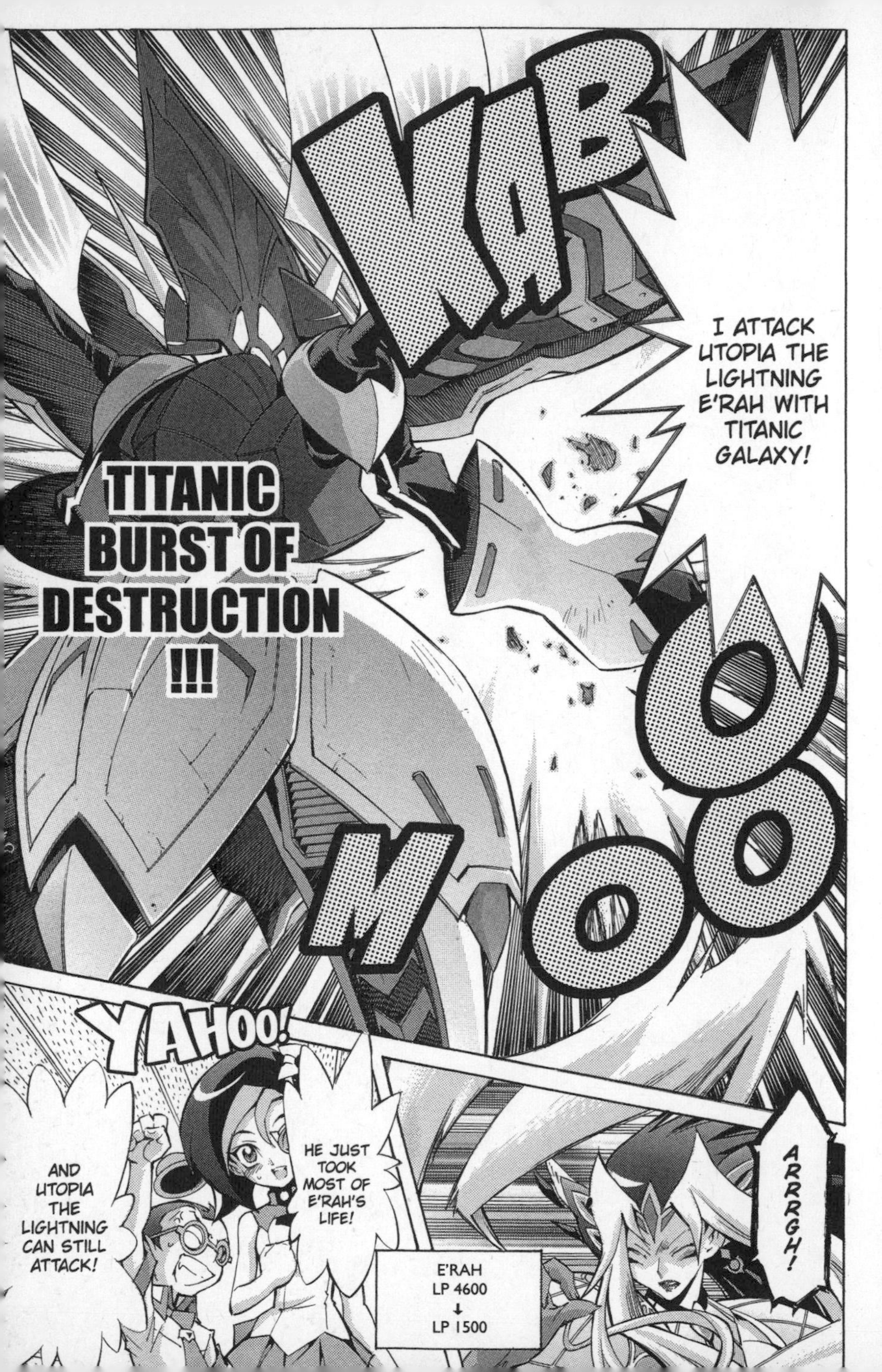
I ATTACK UTOPIA THE LIGHTNING E'RAH WITH TITANIC GALAXY!
KABOOOM
TITANIC BURST OF DESTRUCTION !!!
ARRRGH!
E'RAH LP 4600 ↓ LP 1500
HE JUST TOOK MOST OF E'RAH'S LIFE!
YAHOO!
AND UTOPIA THE LIGHTNING CAN STILL ATTACK!

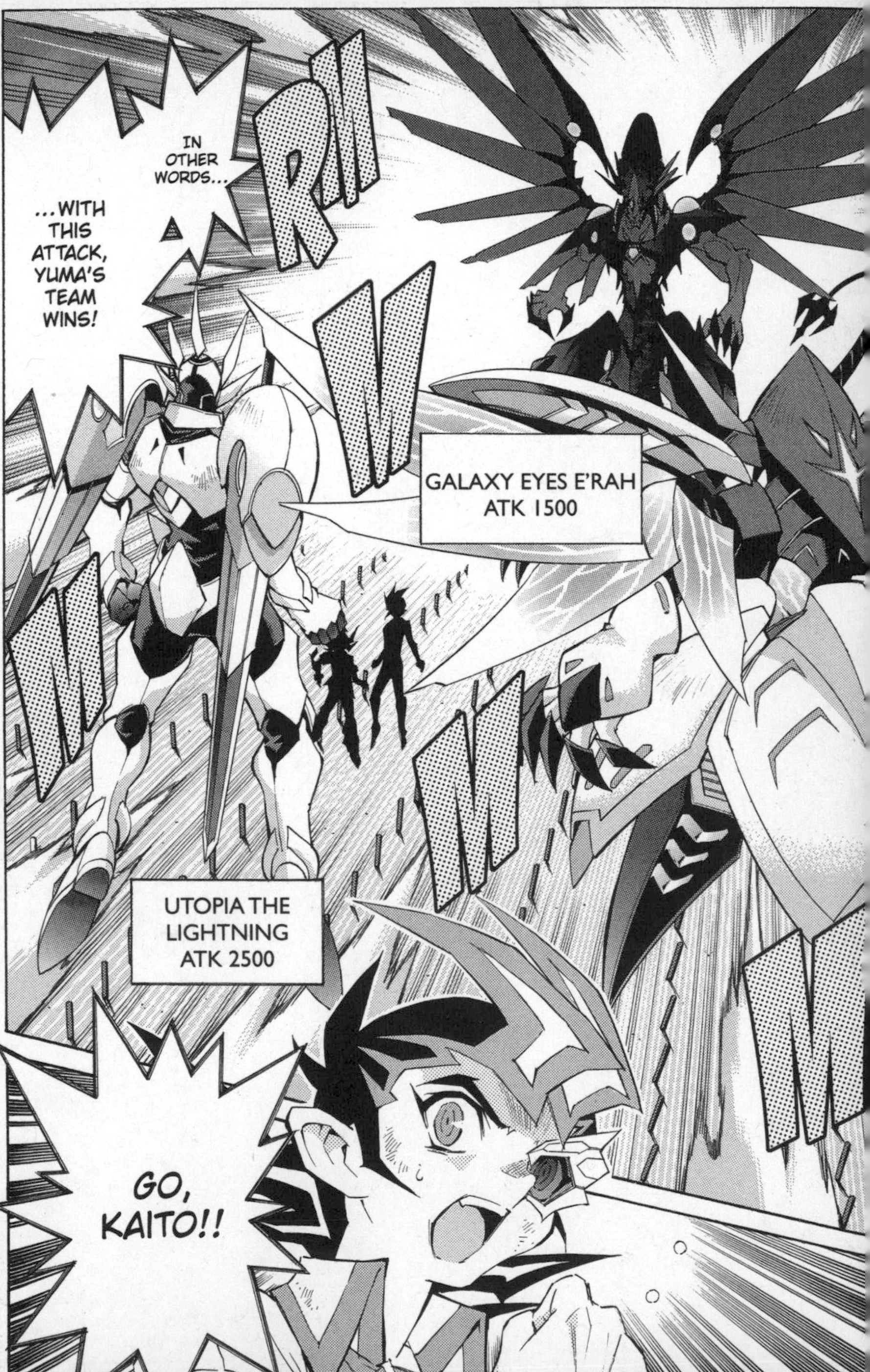
GALAXY EYES E'RAH
ATK 1500
RMMM
IN OTHER WORDS...
...WITH THIS ATTACK, YUMA'S TEAM WINS!
UTOPIA THE LIGHTNING
ATK 2500
GO, KAITO!!

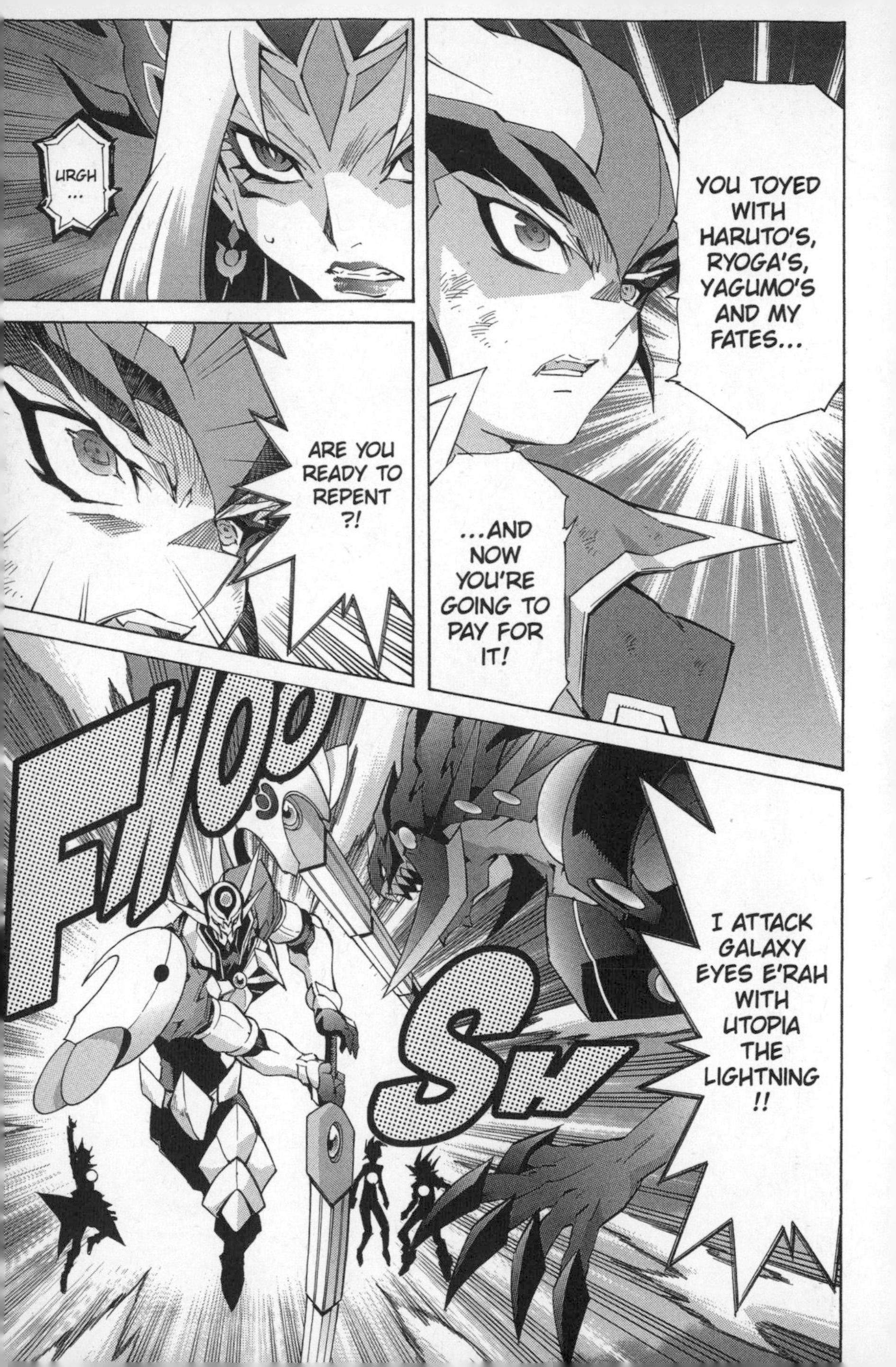
YOU TOYED WITH HARUTO'S, RYOGA'S, YAGUMO'S AND MY FATES...
...AND NOW YOU'RE GOING TO PAY FOR IT!
URGH ...
ARE YOU READY TO REPENT ?!
I ATTACK GALAXY EYES E'RAH WITH UTOPIA THE LIGHTNING !!
FWOO
SH

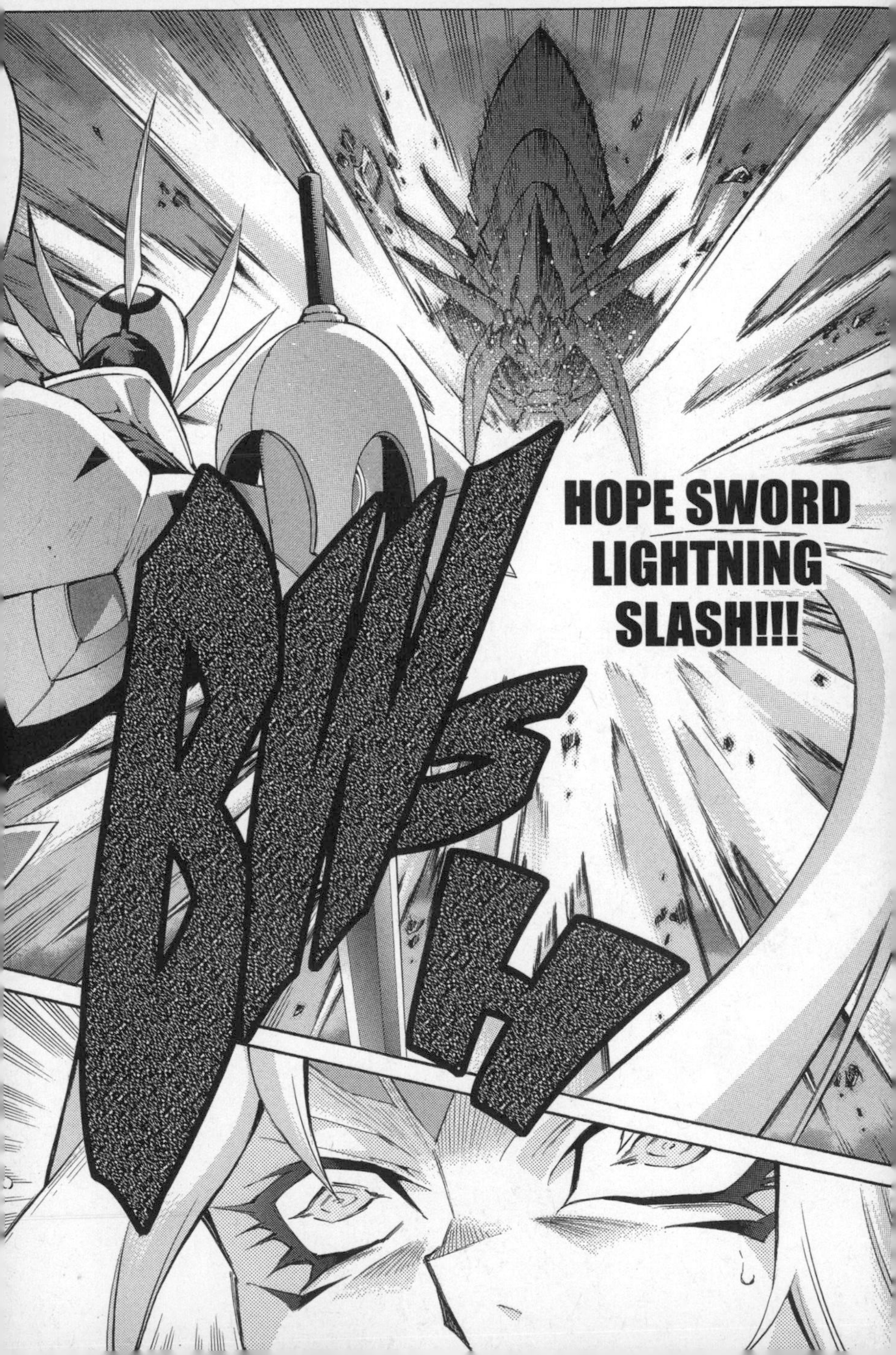
HOPE SWORD LIGHTNING SLASH!!!

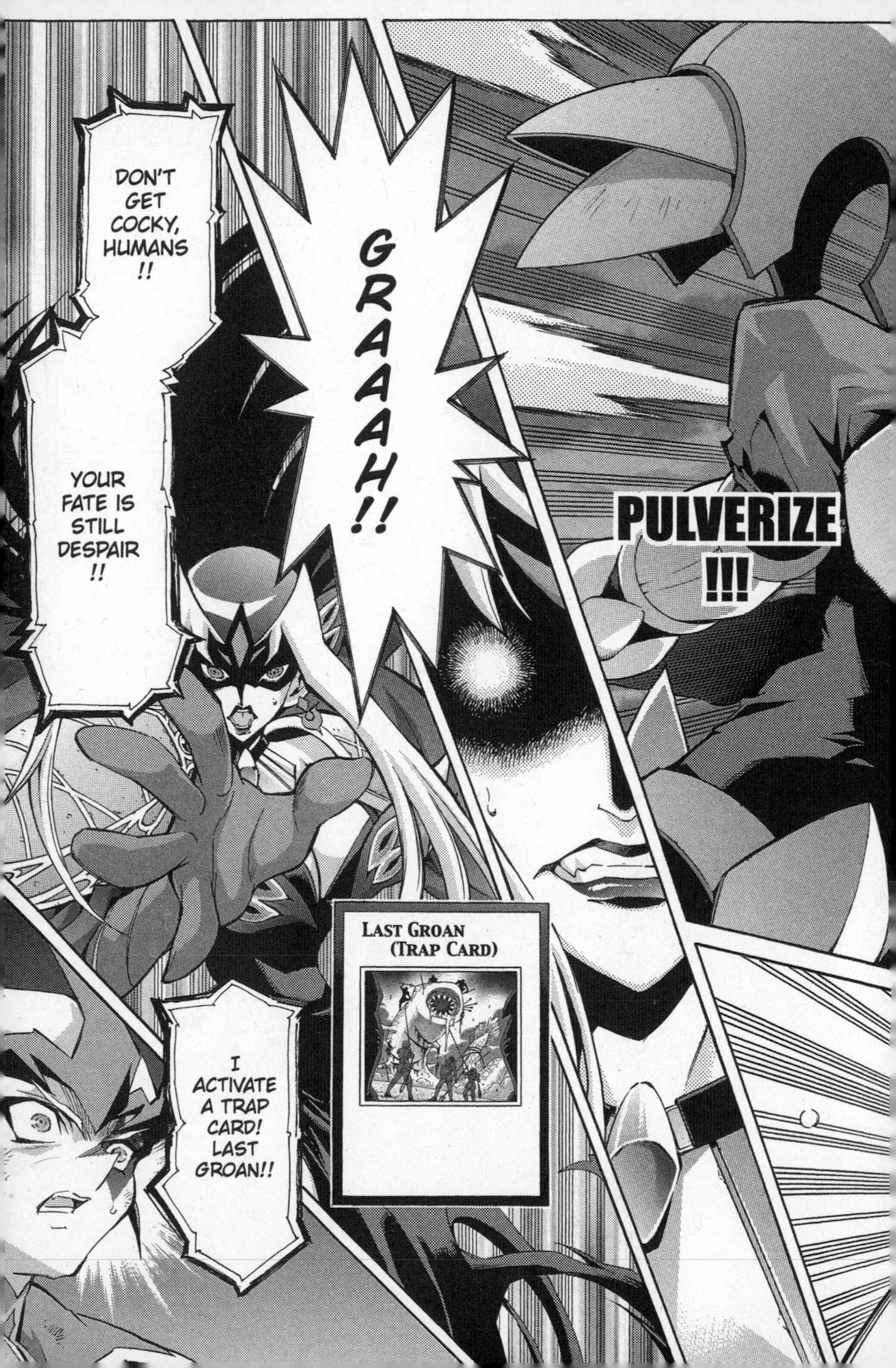
PULVERIZE!!!
GRAAAAH!!
DON'T GET COCKY, HUMANS!!
YOUR FATE IS STILL DESPAIR!!
LAST GROAN (TRAP CARD)
I ACTIVATE A TRAP CARD! LAST GROAN!!

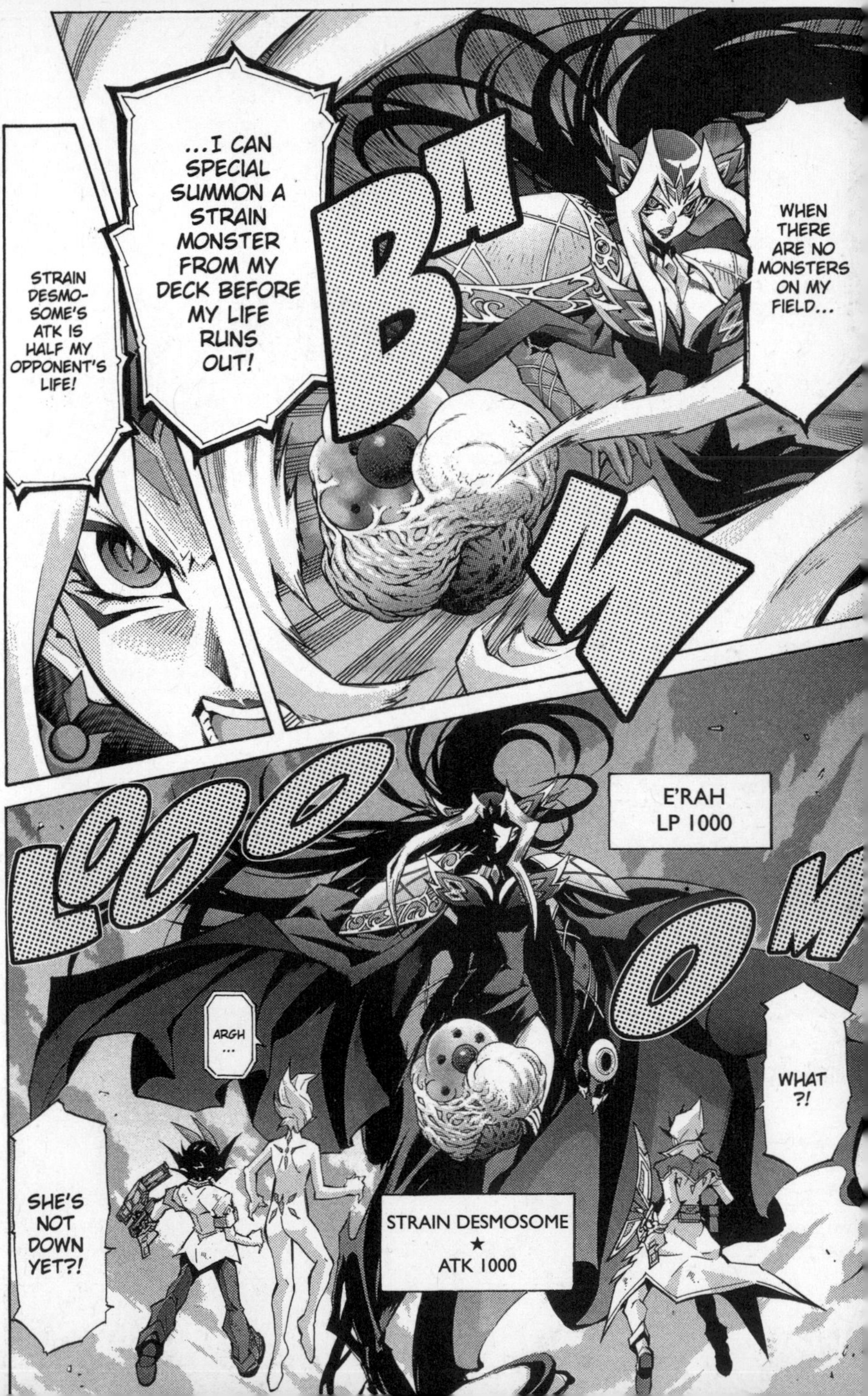
WHEN THERE ARE NO MONSTERS ON MY FIELD...
BA
...I CAN SPECIAL SUMMON A STRAIN MONSTER FROM MY DECK BEFORE MY LIFE RUNS OUT!
M
STRAIN DESMO-SOME'S ATK IS HALF MY OPPONENT'S LIFE!
E'RAH LP 1000
LOOOOOM
WHAT ?!
ARGH ...
STRAIN DESMOSOME ★ ATK 1000
SHE'S NOT DOWN YET?!

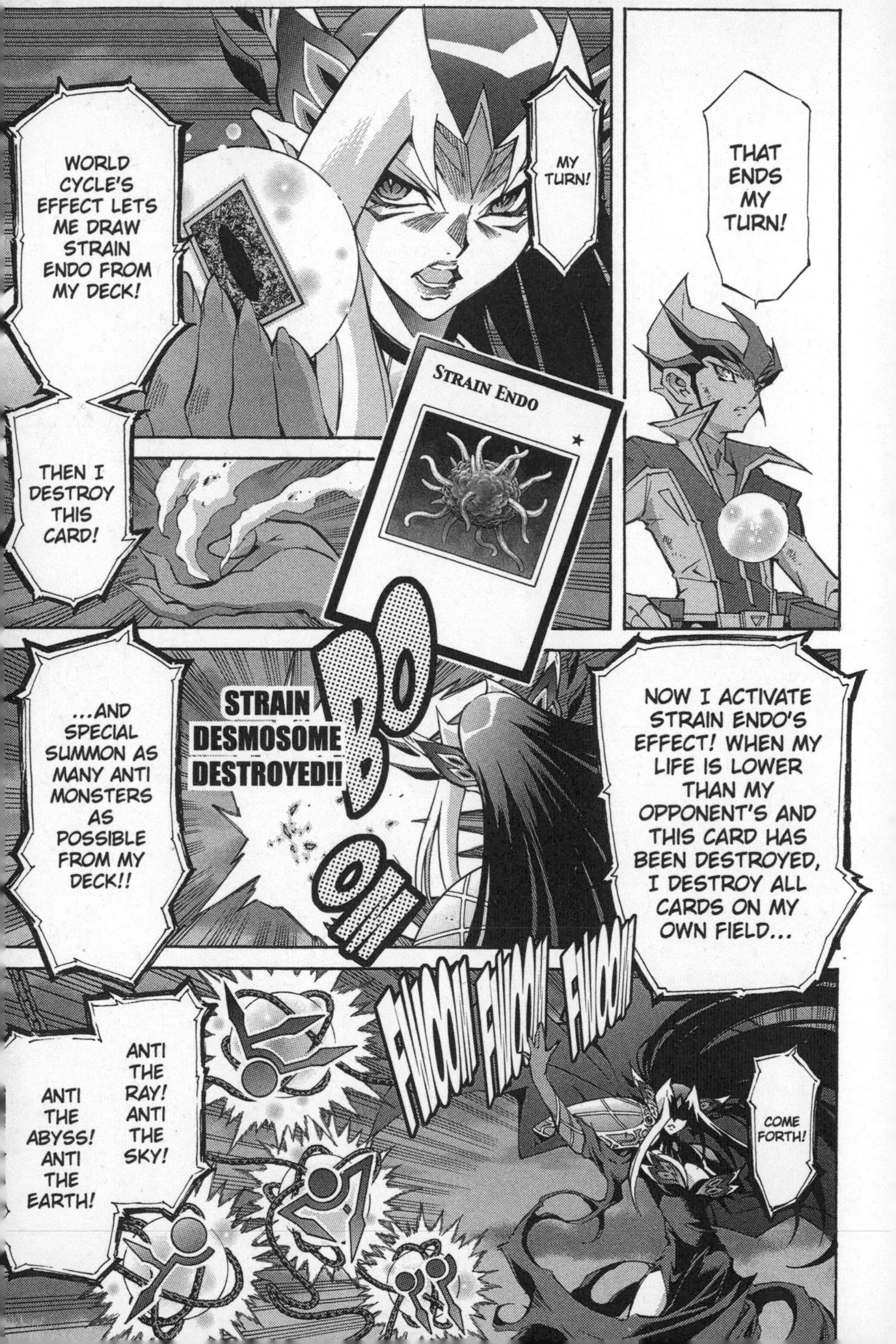
THAT ENDS MY TURN!
MY TURN!
WORLD CYCLE'S EFFECT LETS ME DRAW STRAIN ENDO FROM MY DECK!
THEN I DESTROY THIS CARD!
STRAIN ENDO
NOW I ACTIVATE STRAIN ENDO'S EFFECT! WHEN MY LIFE IS LOWER THAN MY OPPONENT'S AND THIS CARD HAS BEEN DESTROYED, I DESTROY ALL CARDS ON MY OWN FIELD...
BOOM!
STRAIN DESMOSOME DESTROYED!!
...AND SPECIAL SUMMON AS MANY ANTI MONSTERS AS POSSIBLE FROM MY DECK!!
FWOOM! FWOOM! FWOOM!
COME FORTH!
ANTI THE RAY! ANTI THE SKY!
ANTI THE ABYSS! ANTI THE EARTH!

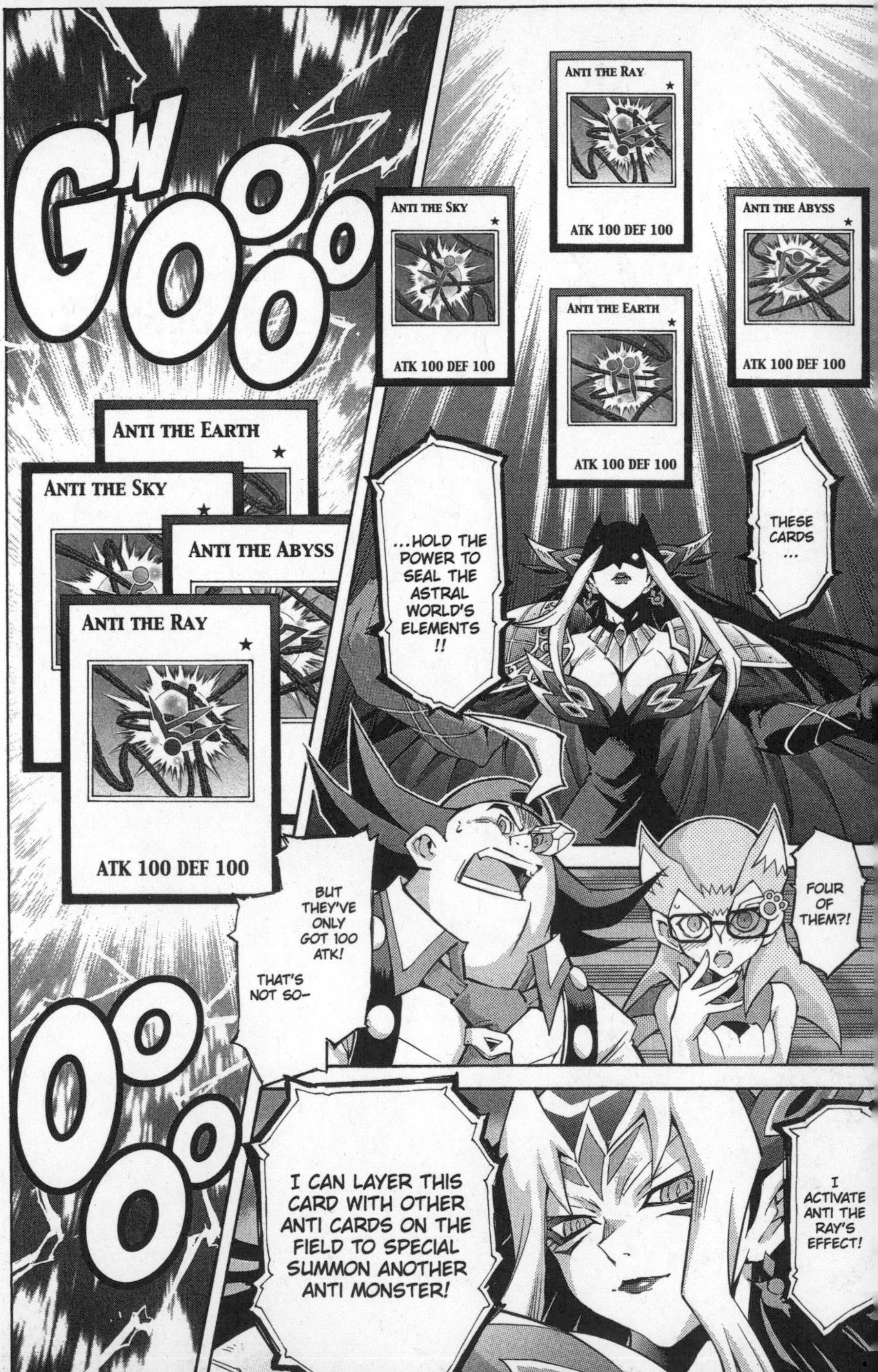
ANTI THE RAY
ATK 100 DEF 100
ANTI THE ABYSS
ATK 100 DEF 100
ANTI THE SKY
ATK 100 DEF 100
ANTI THE EARTH
ATK 100 DEF 100
THESE CARDS ...
...HOLD THE POWER TO SEAL THE ASTRAL WORLD'S ELEMENTS !!
GWOOOO
ANTI THE EARTH
ANTI THE SKY
ANTI THE ABYSS
ANTI THE RAY
ATK 100 DEF 100
FOUR OF THEM?!
BUT THEY'VE ONLY GOT 100 ATK!
THAT'S NOT SO-
OOOO
I ACTIVATE ANTI THE RAY'S EFFECT!
I CAN LAYER THIS CARD WITH OTHER ANTI CARDS ON THE FIELD TO SPECIAL SUMMON ANOTHER ANTI MONSTER!

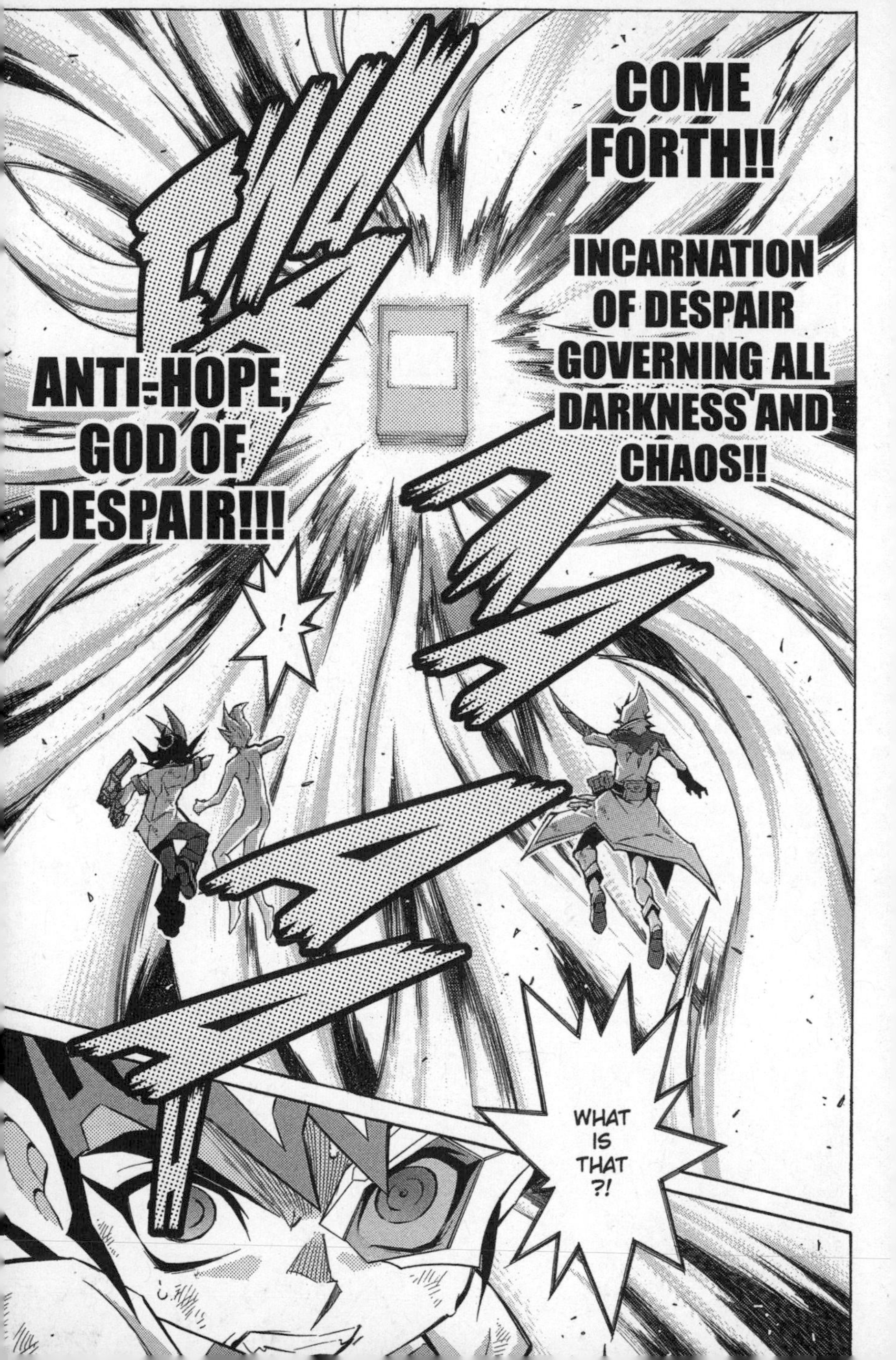
COME FORTH!!
INCARNATION OF DESPAIR GOVERNING ALL DARKNESS AND CHAOS!!
ANTI-HOPE, GOD OF DESPAIR!!!
!
WHAT IS THAT ?!

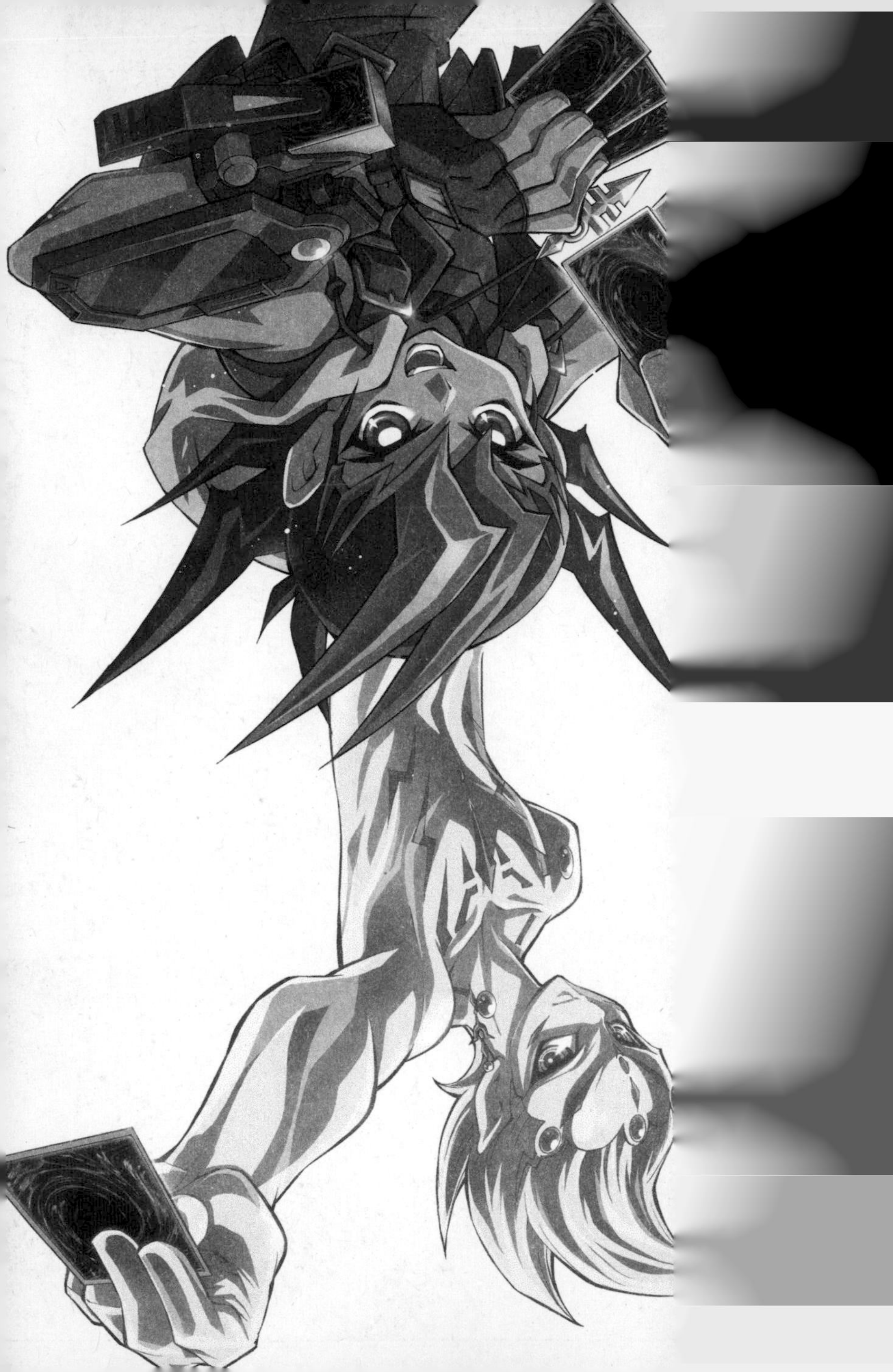

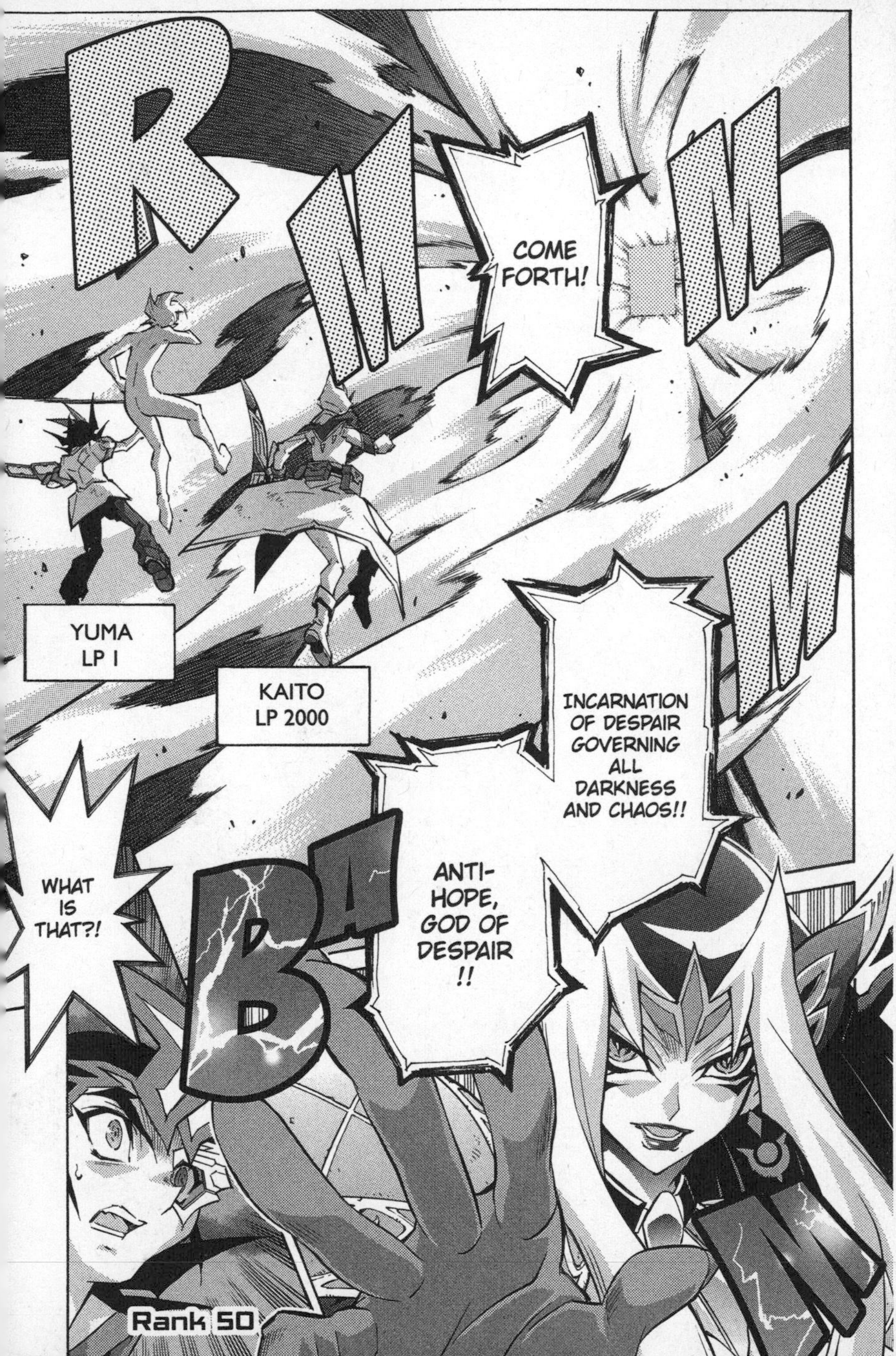
RMMM
COME FORTH!
YUMA LP 1
KAITO LP 2000
INCARNATION OF DESPAIR GOVERNING ALL DARKNESS AND CHAOS!!
ANTI-HOPE, GOD OF DESPAIR !!
BA
WHAT IS THAT?!

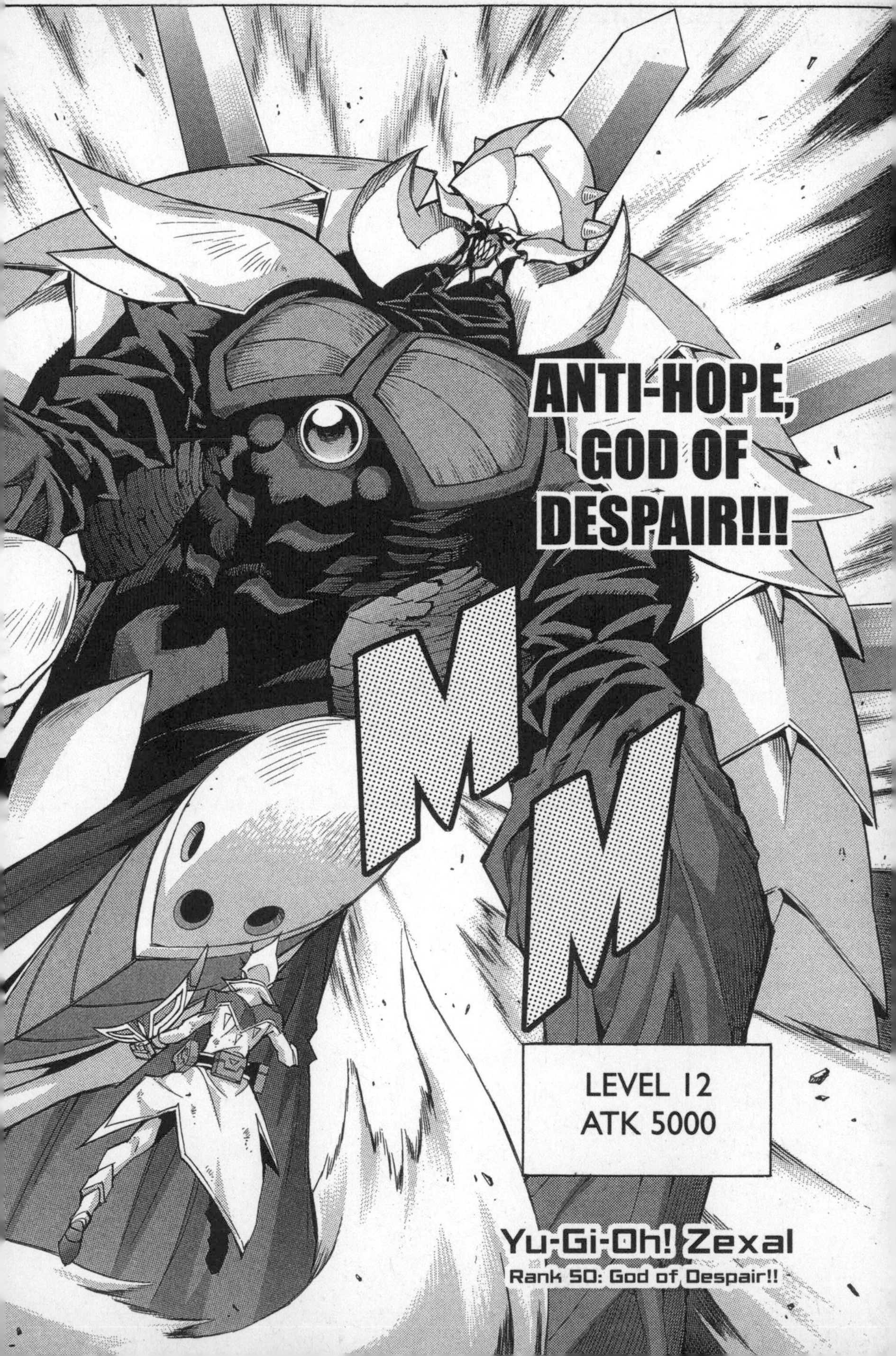
ANTI-HOPE, GOD OF DESPAIR!!!
MMM
LEVEL 12
ATK 5000
Yu-Gi-Oh! Zexal
Rank 50: God of Despair!!

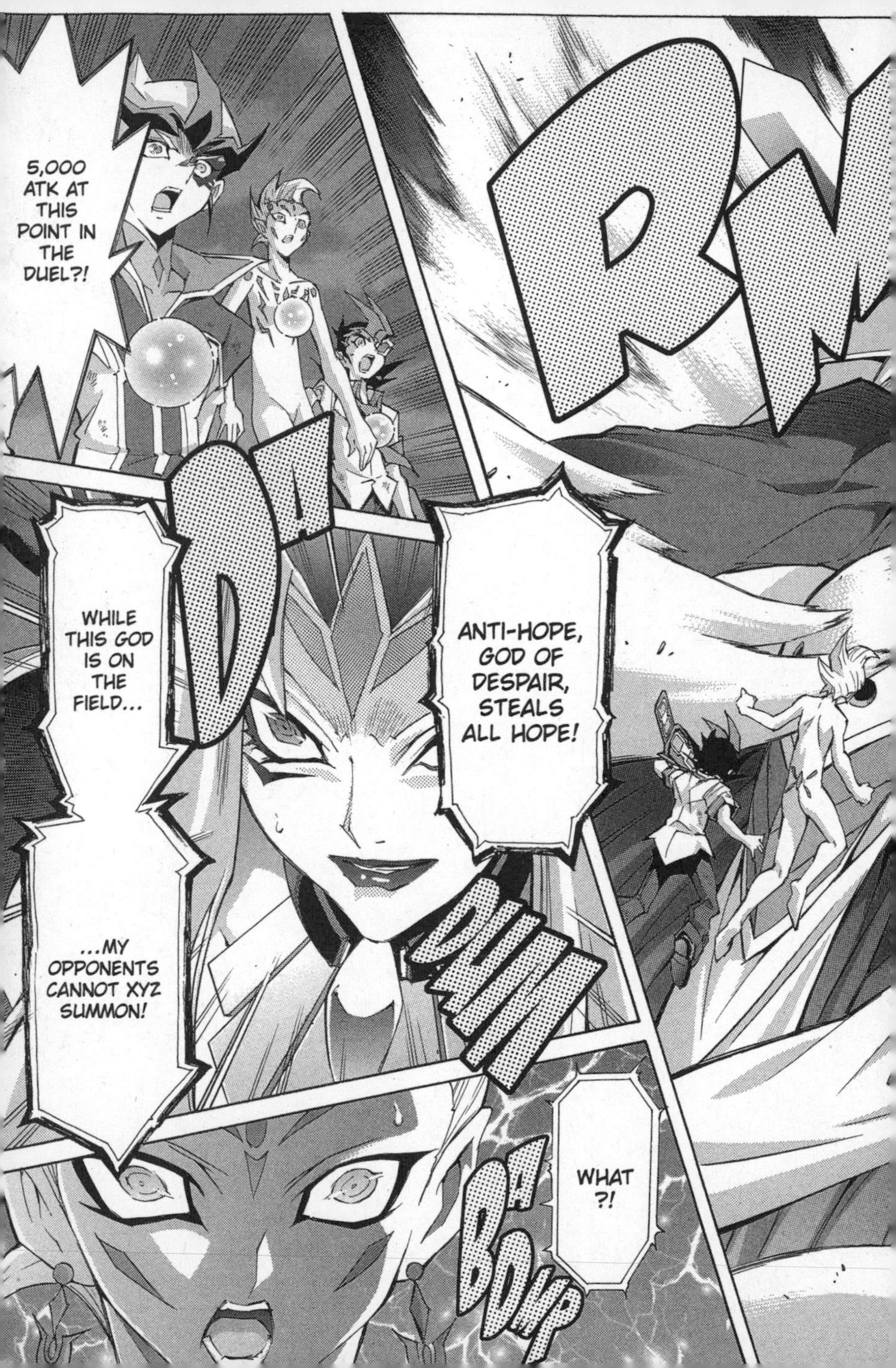
5,000 ATK AT THIS POINT IN THE DUEL?!
ANTI-HOPE, GOD OF DESPAIR, STEALS ALL HOPE!
WHILE THIS GOD IS ON THE FIELD...
...MY OPPONENTS CANNOT XYZ SUMMON!
WHAT ?!

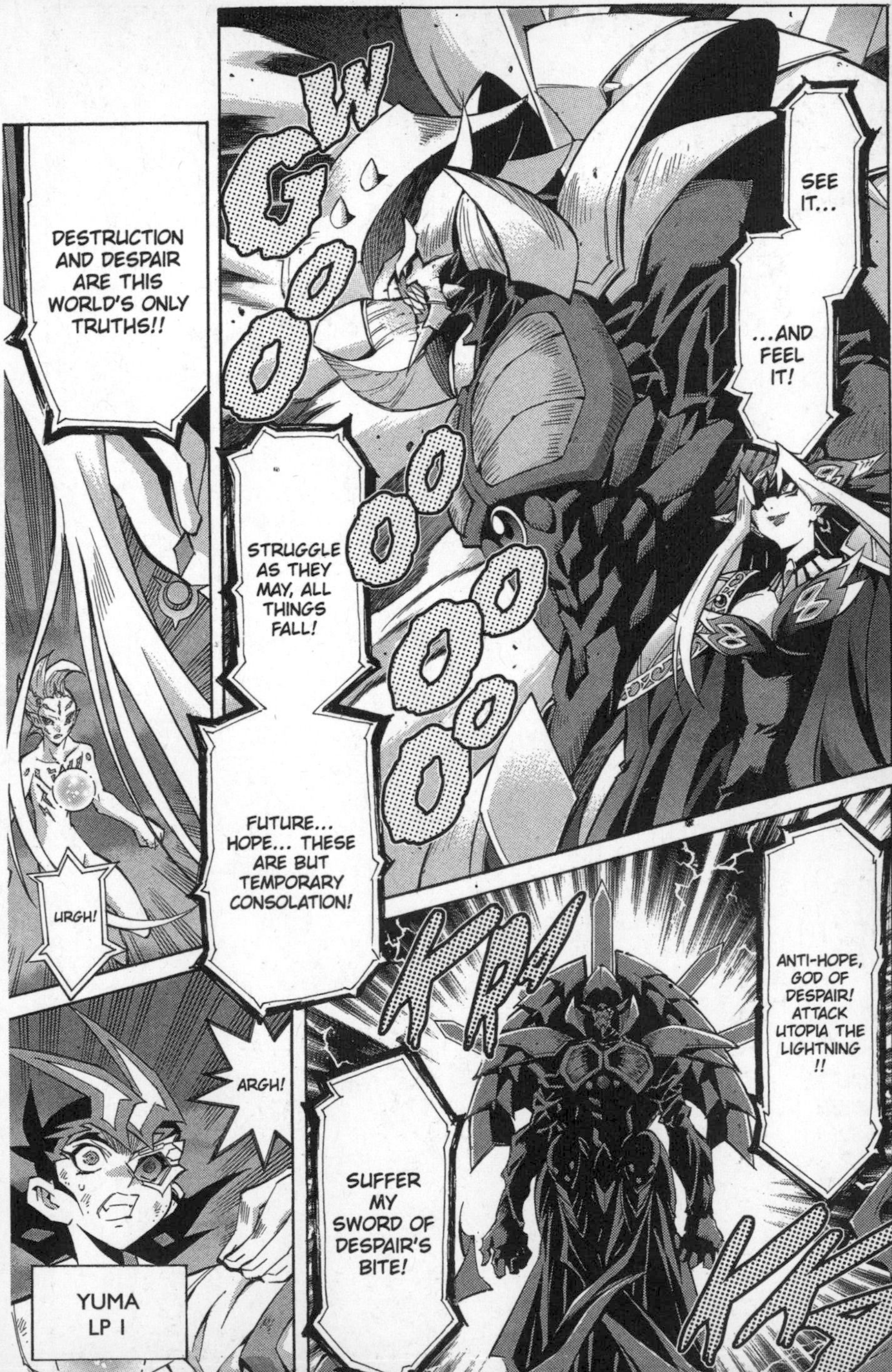
SEE IT...
...AND FEEL IT!
GWOOOOOOOOO
STRUGGLE AS THEY MAY, ALL THINGS FALL!
FUTURE... HOPE... THESE ARE BUT TEMPORARY CONSOLATION!
DESTRUCTION AND DESPAIR ARE THIS WORLD'S ONLY TRUTHS!!
URGH!
ANTI-HOPE, GOD OF DESPAIR! ATTACK UTOPIA THE LIGHTNING!!
KRA
SUFFER MY SWORD OF DESPAIR'S BITE!
KKK
ARGH!
YUMA LP 1

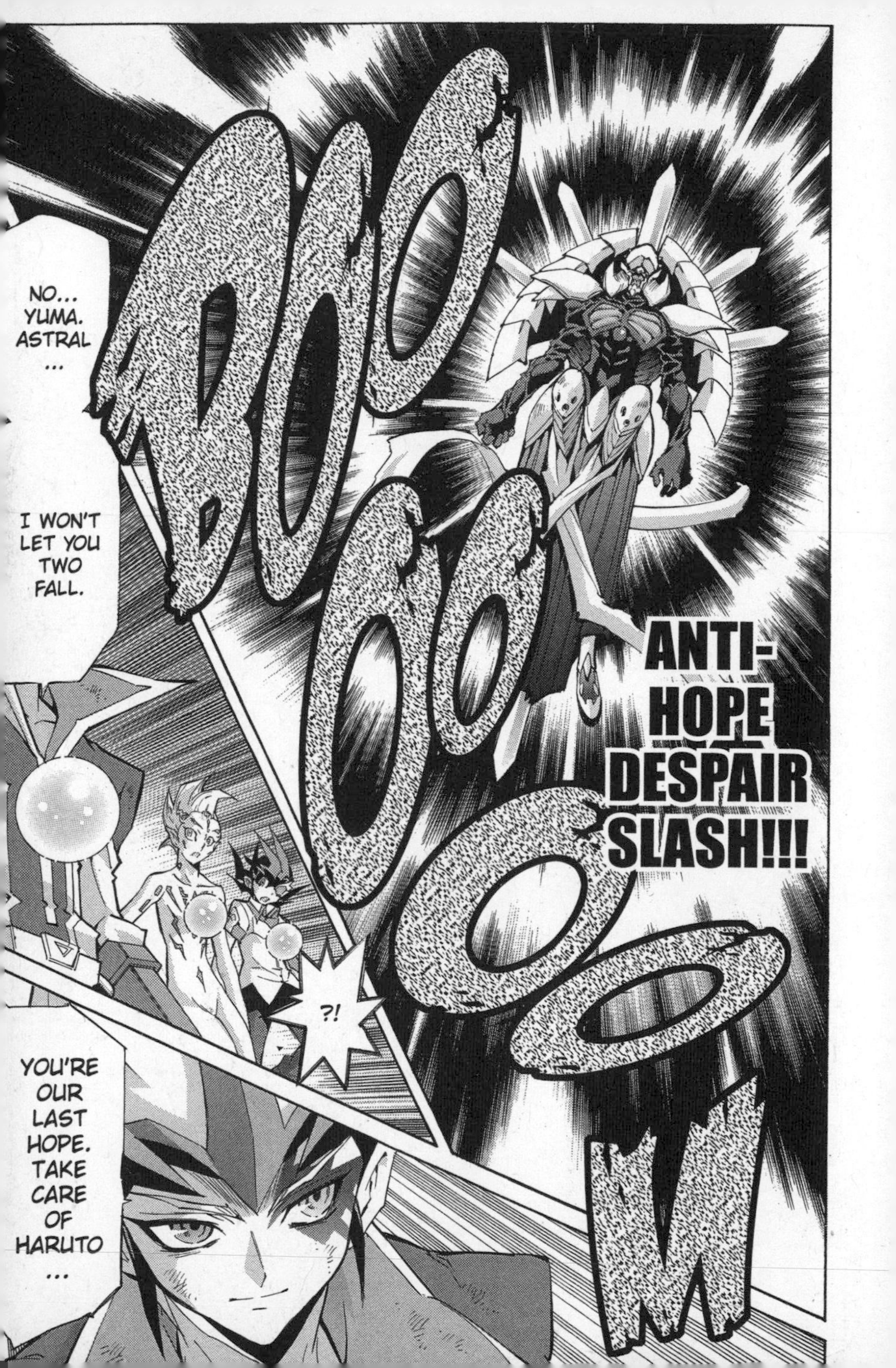
ANTI-HOPE DESPAIR SLASH!!!
BOOOOOOOM
NO... YUMA. ASTRAL...
I WON'T LET YOU TWO FALL.
?!
YOU'RE OUR LAST HOPE. TAKE CARE OF HARUTO...

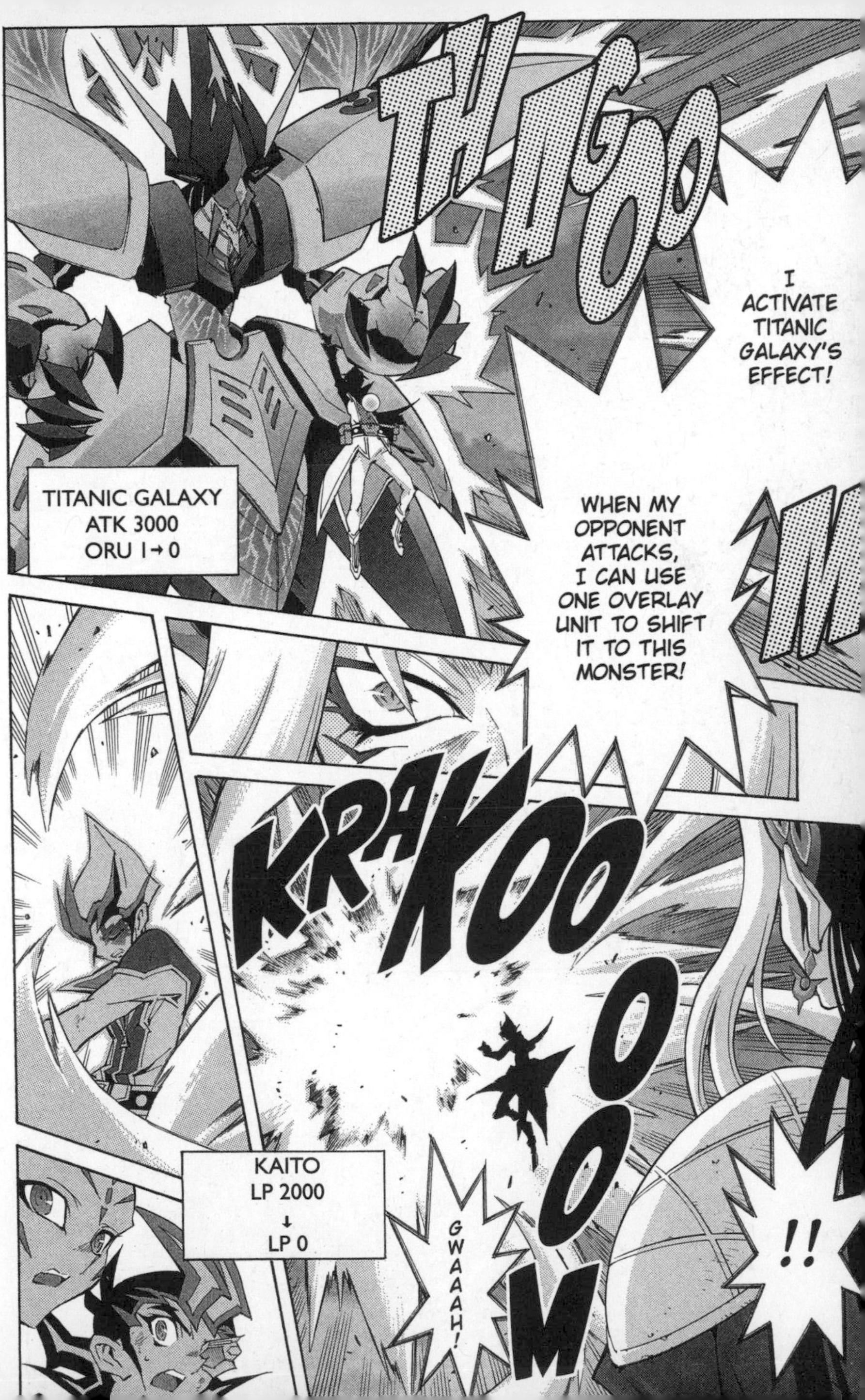
I ACTIVATE TITANIC GALAXY'S EFFECT!
THWOOM
TITANIC GALAXY
ATK 3000
ORU 1 → 0
WHEN MY OPPONENT ATTACKS, I CAN USE ONE OVERLAY UNIT TO SHIFT IT TO THIS MONSTER!
KRAKOOOOM
!!
GWAAAH!
KAITO
LP 2000
↓
LP 0

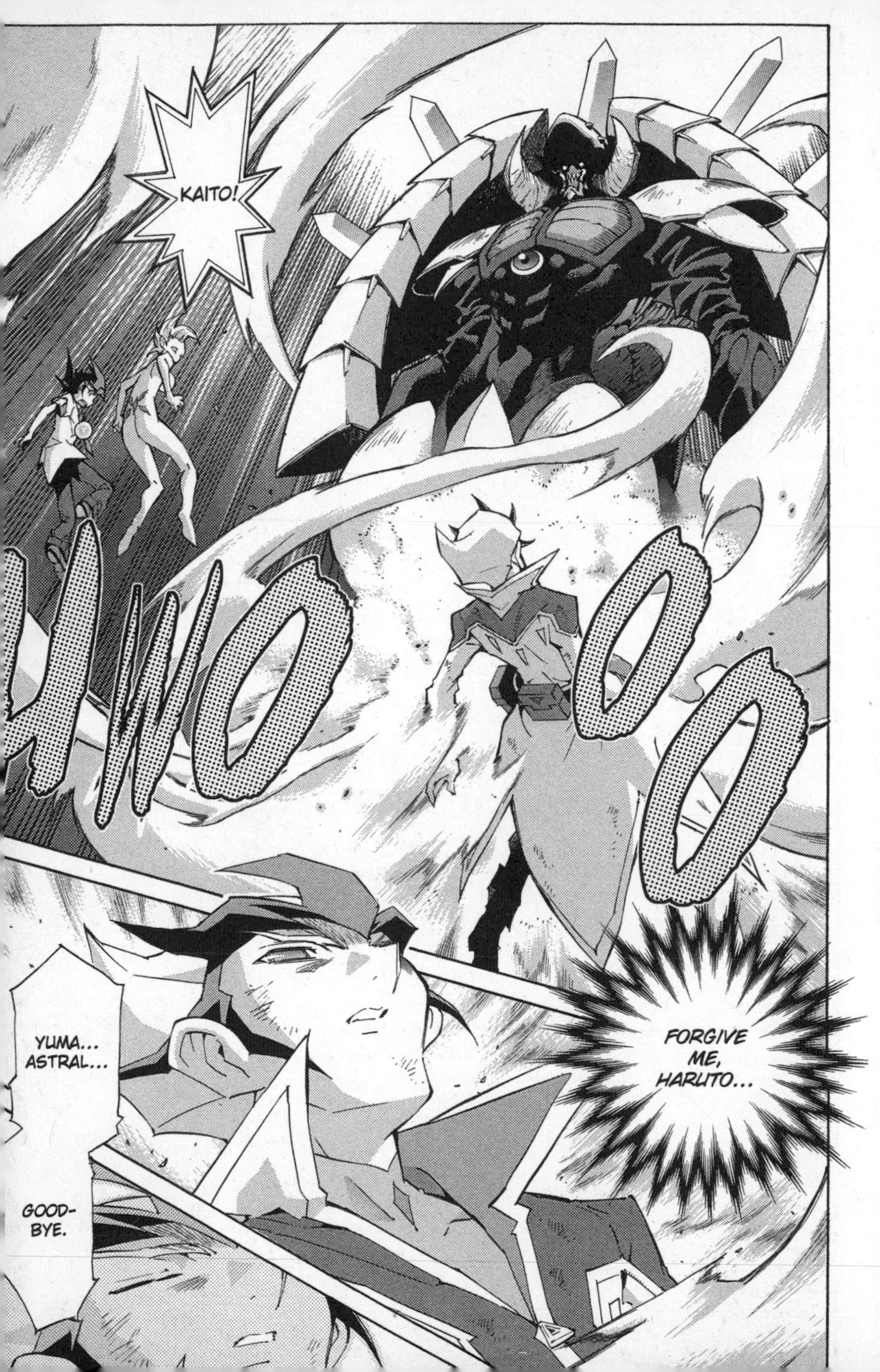
KAITO!
WOOO
FORGIVE ME, HARUTO...
YUMA... ASTRAL...
GOOD-BYE.

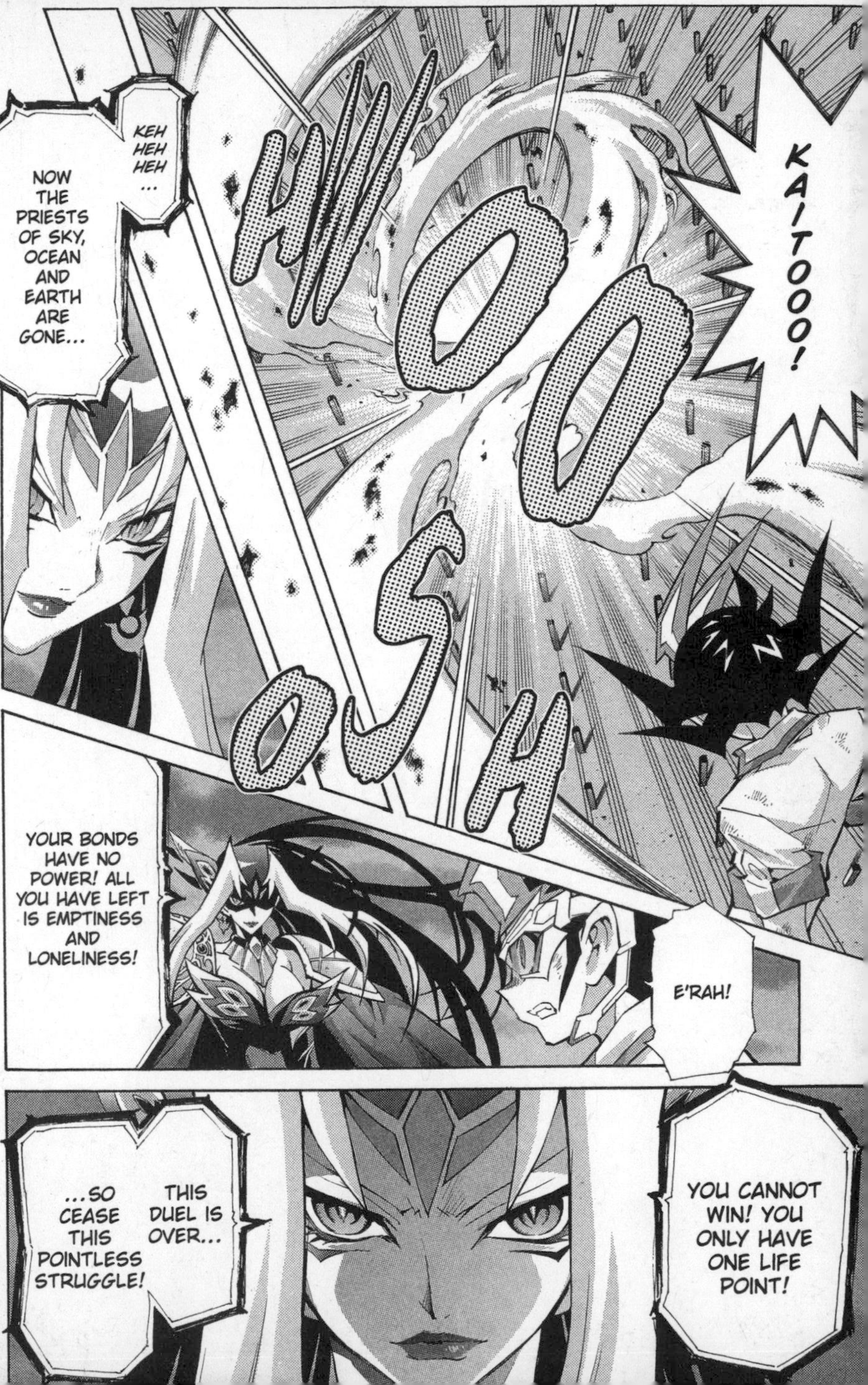
KAITOOO!
WHOOOSH
KEH HEH HEH...
NOW THE PRIESTS OF SKY, OCEAN AND EARTH ARE GONE...
E'RAH!
YOUR BONDS HAVE NO POWER! ALL YOU HAVE LEFT IS EMPTINESS AND LONELINESS!
YOU CANNOT WIN! YOU ONLY HAVE ONE LIFE POINT!
THIS DUEL IS OVER...
...SO CEASE THIS POINTLESS STRUGGLE!

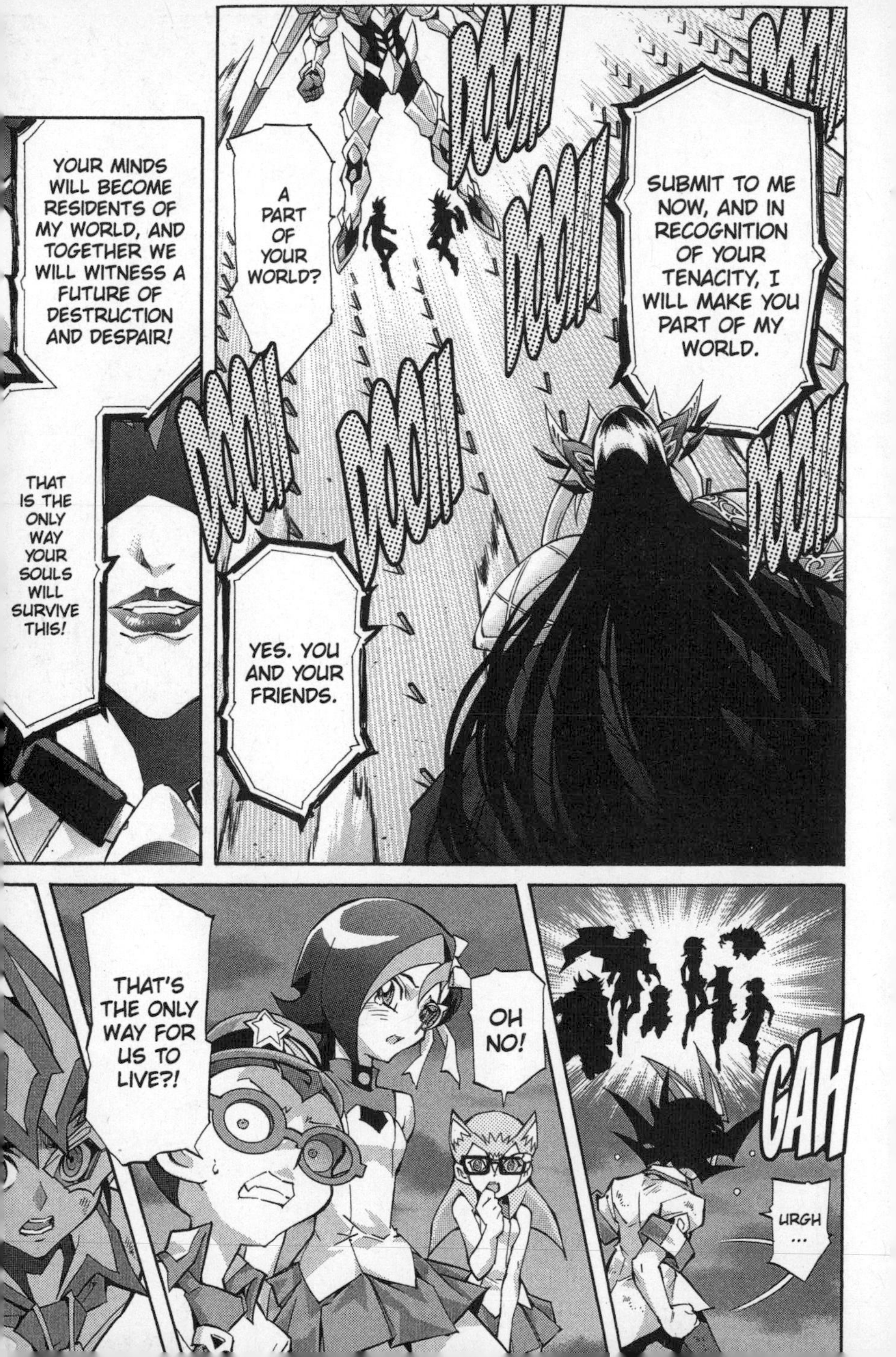
SUBMIT TO ME NOW, AND IN RECOGNITION OF YOUR TENACITY, I WILL MAKE YOU PART OF MY WORLD.
GAH
DOOM
DOOM
A PART OF YOUR WORLD?
DOOM
DOOM
YES. YOU AND YOUR FRIENDS.
YOUR MINDS WILL BECOME RESIDENTS OF MY WORLD, AND TOGETHER WE WILL WITNESS A FUTURE OF DESTRUCTION AND DESPAIR!
THAT IS THE ONLY WAY YOUR SOULS WILL SURVIVE THIS!
GAH
URGH...
OH NO!
THAT'S THE ONLY WAY FOR US TO LIVE?!

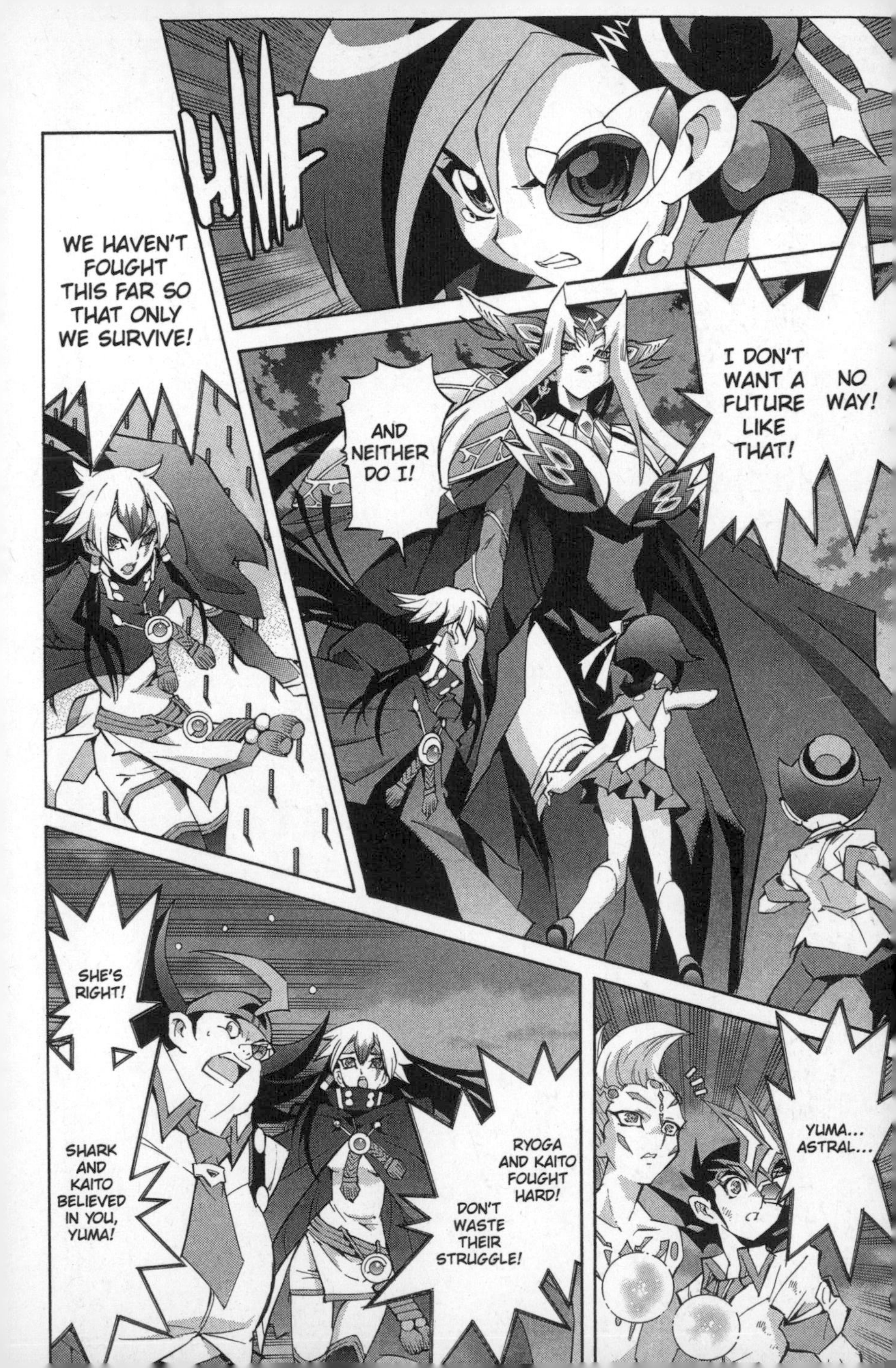
HMF
WE HAVEN'T FOUGHT THIS FAR SO THAT ONLY WE SURVIVE!
NO WAY!
I DON'T WANT A FUTURE LIKE THAT!
AND NEITHER DO I!
YUMA... ASTRAL...
RYOGA AND KAITO FOUGHT HARD!
DON'T WASTE THEIR STRUGGLE!
SHE'S RIGHT!
SHARK AND KAITO BELIEVED IN YOU, YUMA!

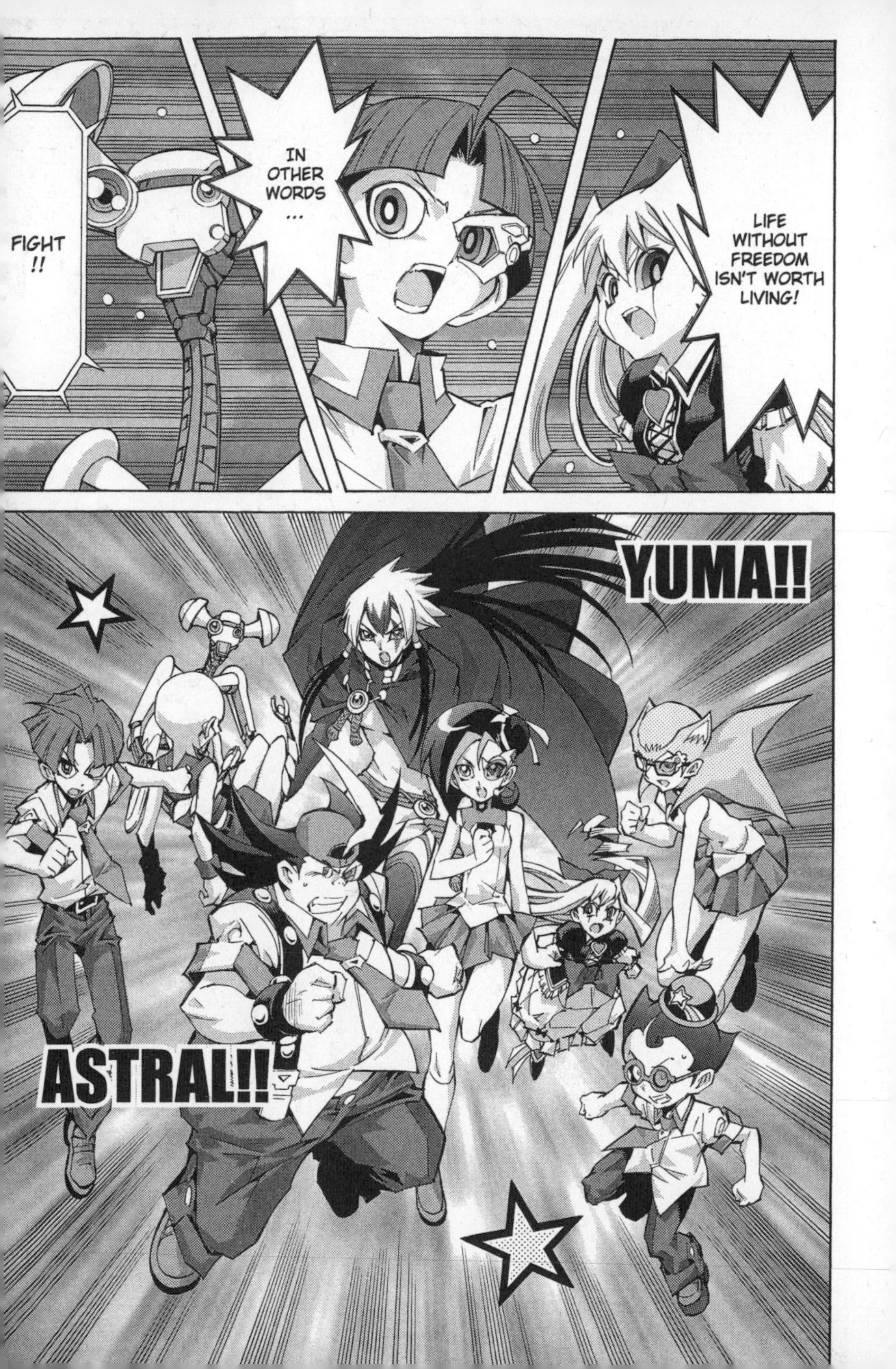
LIFE WITHOUT FREEDOM ISN'T WORTH LIVING!
IN OTHER WORDS ...
FIGHT !!
YUMA!!
ASTRAL!!

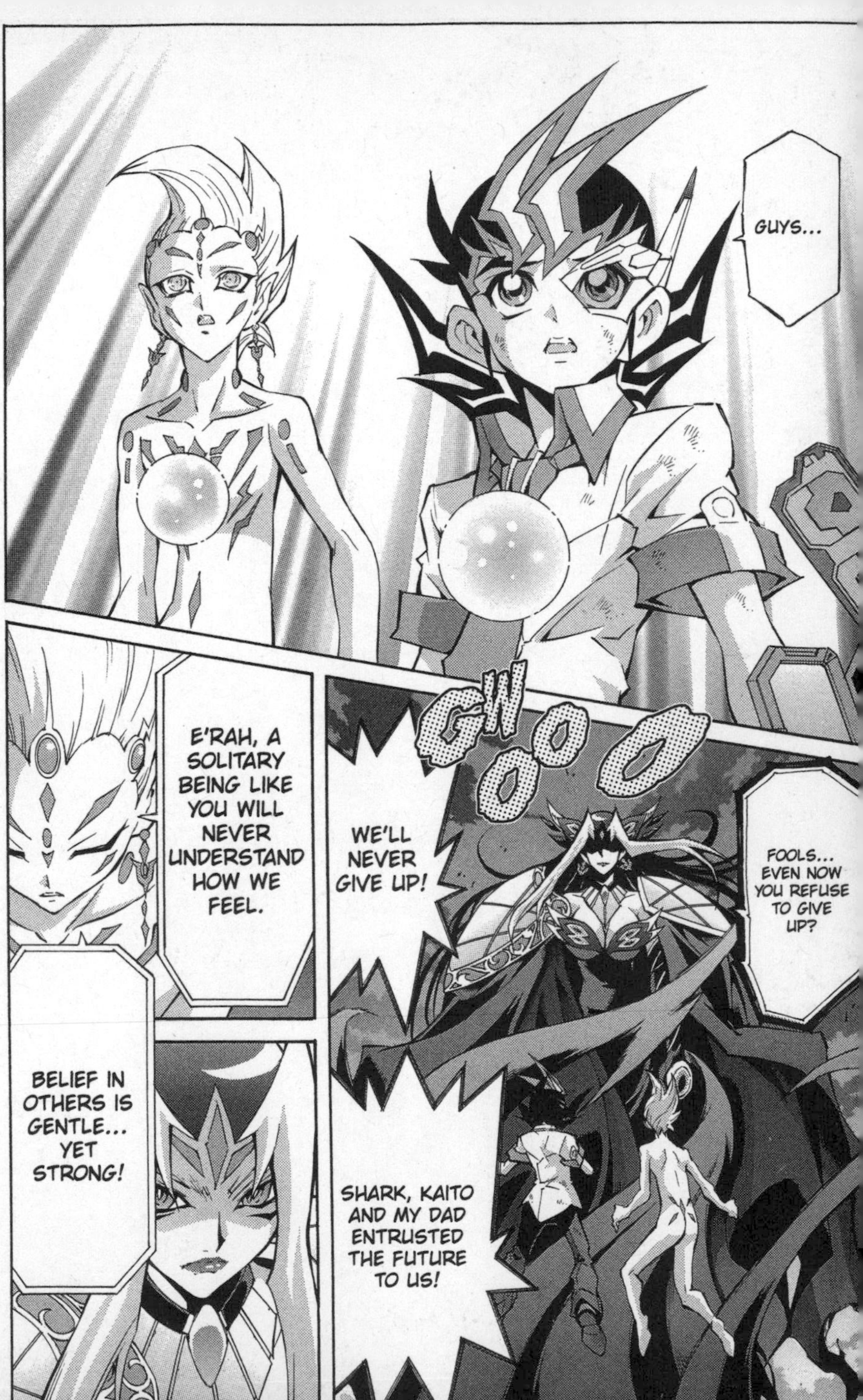
GUYS...
GWOOOO
FOOLS... EVEN NOW YOU REFUSE TO GIVE UP?
WE'LL NEVER GIVE UP!
SHARK, KAITO AND MY DAD ENTRUSTED THE FUTURE TO US!
E'RAH, A SOLITARY BEING LIKE YOU WILL NEVER UNDERSTAND HOW WE FEEL.
BELIEF IN OTHERS IS GENTLE... YET STRONG!

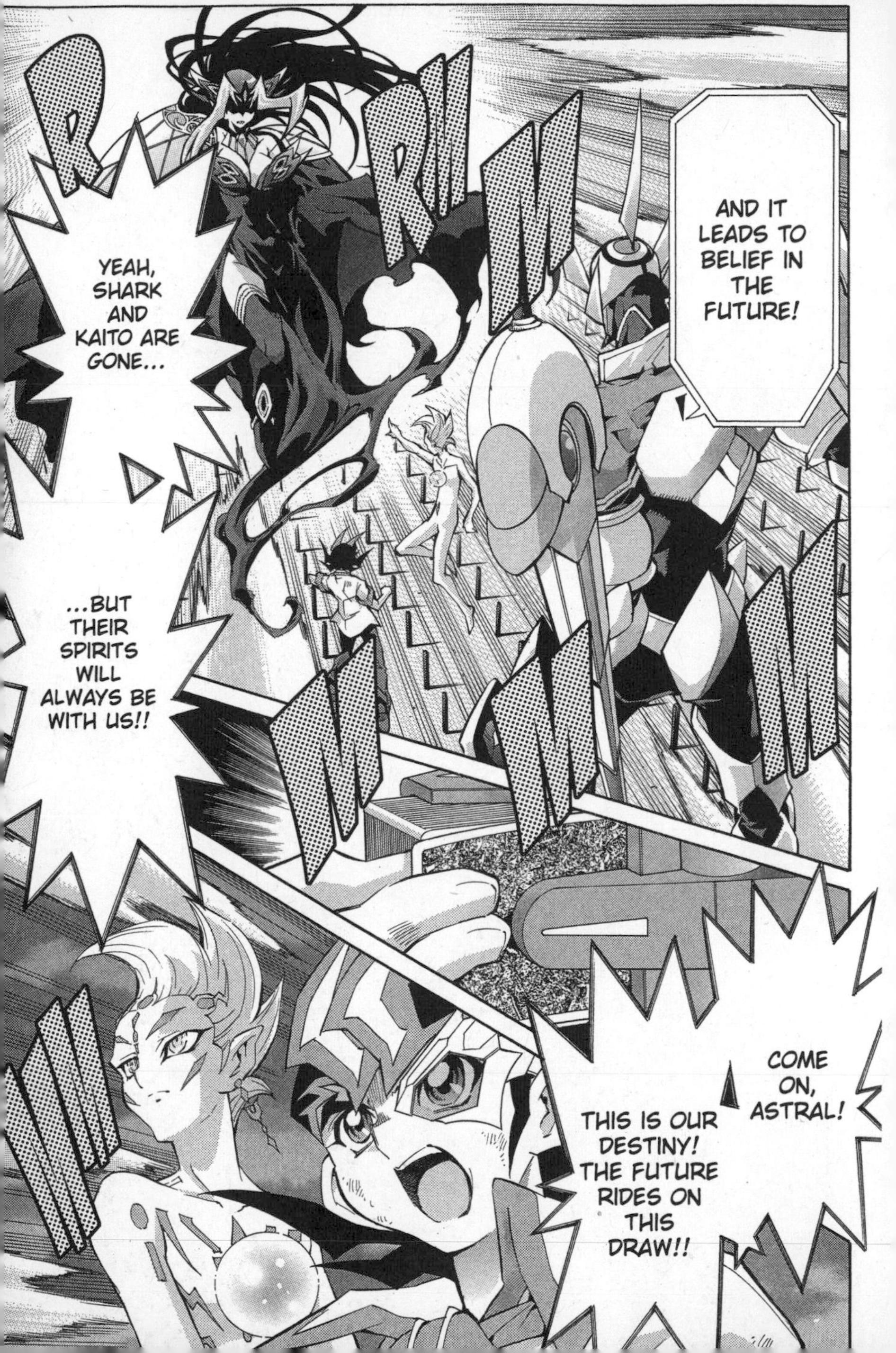
AND IT LEADS TO BELIEF IN THE FUTURE!
YEAH, SHARK AND KAITO ARE GONE...
...BUT THEIR SPIRITS WILL ALWAYS BE WITH US!!
COME ON, ASTRAL!
THIS IS OUR DESTINY! THE FUTURE RIDES ON THIS DRAW!!

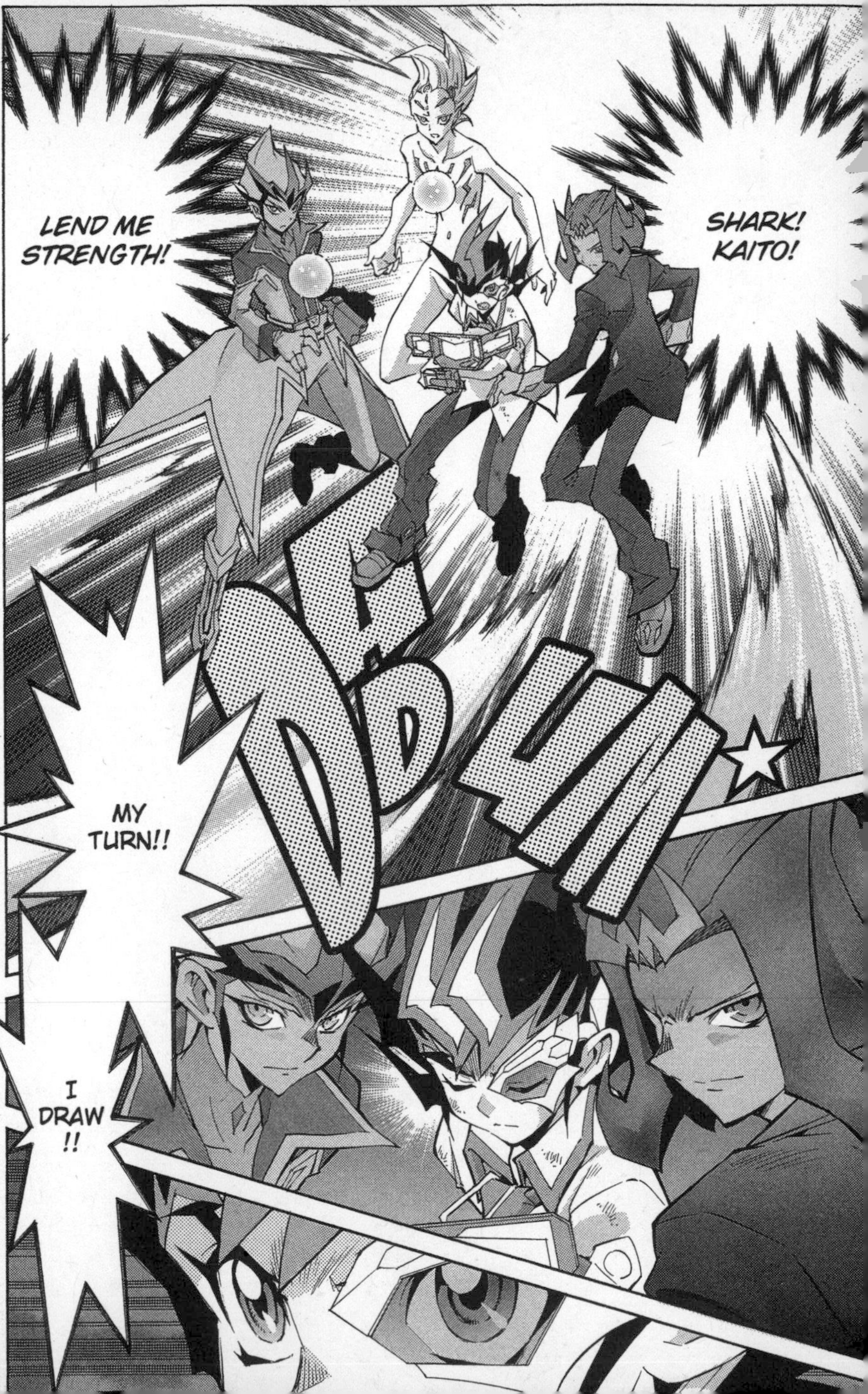
SHARK! KAITO!
LEND ME STRENGTH!
MY TURN!!
I DRAW!!

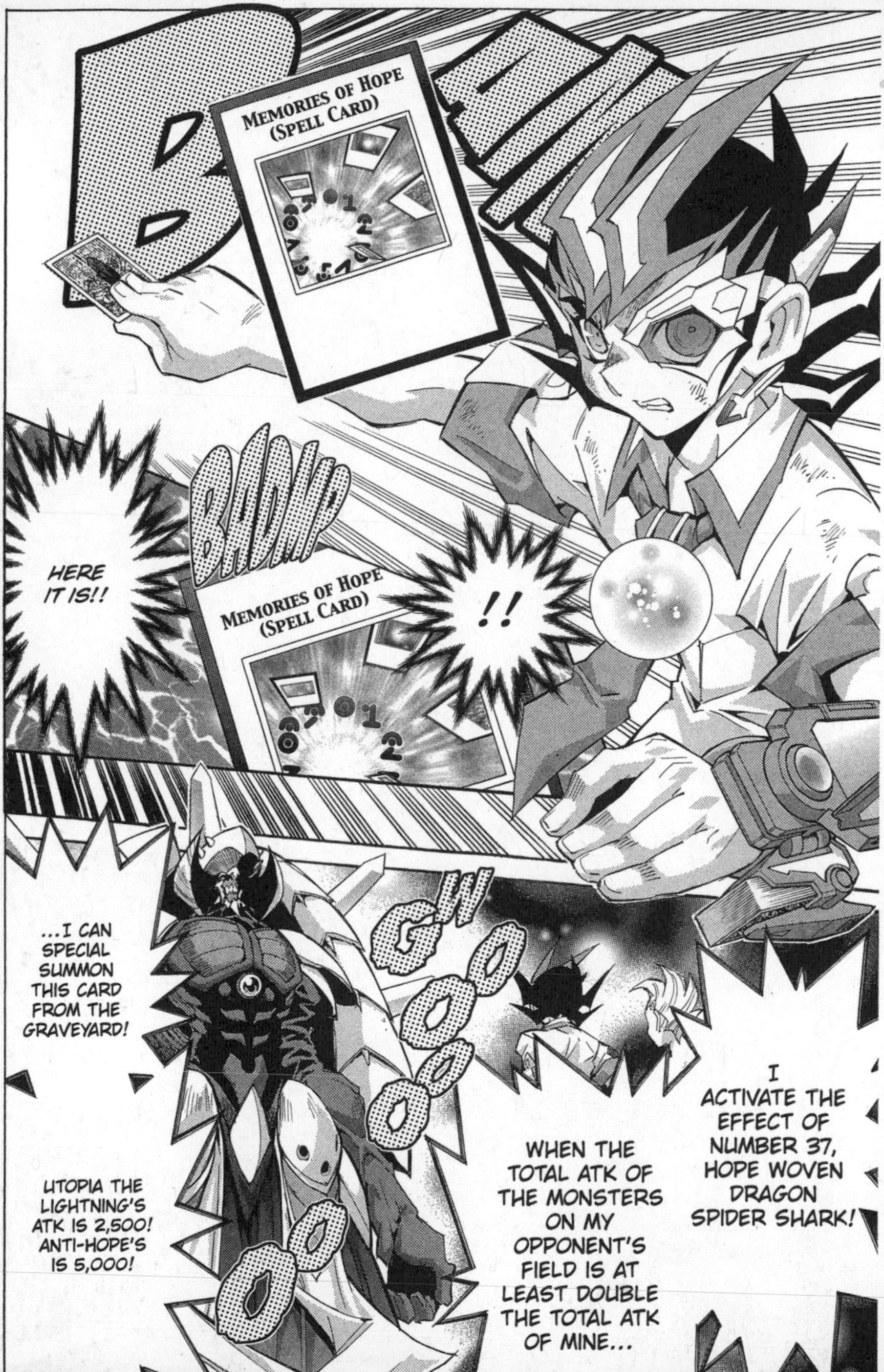
MEMORIES OF HOPE
(SPELL CARD)
!!
BADUMP
HERE IT IS!!
MEMORIES OF HOPE
(SPELL CARD)
I ACTIVATE THE EFFECT OF NUMBER 37, HOPE WOVEN DRAGON SPIDER SHARK!
WHEN THE TOTAL ATK OF THE MONSTERS ON MY OPPONENT'S FIELD IS AT LEAST DOUBLE THE TOTAL ATK OF MINE...
GWOOOOOO
...I CAN SPECIAL SUMMON THIS CARD FROM THE GRAVEYARD!
UTOPIA THE LIGHTNING'S ATK IS 2,500! ANTI-HOPE'S IS 5,000!

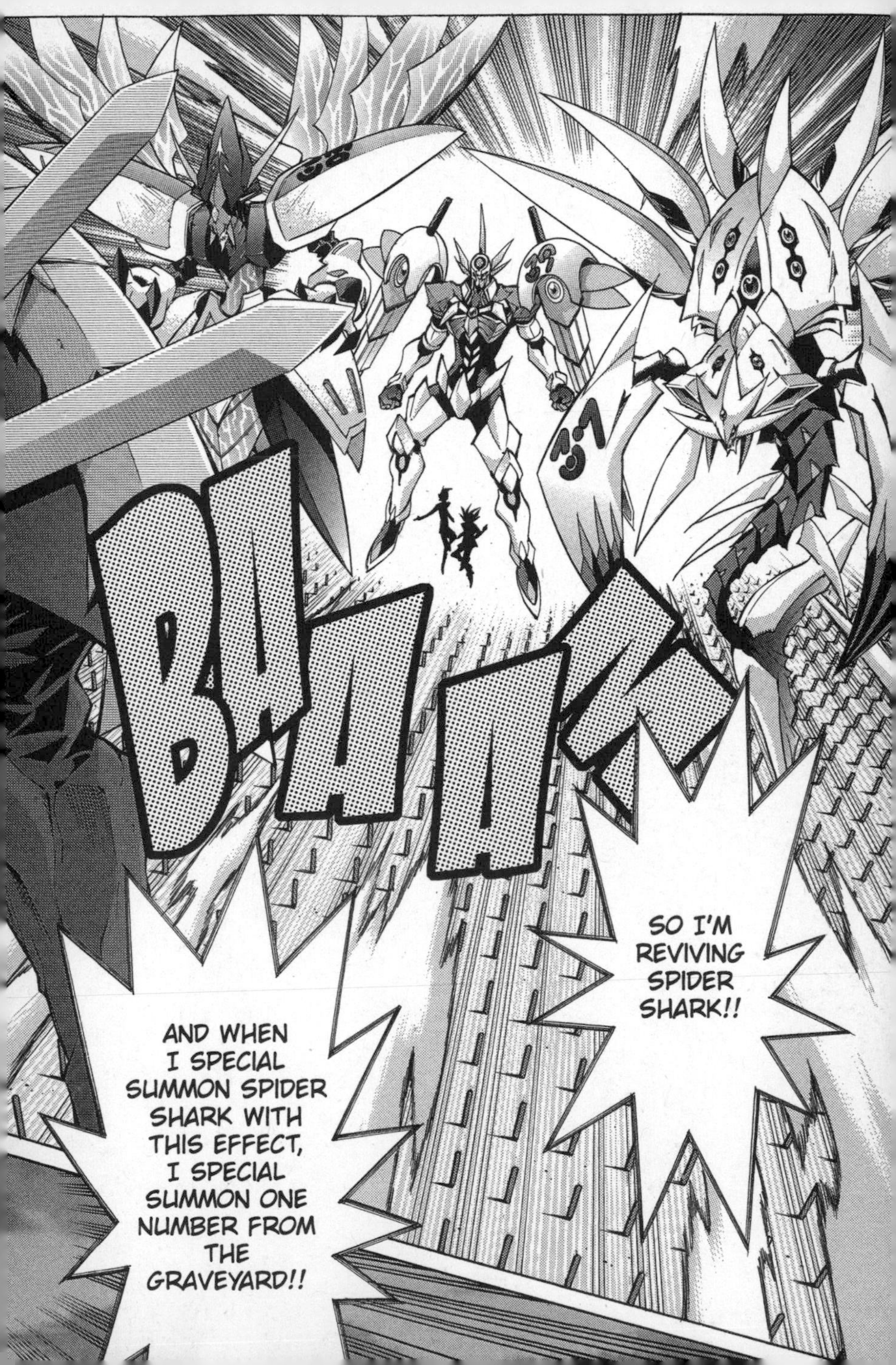
BAAAT
SO I'M REVIVING SPIDER SHARK!!
AND WHEN I SPECIAL SUMMON SPIDER SHARK WITH THIS EFFECT, I SPECIAL SUMMON ONE NUMBER FROM THE GRAVEYARD!!

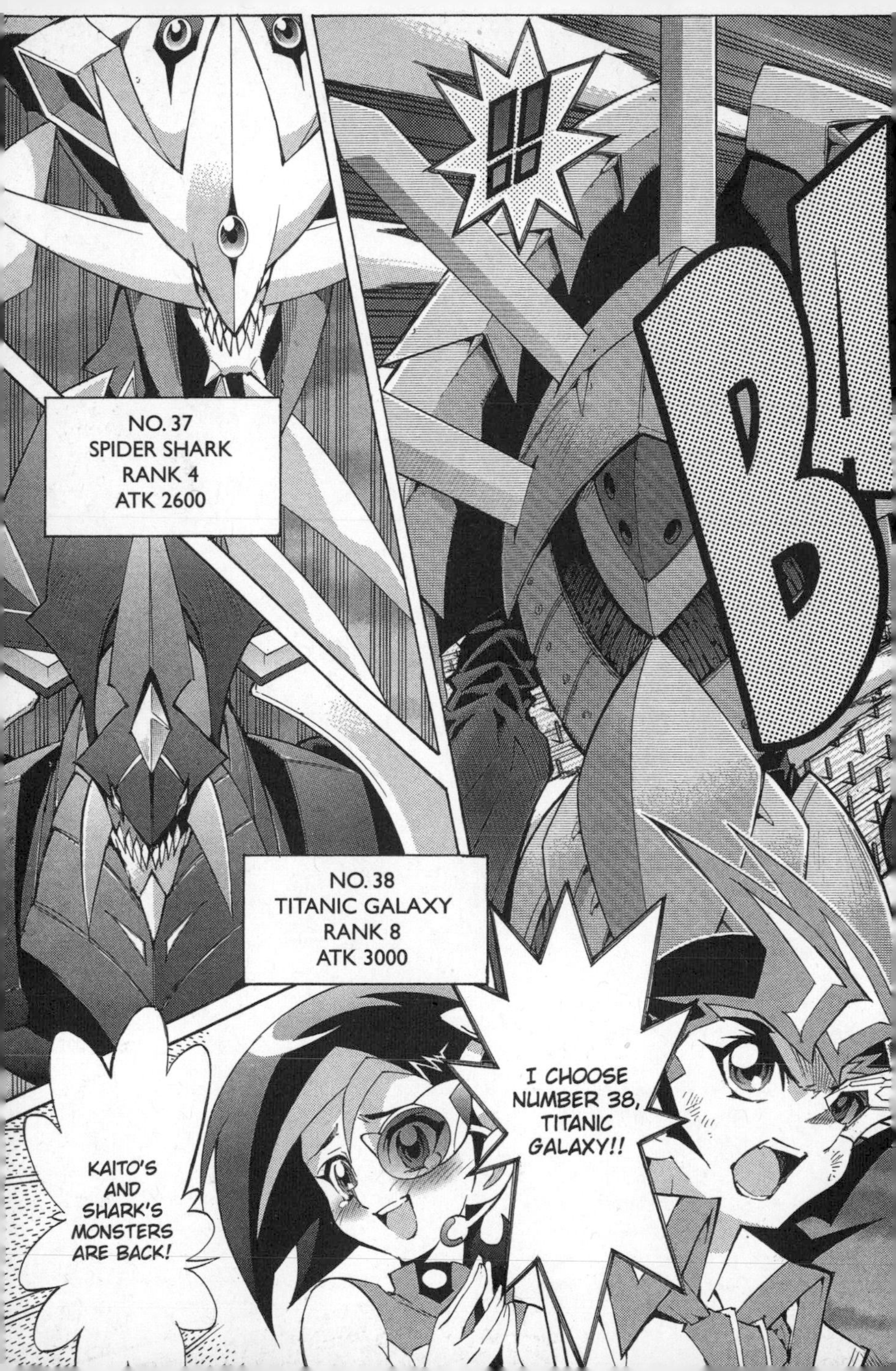
!!
NO. 37
SPIDER SHARK
RANK 4
ATK 2600
NO. 38
TITANIC GALAXY
RANK 8
ATK 3000
I CHOOSE NUMBER 38, TITANIC GALAXY!!
KAITO'S AND SHARK'S MONSTERS ARE BACK!

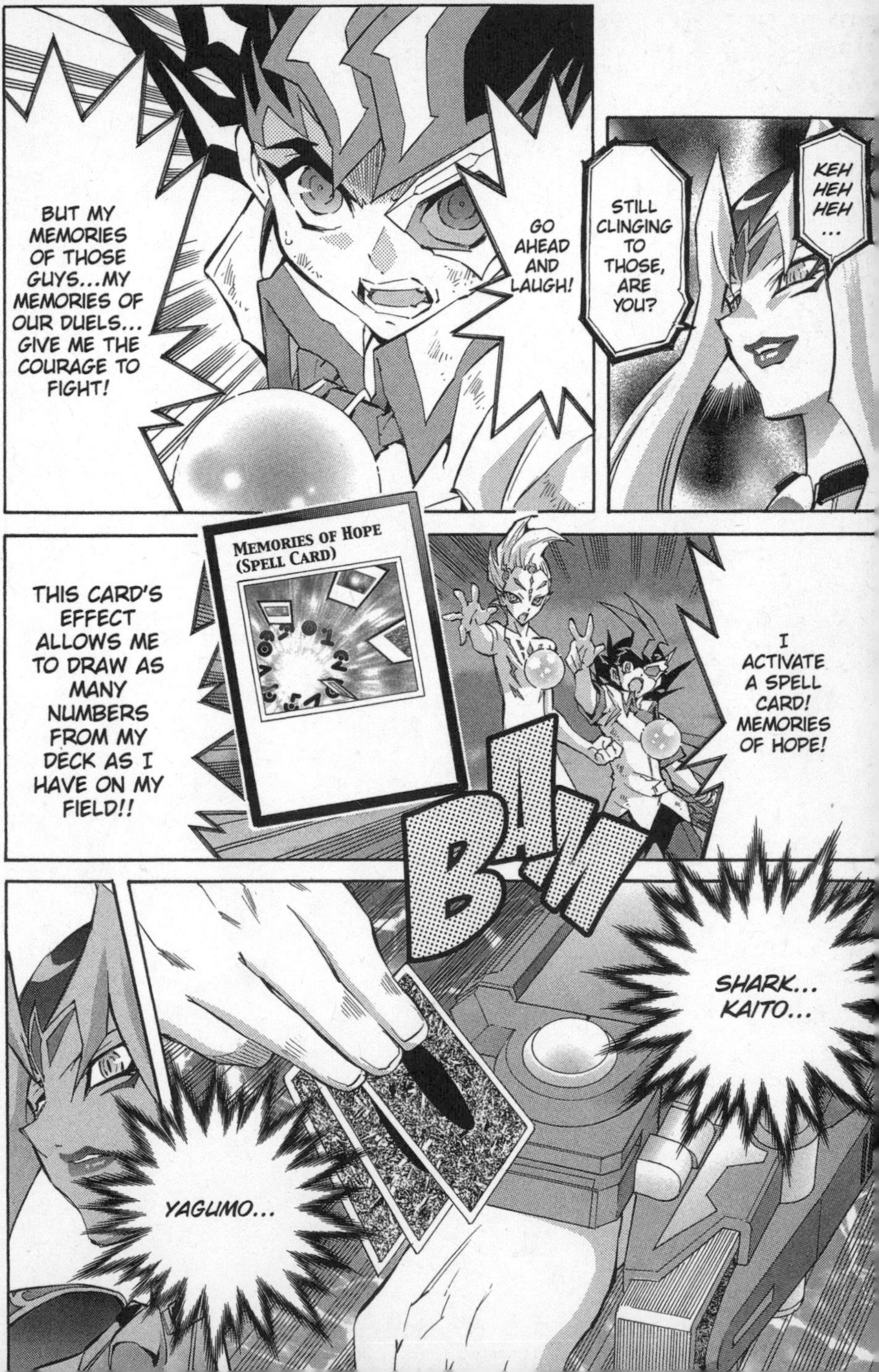
KEH HEH HEH ...
STILL CLINGING TO THOSE, ARE YOU?
GO AHEAD AND LAUGH!
BUT MY MEMORIES OF THOSE GUYS...MY MEMORIES OF OUR DUELS... GIVE ME THE COURAGE TO FIGHT!
I ACTIVATE A SPELL CARD! MEMORIES OF HOPE!
MEMORIES OF HOPE (SPELL CARD)
THIS CARD'S EFFECT ALLOWS ME TO DRAW AS MANY NUMBERS FROM MY DECK AS I HAVE ON MY FIELD!!
BAM
SHARK... KAITO...
YAGUMO...

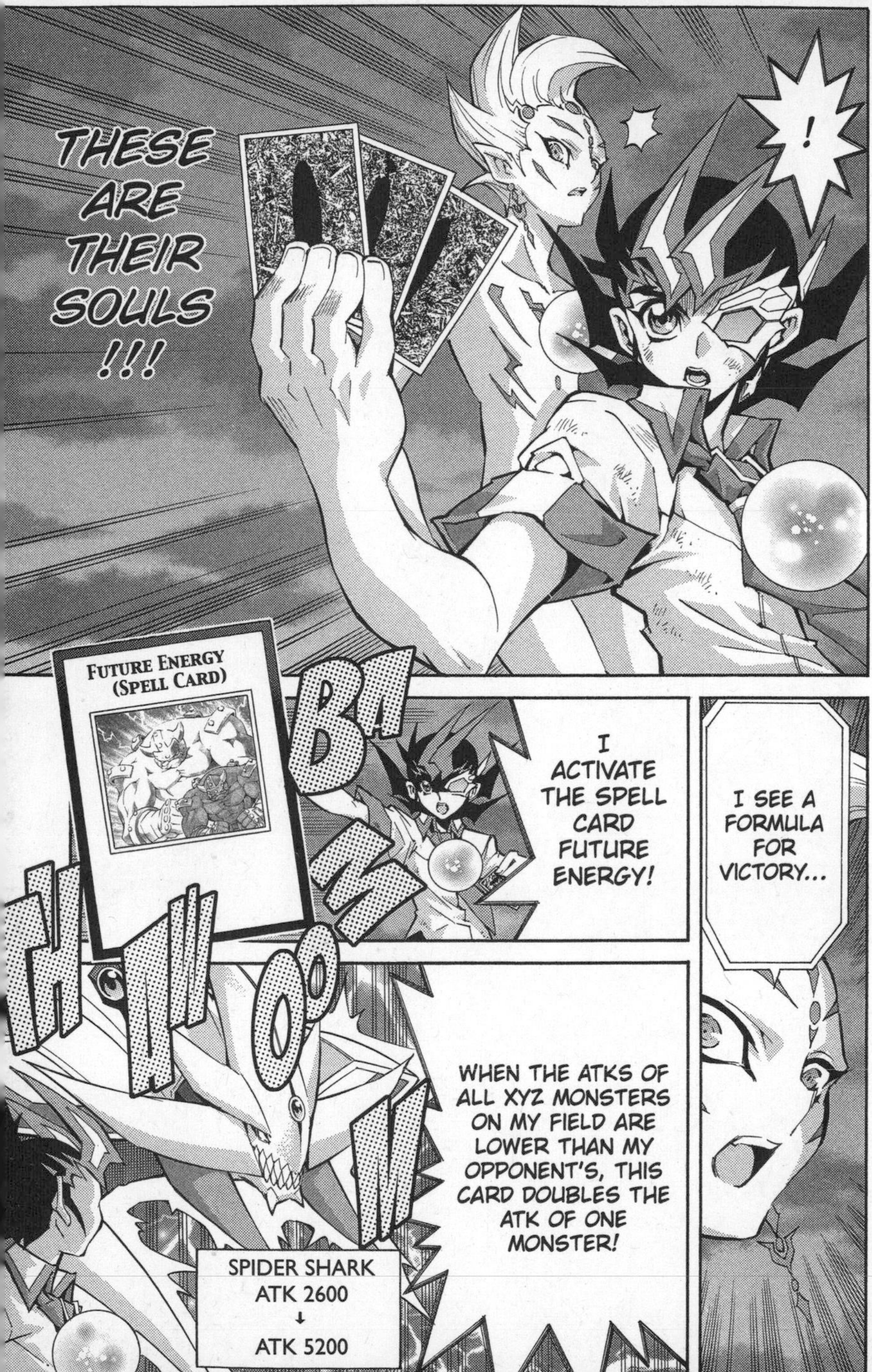
!
THESE ARE THEIR SOULS!!!
I SEE A FORMULA FOR VICTORY...
I ACTIVATE THE SPELL CARD FUTURE ENERGY!
BAM
FUTURE ENERGY (SPELL CARD)
THWOOM
WHEN THE ATKS OF ALL XYZ MONSTERS ON MY FIELD ARE LOWER THAN MY OPPONENT'S, THIS CARD DOUBLES THE ATK OF ONE MONSTER!
SPIDER SHARK
ATK 2600
↓
ATK 5200

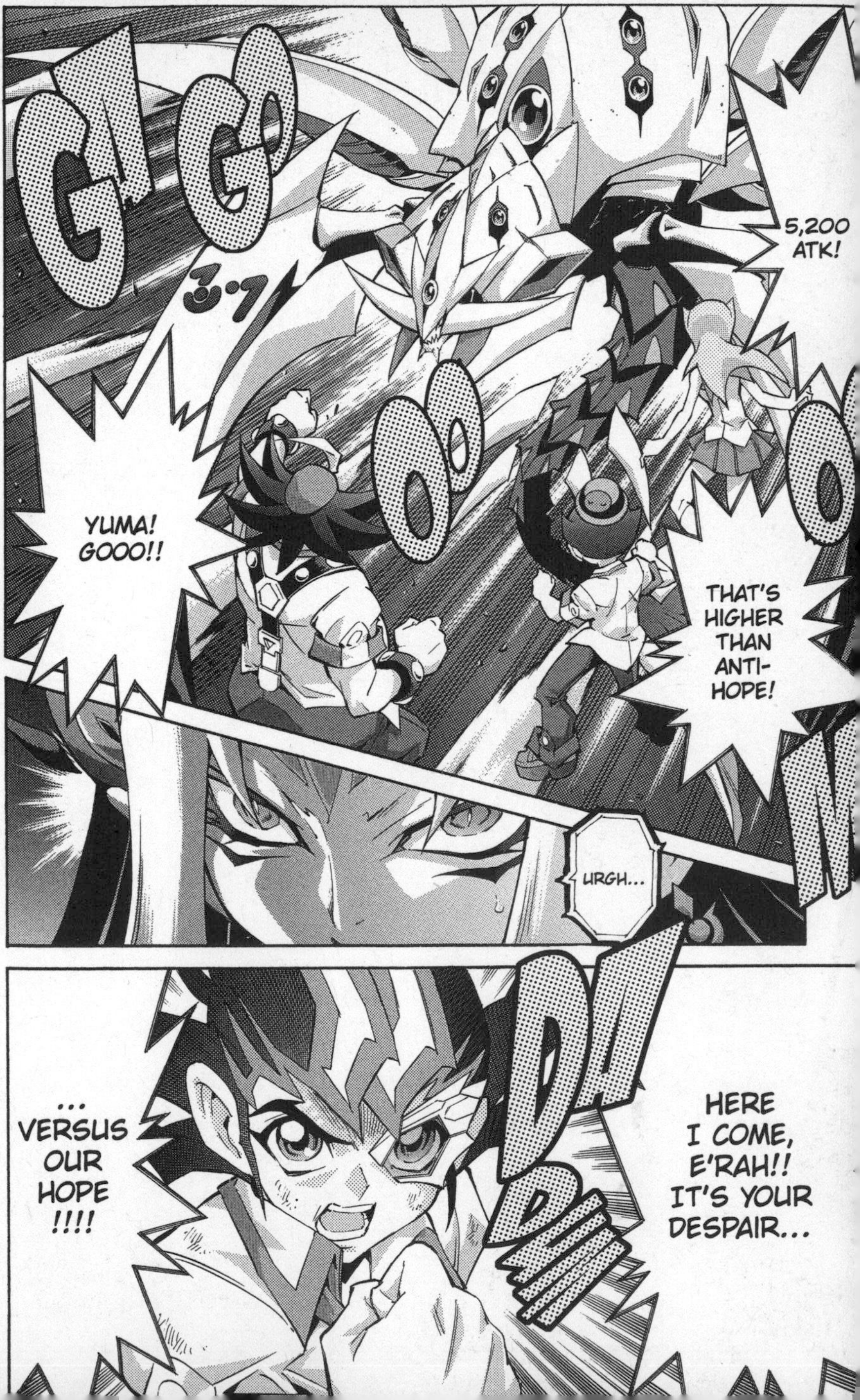
5,200 ATK!
THAT'S HIGHER THAN ANTI-HOPE!
YUMA! GOOO!!
URGH...
HERE I COME, E'RAH!! IT'S YOUR DESPAIR...
... VERSUS OUR HOPE !!!!

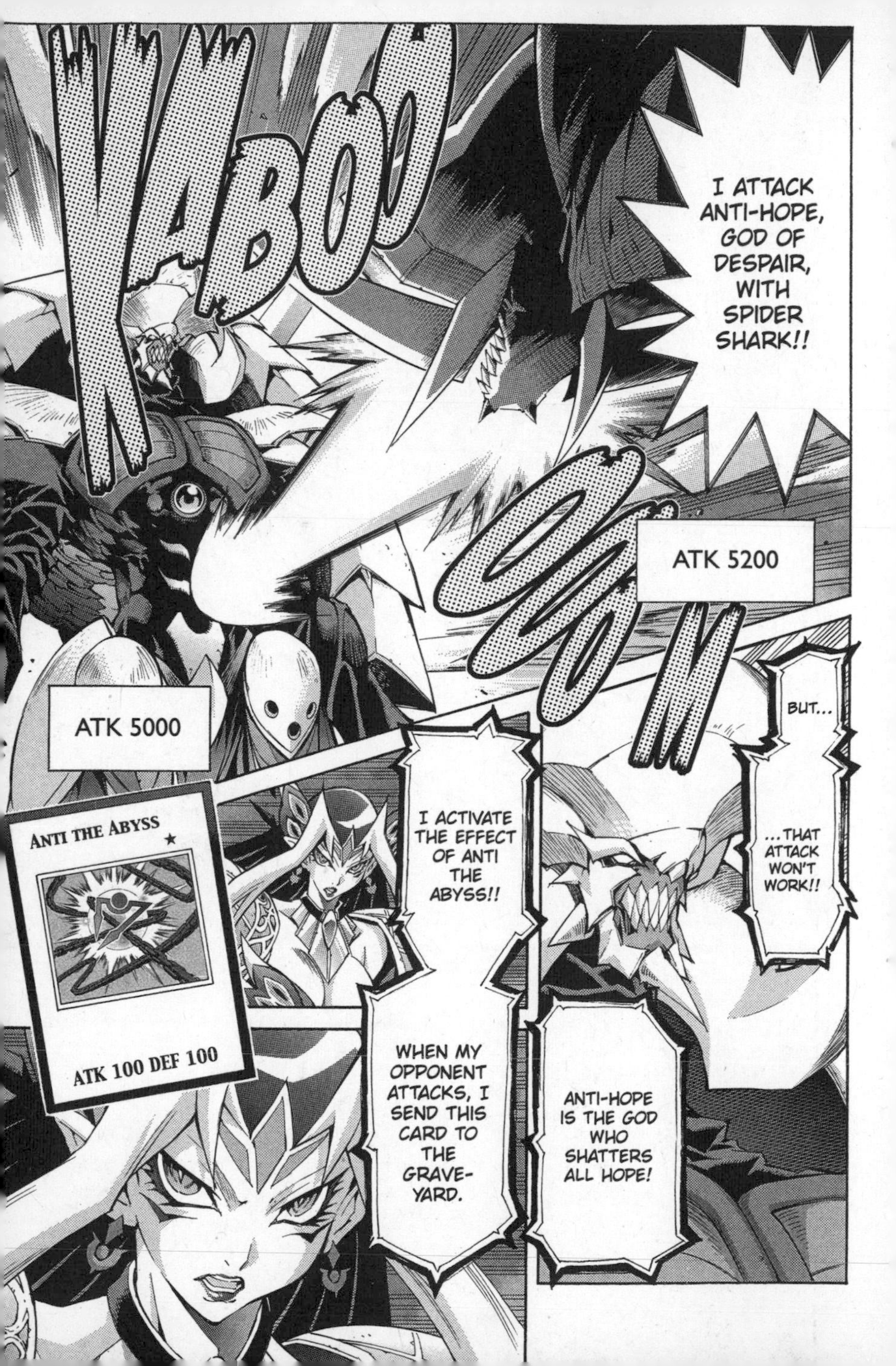
I ATTACK ANTI-HOPE, GOD OF DESPAIR, WITH SPIDER SHARK!!
ATK 5200
ATK 5000
BUT...
...THAT ATTACK WON'T WORK!!
I ACTIVATE THE EFFECT OF ANTI THE ABYSS!!
ANTI THE ABYSS ★
ATK 100 DEF 100
ANTI-HOPE IS THE GOD WHO SHATTERS ALL HOPE!
WHEN MY OPPONENT ATTACKS, I SEND THIS CARD TO THE GRAVE-YARD.

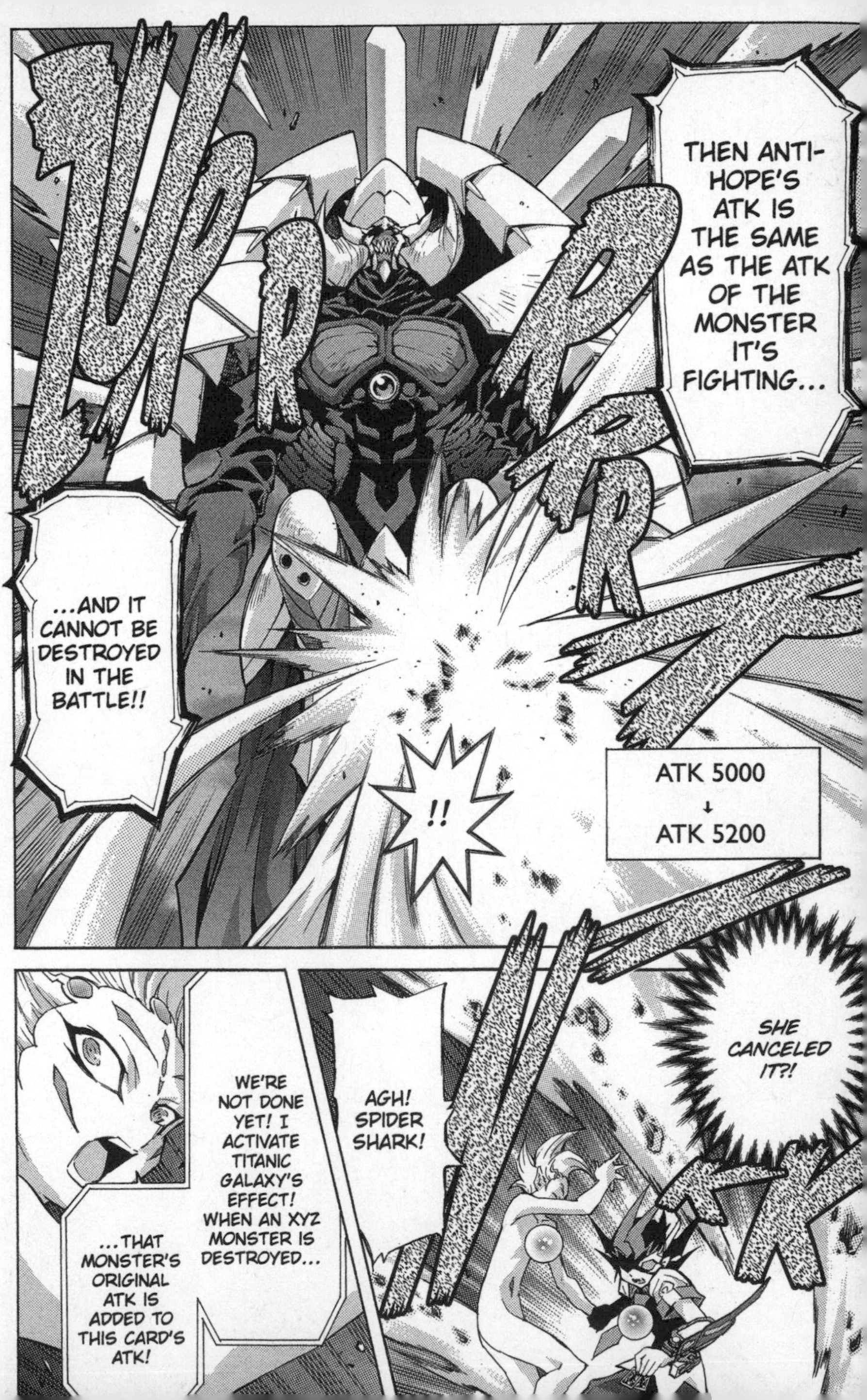
THEN ANTI-HOPE'S ATK IS THE SAME AS THE ATK OF THE MONSTER IT'S FIGHTING...
...AND IT CANNOT BE DESTROYED IN THE BATTLE!!
ATK 5000 ↓ ATK 5200
!!
SHE CANCELED IT?!
AGH! SPIDER SHARK!
WE'RE NOT DONE YET! I ACTIVATE TITANIC GALAXY'S EFFECT! WHEN AN XYZ MONSTER IS DESTROYED...
...THAT MONSTER'S ORIGINAL ATK IS ADDED TO THIS CARD'S ATK!

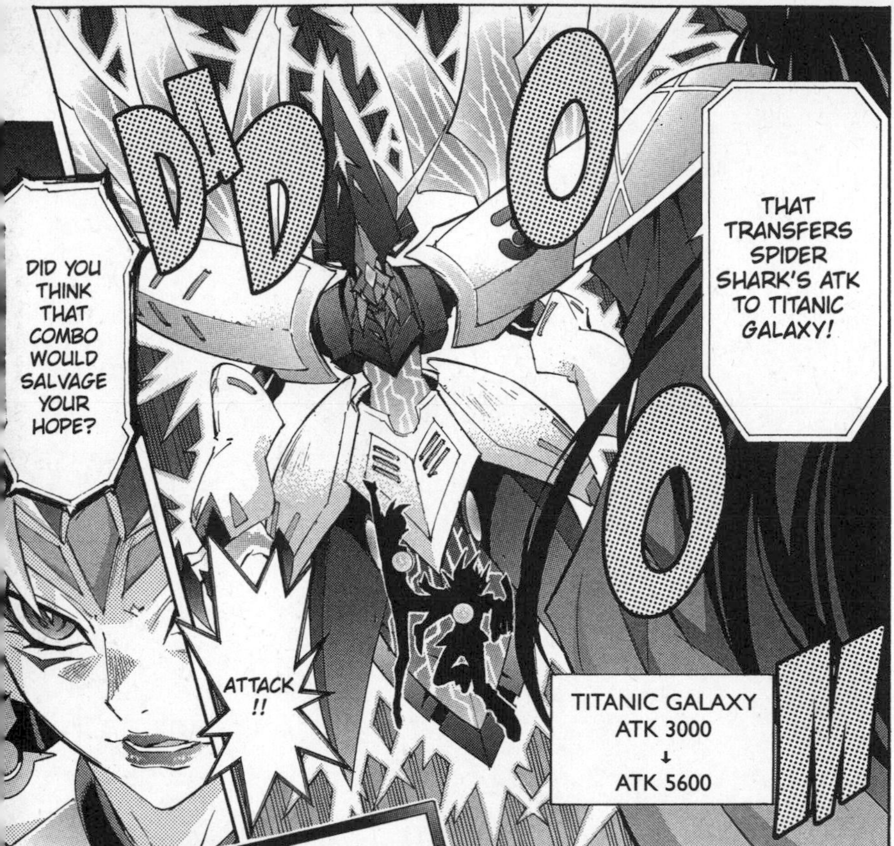
THAT TRANSFERS SPIDER SHARK'S ATK TO TITANIC GALAXY!
DA-DO
DID YOU THINK THAT COMBO WOULD SALVAGE YOUR HOPE?
OOM
TITANIC GALAXY ATK 3000 ↓ ATK 5600
ATTACK !!
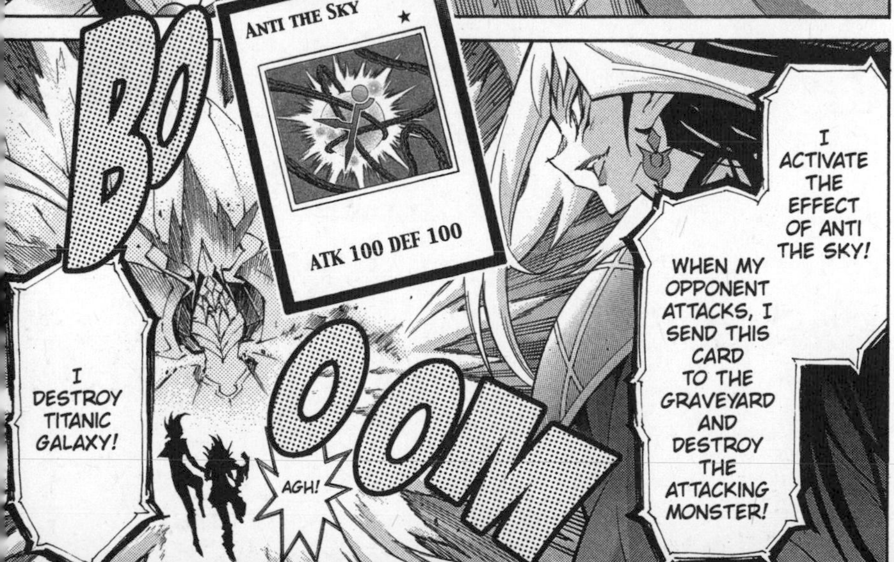
I ACTIVATE THE EFFECT OF ANTI THE SKY!
WHEN MY OPPONENT ATTACKS, I SEND THIS CARD TO THE GRAVEYARD AND DESTROY THE ATTACKING MONSTER!
ANTI THE SKY
ATK 100 DEF 100
BOOOOM
I DESTROY TITANIC GALAXY!
AGH!

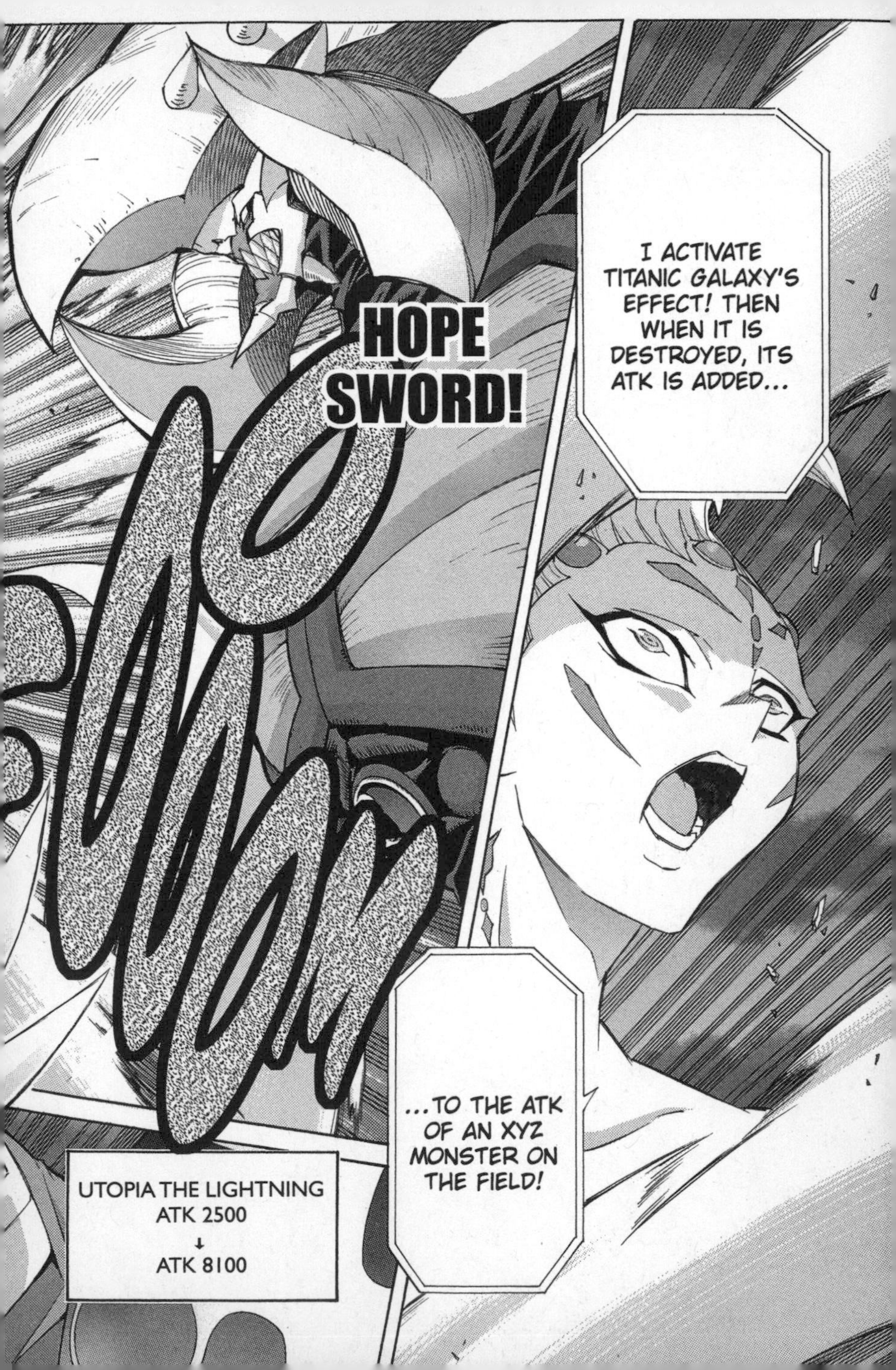
I ACTIVATE TITANIC GALAXY'S EFFECT! THEN WHEN IT IS DESTROYED, ITS ATK IS ADDED...
HOPE SWORD!
...TO THE ATK OF AN XYZ MONSTER ON THE FIELD!
UTOPIA THE LIGHTNING
ATK 2500
↓
ATK 8100

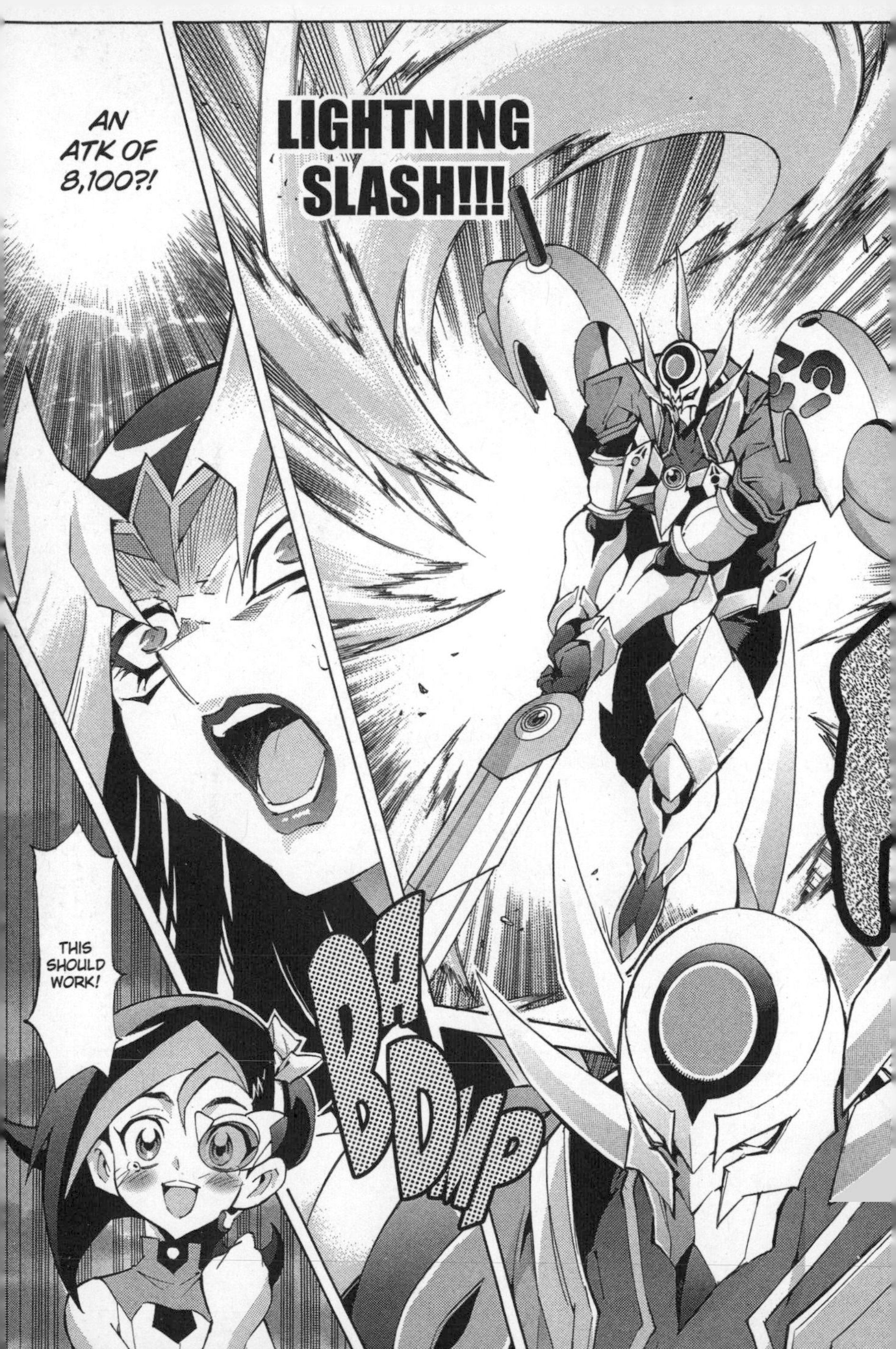
LIGHTNING SLASH!!!
AN ATK OF 8,100?!
BA-BDIP
THIS SHOULD WORK!

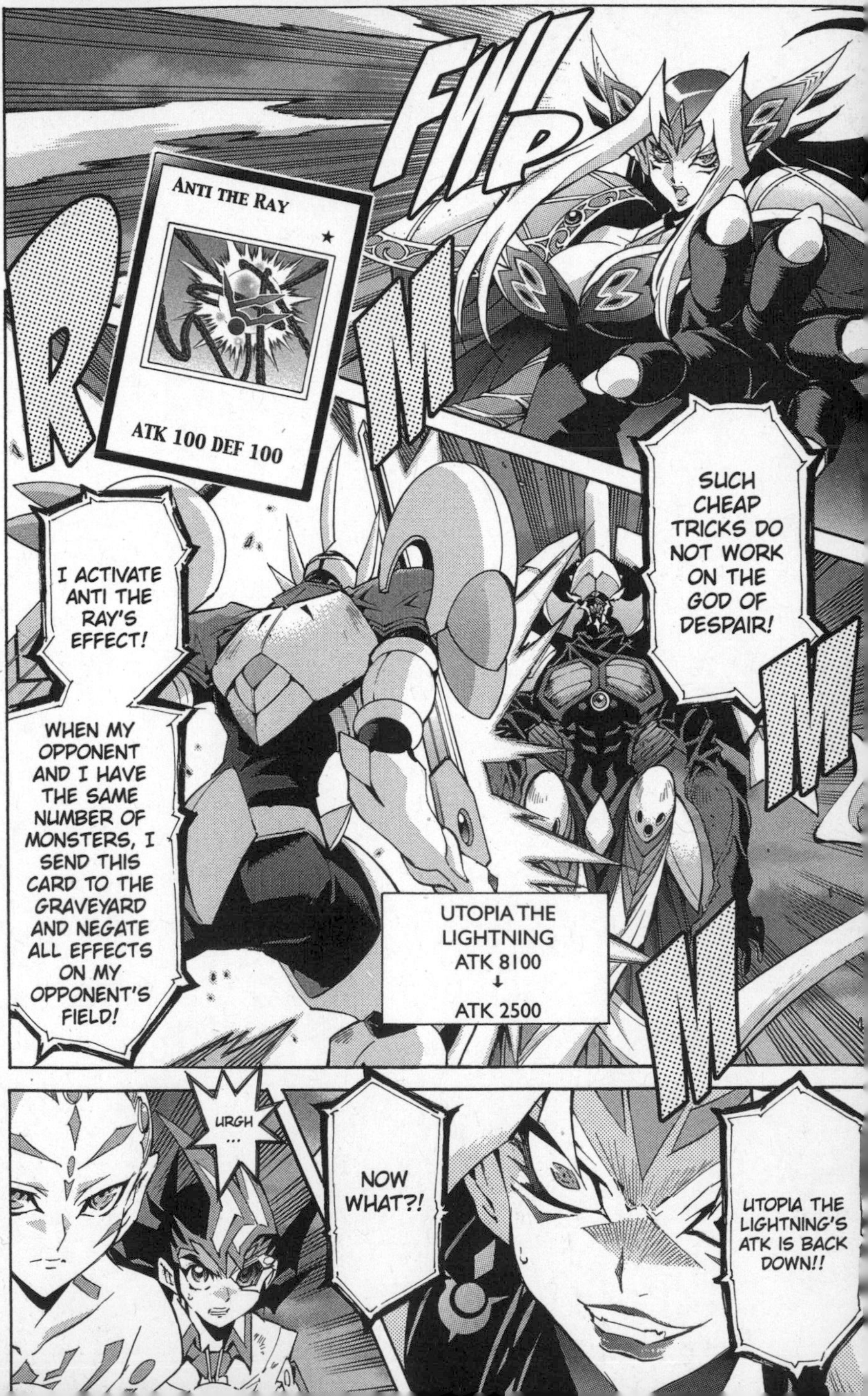
FWIP
SUCH CHEAP TRICKS DO NOT WORK ON THE GOD OF DESPAIR!
ANTI THE RAY
ATK 100 DEF 100
RMMM
I ACTIVATE ANTI THE RAY'S EFFECT!
WHEN MY OPPONENT AND I HAVE THE SAME NUMBER OF MONSTERS, I SEND THIS CARD TO THE GRAVEYARD AND NEGATE ALL EFFECTS ON MY OPPONENT'S FIELD!
UTOPIA THE LIGHTNING ATK 8100 ↓ ATK 2500
MMM
UTOPIA THE LIGHTNING'S ATK IS BACK DOWN!!
NOW WHAT?!
URGH ...

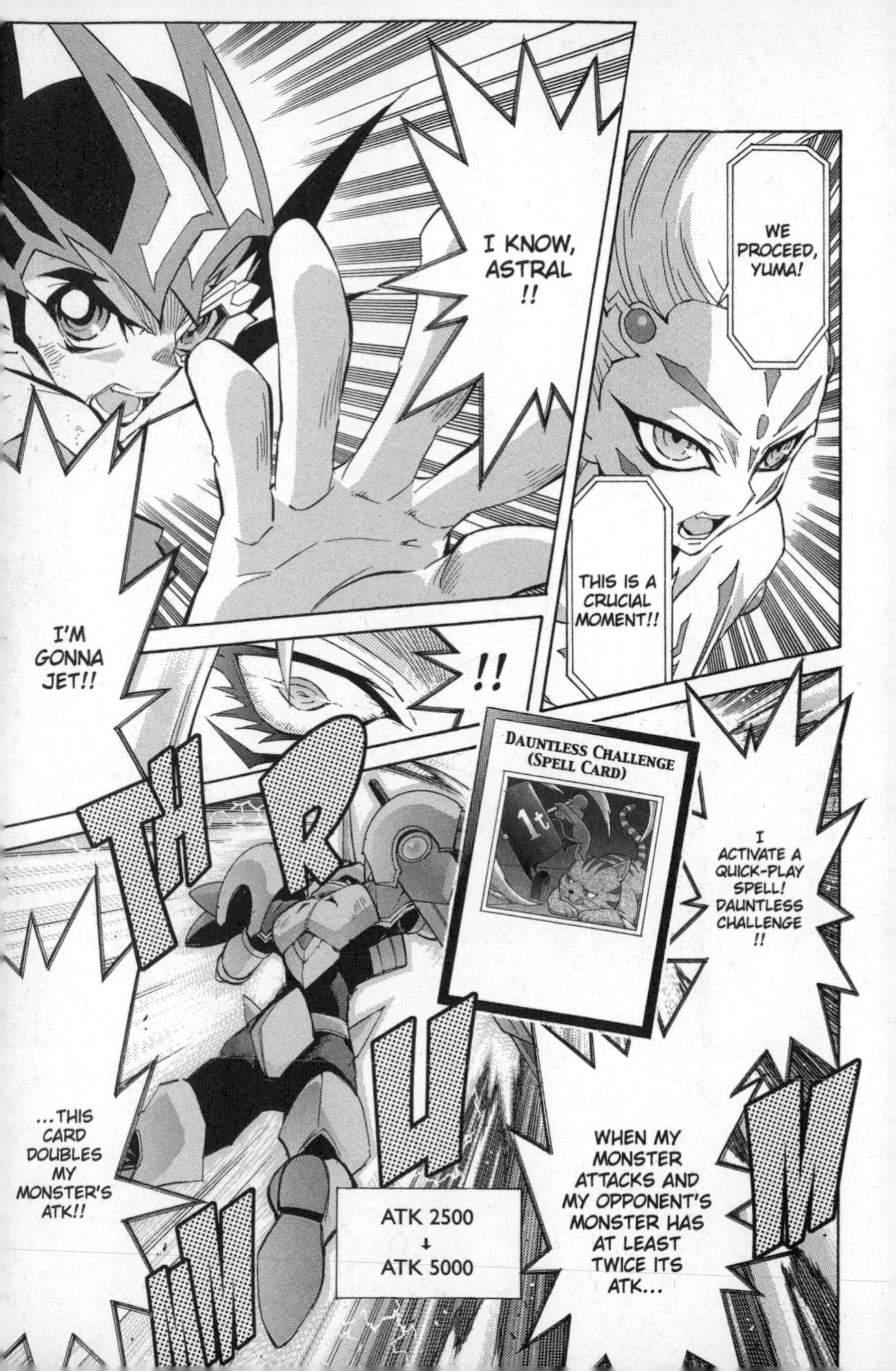
WE PROCEED, YUMA!
THIS IS A CRUCIAL MOMENT!!
I KNOW, ASTRAL !!
!!
I'M GONNA JET!!
I ACTIVATE A QUICK-PLAY SPELL! DAUNTLESS CHALLENGE !!
DAUNTLESS CHALLENGE (SPELL CARD)
1t
THRUM
WHEN MY MONSTER ATTACKS AND MY OPPONENT'S MONSTER HAS AT LEAST TWICE ITS ATK...
ATK 2500 → ATK 5000
...THIS CARD DOUBLES MY MONSTER'S ATK!!

UTOPIA THE LIGHTNING AND ANTI-HOPE, GOD OF DESPAIR...
THEN, WHEN I'VE DESTROYED AN ENEMY MONSTER, I DESTROY ONE OF MY OPPONENT'S SPELL CARDS!

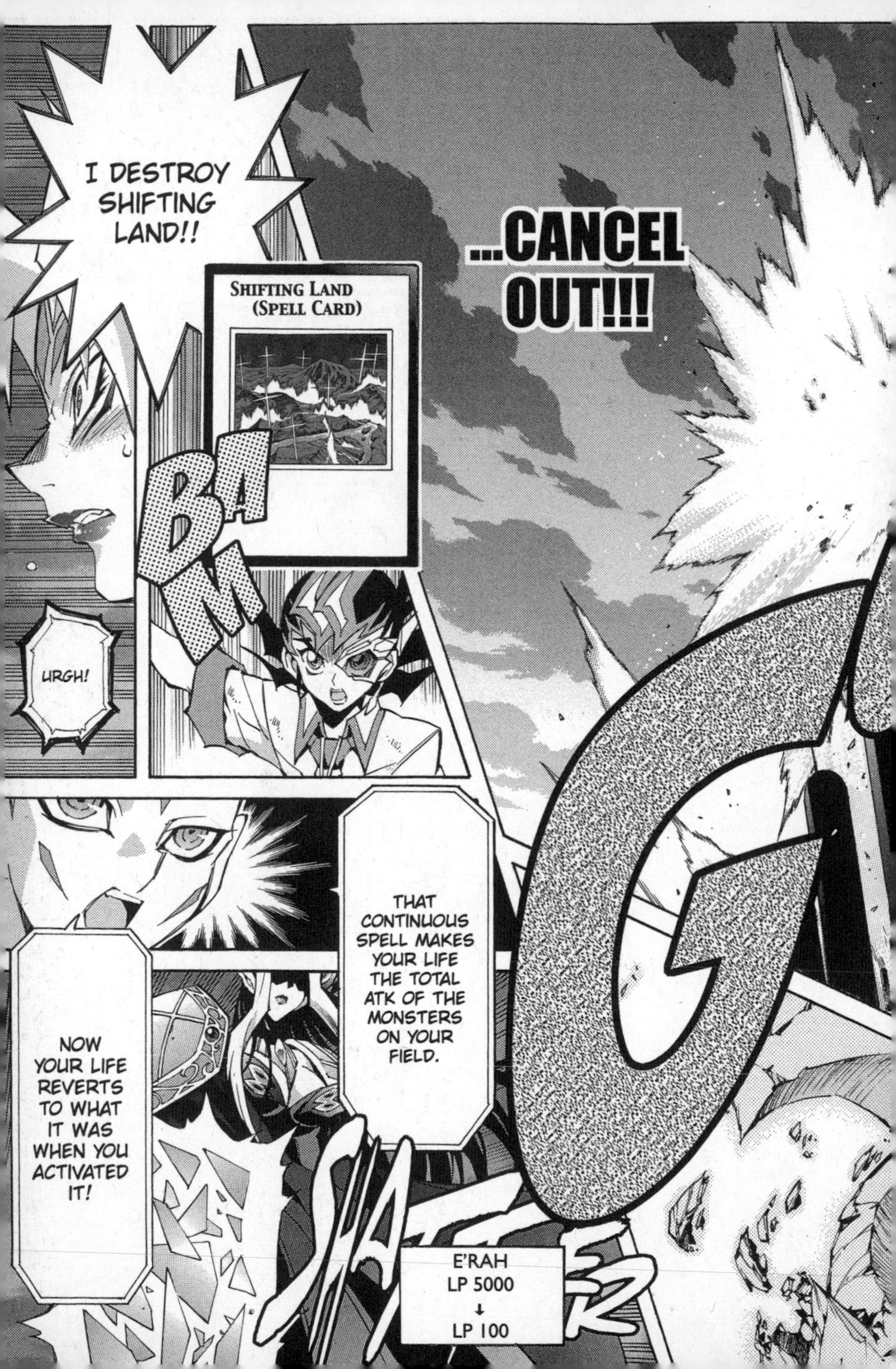
...CANCEL OUT!!!
I DESTROY SHIFTING LAND!!
SHIFTING LAND (SPELL CARD)
BAM
URGH!
THAT CONTINUOUS SPELL MAKES YOUR LIFE THE TOTAL ATK OF THE MONSTERS ON YOUR FIELD.
NOW YOUR LIFE REVERTS TO WHAT IT WAS WHEN YOU ACTIVATED IT!
E'RAH LP 5000 ↓ LP 100

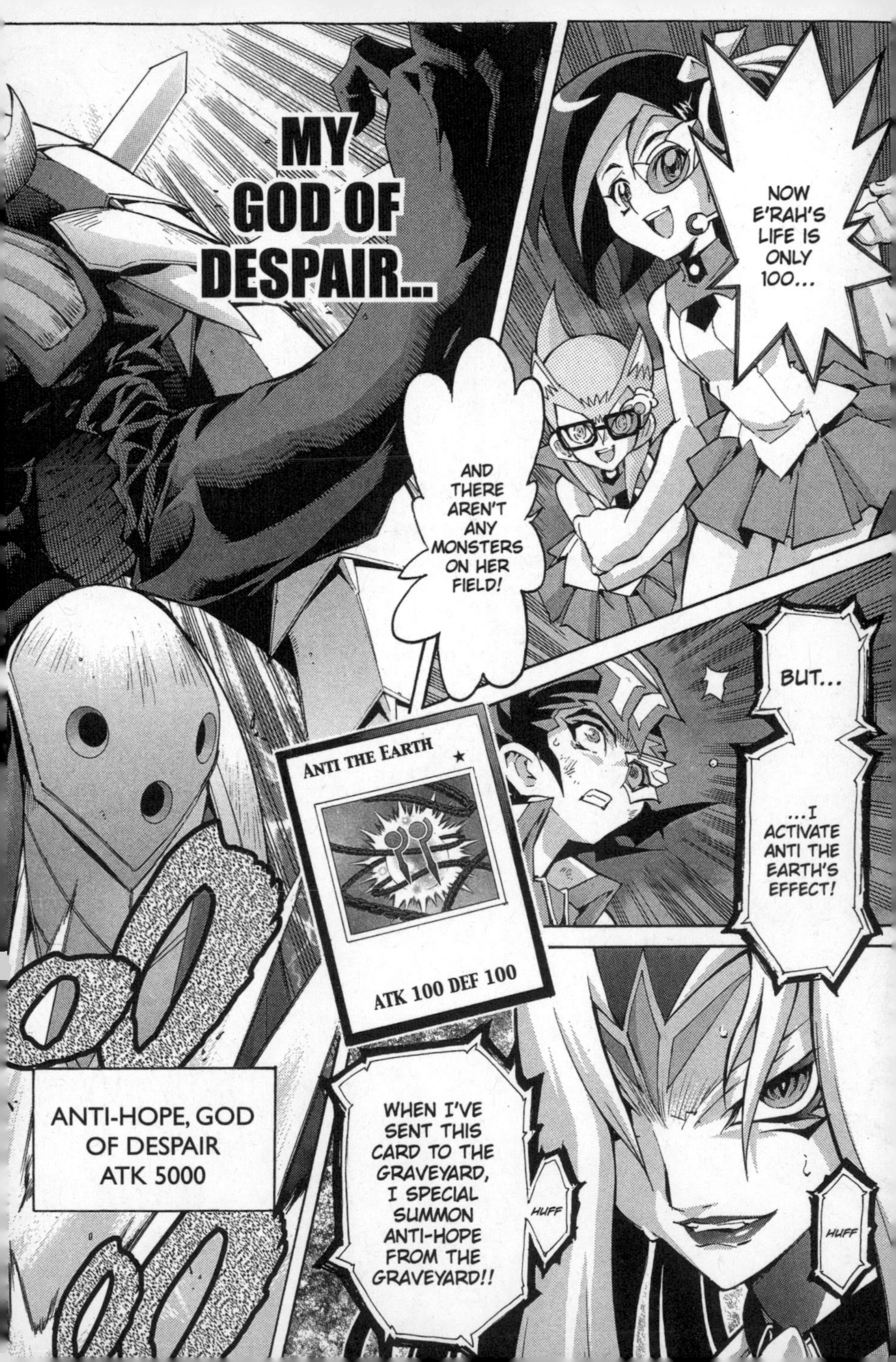
NOW E'RAH'S LIFE IS ONLY 100...
AND THERE AREN'T ANY MONSTERS ON HER FIELD!
MY GOD OF DESPAIR...
BUT...
...I ACTIVATE ANTI THE EARTH'S EFFECT!
ANTI THE EARTH
ATK 100 DEF 100
HUFF
HUFF
WHEN I'VE SENT THIS CARD TO THE GRAVEYARD, I SPECIAL SUMMON ANTI-HOPE FROM THE GRAVEYARD!!
ANTI-HOPE, GOD OF DESPAIR ATK 5000

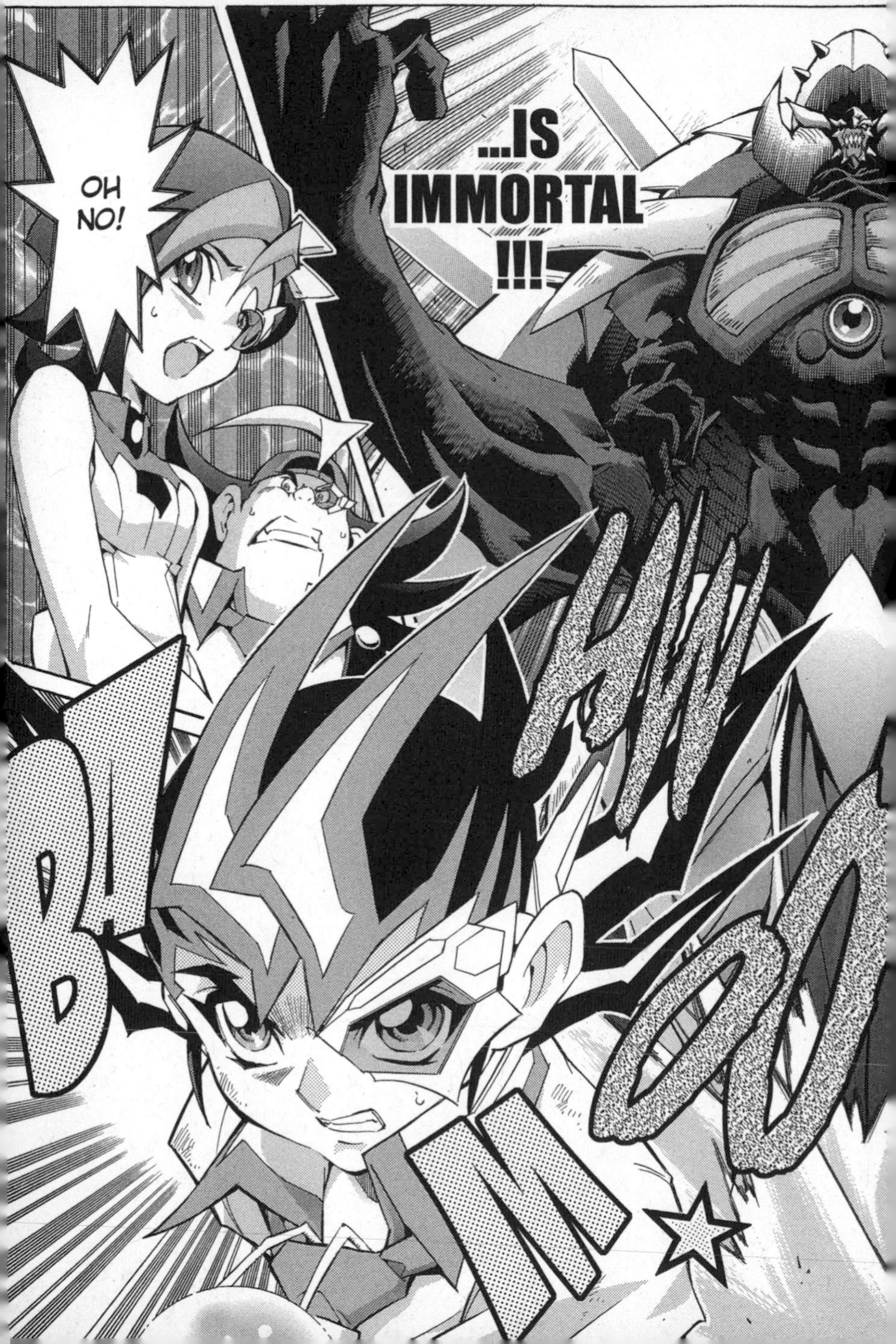
...IS IMMORTAL!!!
OH NO!

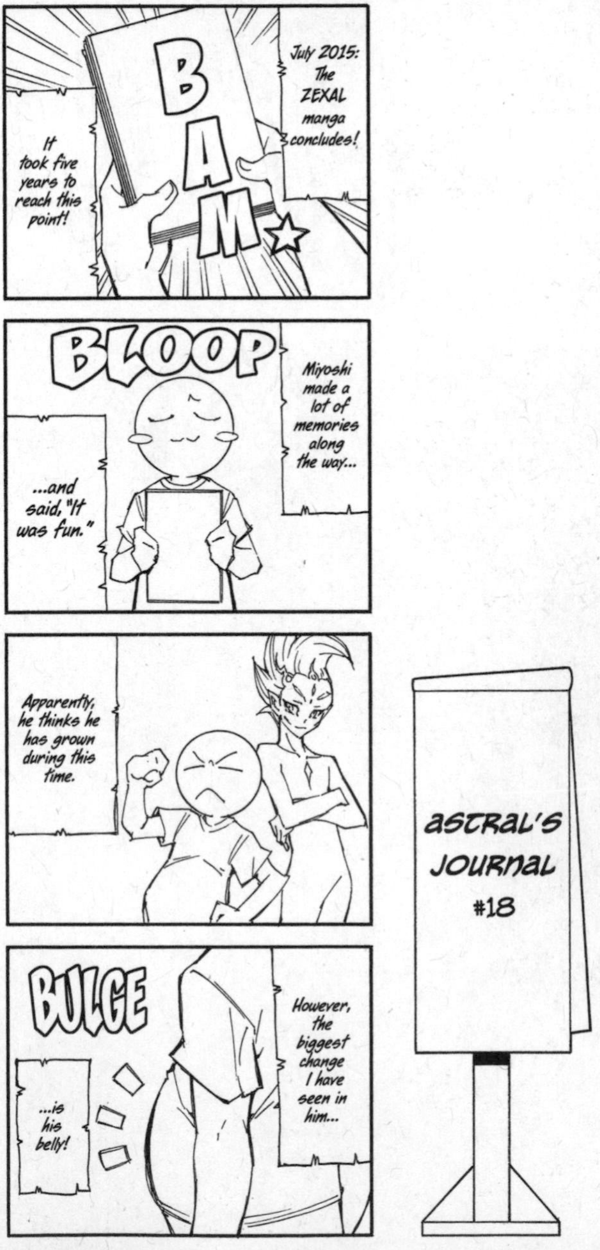
astral's journal #18
July 2015: The ZEXAL manga concludes!
BAM☆
It took five years to reach this point!
BLOOP
Miyoshi made a lot of memories along the way...
...and said, "It was fun."
Apparently, he thinks he has grown during this time.
However, the biggest change I have seen in him...
BULGE
...is his belly!

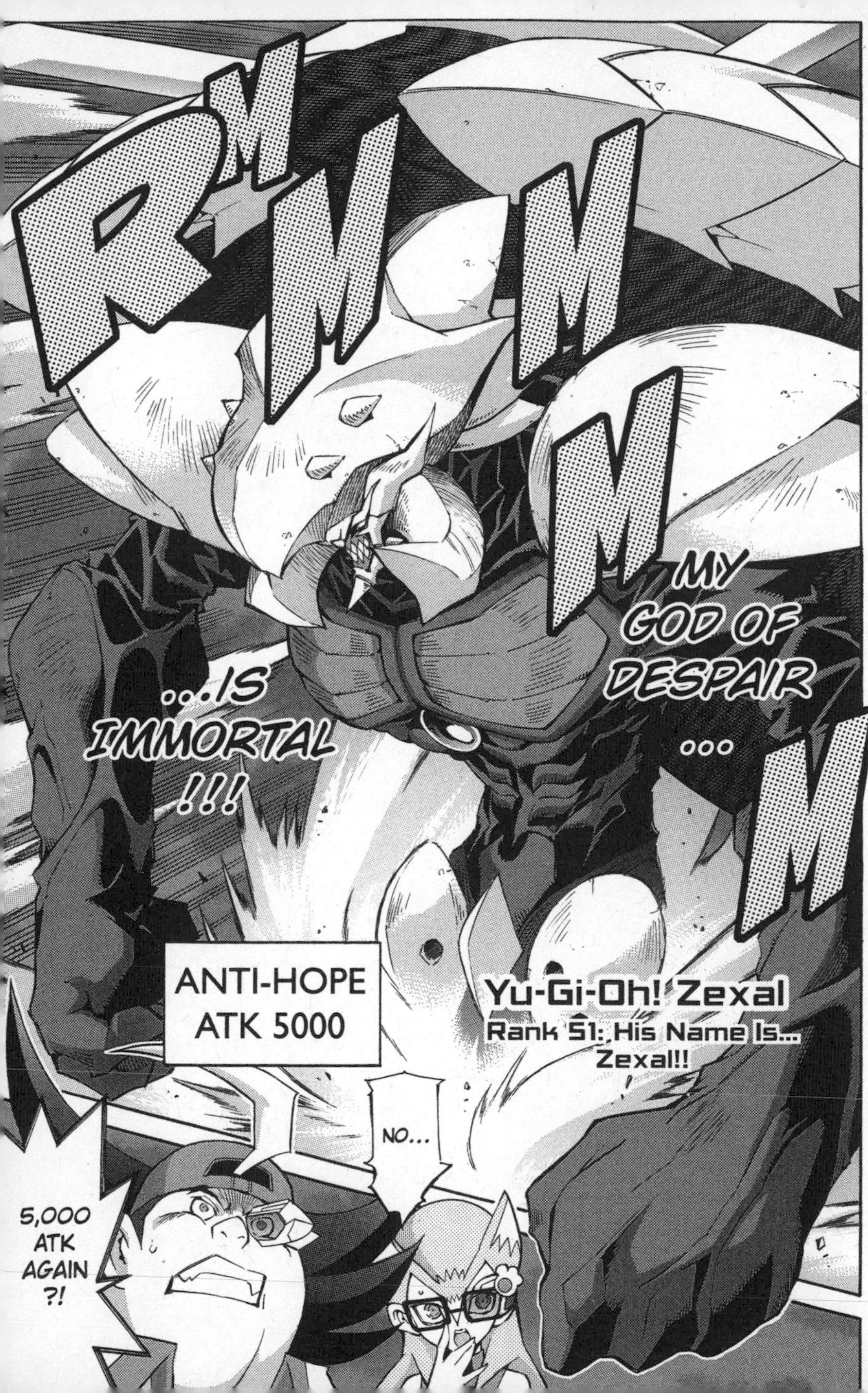
RMMMMM
MY GOD OF DESPAIR...
...IS IMMORTAL!!!
ANTI-HOPE ATK 5000
Yu-Gi-Oh! Zexal
Rank 51: His Name Is... Zexal!!
NO...
5,000 ATK AGAIN?!

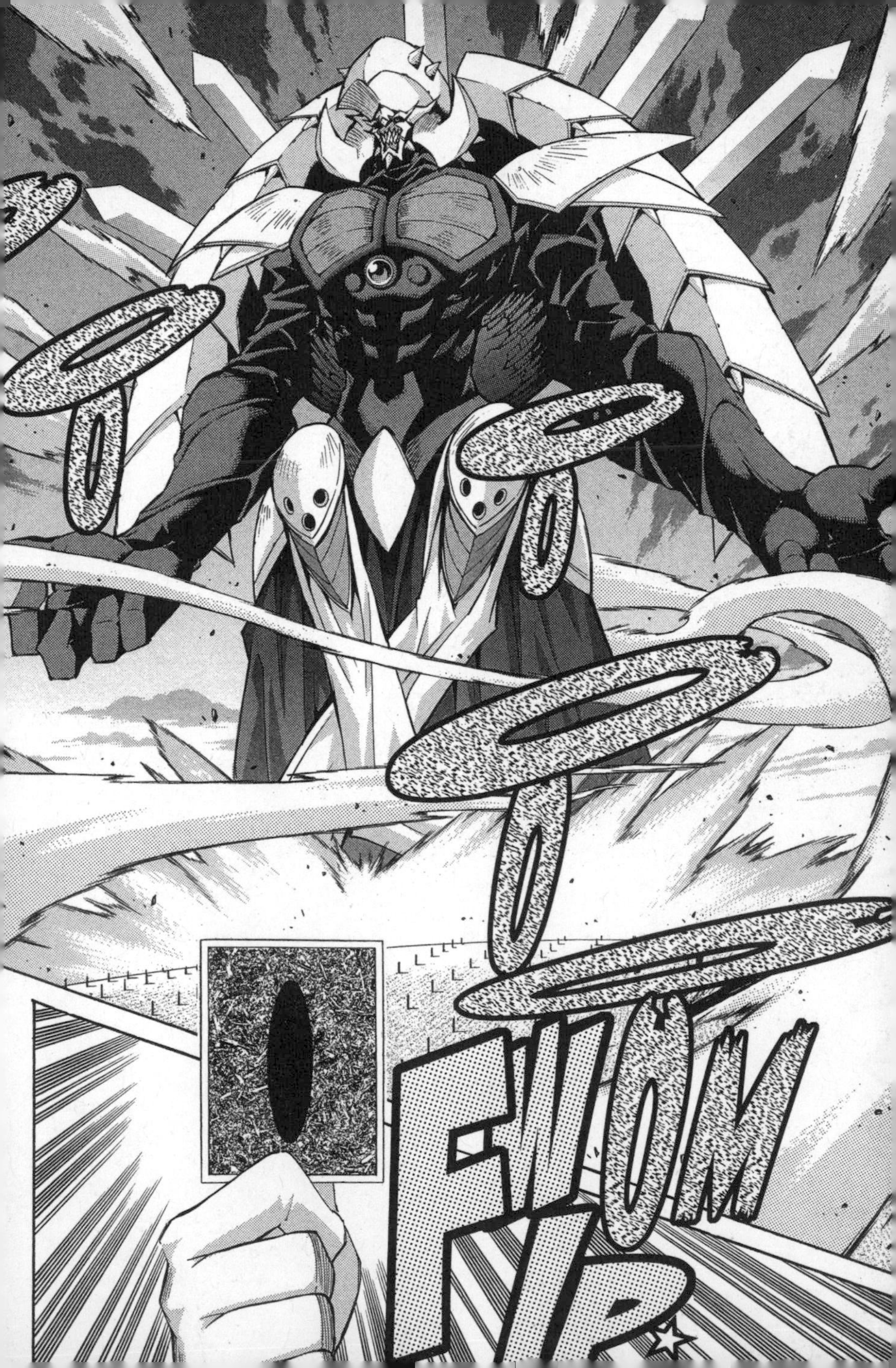
FWOM

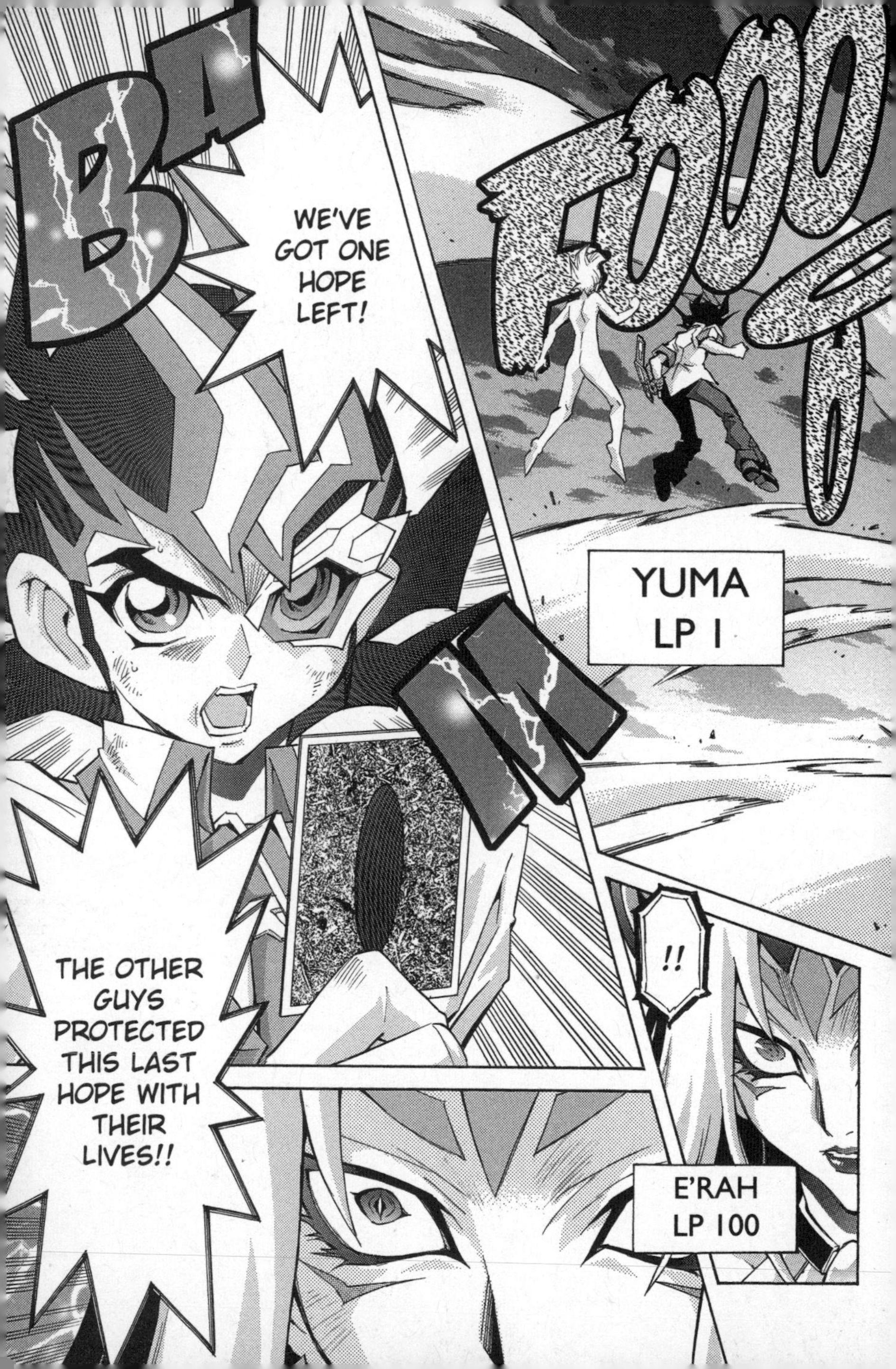
FOOOO
YUMA
LP 1
BAM
WE'VE GOT ONE HOPE LEFT!
THE OTHER GUYS PROTECTED THIS LAST HOPE WITH THEIR LIVES!!
!!
E'RAH
LP 100

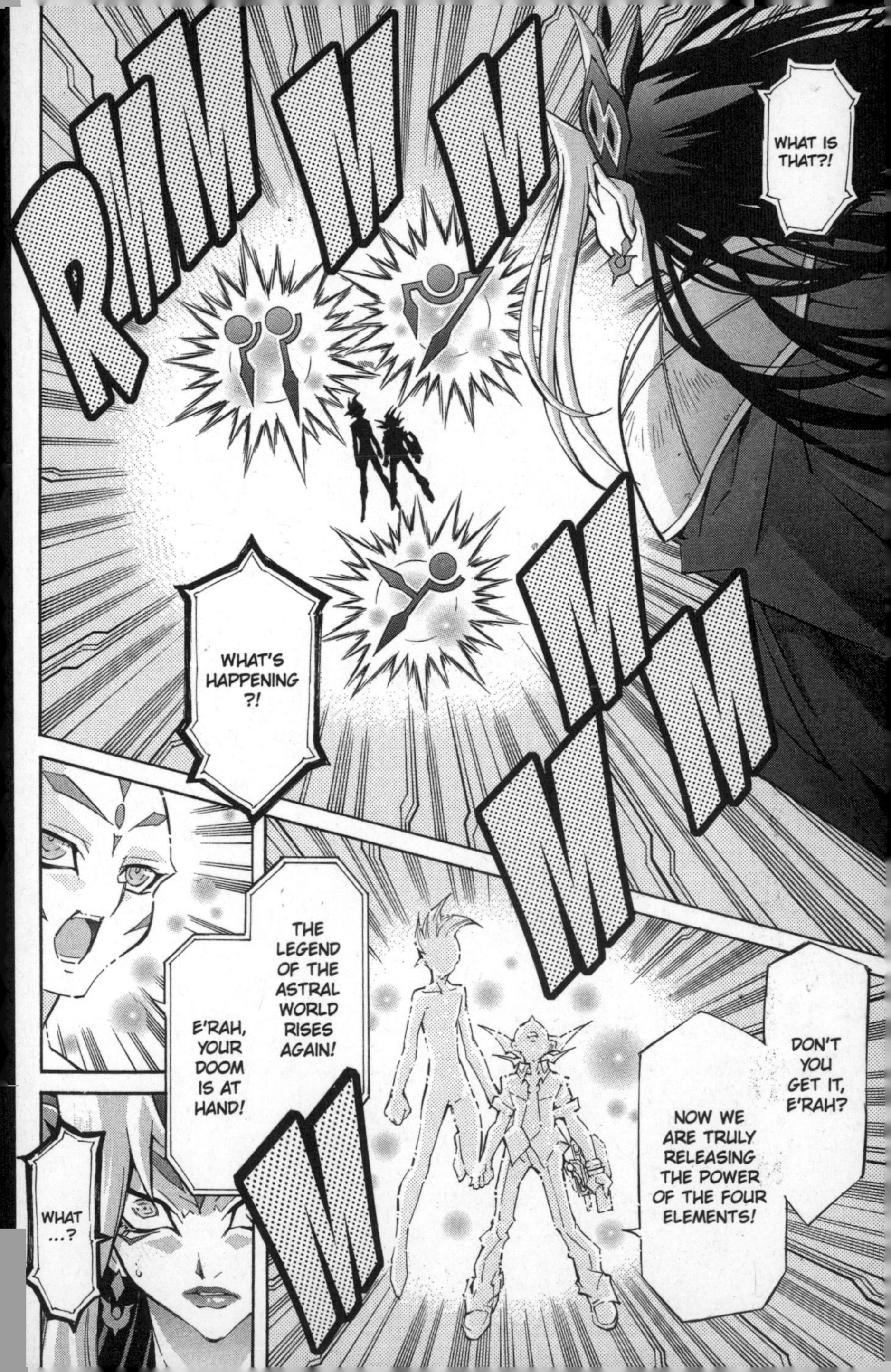
WHAT IS THAT?!
RMMM MM MM
MMM MMM MMM
WHAT'S HAPPENING ?!
DON'T YOU GET IT, E'RAH?
NOW WE ARE TRULY RELEASING THE POWER OF THE FOUR ELEMENTS!
THE LEGEND OF THE ASTRAL WORLD RISES AGAIN!
E'RAH, YOUR DOOM IS AT HAND!
WHAT ...?

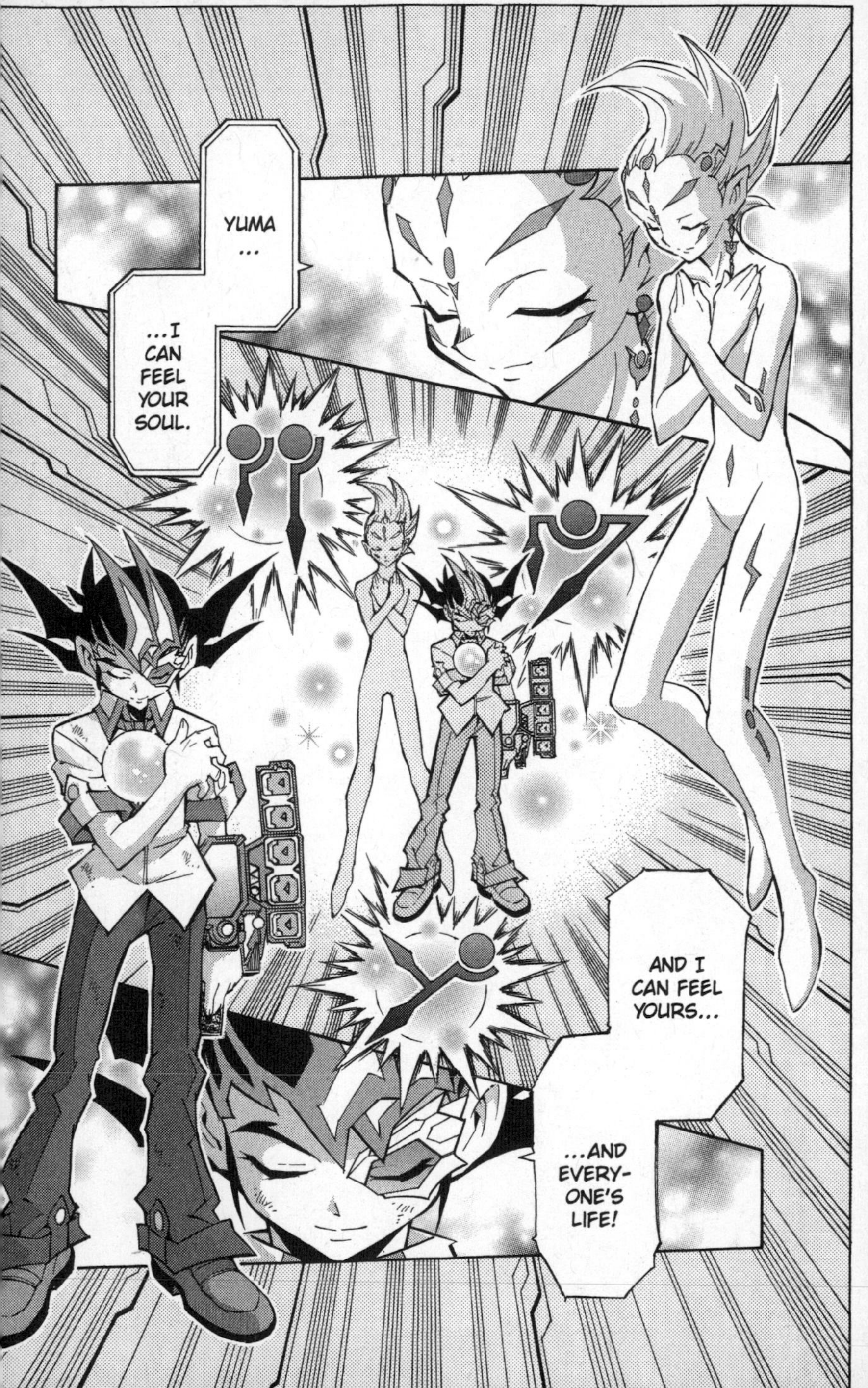
YUMA ...
...I CAN FEEL YOUR SOUL.
AND I CAN FEEL YOURS...
...AND EVERY-ONE'S LIFE!

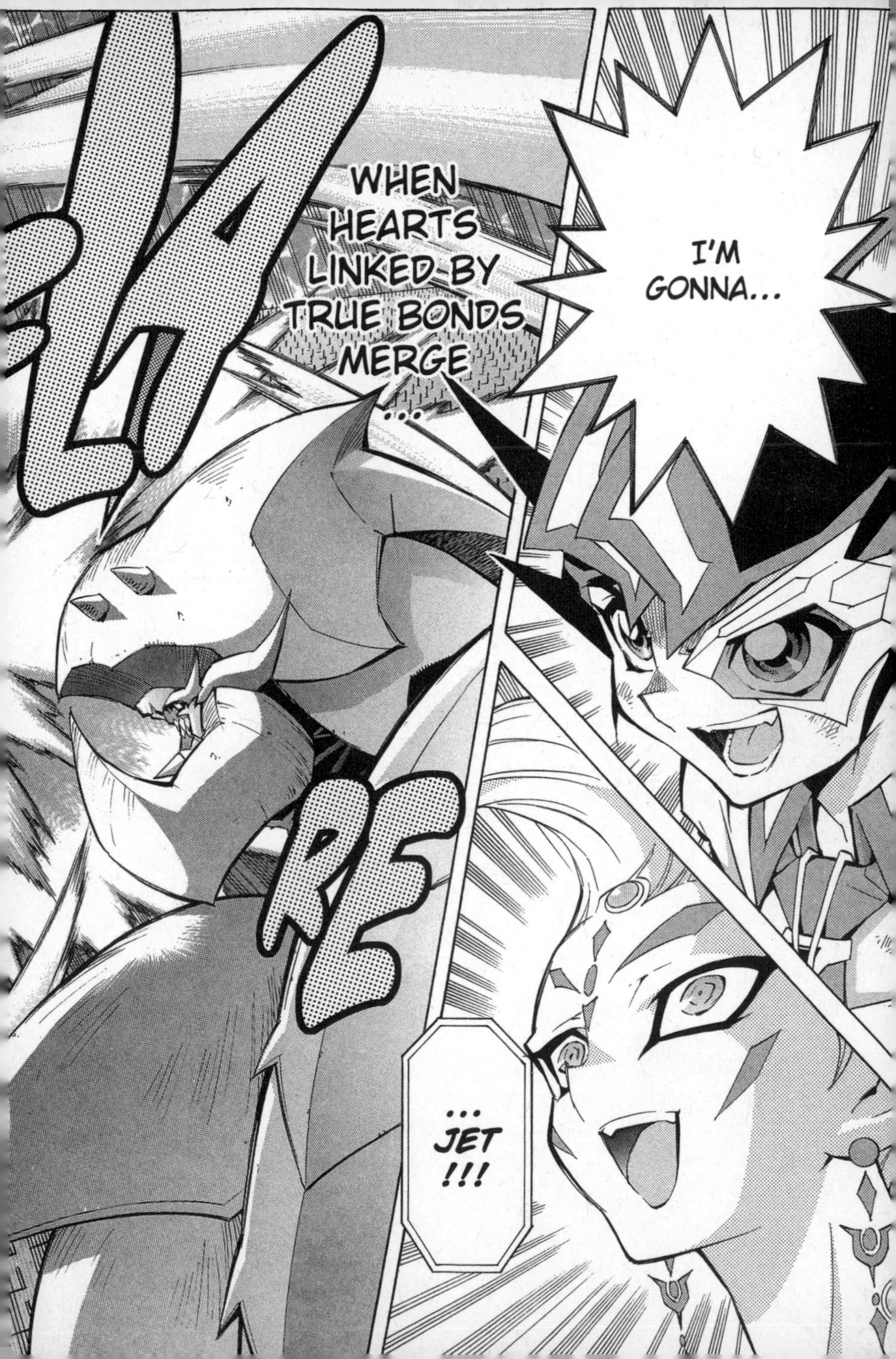
I'M GONNA...
WHEN HEARTS LINKED BY TRUE BONDS MERGE...
...JET!!!
RE
JA

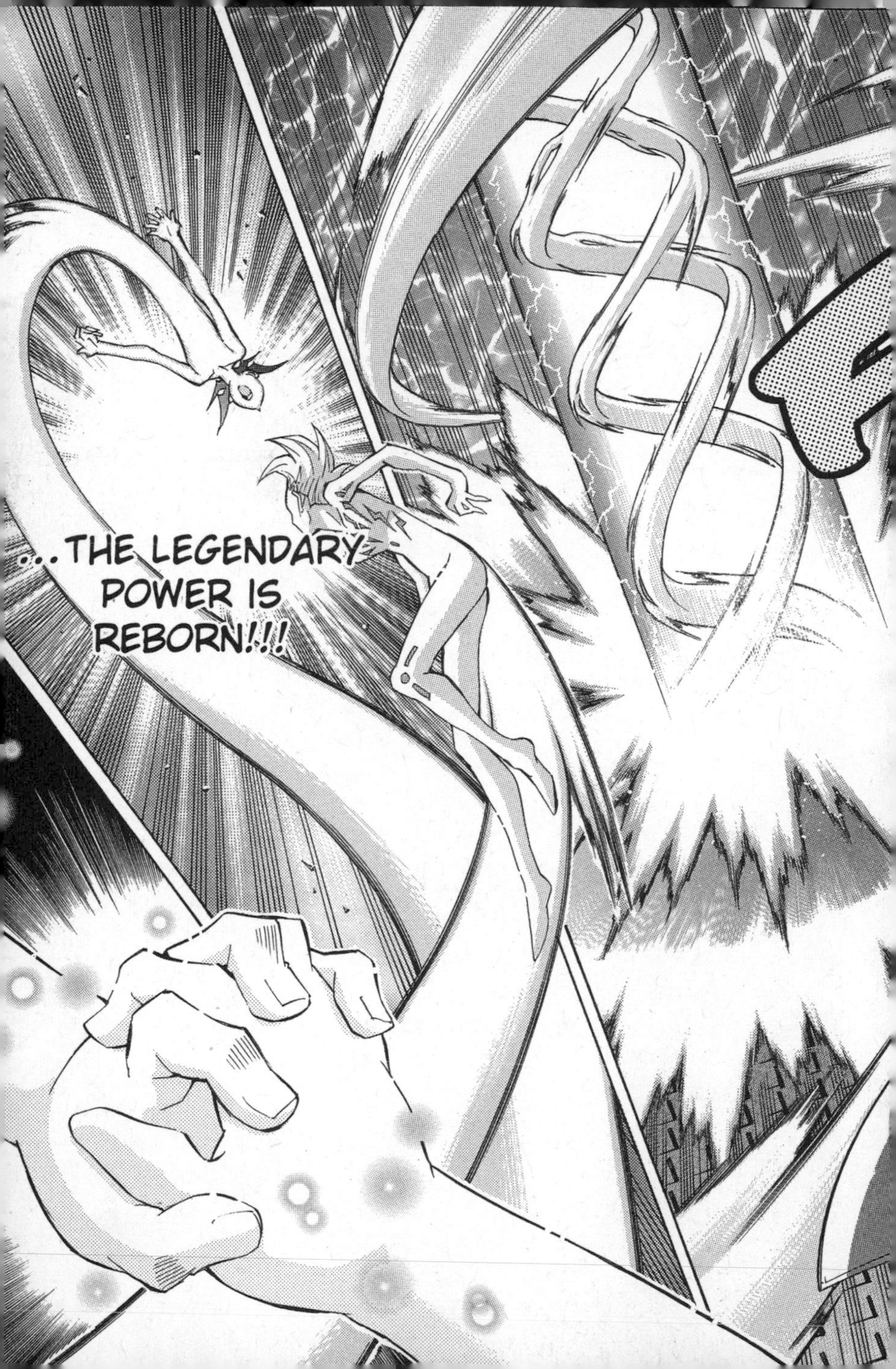
...THE LEGENDARY POWER IS REBORN!!!

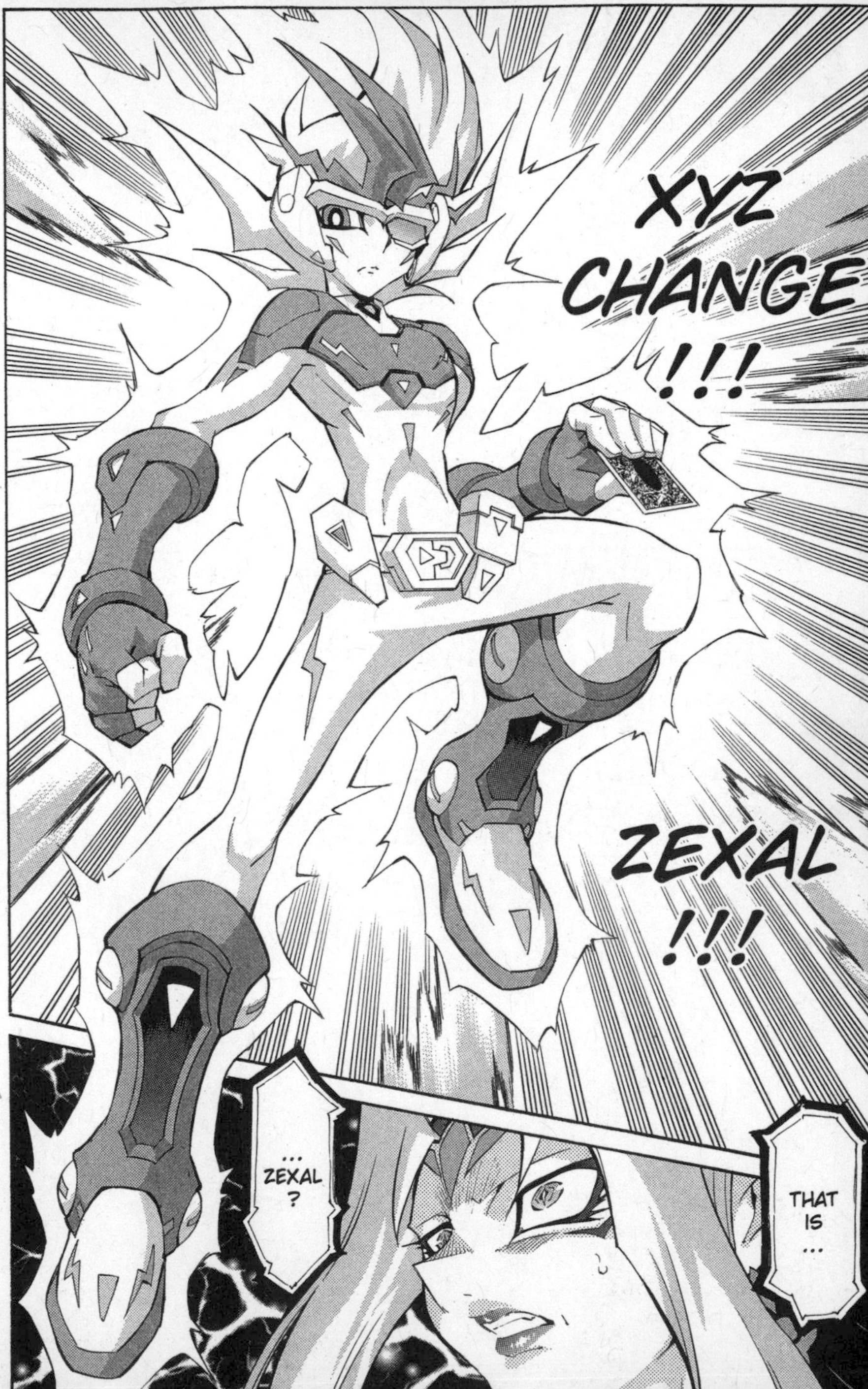
XYZ CHANGE !!!
ZEXAL !!!
THAT IS ...
... ZEXAL ?

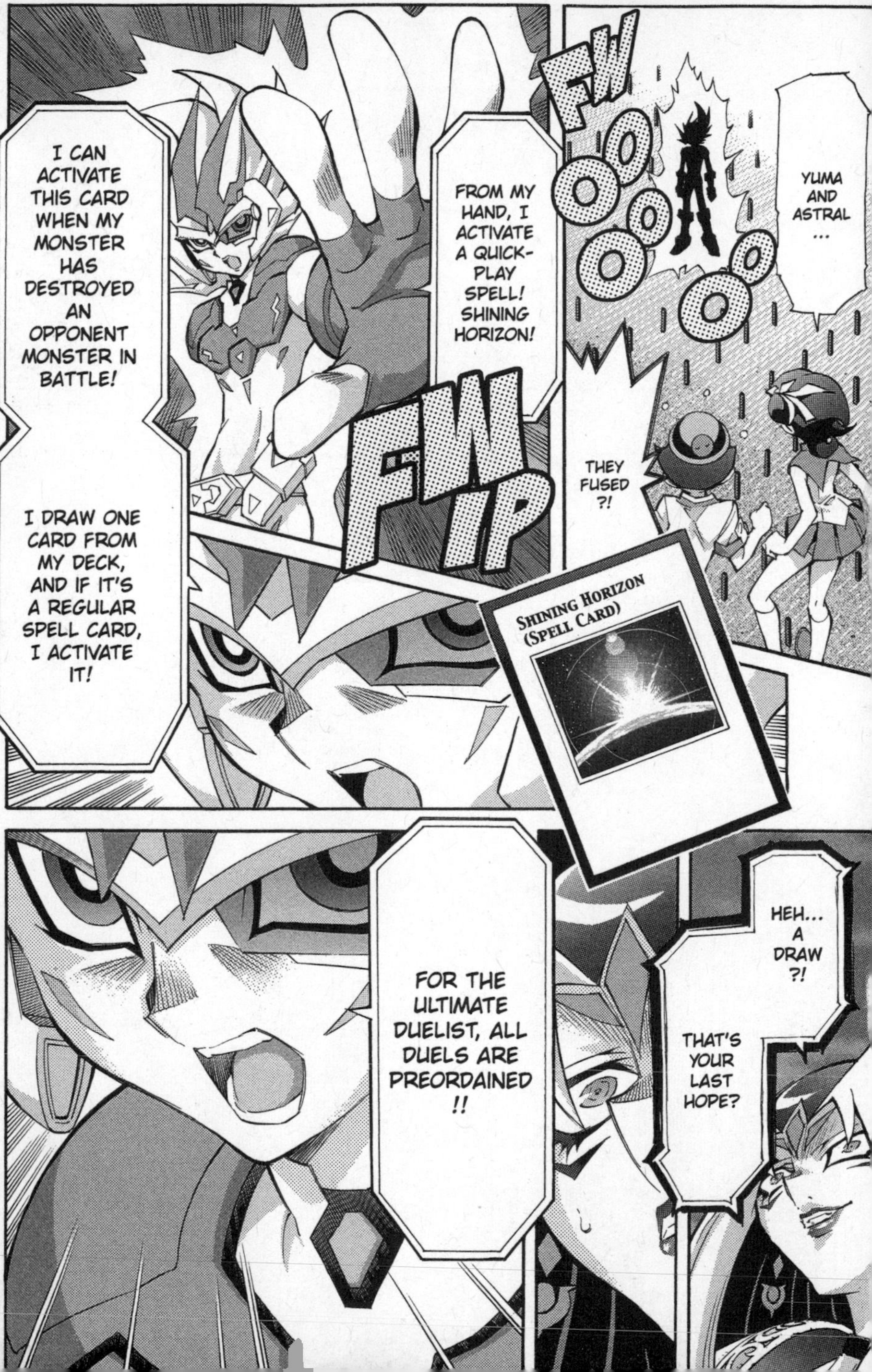
YUMA AND ASTRAL ...
FWOOOOOO
THEY FUSED ?!
FROM MY HAND, I ACTIVATE A QUICK-PLAY SPELL! SHINING HORIZON!
FWIP
I CAN ACTIVATE THIS CARD WHEN MY MONSTER HAS DESTROYED AN OPPONENT MONSTER IN BATTLE!
I DRAW ONE CARD FROM MY DECK, AND IF IT'S A REGULAR SPELL CARD, I ACTIVATE IT!
SHINING HORIZON (SPELL CARD)
HEH... A DRAW ?!
THAT'S YOUR LAST HOPE?
FOR THE ULTIMATE DUELIST, ALL DUELS ARE PREORDAINED !!

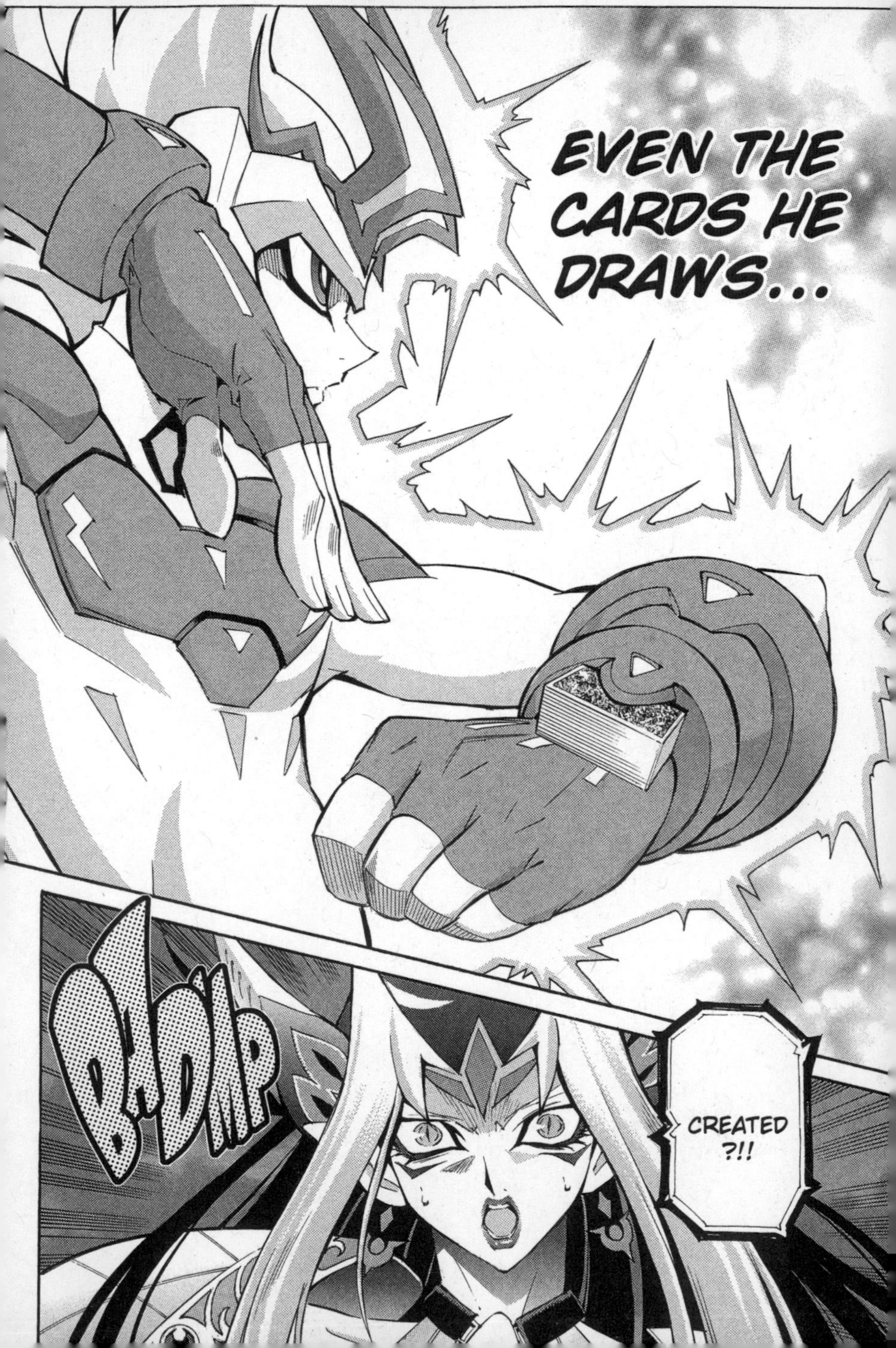
EVEN THE CARDS HE DRAWS...
BA-DUMP
CREATED ?!!

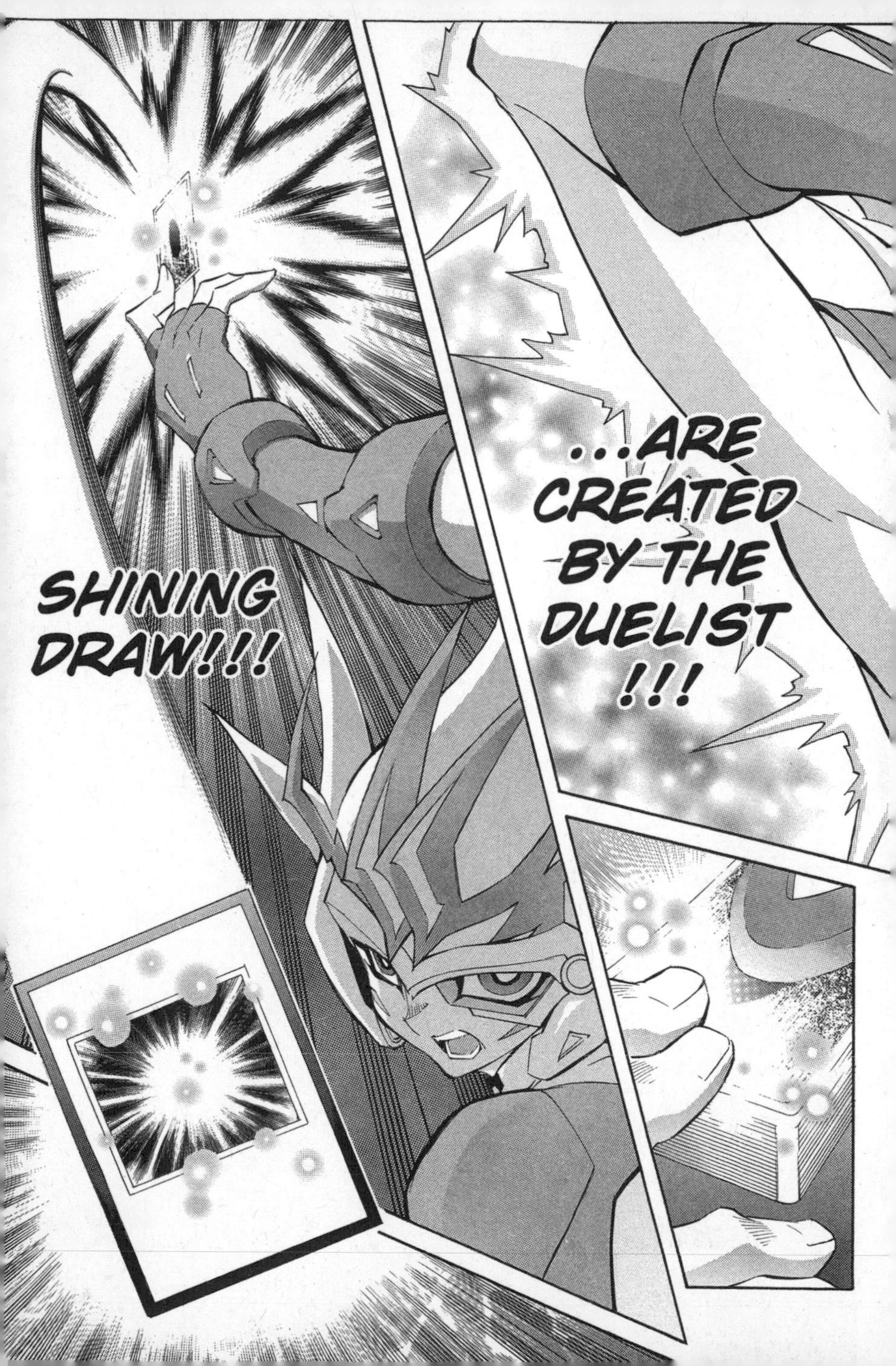
...ARE CREATED BY THE DUELIST !!!
SHINING DRAW!!!

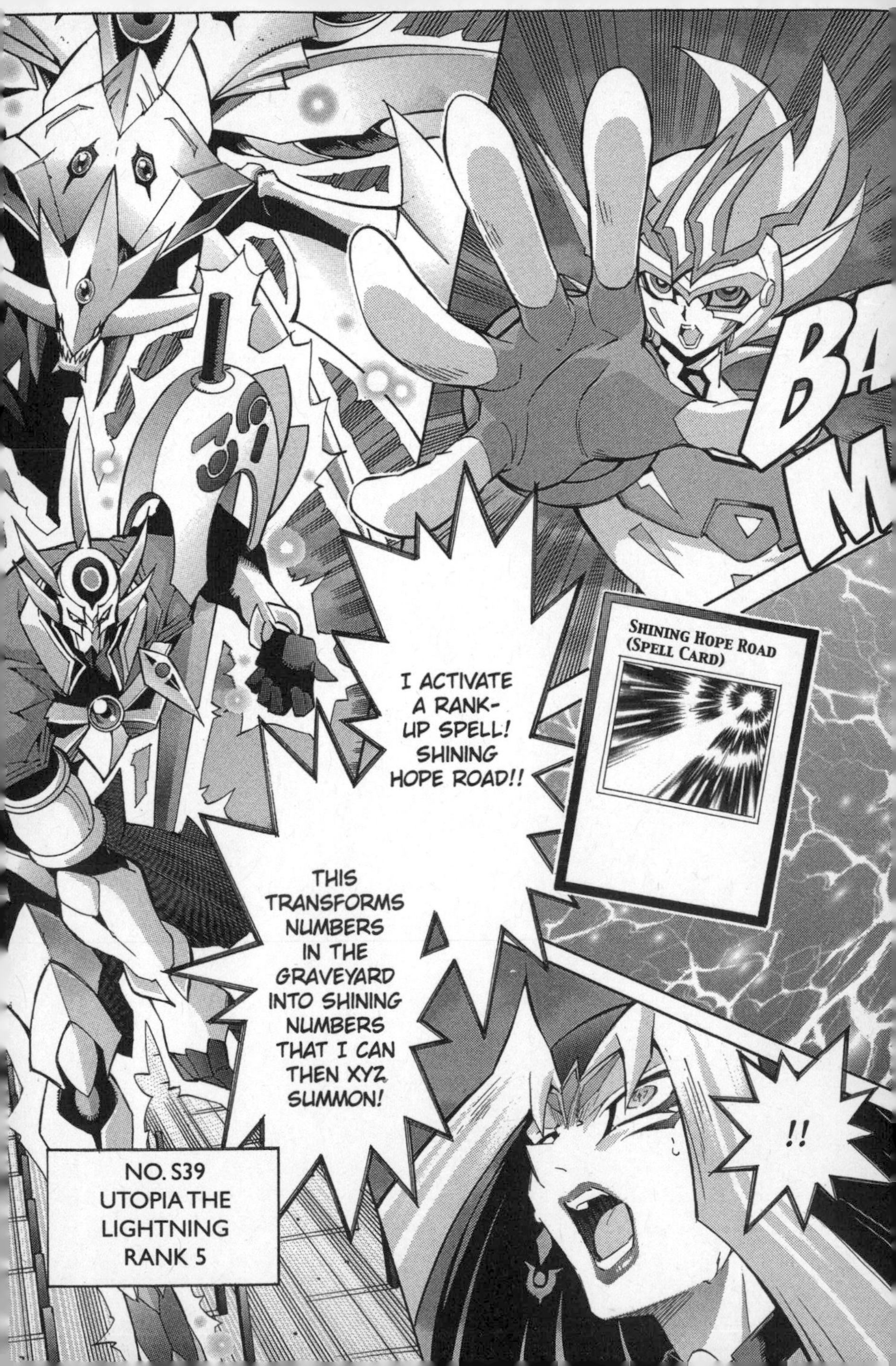
BAM
SHINING HOPE ROAD
(SPELL CARD)
I ACTIVATE A RANK-UP SPELL! SHINING HOPE ROAD!!
THIS TRANSFORMS NUMBERS IN THE GRAVEYARD INTO SHINING NUMBERS THAT I CAN THEN XYZ SUMMON!
!!
NO. S39 UTOPIA THE LIGHTNING RANK 5

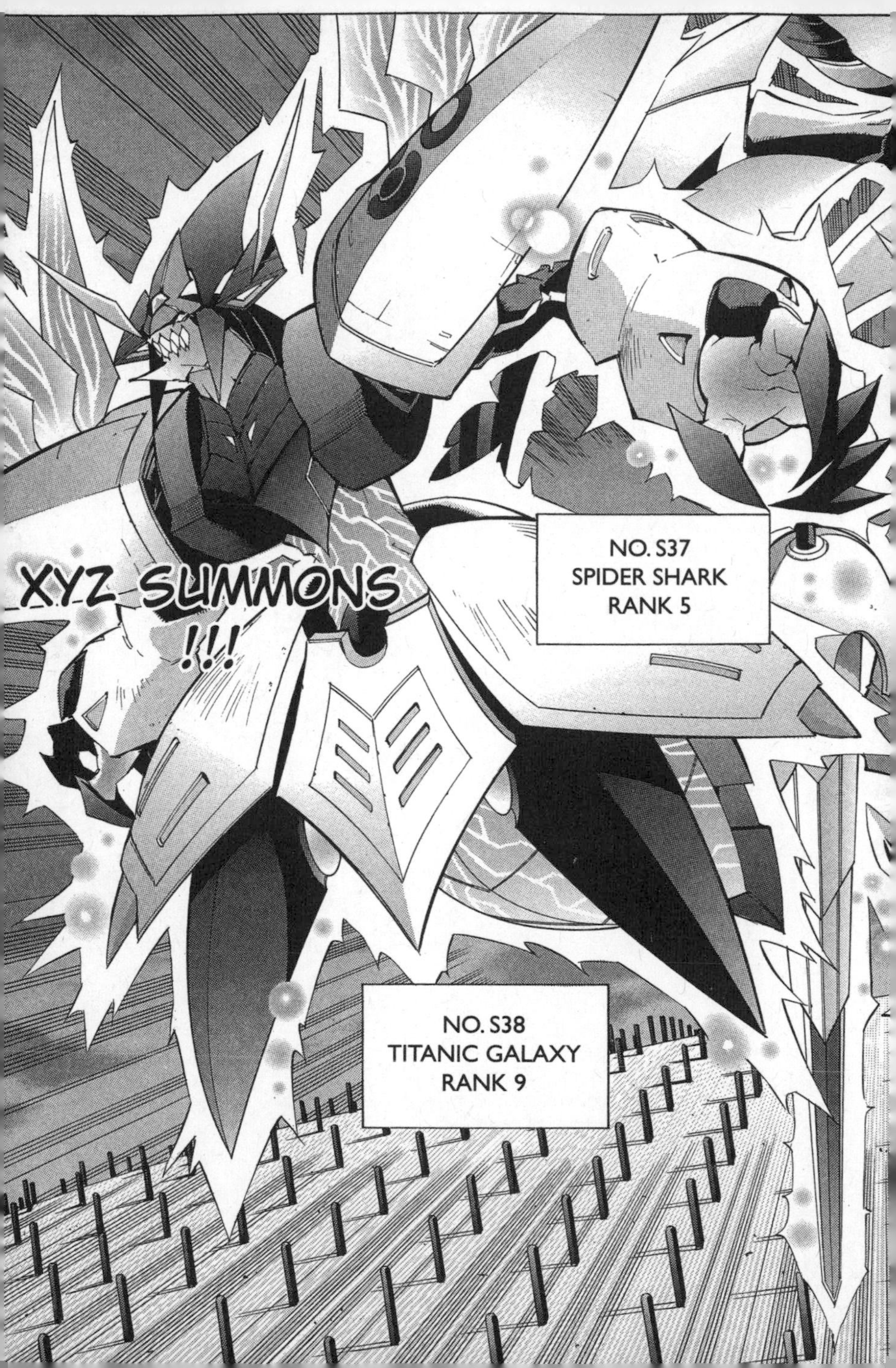
NO. S37
SPIDER SHARK
RANK 5
XYZ SUMMONS !!!
NO. S38
TITANIC GALAXY
RANK 9

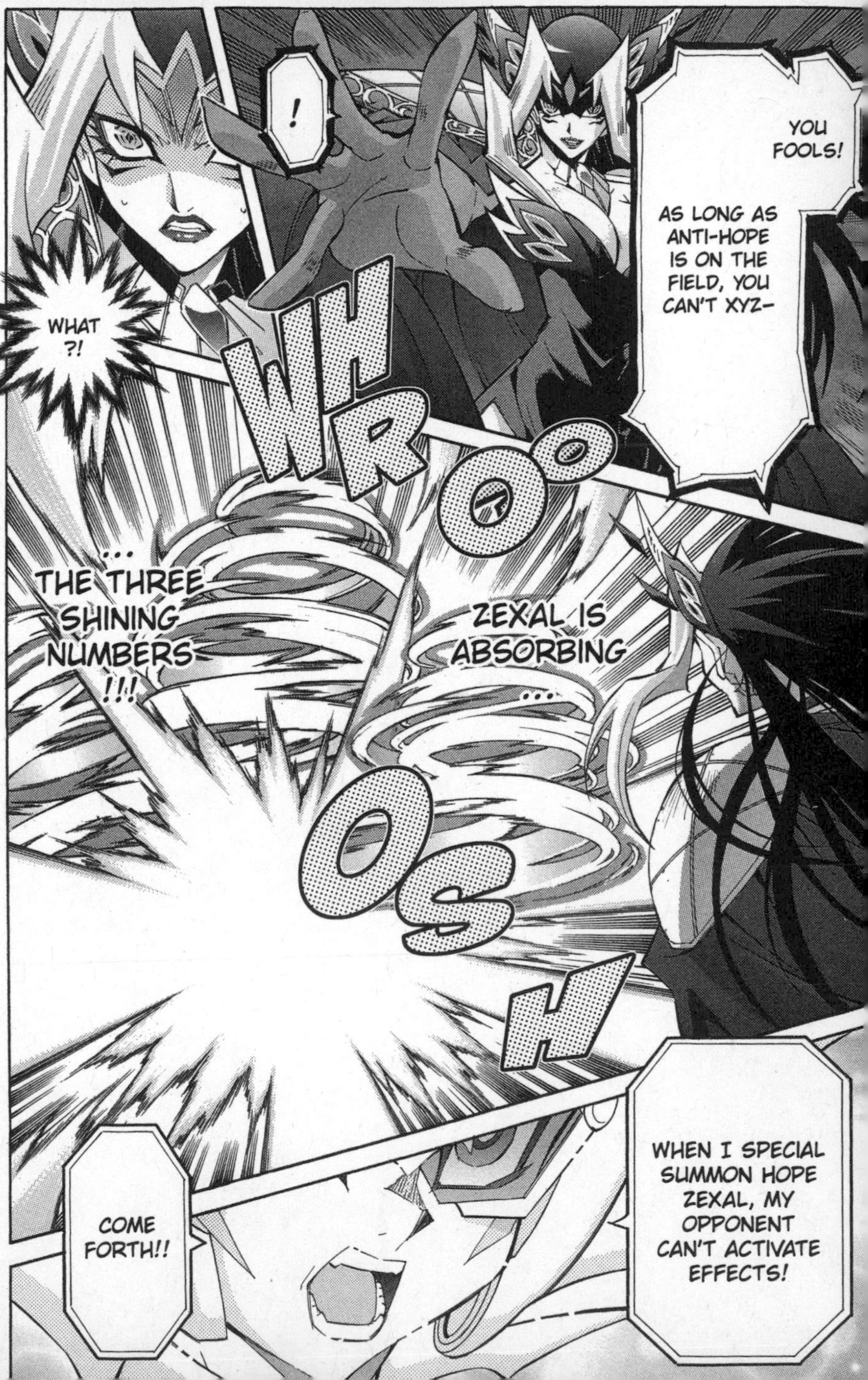
YOU FOOLS!
AS LONG AS ANTI-HOPE IS ON THE FIELD, YOU CAN'T XYZ-
!
WHAT ?!
WHROOOSH
ZEXAL IS ABSORBING ...
... THE THREE SHINING NUMBERS !!!
WHEN I SPECIAL SUMMON HOPE ZEXAL, MY OPPONENT CAN'T ACTIVATE EFFECTS!
COME FORTH!!

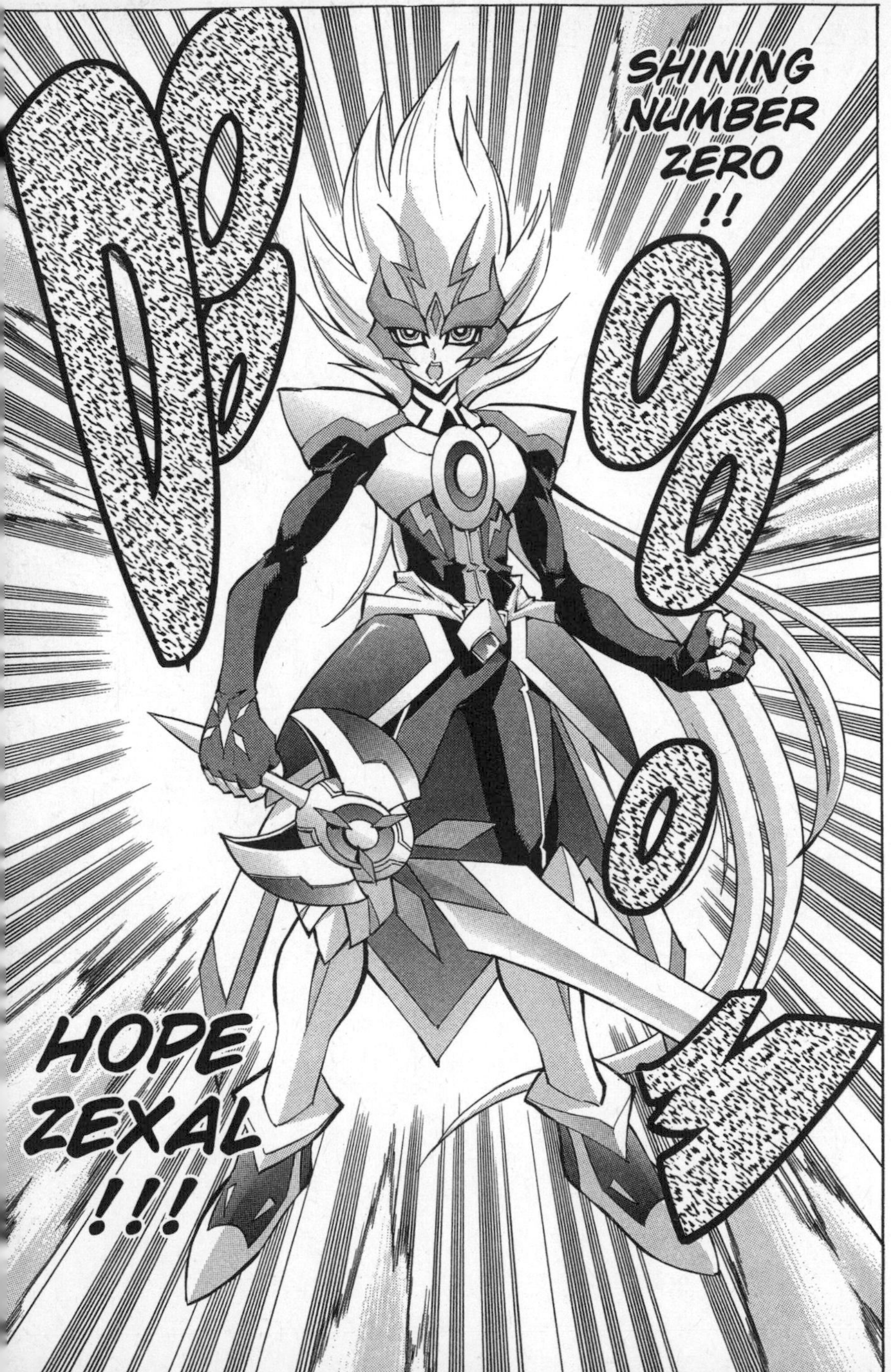
SHINING NUMBER ZERO!!
DOOOON
HOPE ZEXAL!!!

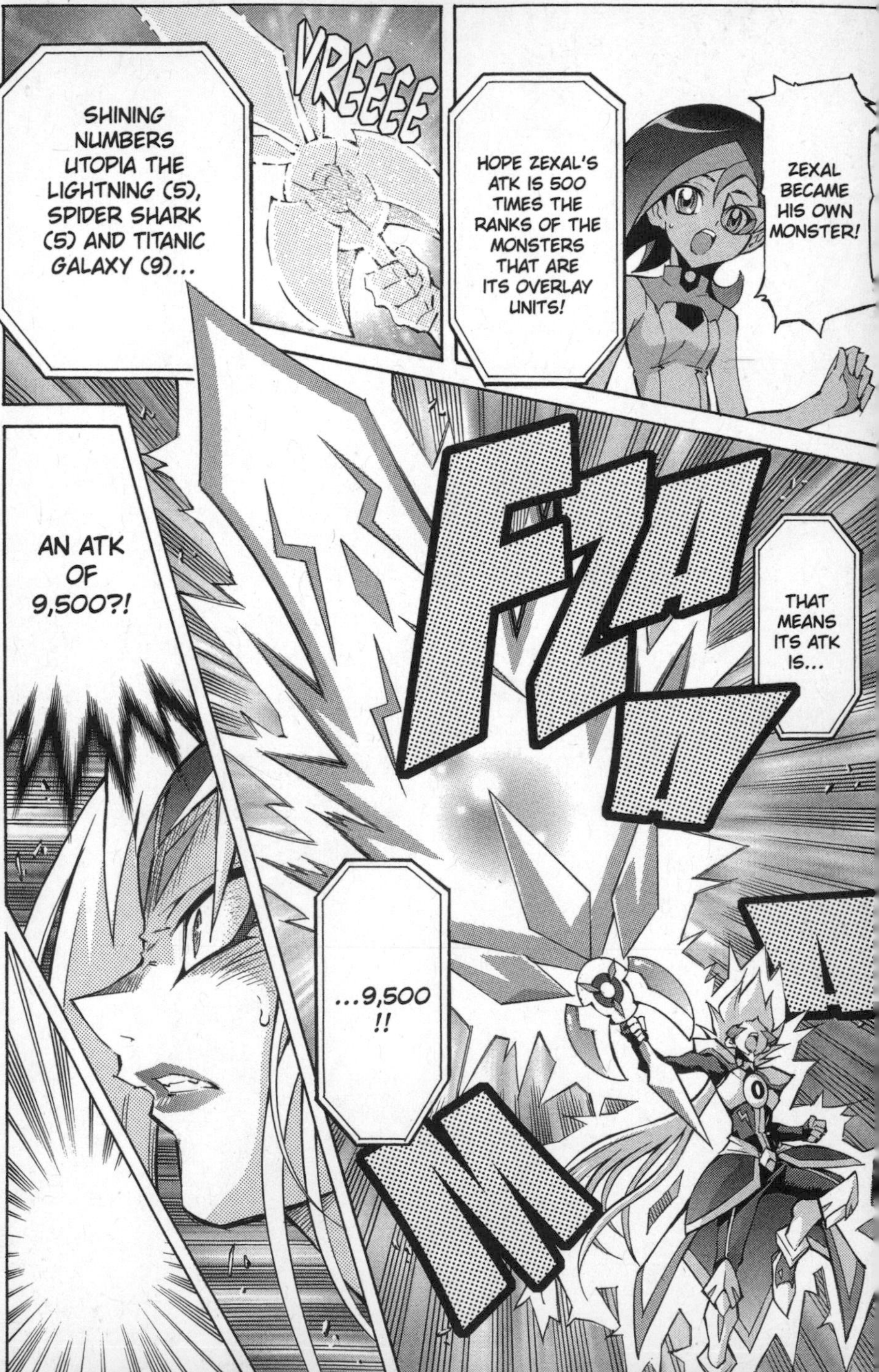
ZEXAL BECAME HIS OWN MONSTER!
HOPE ZEXAL'S ATK IS 500 TIMES THE RANKS OF THE MONSTERS THAT ARE ITS OVERLAY UNITS!
VREEEE
SHINING NUMBERS UTOPIA THE LIGHTNING (5), SPIDER SHARK (5) AND TITANIC GALAXY (9)...
THAT MEANS ITS ATK IS...
FZAA
AN ATK OF 9,500?!
...9,500 !!

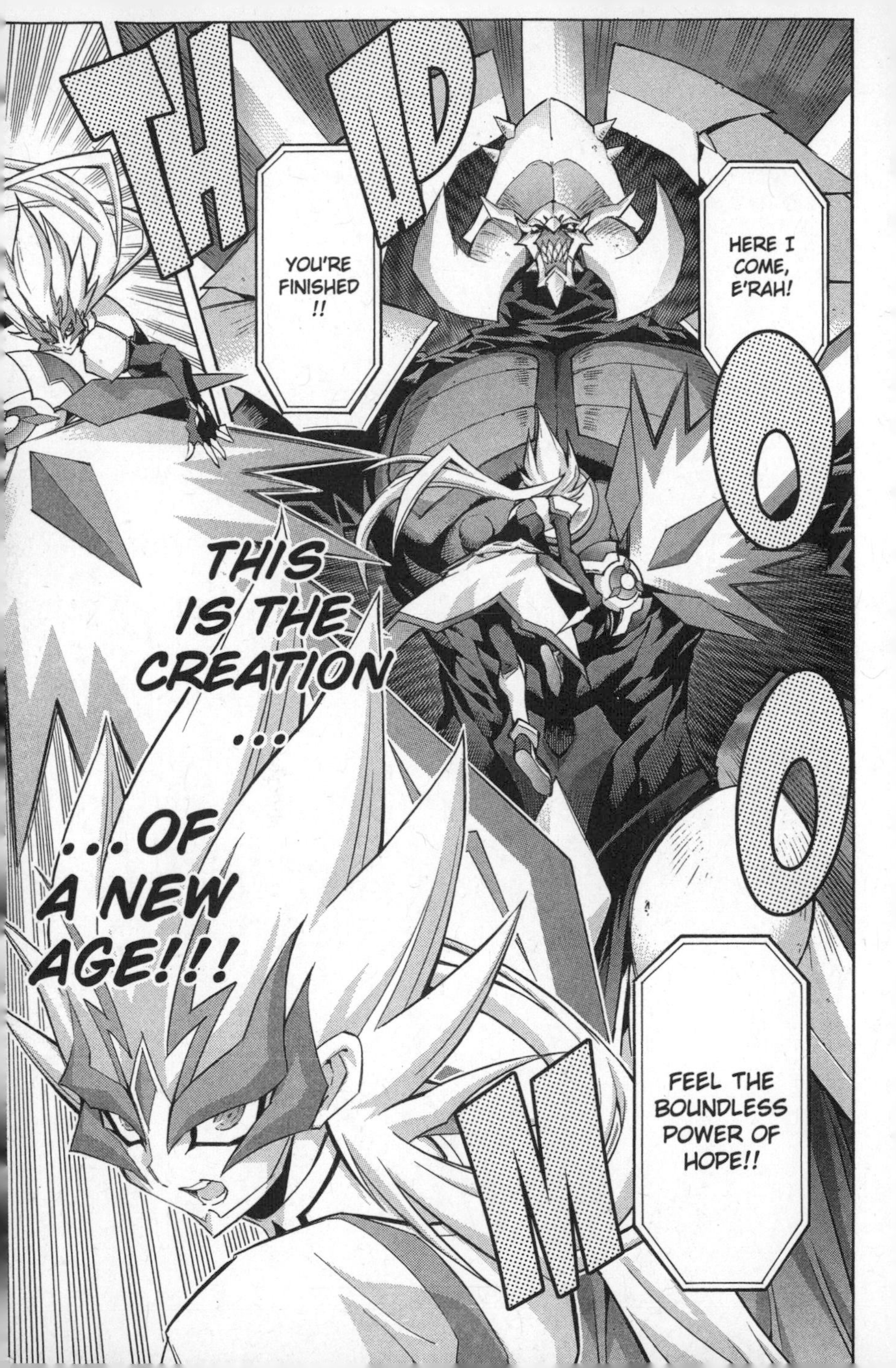
HERE I COME, E'RAH!
YOU'RE FINISHED!!
THUD
FEEL THE BOUNDLESS POWER OF HOPE!!
THIS IS THE CREATION...
...OF A NEW AGE!!!

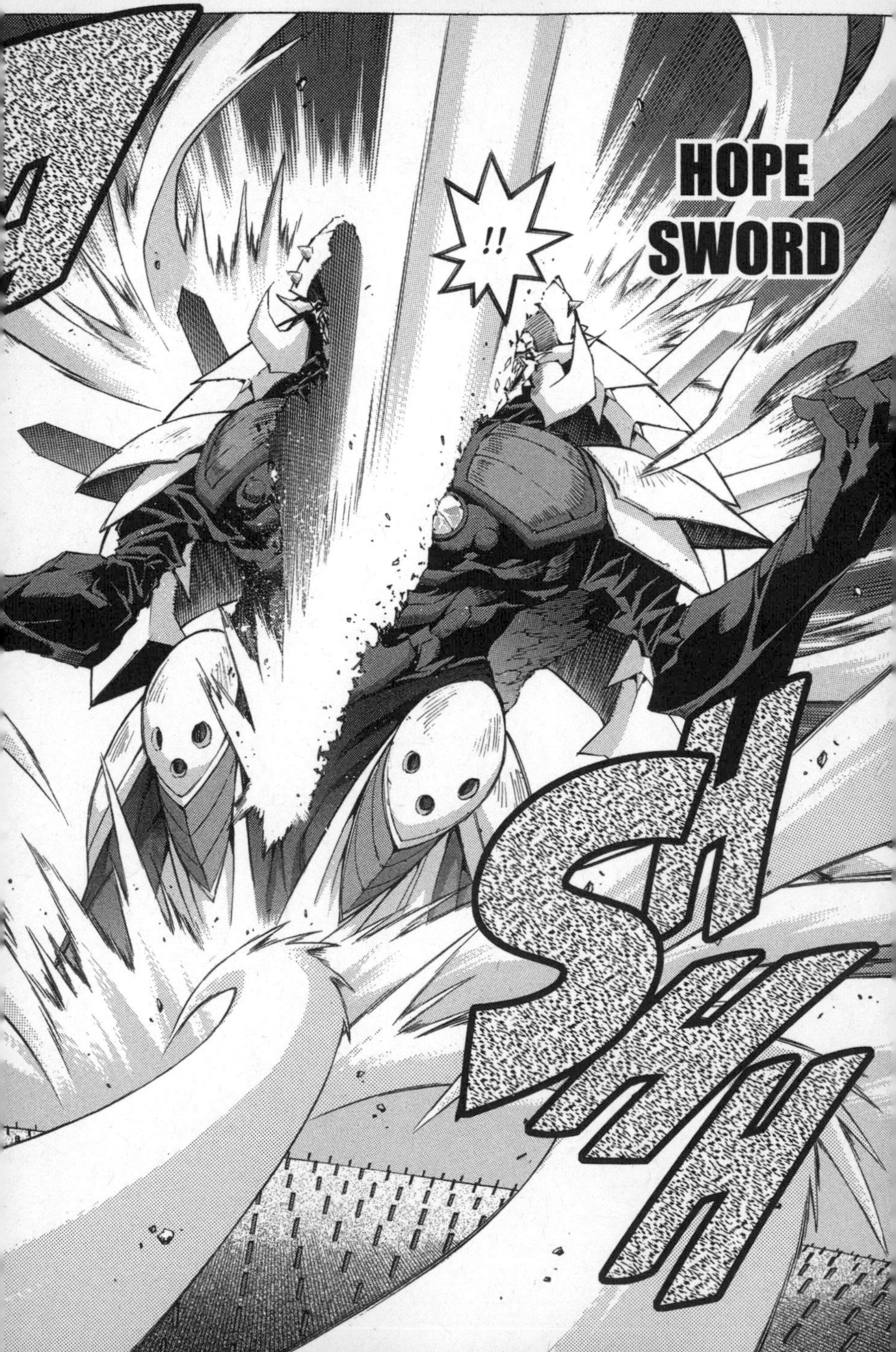
HOPE SWORD
!!
SHHH

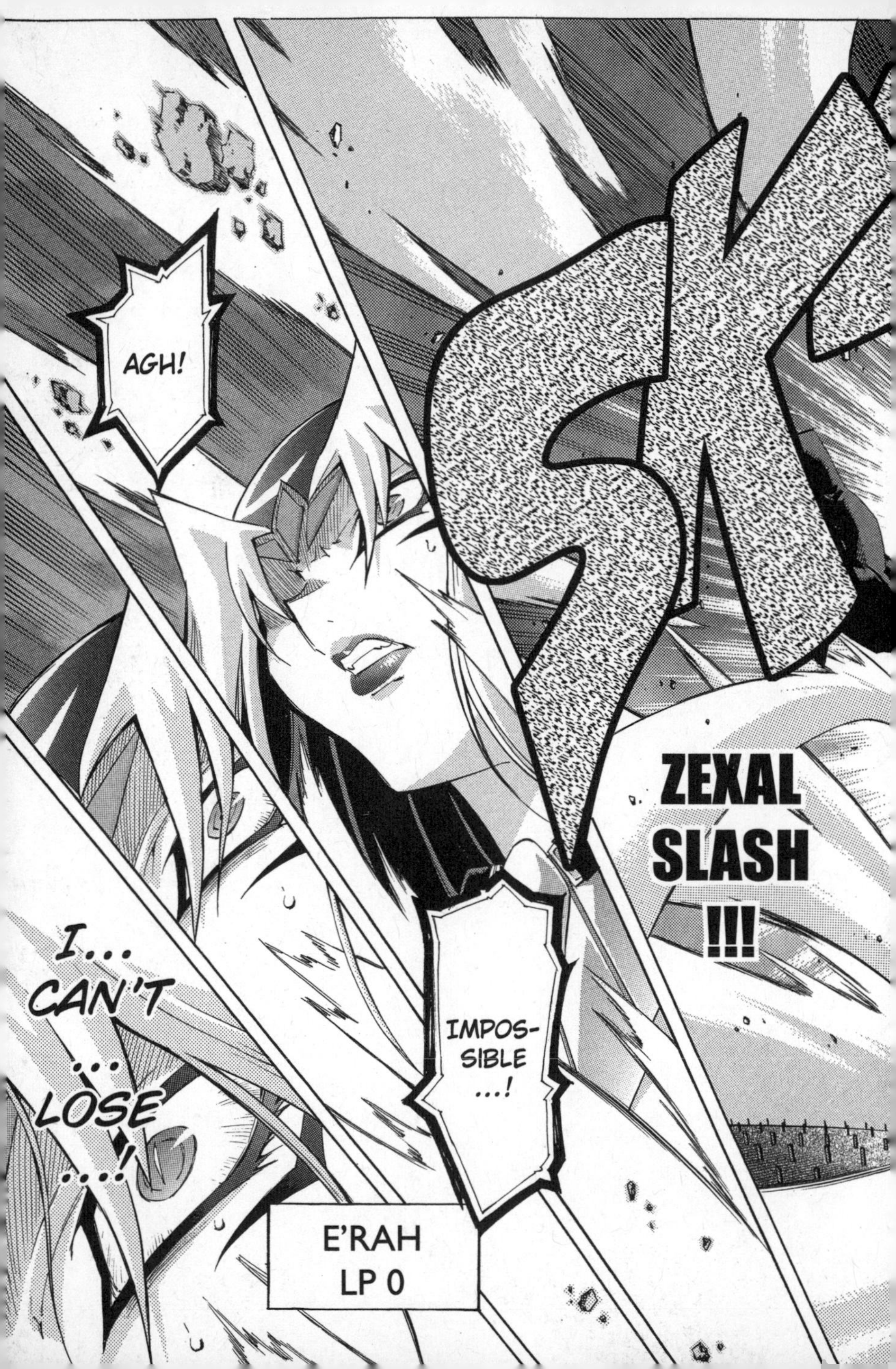
ZEXAL SLASH !!!
AGH!
IMPOSSIBLE ...!
I... CAN'T ... LOSE ...!
E'RAH LP 0

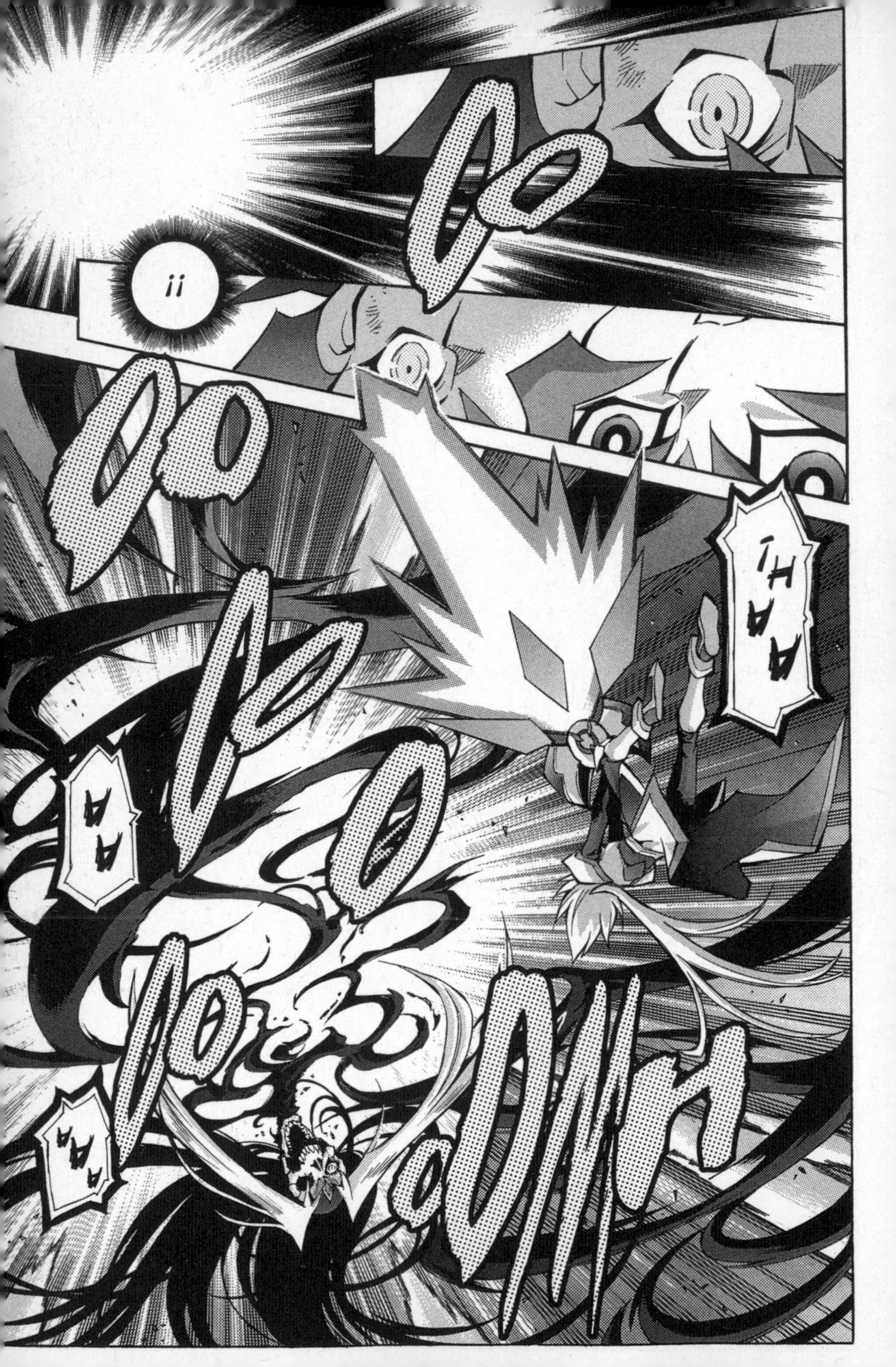
!!
AAH!
AA
AAA

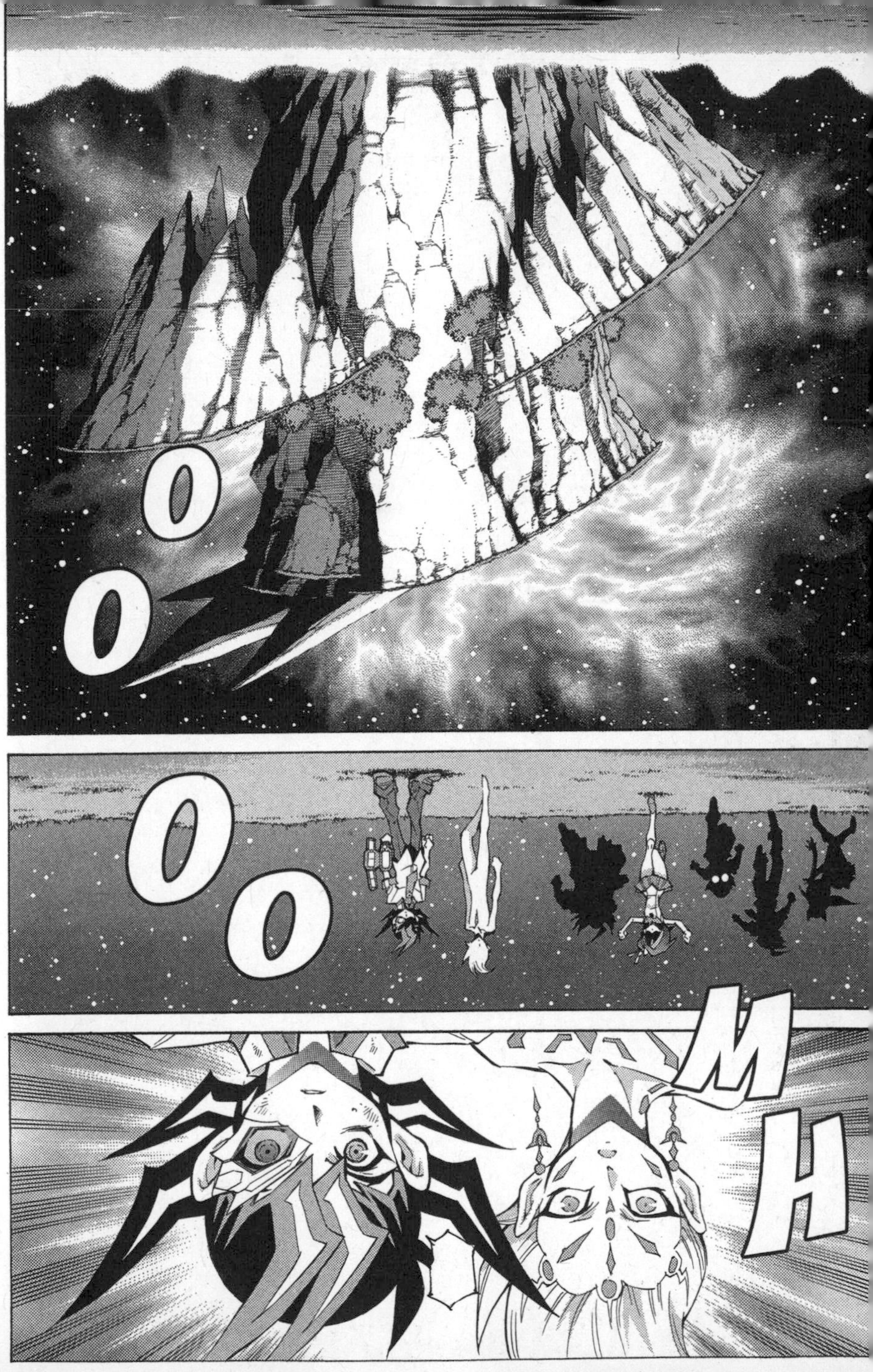
OO
OO
MH

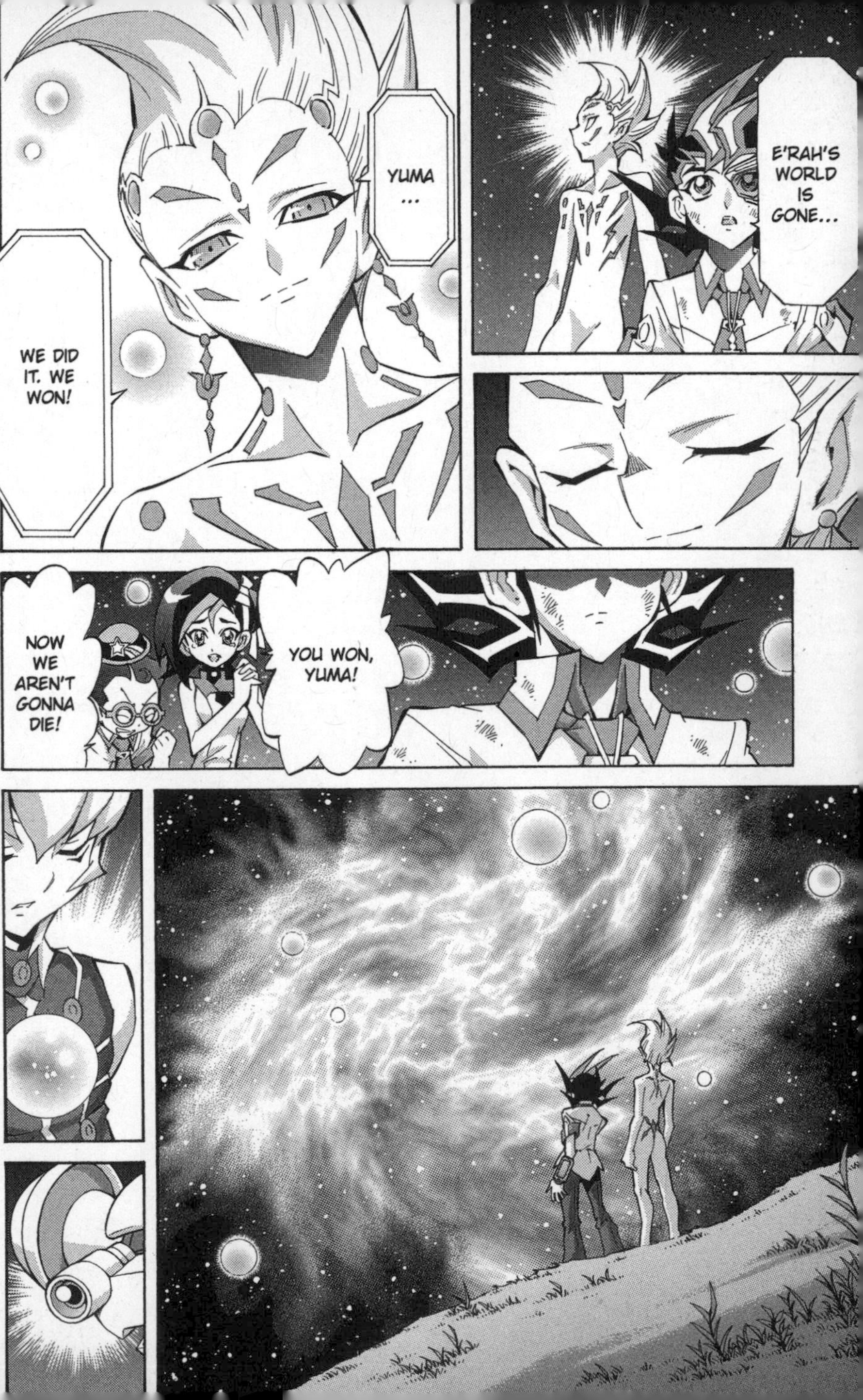
E'RAH'S WORLD IS GONE...
YUMA ...
WE DID IT. WE WON!
YOU WON, YUMA!
NOW WE AREN'T GONNA DIE!

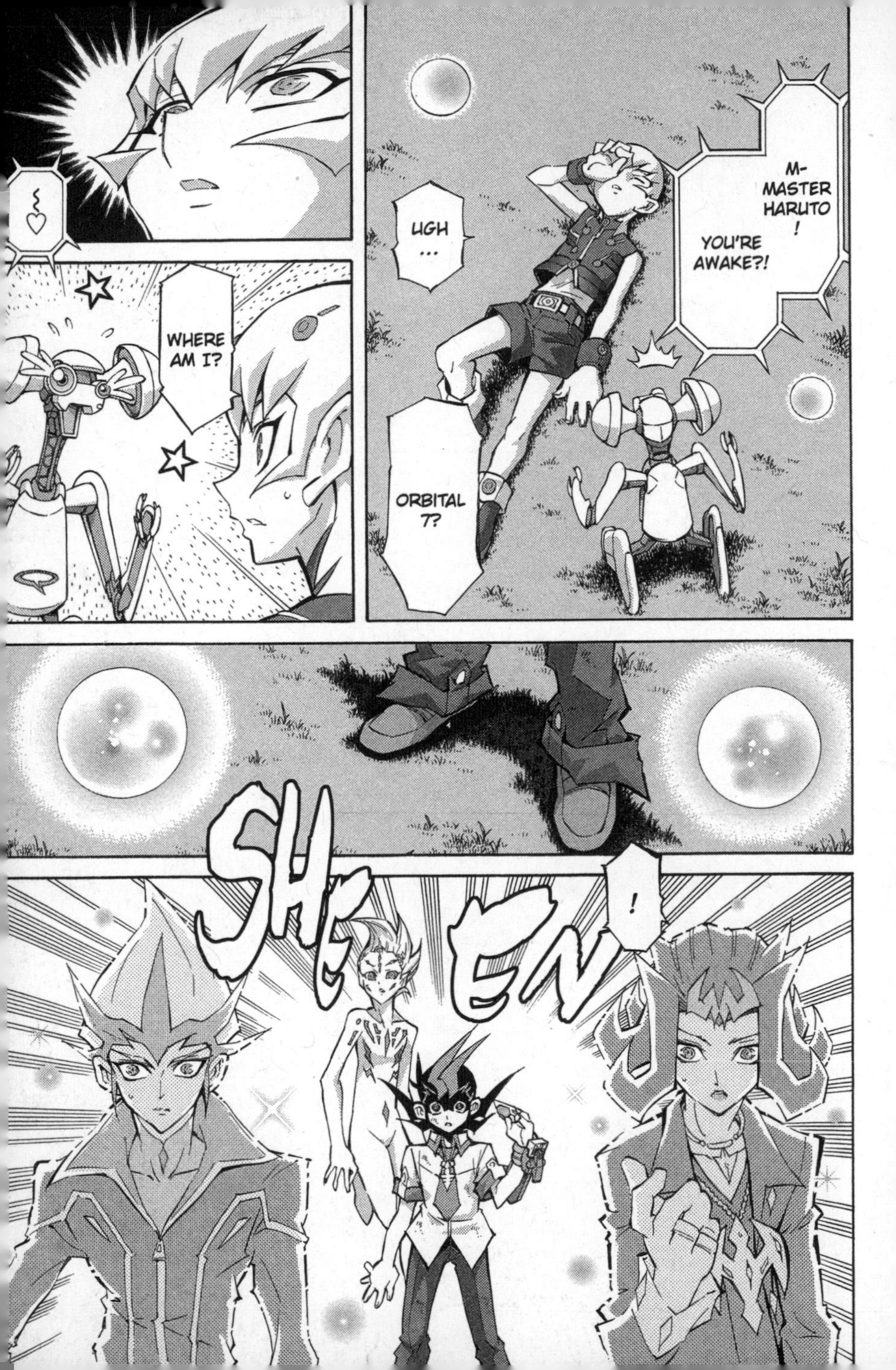
M-MASTER HARUTO!
YOU'RE AWAKE?!
UGH...
ORBITAL 7?
WHERE AM I?
~♡
SHEEN
!

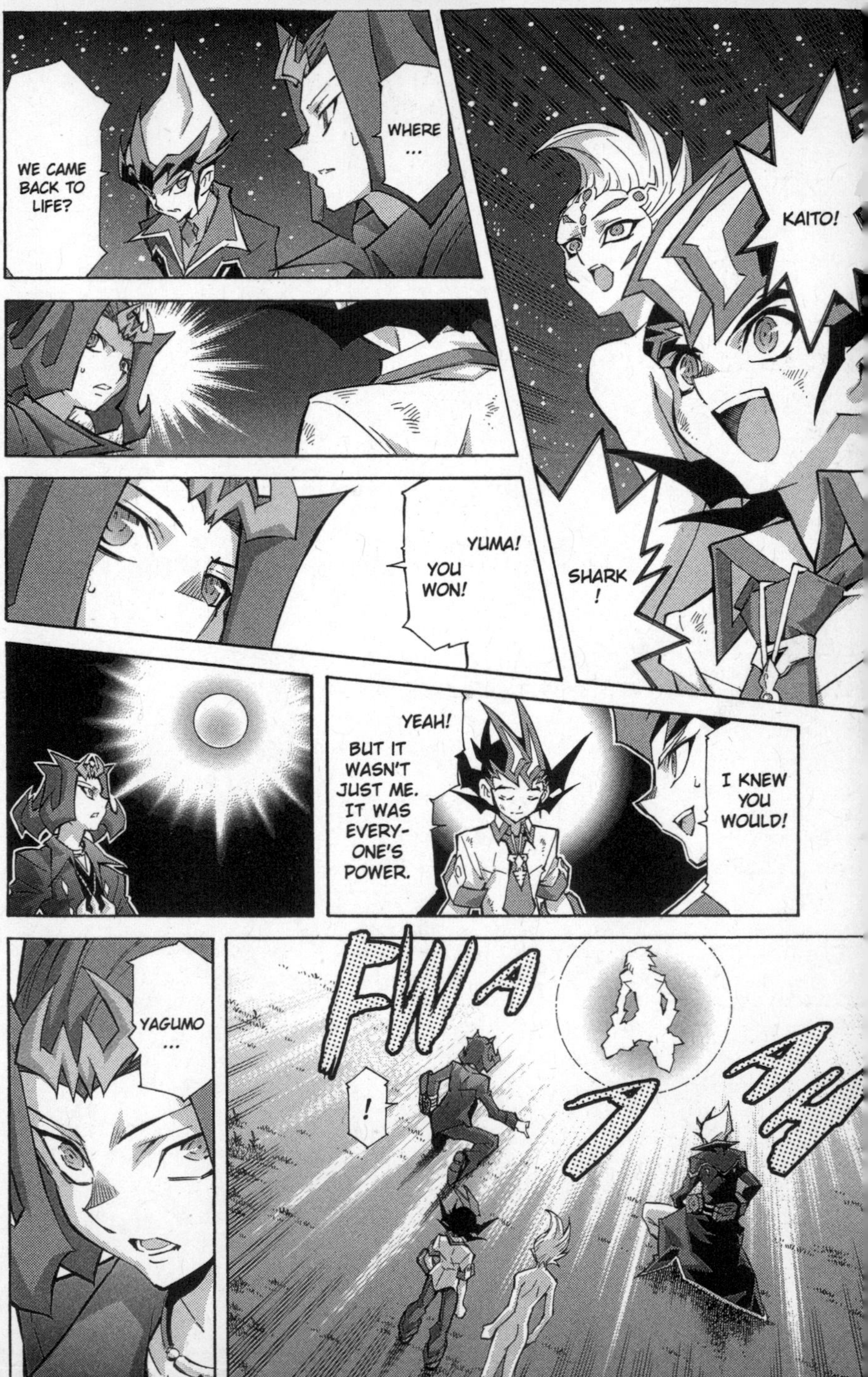
KAITO!
SHARK!
WHERE...
WE CAME BACK TO LIFE?
YUMA! YOU WON!
I KNEW YOU WOULD!
YEAH!
BUT IT WASN'T JUST ME. IT WAS EVERY-ONE'S POWER.
FWAAAH
!
YAGUMO...

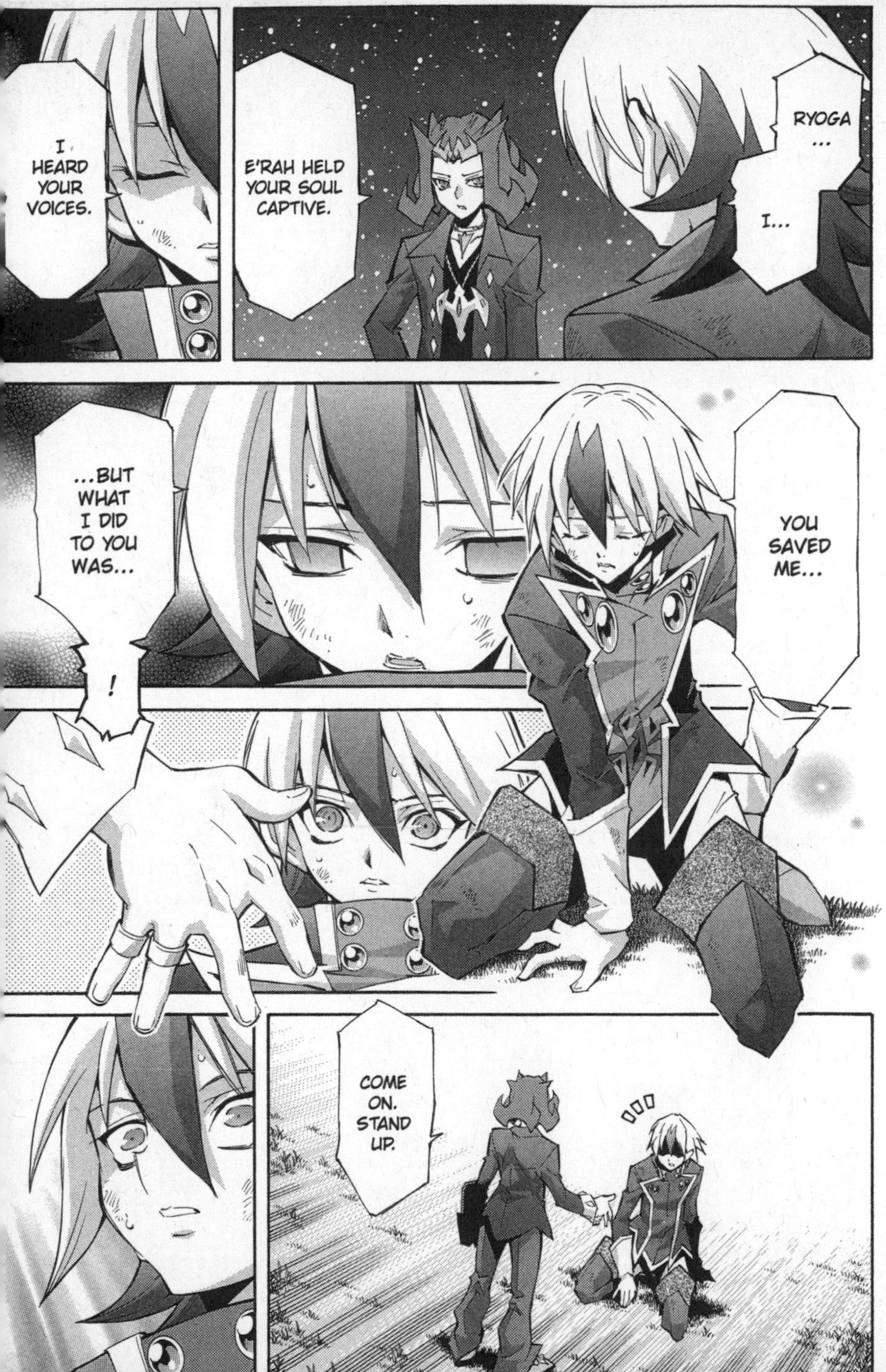
RYOGA ...
I...
E'RAH HELD YOUR SOUL CAPTIVE.
I HEARD YOUR VOICES.
YOU SAVED ME...
...BUT WHAT I DID TO YOU WAS...
!
COME ON. STAND UP.

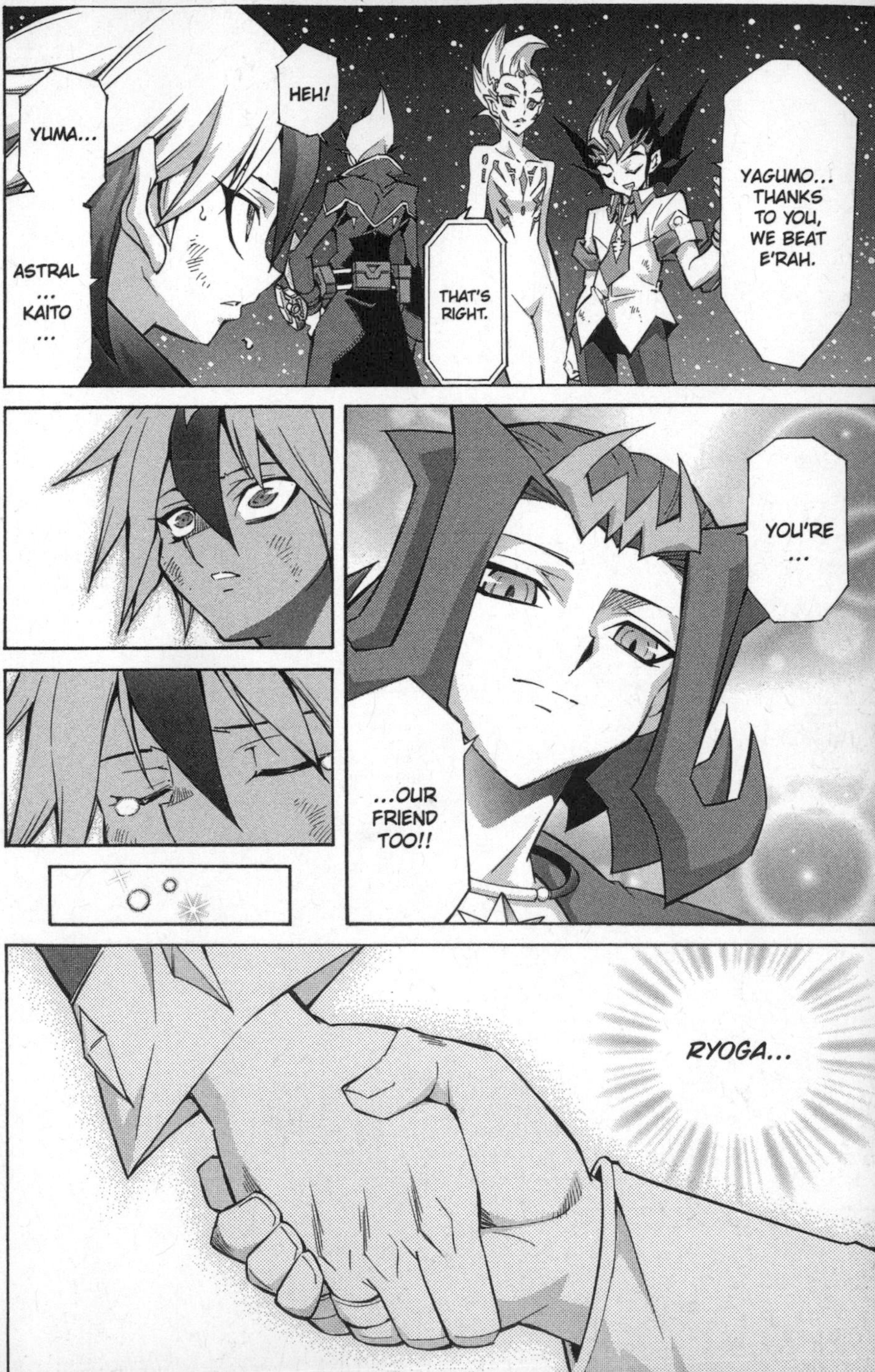
YAGUMO... THANKS TO YOU, WE BEAT E'RAH.
THAT'S RIGHT.
HEH!
YUMA...
ASTRAL ... KAITO ...
YOU'RE ...
...OUR FRIEND TOO!!
RYOGA...

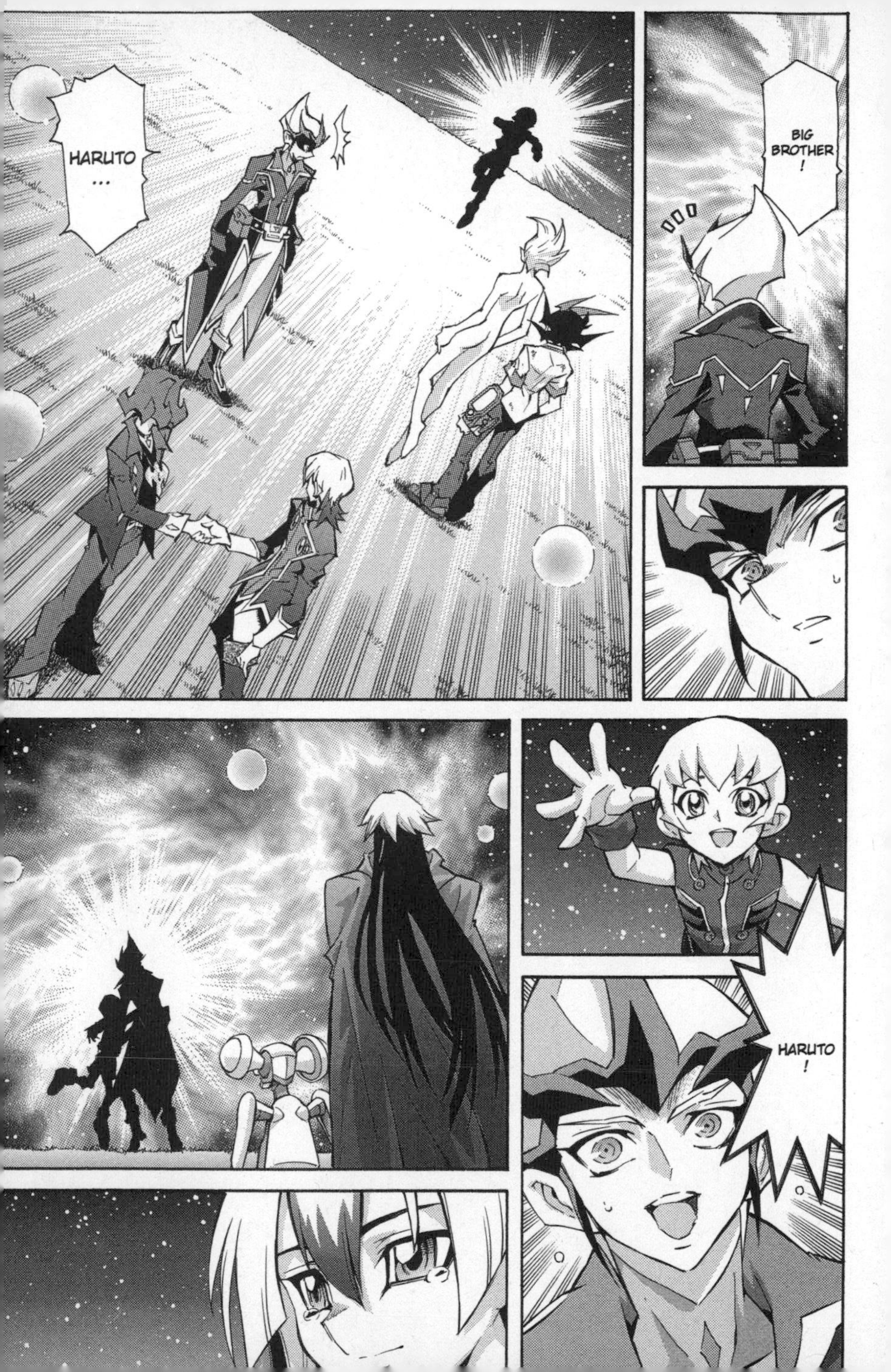
BIG BROTHER!
HARUTO...
HARUTO!

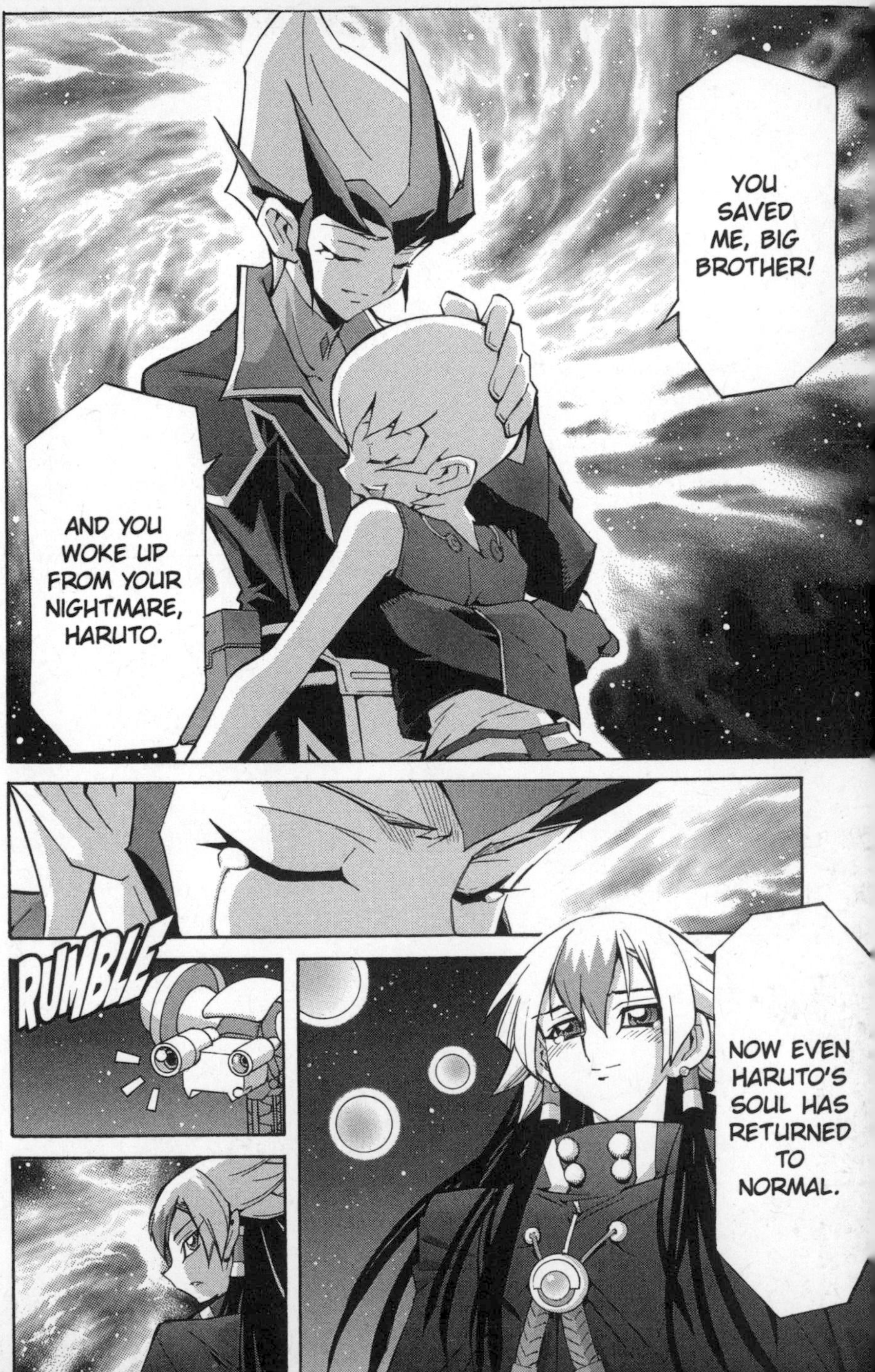
YOU SAVED ME, BIG BROTHER!
AND YOU WOKE UP FROM YOUR NIGHTMARE, HARUTO.
NOW EVEN HARUTO'S SOUL HAS RETURNED TO NORMAL.
RUMBLE

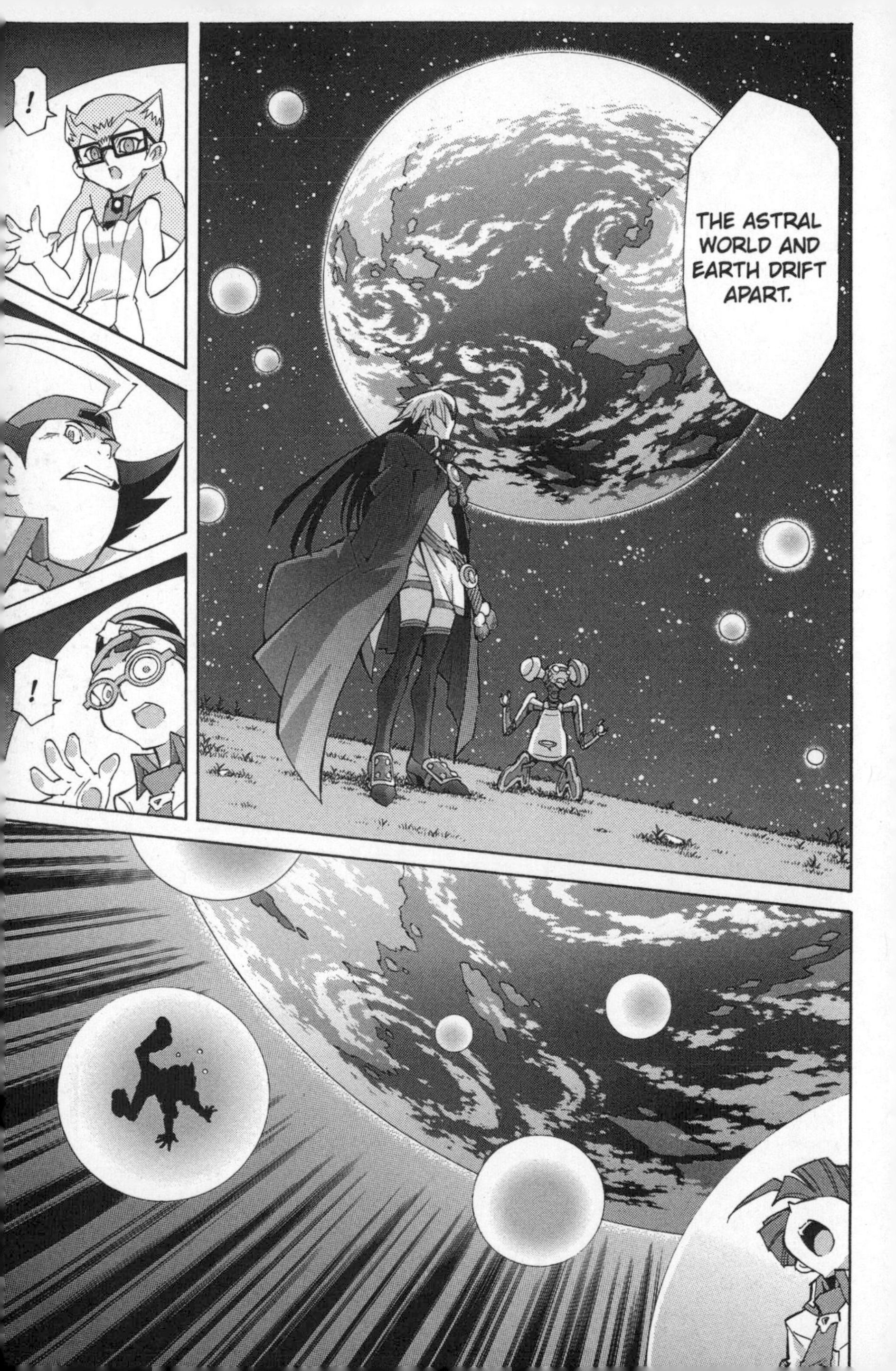
THE ASTRAL WORLD AND EARTH DRIFT APART.
!
!

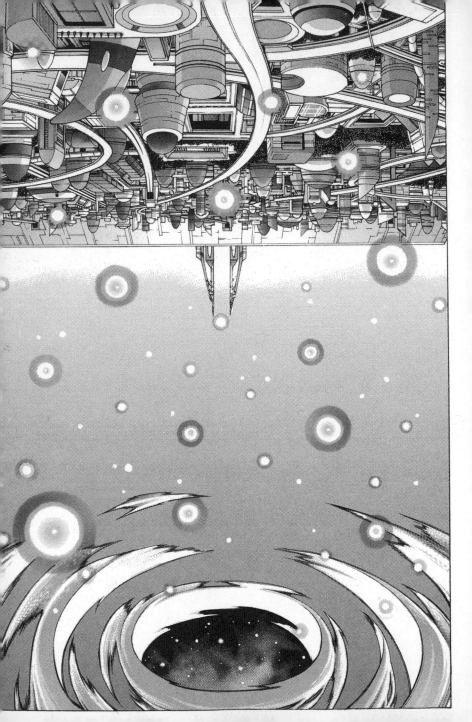

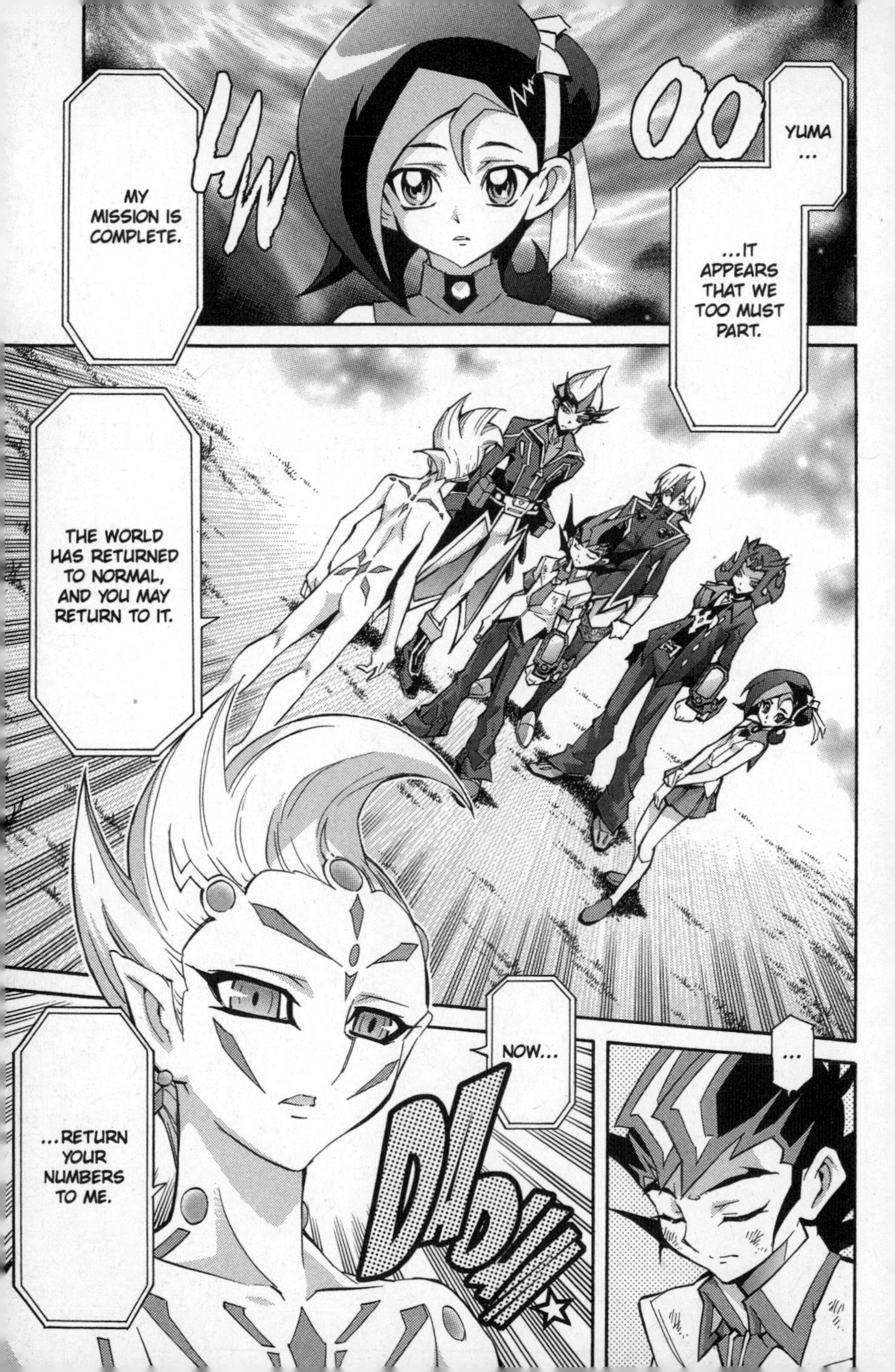
YUMA...
...IT APPEARS THAT WE TOO MUST PART.
HWOO
MY MISSION IS COMPLETE.
THE WORLD HAS RETURNED TO NORMAL, AND YOU MAY RETURN TO IT.
...
NOW...
...RETURN YOUR NUMBERS TO ME.

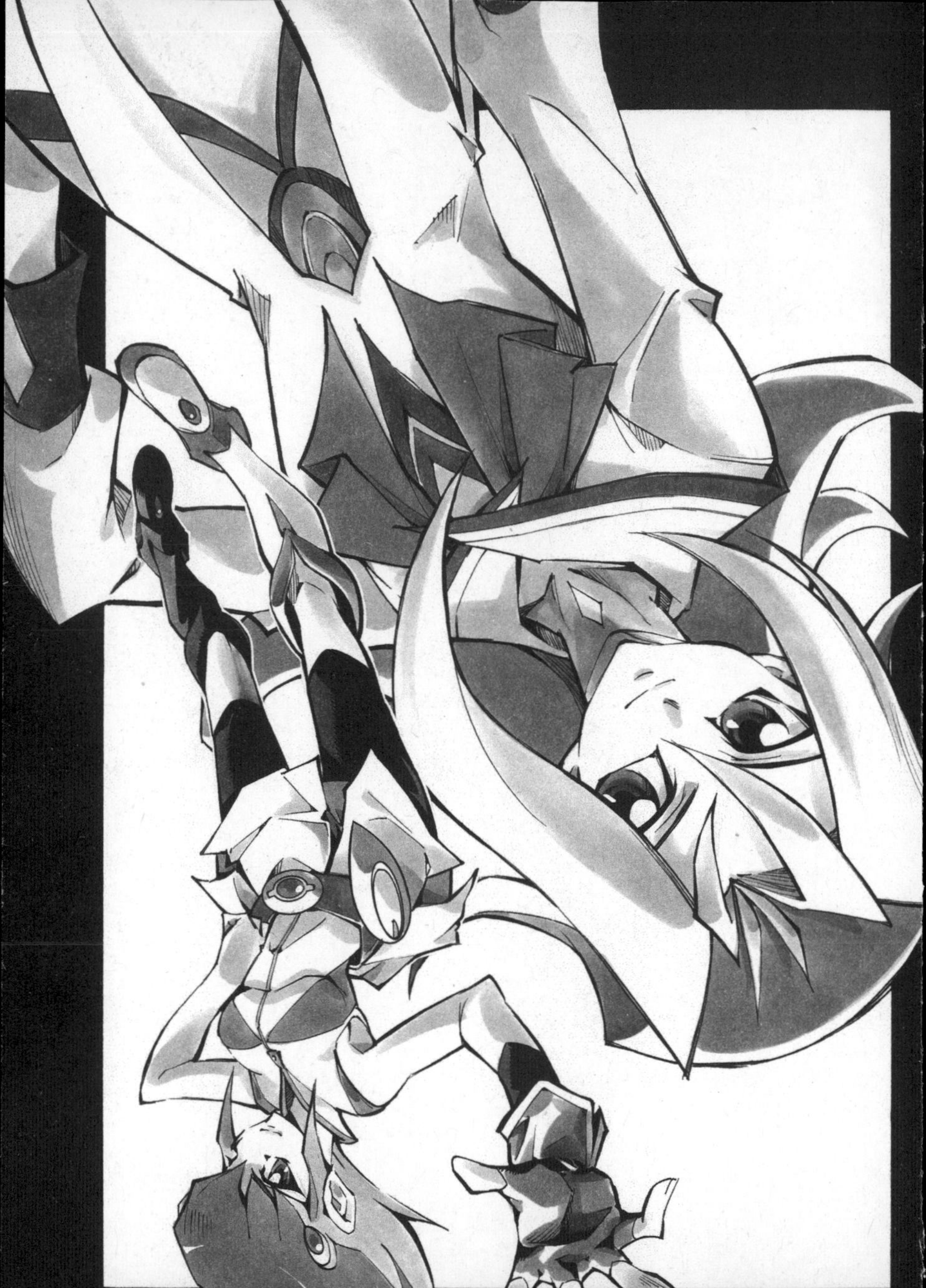

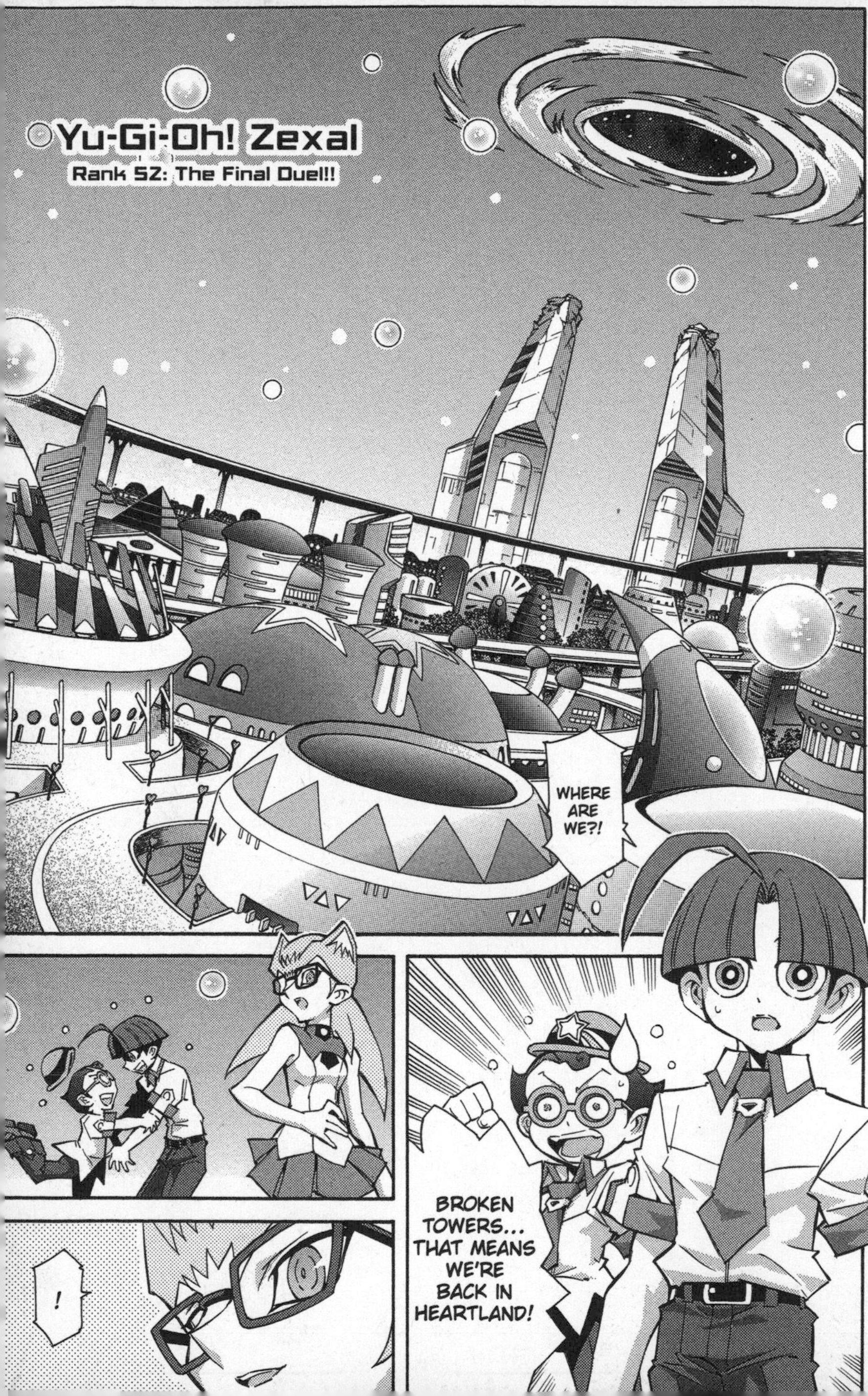
Yu-Gi-Oh! Zexal
Rank 52: The Final Duel!!
WHERE ARE WE?!
BROKEN TOWERS... THAT MEANS WE'RE BACK IN HEARTLAND!
!

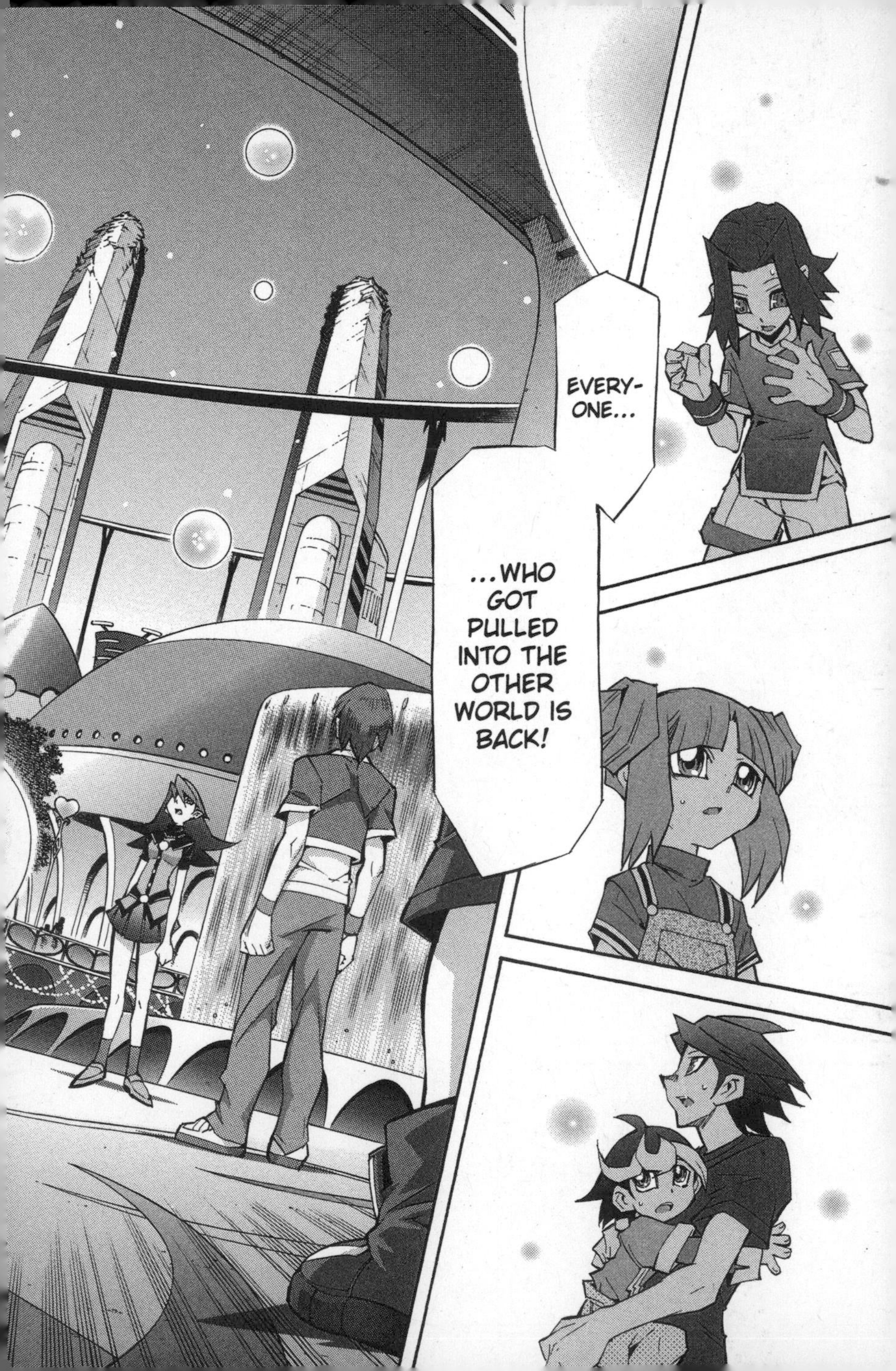
EVERY-ONE...
...WHO GOT PULLED INTO THE OTHER WORLD IS BACK!

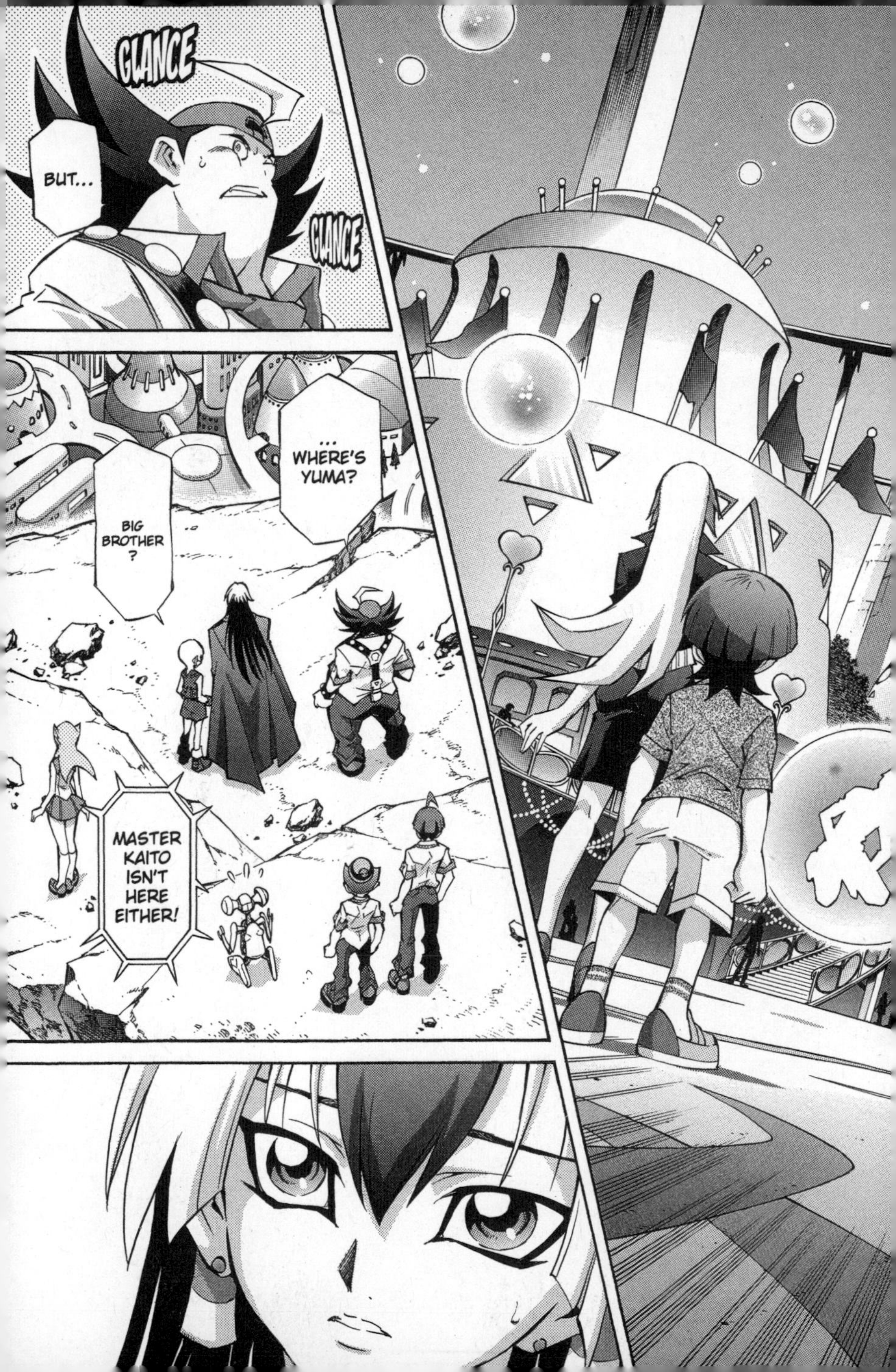
GLANCE
GLANCE
BUT…
… WHERE'S YUMA?
BIG BROTHER?
MASTER KAITO ISN'T HERE EITHER!

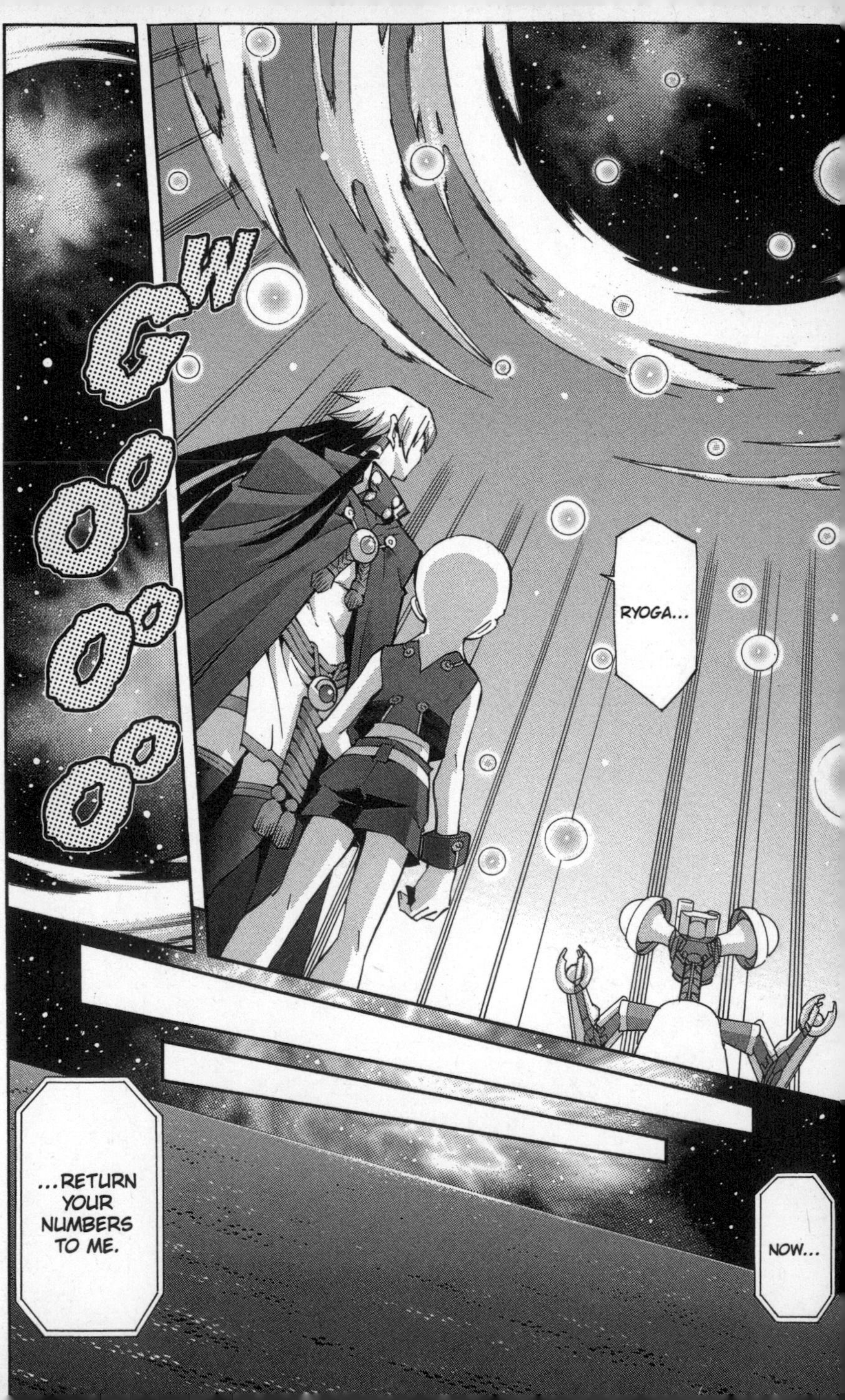
GWOOOOOO
RYOGA...
NOW...
...RETURN YOUR NUMBERS TO ME.

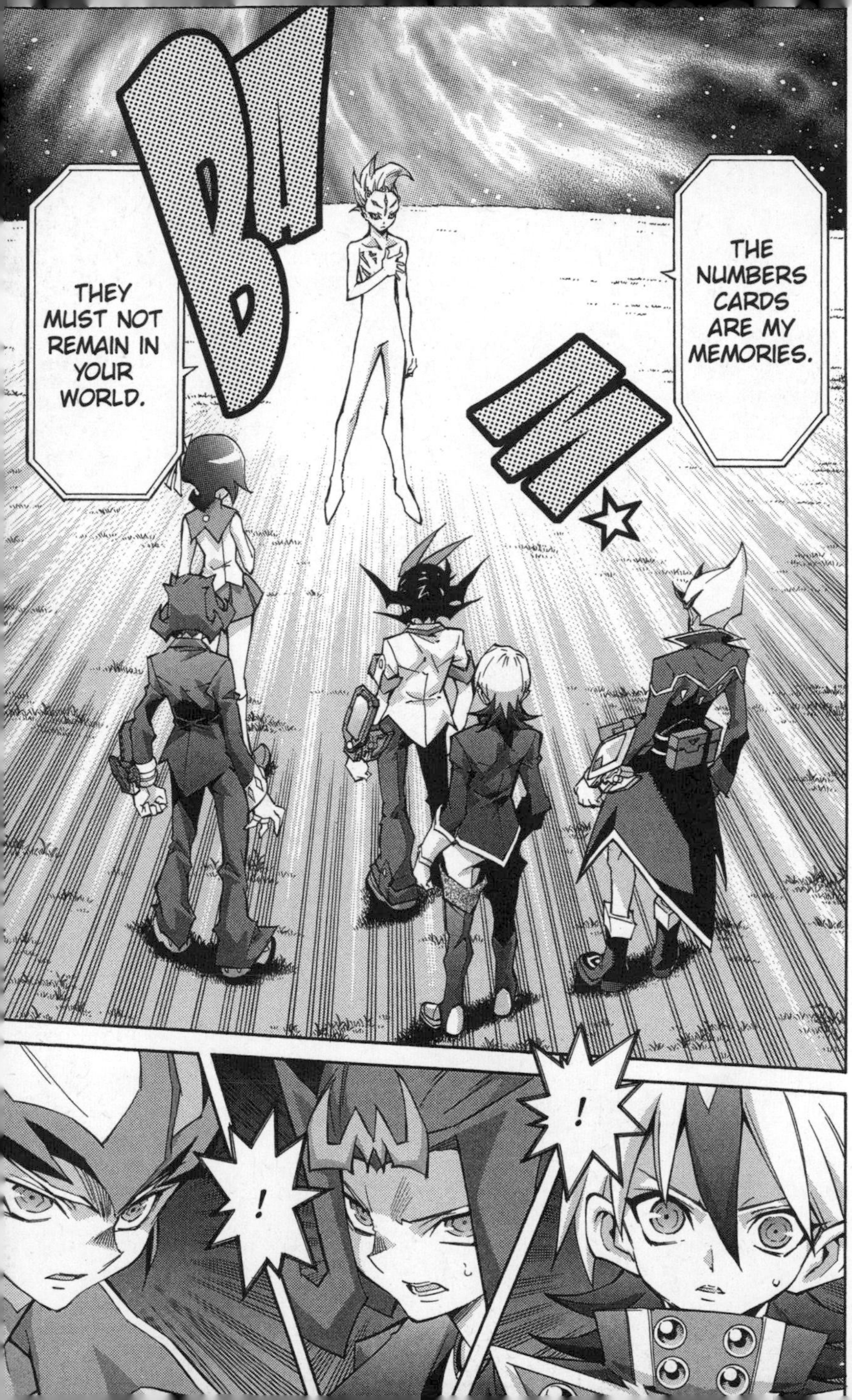
THE NUMBERS CARDS ARE MY MEMORIES.
BA
THEY MUST NOT REMAIN IN YOUR WORLD.
!
!

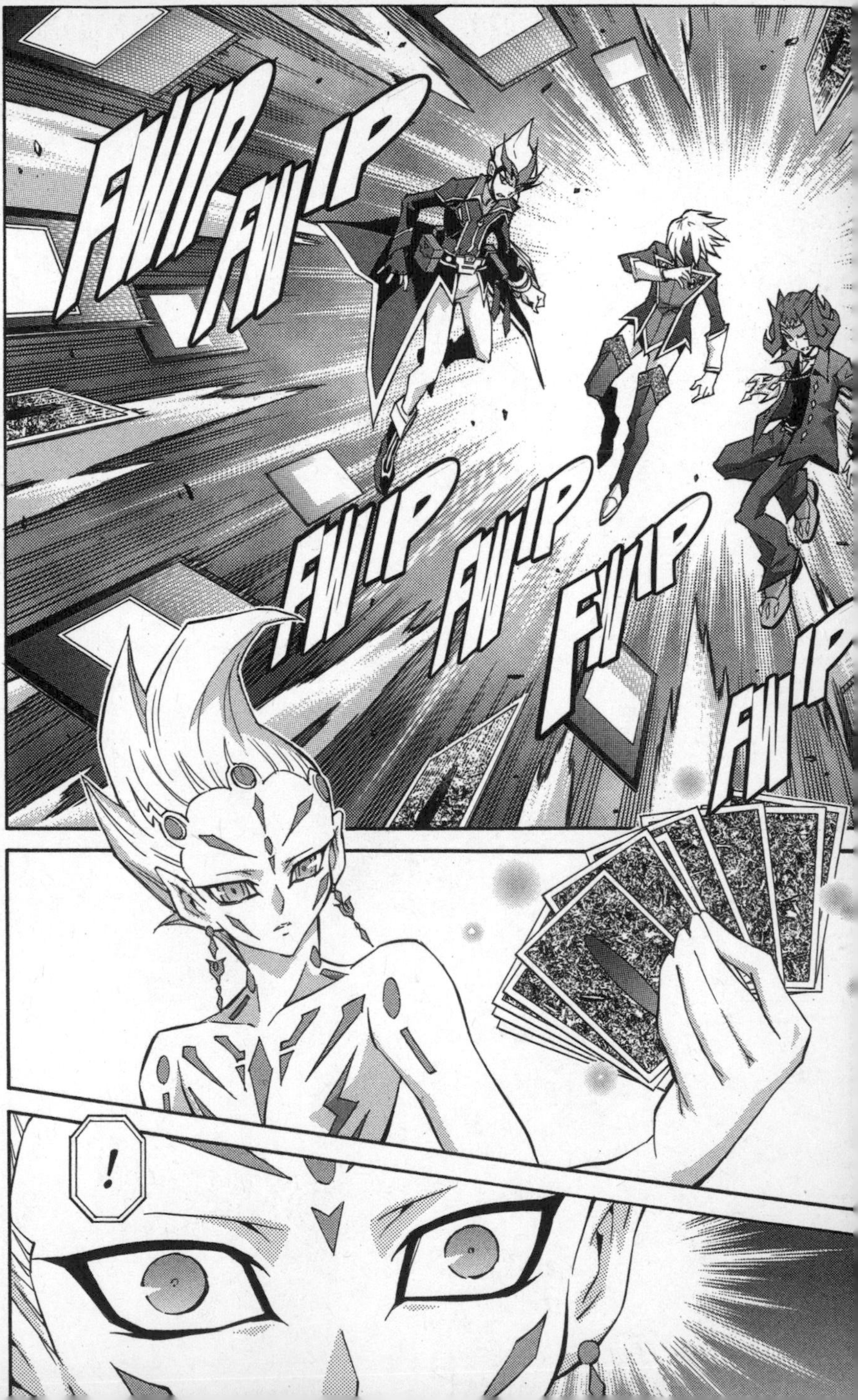
FWIP
FWIP
FWIP
FWIP
FWIP
FWIP
FWIP
!

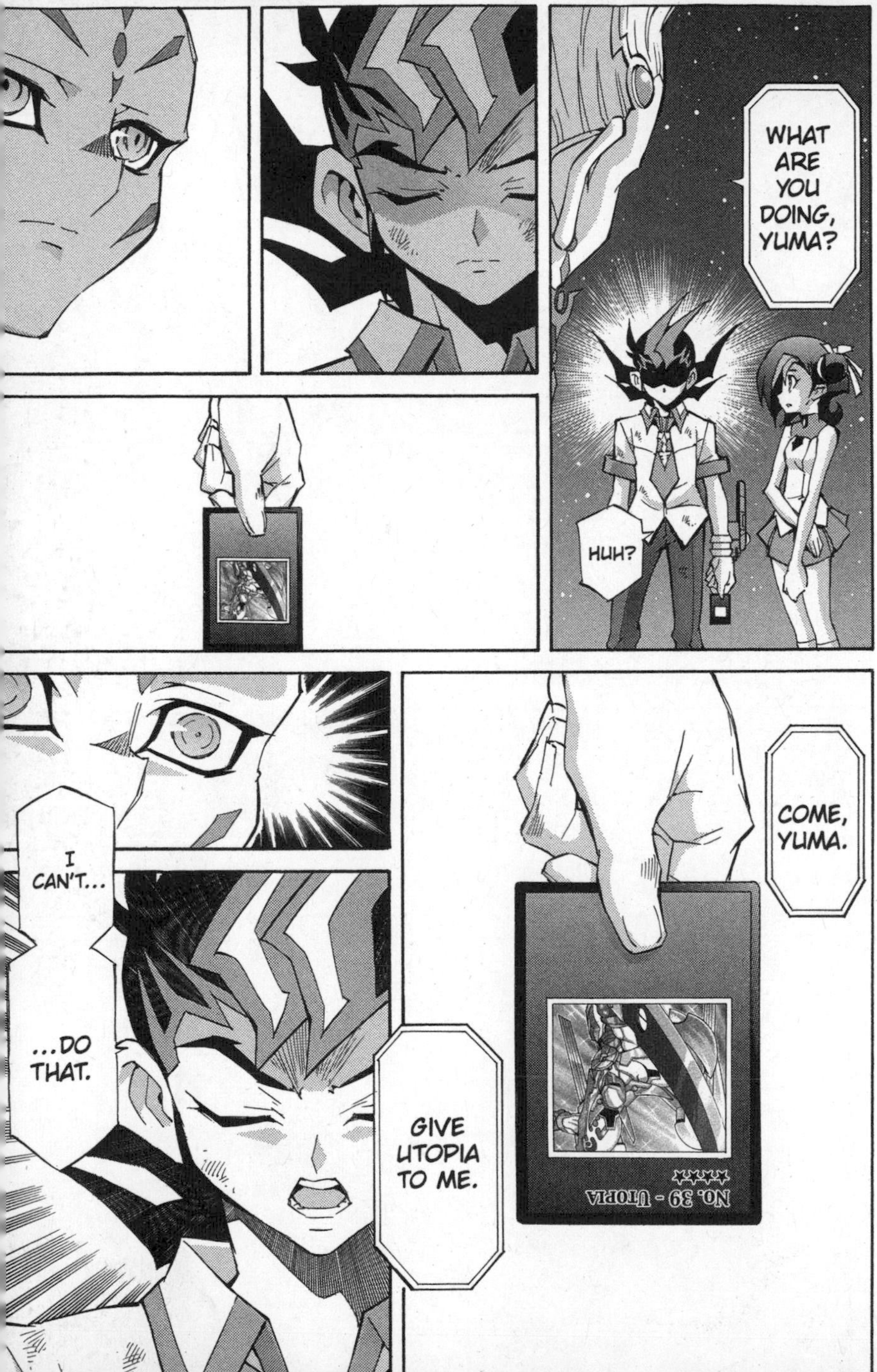

WHAT ARE YOU DOING, YUMA?
HUH?
COME, YUMA.
No. 39 - Utopia
GIVE UTOPIA TO ME.
I CAN'T...
...DO THAT.

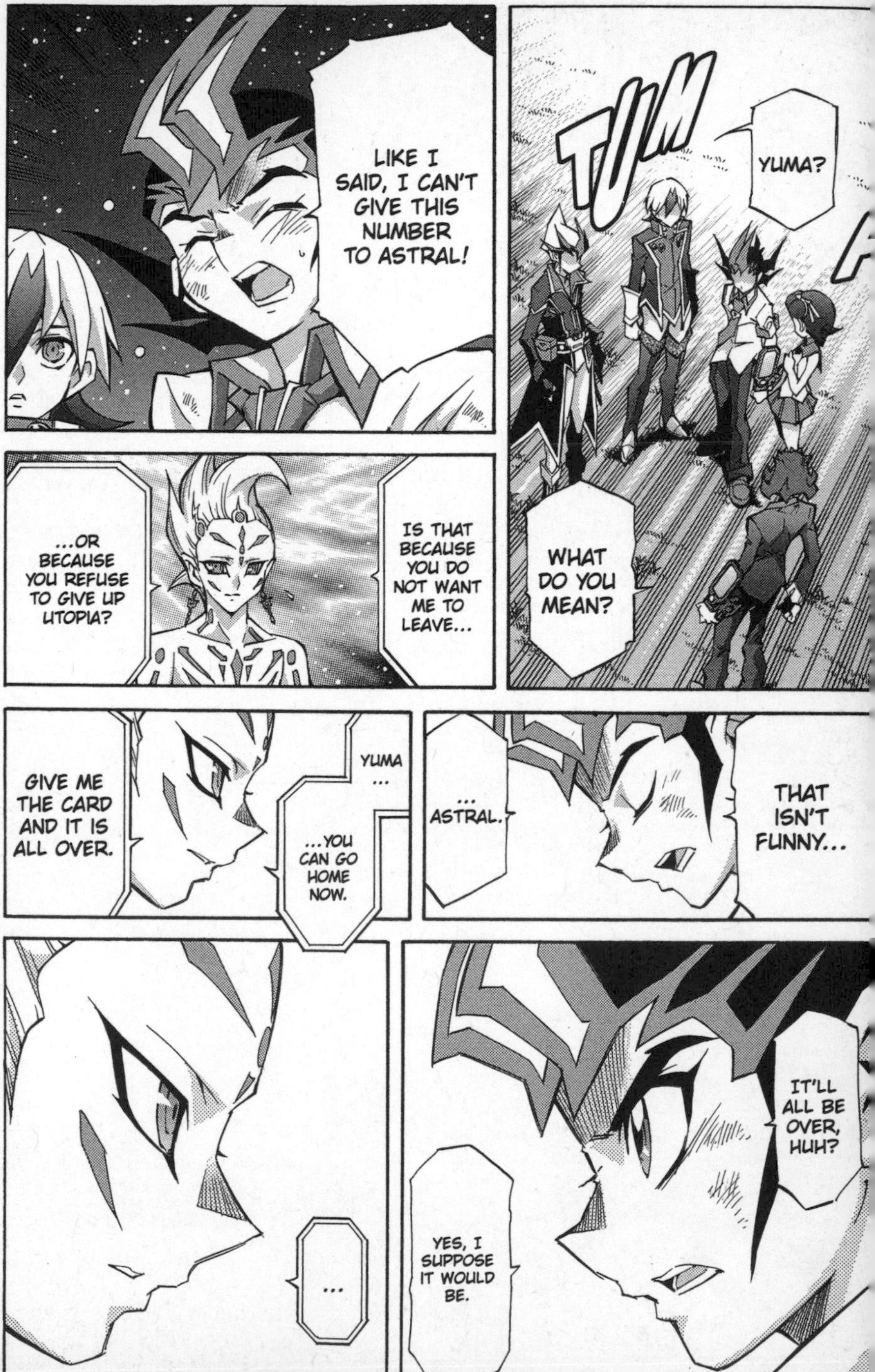
YUMA?
TUM
WHAT DO YOU MEAN?
LIKE I SAID, I CAN'T GIVE THIS NUMBER TO ASTRAL!
IS THAT BECAUSE YOU DO NOT WANT ME TO LEAVE...
...OR BECAUSE YOU REFUSE TO GIVE UP UTOPIA?
THAT ISN'T FUNNY...
...ASTRAL.
YUMA...
...YOU CAN GO HOME NOW.
GIVE ME THE CARD AND IT IS ALL OVER.
IT'LL ALL BE OVER, HUH?
YES, I SUPPOSE IT WOULD BE.
...

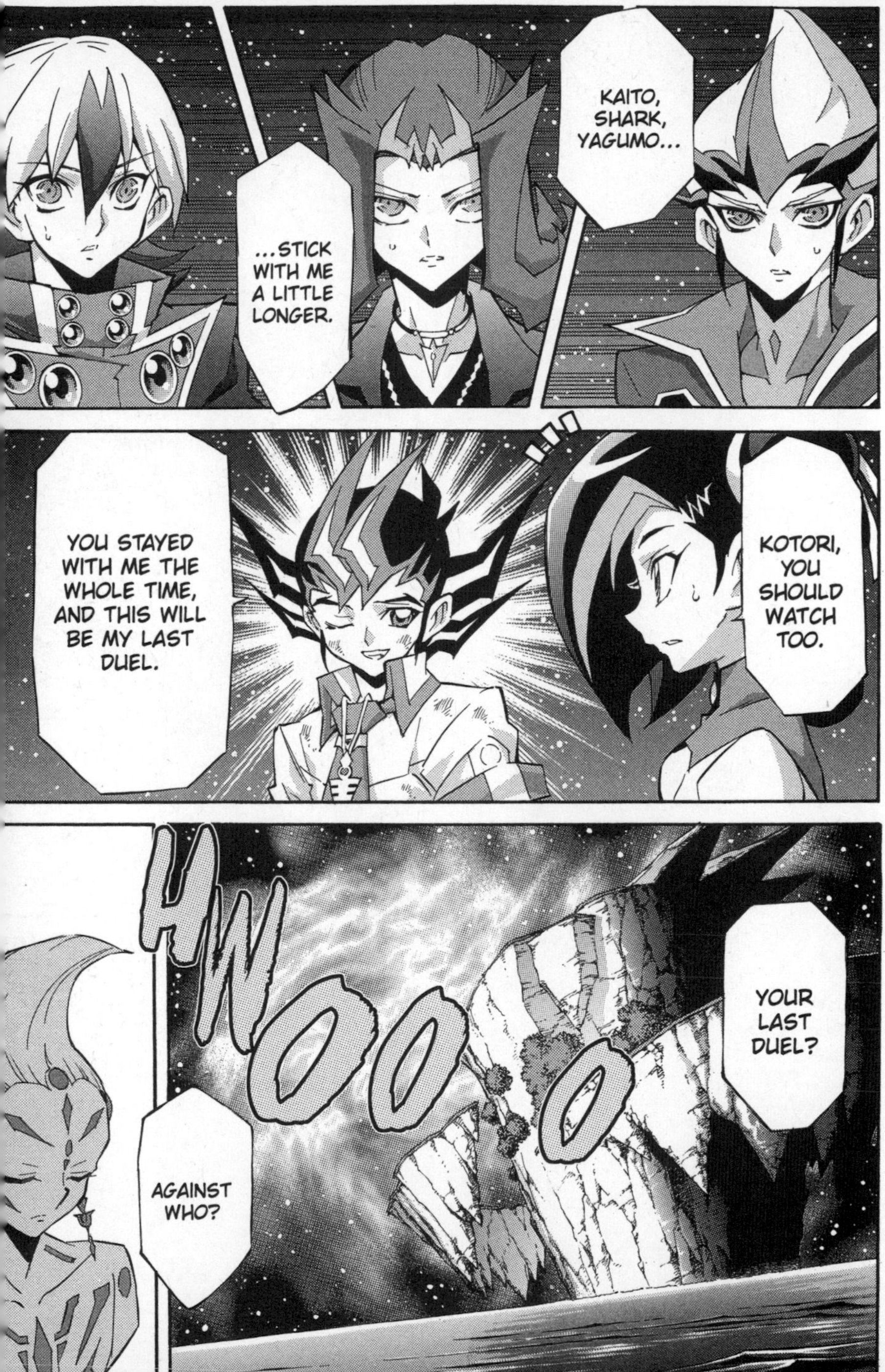
KAITO, SHARK, YAGUMO...
...STICK WITH ME A LITTLE LONGER.
KOTORI, YOU SHOULD WATCH TOO.
YOU STAYED WITH ME THE WHOLE TIME, AND THIS WILL BE MY LAST DUEL.
...
YOUR LAST DUEL?
HWOOO
AGAINST WHO?

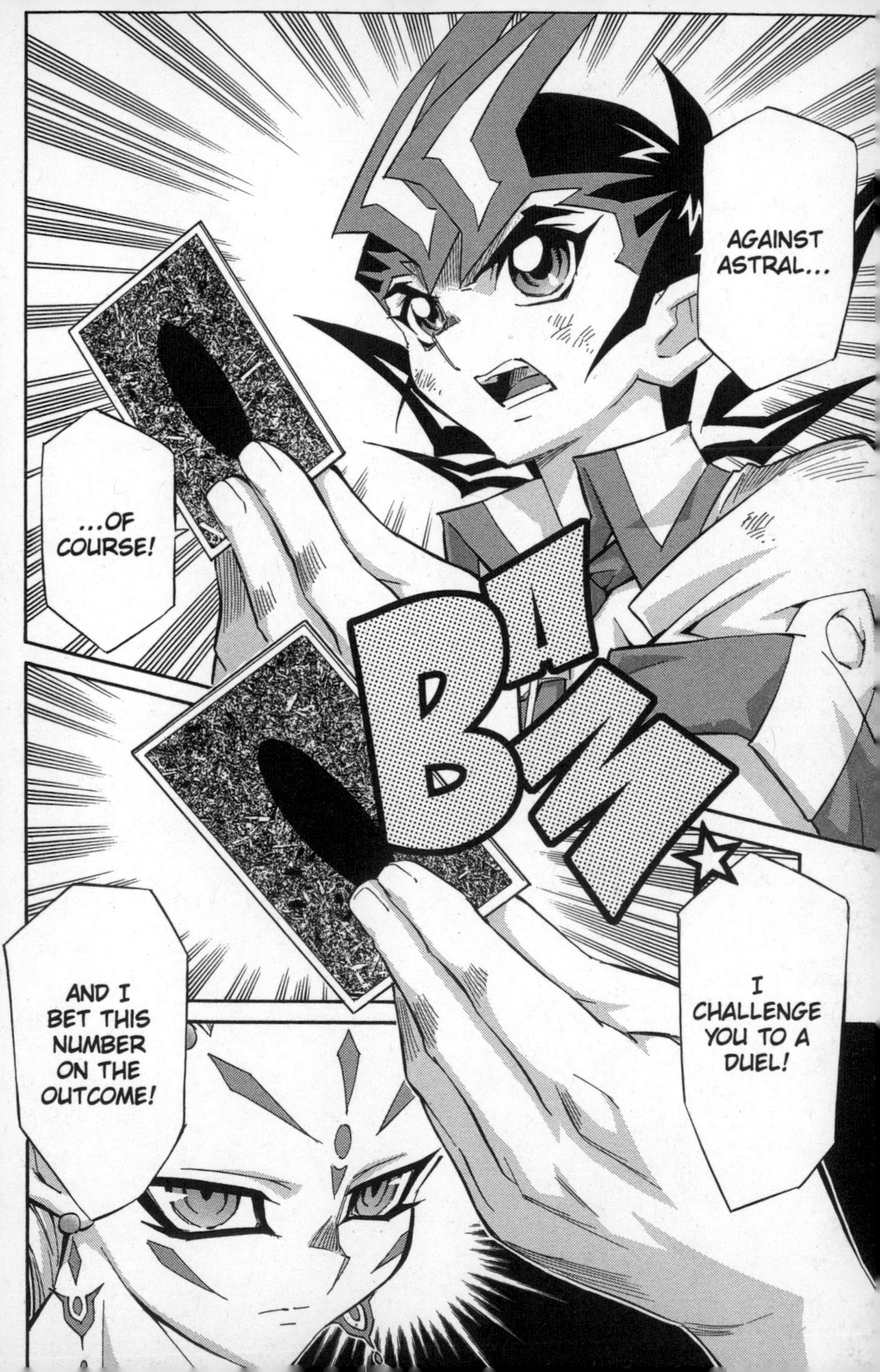
AGAINST ASTRAL...
...OF COURSE!
BAM
I CHALLENGE YOU TO A DUEL!
AND I BET THIS NUMBER ON THE OUTCOME!

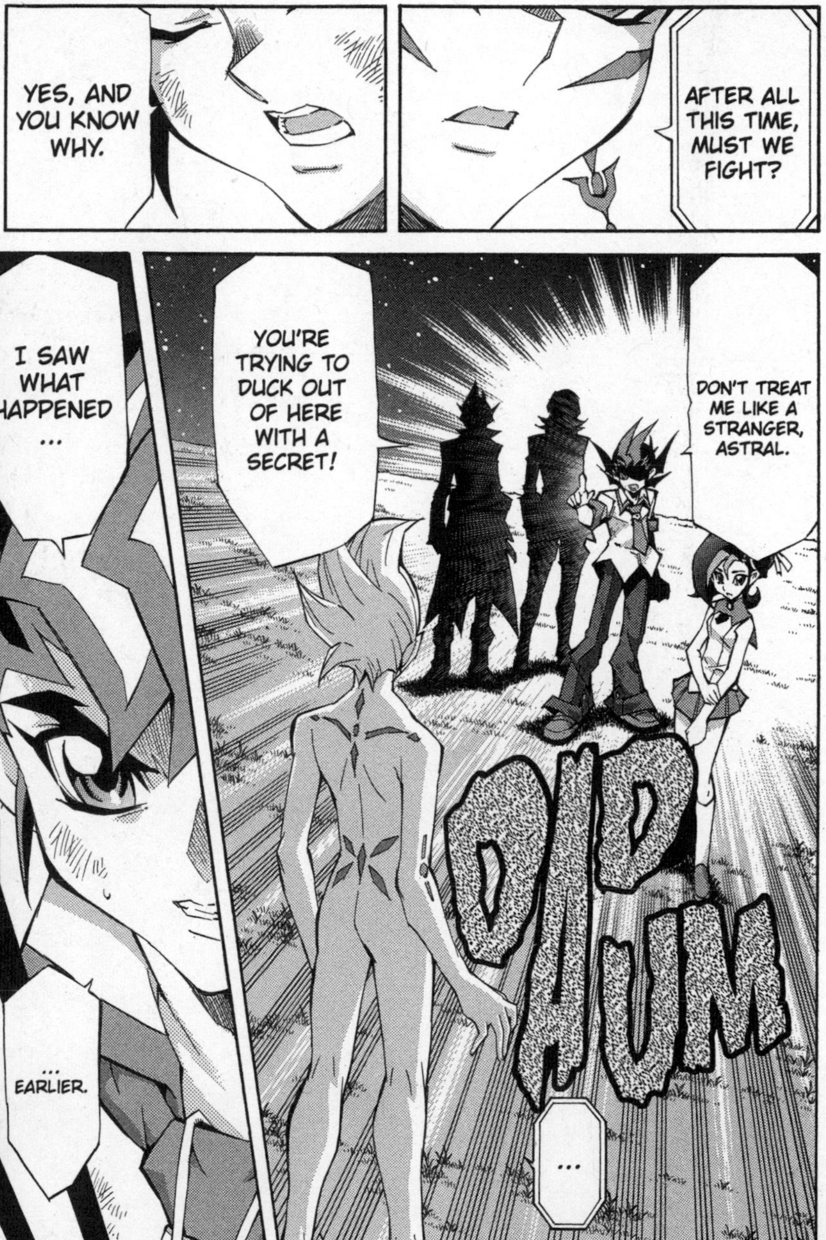
AFTER ALL THIS TIME, MUST WE FIGHT?
YES, AND YOU KNOW WHY.
DON'T TREAT ME LIKE A STRANGER, ASTRAL.
YOU'RE TRYING TO DUCK OUT OF HERE WITH A SECRET!
I SAW WHAT HAPPENED ...
... EARLIER.
...

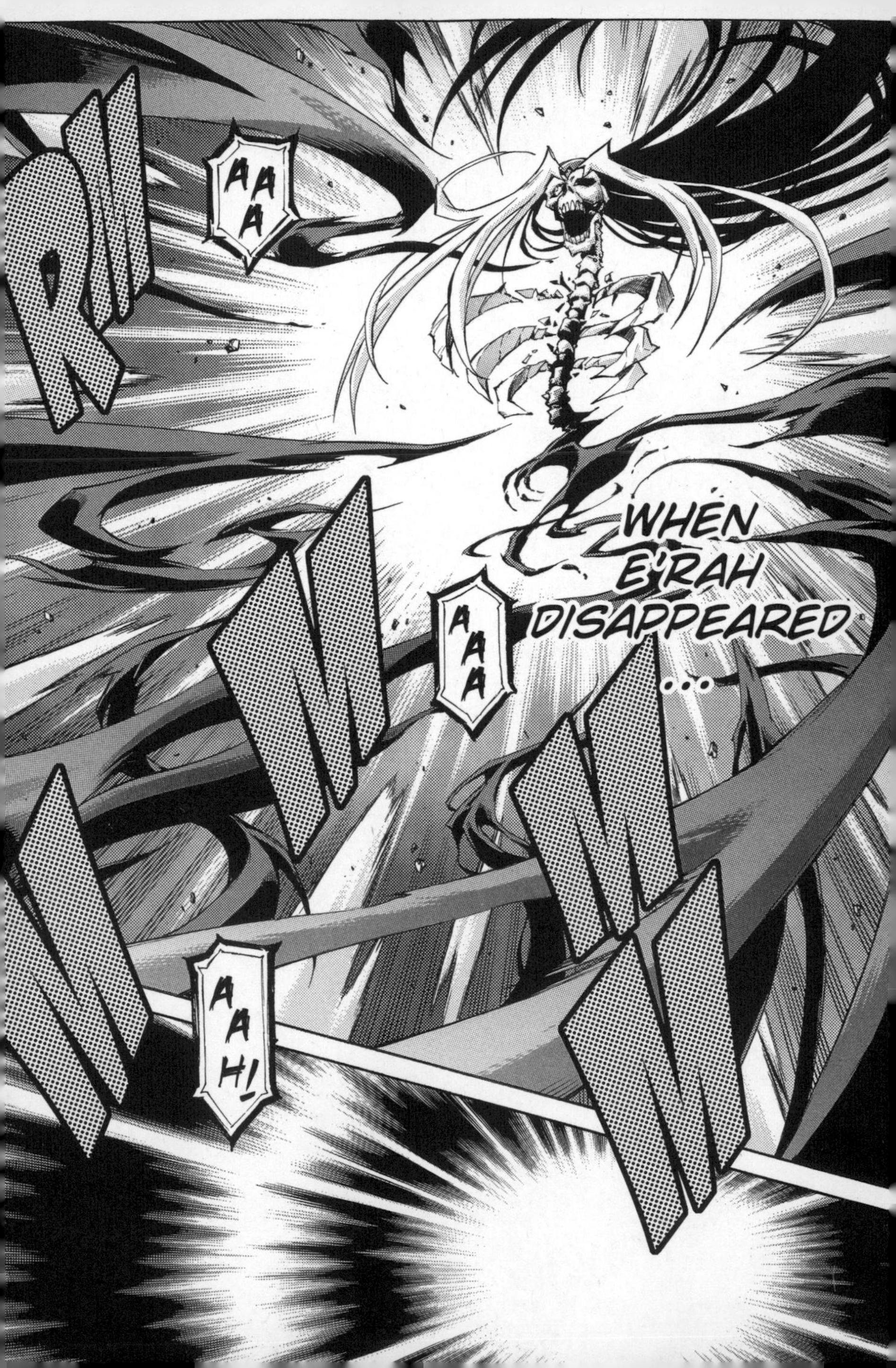
AAA
WHEN E'RAH DISAPPEARED...
AAA
AAH!

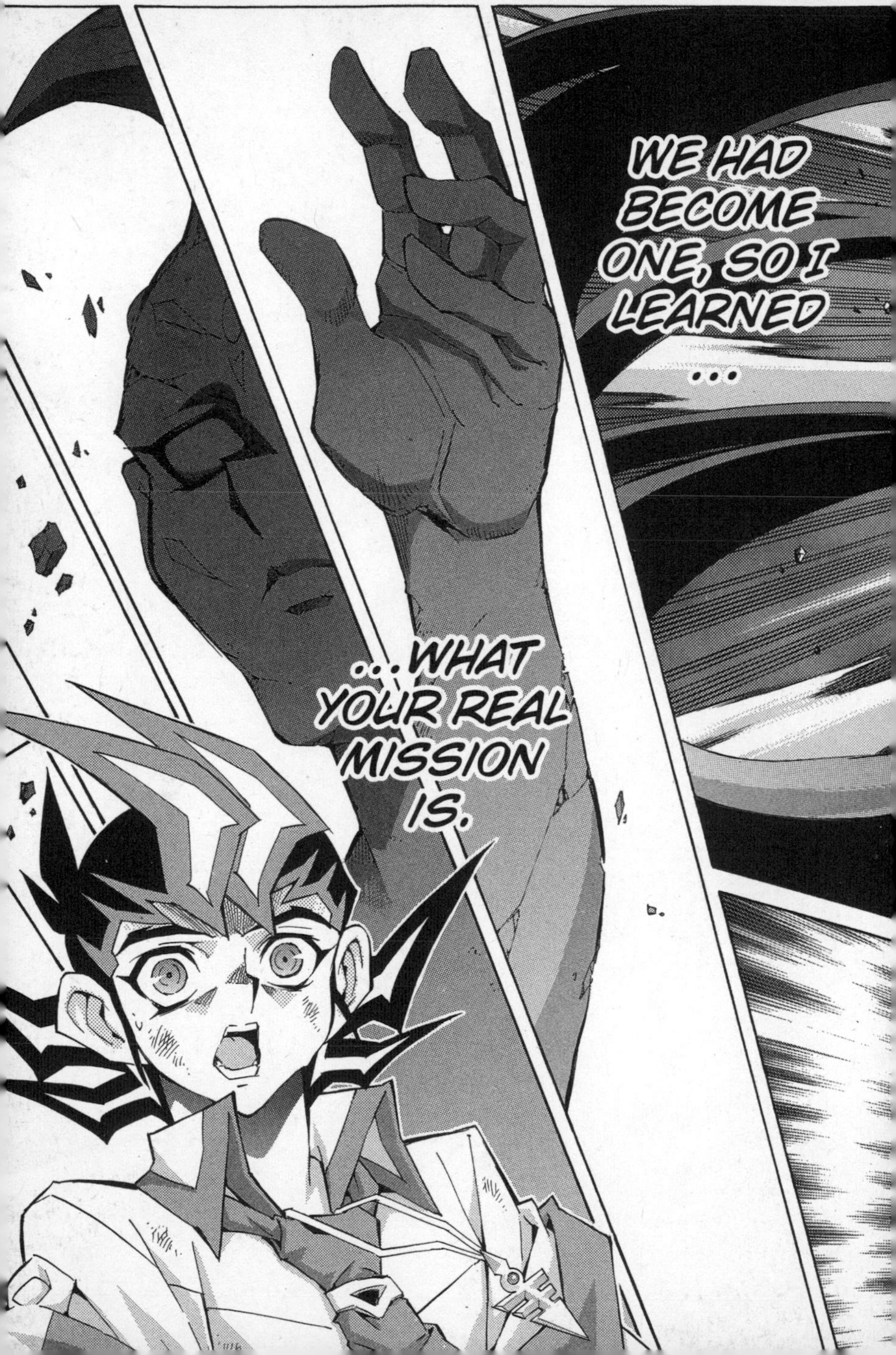
WE HAD BECOME ONE, SO I LEARNED
...
...WHAT YOUR REAL MISSION IS.

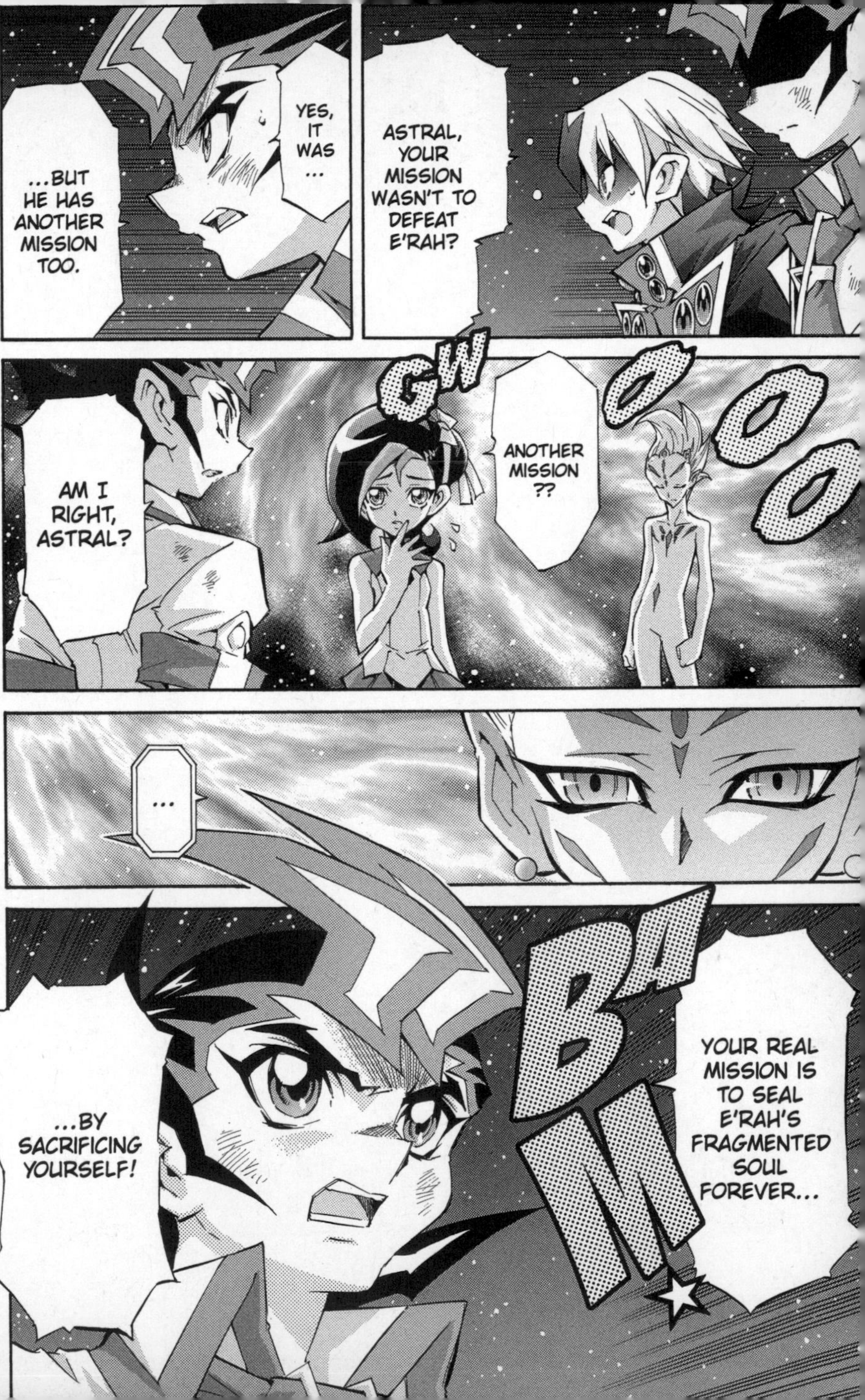
ASTRAL, YOUR MISSION WASN'T TO DEFEAT E'RAH?
YES, IT WAS ...
...BUT HE HAS ANOTHER MISSION TOO.
GWOOO
ANOTHER MISSION ??
AM I RIGHT, ASTRAL?
...
YOUR REAL MISSION IS TO SEAL E'RAH'S FRAGMENTED SOUL FOREVER...
BAM
...BY SACRIFICING YOURSELF!

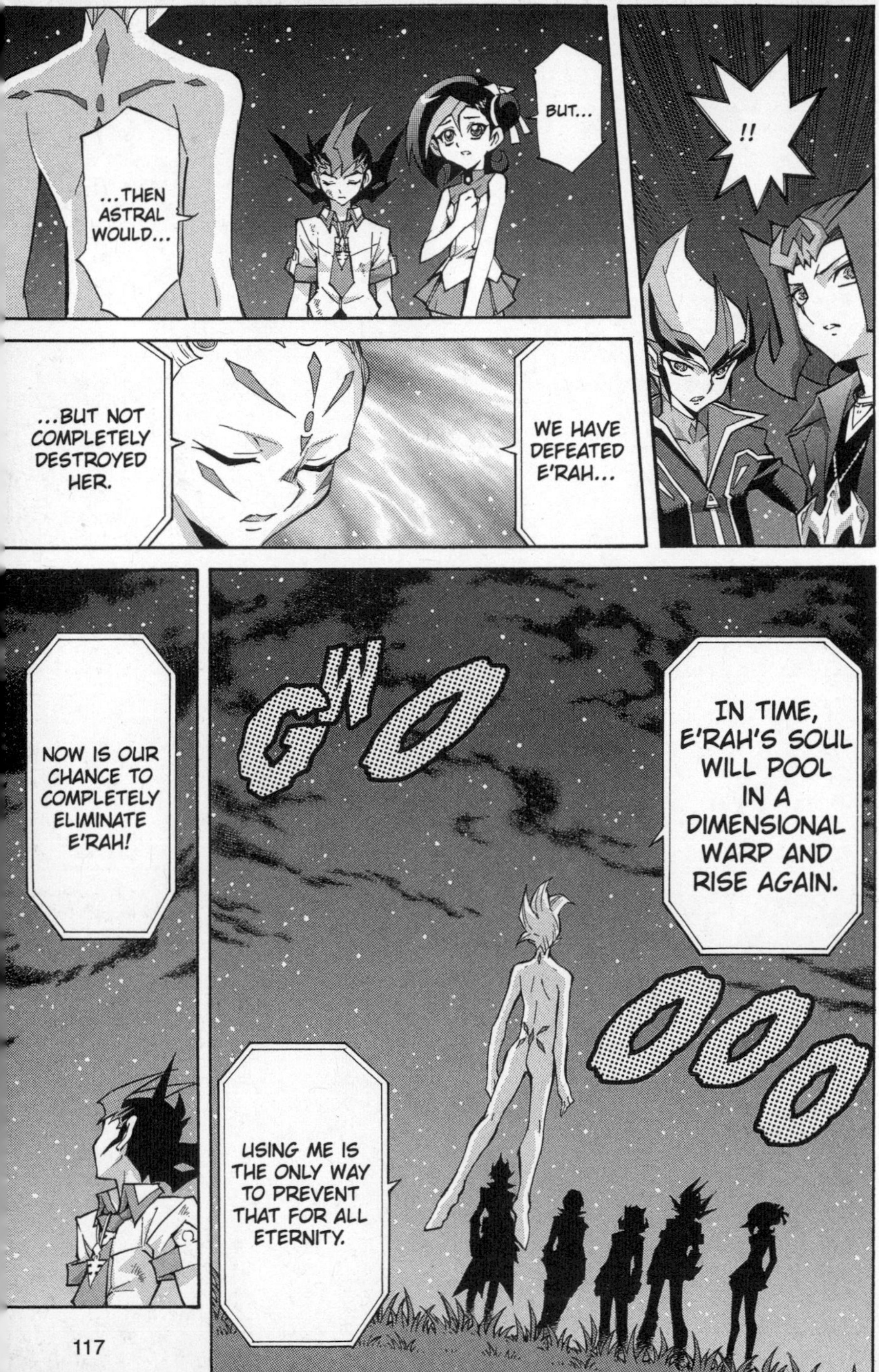
!!
BUT...
...THEN ASTRAL WOULD...
WE HAVE DEFEATED E'RAH...
...BUT NOT COMPLETELY DESTROYED HER.
IN TIME, E'RAH'S SOUL WILL POOL IN A DIMENSIONAL WARP AND RISE AGAIN.
GWOOO
USING ME IS THE ONLY WAY TO PREVENT THAT FOR ALL ETERNITY.
NOW IS OUR CHANCE TO COMPLETELY ELIMINATE E'RAH!

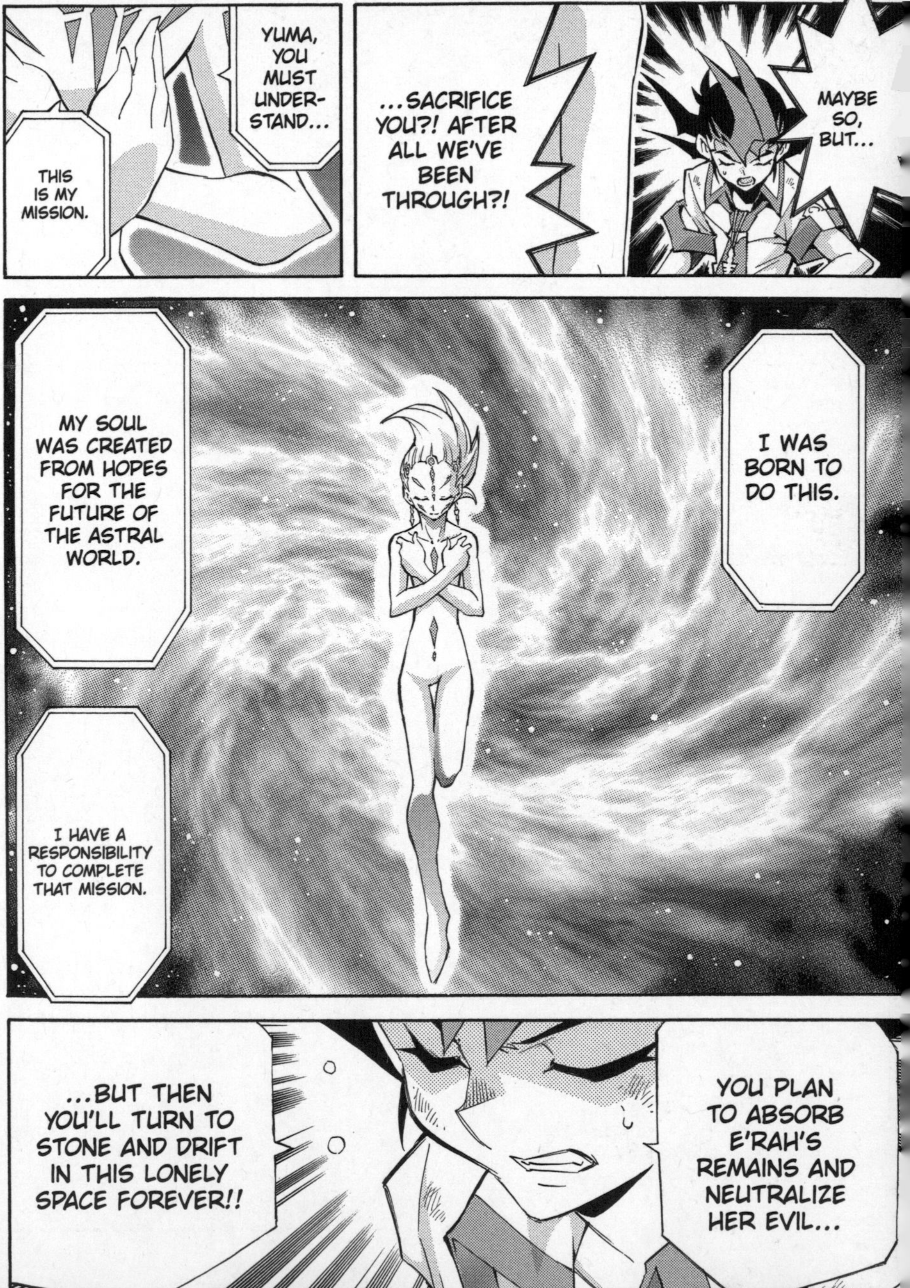
MAYBE SO, BUT...
...SACRIFICE YOU?! AFTER ALL WE'VE BEEN THROUGH?!
YUMA, YOU MUST UNDER-STAND...
THIS IS MY MISSION.
I WAS BORN TO DO THIS.
MY SOUL WAS CREATED FROM HOPES FOR THE FUTURE OF THE ASTRAL WORLD.
I HAVE A RESPONSIBILITY TO COMPLETE THAT MISSION.
YOU PLAN TO ABSORB E'RAH'S REMAINS AND NEUTRALIZE HER EVIL...
...BUT THEN YOU'LL TURN TO STONE AND DRIFT IN THIS LONELY SPACE FOREVER!!

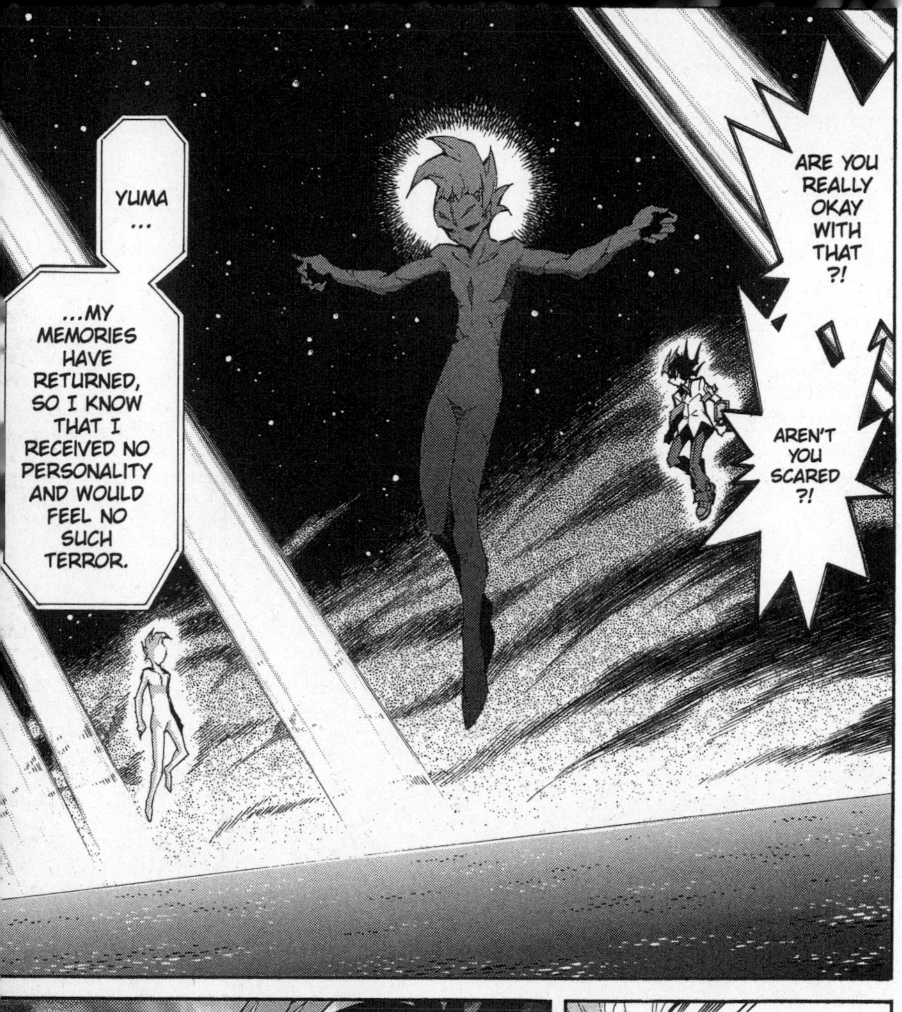
ARE YOU REALLY OKAY WITH THAT ?!
AREN'T YOU SCARED ?!
YUMA ...
...MY MEMORIES HAVE RETURNED, SO I KNOW THAT I RECEIVED NO PERSONALITY AND WOULD FEEL NO SUCH TERROR.
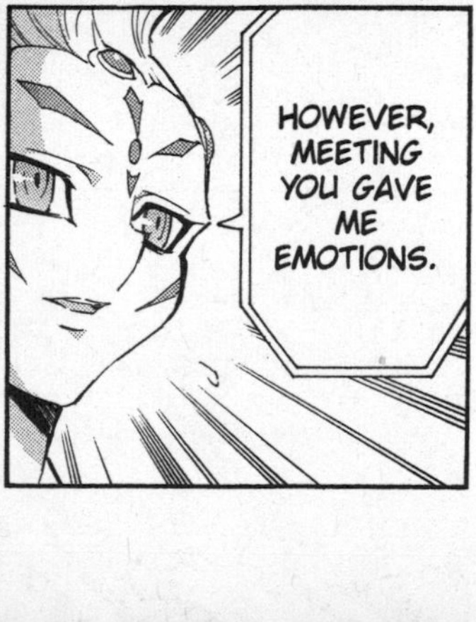
HOWEVER, MEETING YOU GAVE ME EMOTIONS.
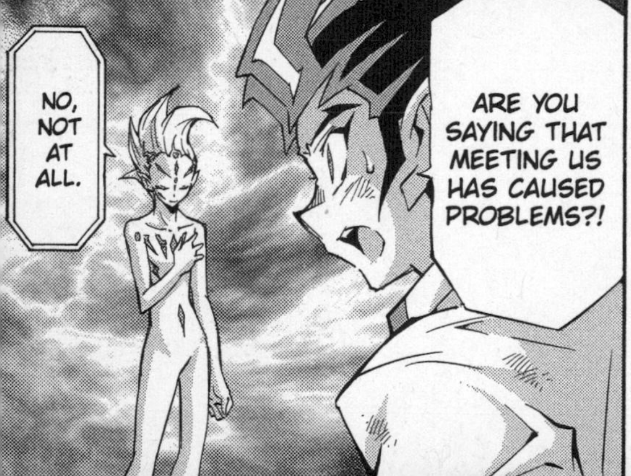
ARE YOU SAYING THAT MEETING US HAS CAUSED PROBLEMS?!
NO, NOT AT ALL.

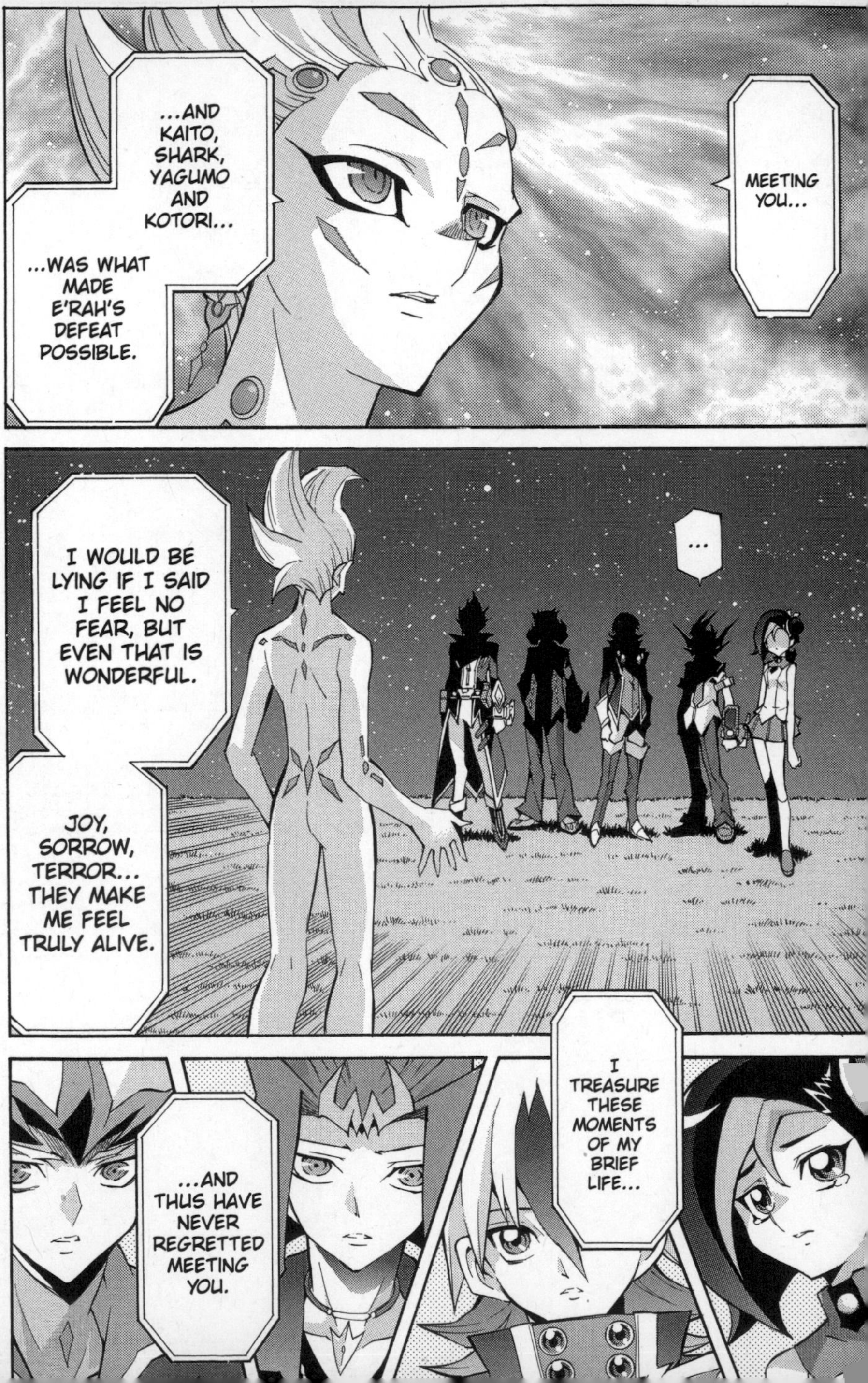
MEETING YOU...
...AND KAITO, SHARK, YAGUMO AND KOTORI...
...WAS WHAT MADE E'RAH'S DEFEAT POSSIBLE.
...
I WOULD BE LYING IF I SAID I FEEL NO FEAR, BUT EVEN THAT IS WONDERFUL.
JOY, SORROW, TERROR... THEY MAKE ME FEEL TRULY ALIVE.
I TREASURE THESE MOMENTS OF MY BRIEF LIFE...
...AND THUS HAVE NEVER REGRETTED MEETING YOU.

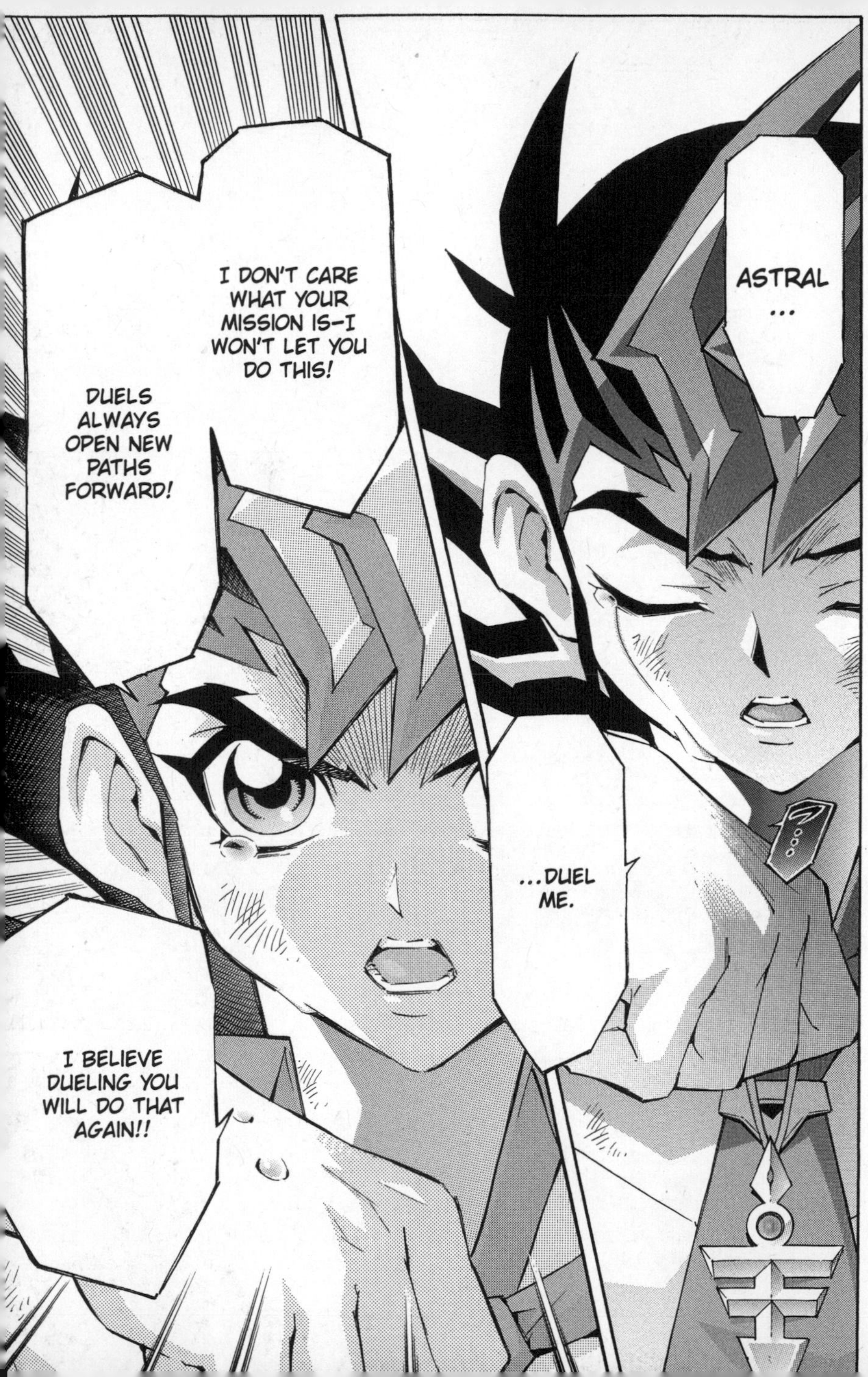
ASTRAL ...
...DUEL ME.
I DON'T CARE WHAT YOUR MISSION IS—I WON'T LET YOU DO THIS!
DUELS ALWAYS OPEN NEW PATHS FORWARD!
I BELIEVE DUELING YOU WILL DO THAT AGAIN!!

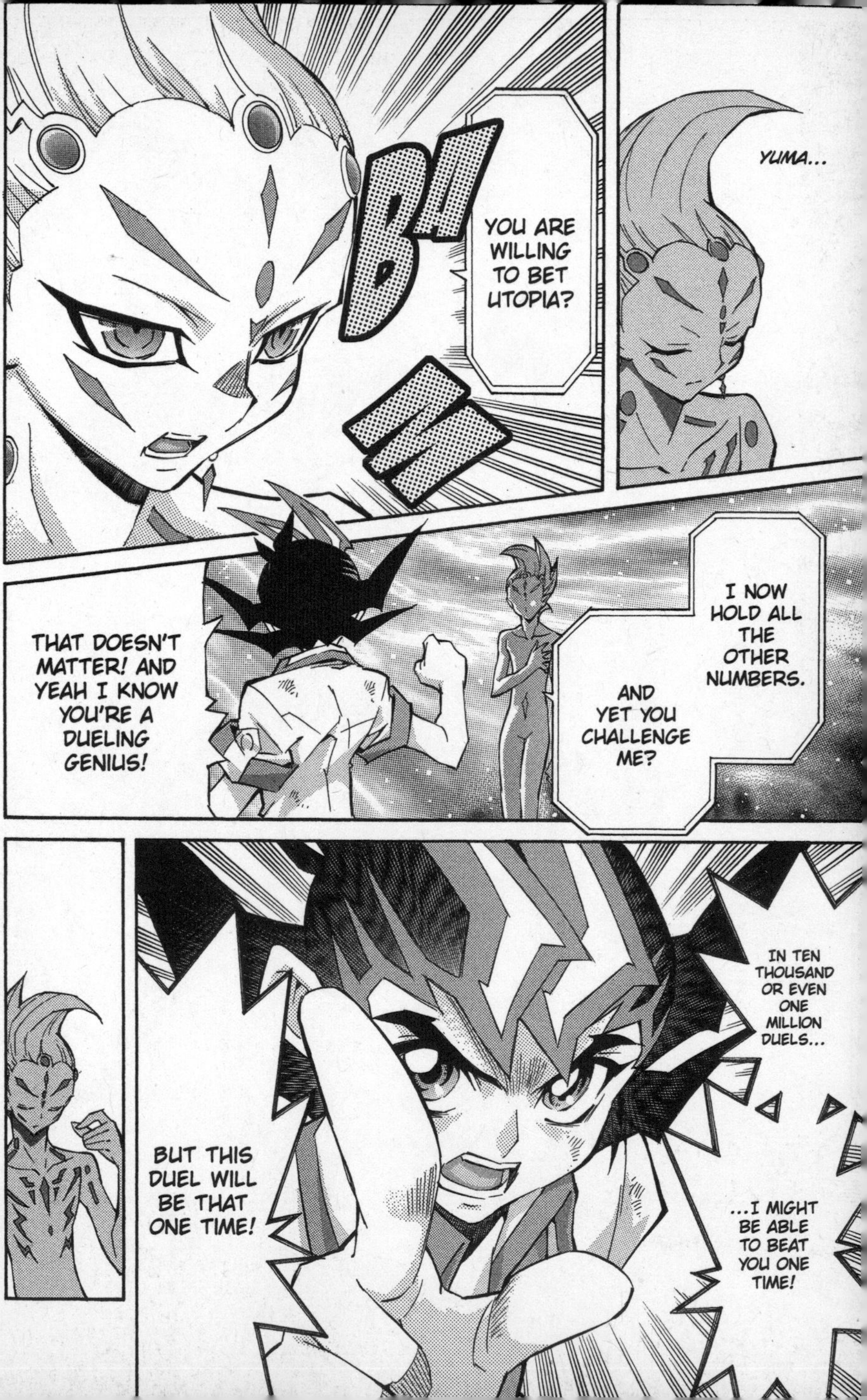
YUMA...
YOU ARE WILLING TO BET UTOPIA?
BAM
I NOW HOLD ALL THE OTHER NUMBERS.
AND YET YOU CHALLENGE ME?
THAT DOESN'T MATTER! AND YEAH I KNOW YOU'RE A DUELING GENIUS!
IN TEN THOUSAND OR EVEN ONE MILLION DUELS...
...I MIGHT BE ABLE TO BEAT YOU ONE TIME!
BUT THIS DUEL WILL BE THAT ONE TIME!

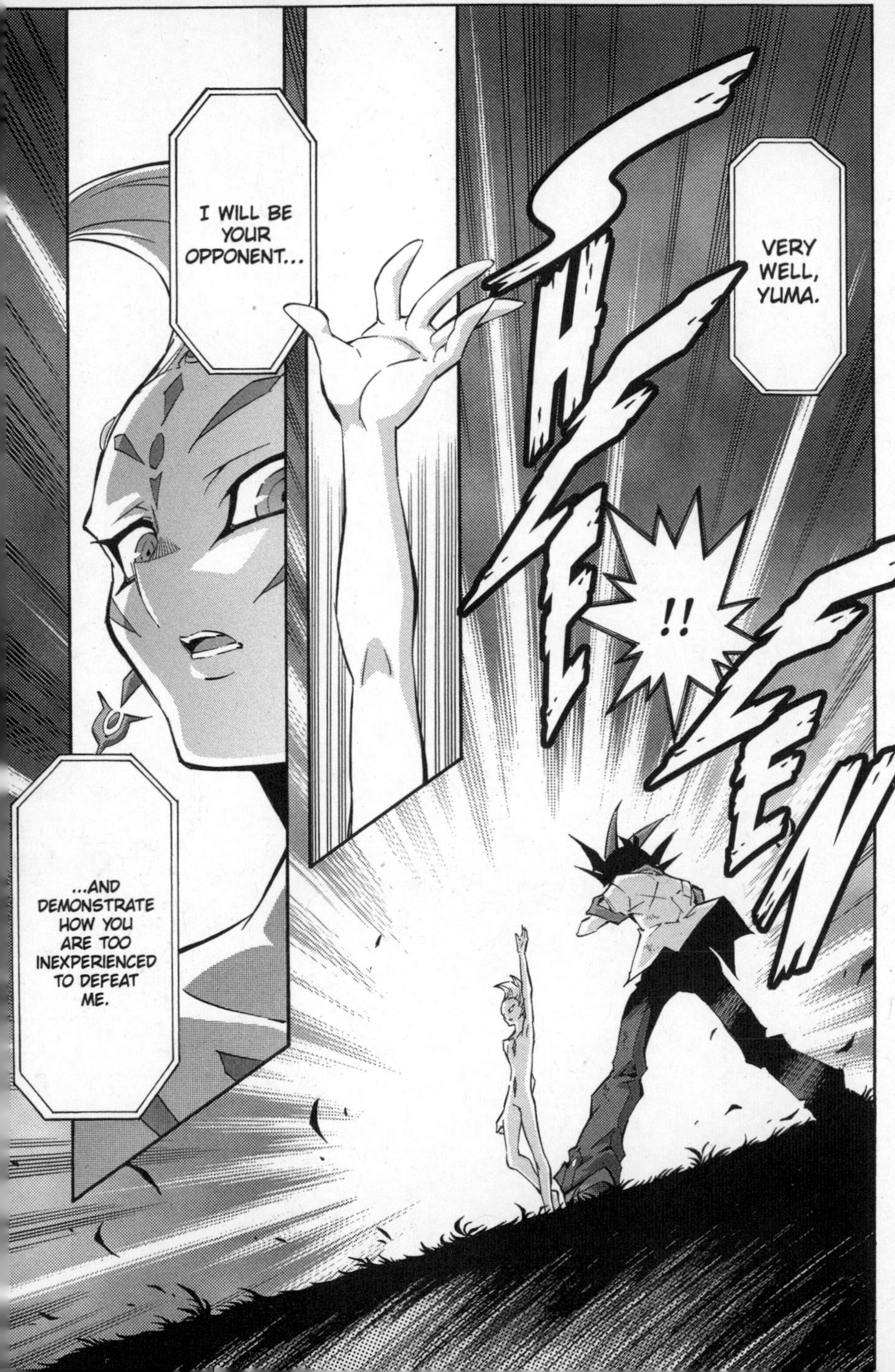
VERY WELL, YUMA.
SHEEN
!!
I WILL BE YOUR OPPONENT...
...AND DEMONSTRATE HOW YOU ARE TOO INEXPERIENCED TO DEFEAT ME.

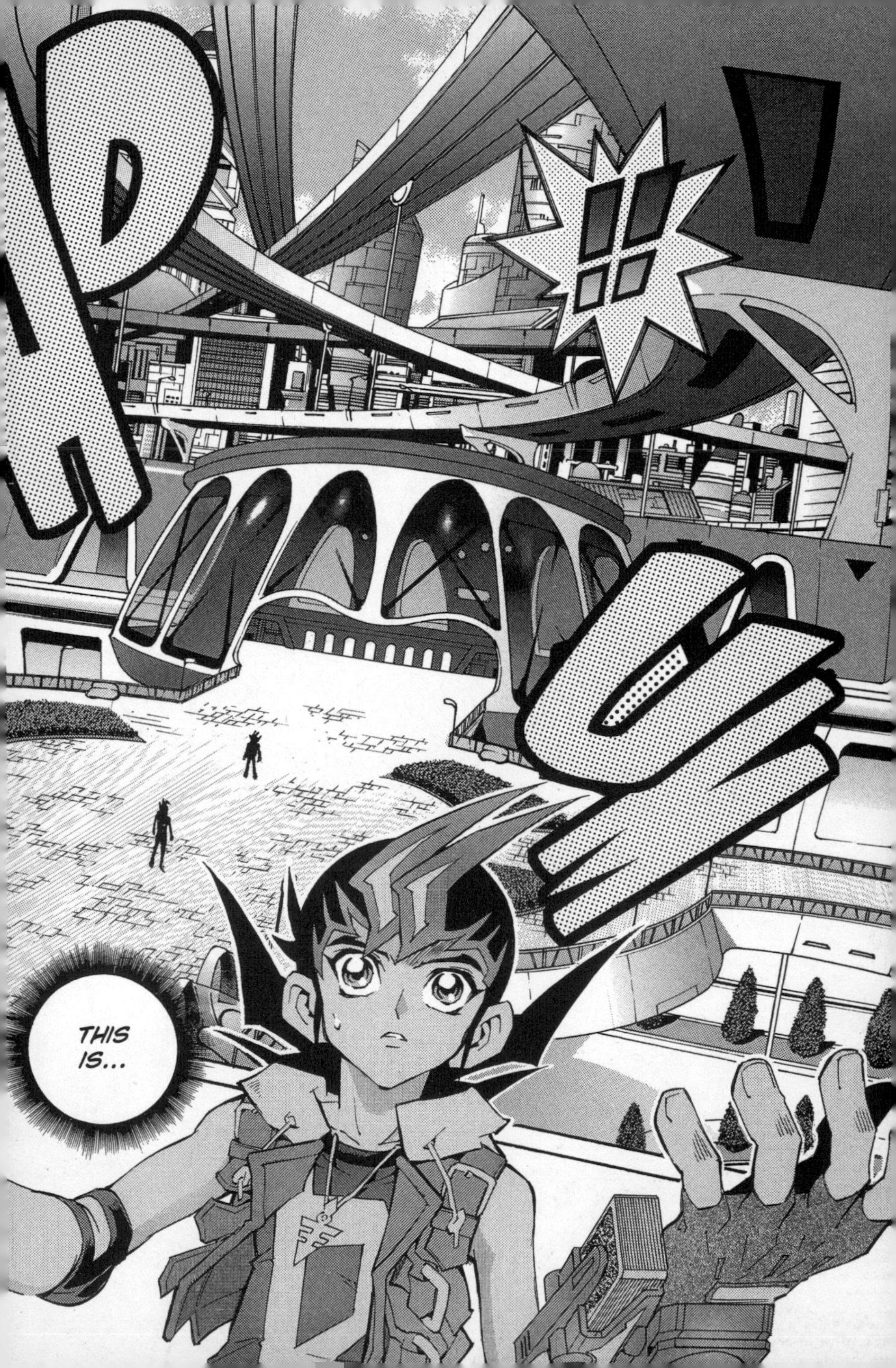
THIS IS...

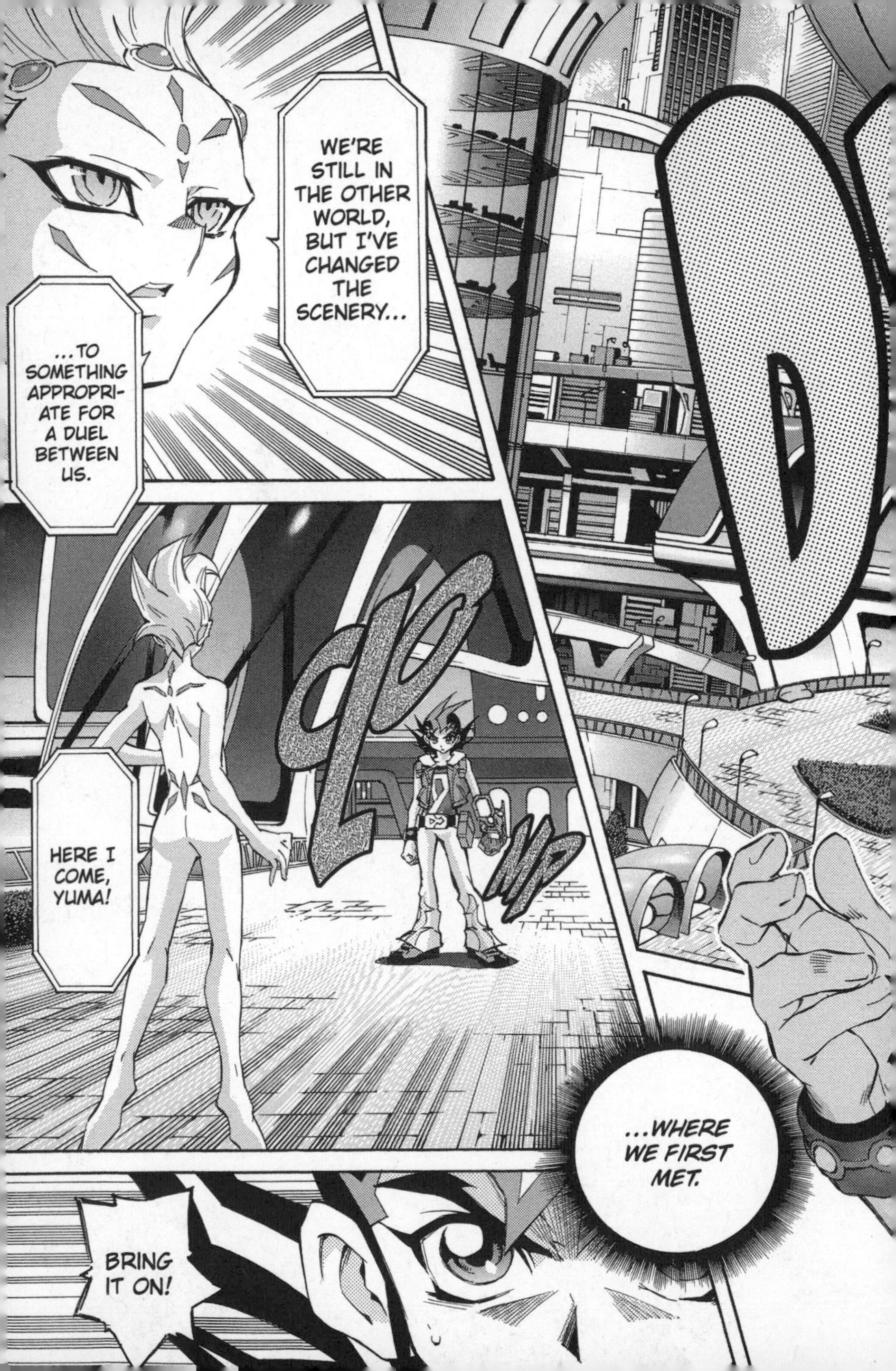
...WHERE WE FIRST MET.
WE'RE STILL IN THE OTHER WORLD, BUT I'VE CHANGED THE SCENERY...
...TO SOMETHING APPROPRIATE FOR A DUEL BETWEEN US.
HERE I COME, YUMA!
BRING IT ON!

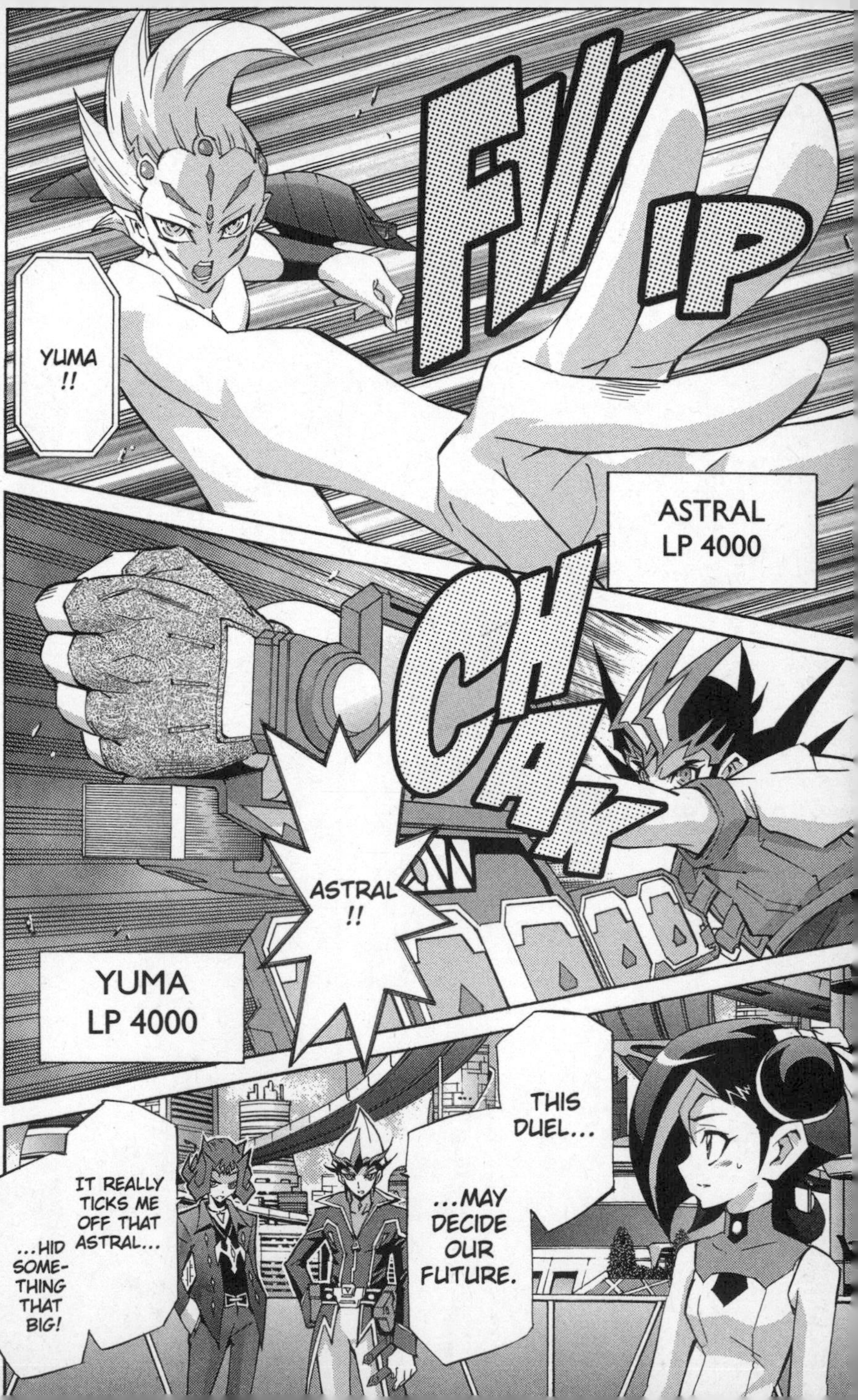
FWIP
YUMA !!
ASTRAL LP 4000
CHCHAK
ASTRAL !!
YUMA LP 4000
THIS DUEL...
...MAY DECIDE OUR FUTURE.
IT REALLY TICKS ME OFF THAT ASTRAL...
...HID SOMETHING THAT BIG!

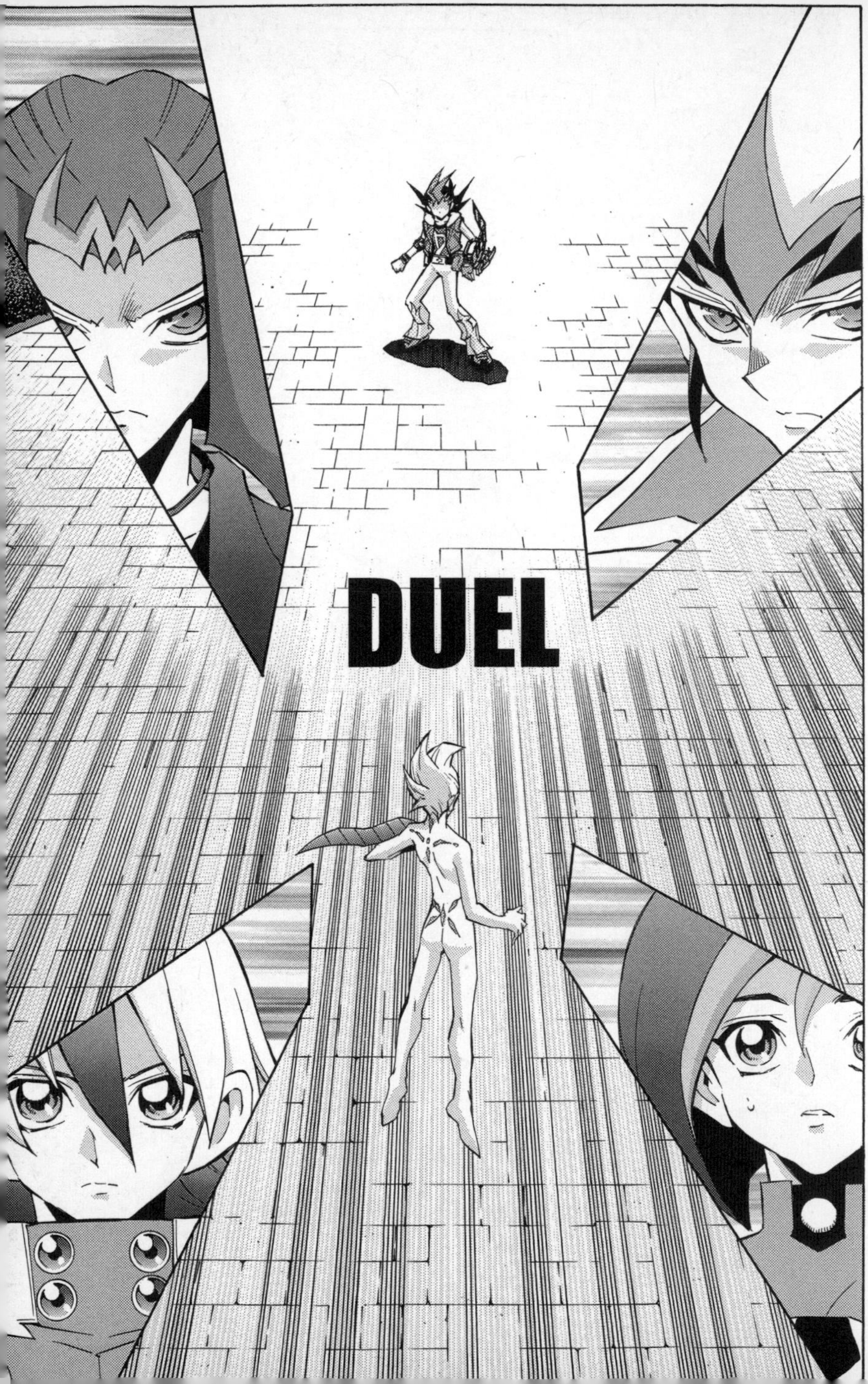
DUEL

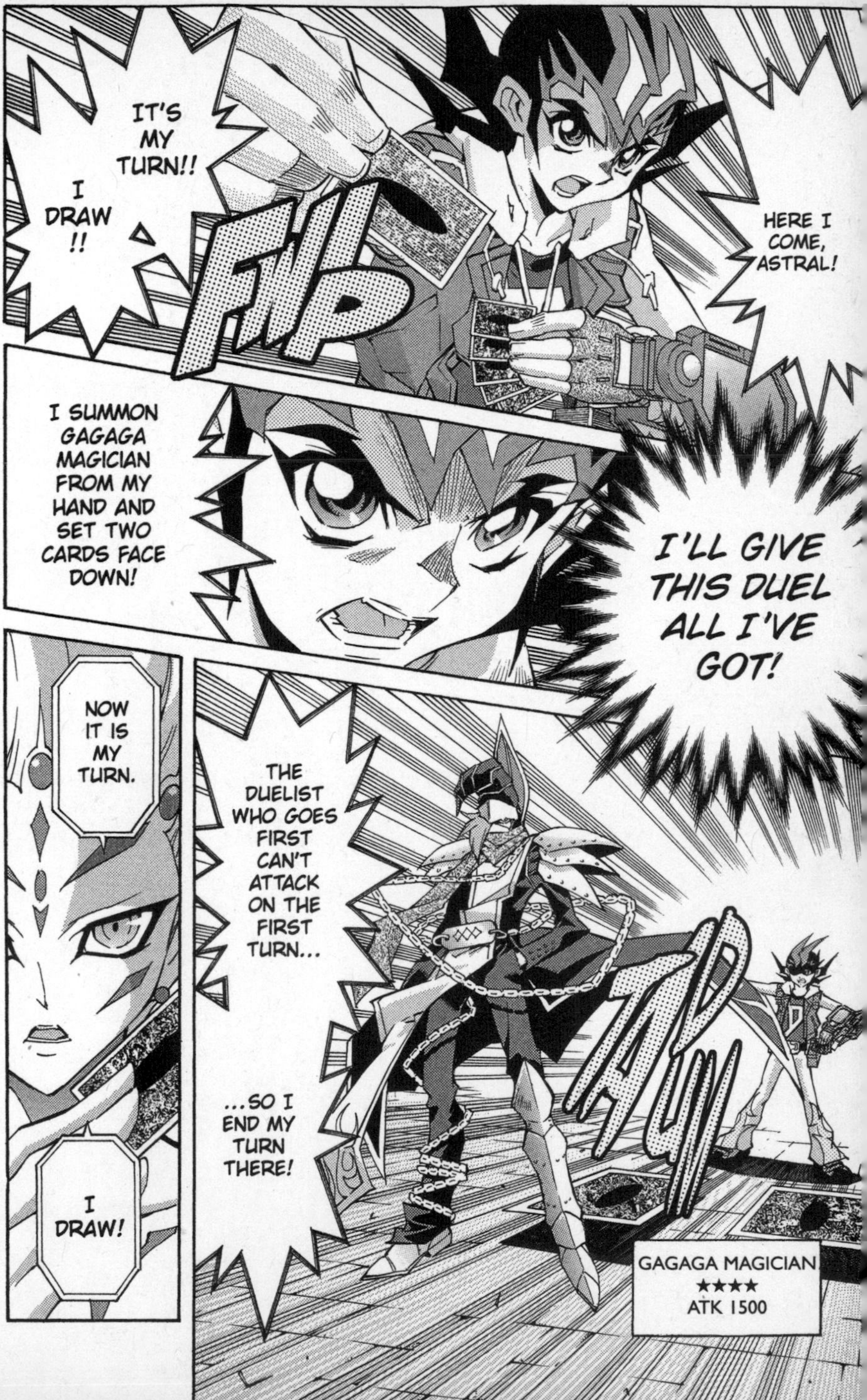
HERE I COME, ASTRAL!
IT'S MY TURN!!
I DRAW!!
I SUMMON GAGAGA MAGICIAN FROM MY HAND AND SET TWO CARDS FACE DOWN!
I'LL GIVE THIS DUEL ALL I'VE GOT!
THE DUELIST WHO GOES FIRST CAN'T ATTACK ON THE FIRST TURN...
...SO I END MY TURN THERE!
GAGAGA MAGICIAN
★★★★
ATK 1500
NOW IT IS MY TURN.
I DRAW!

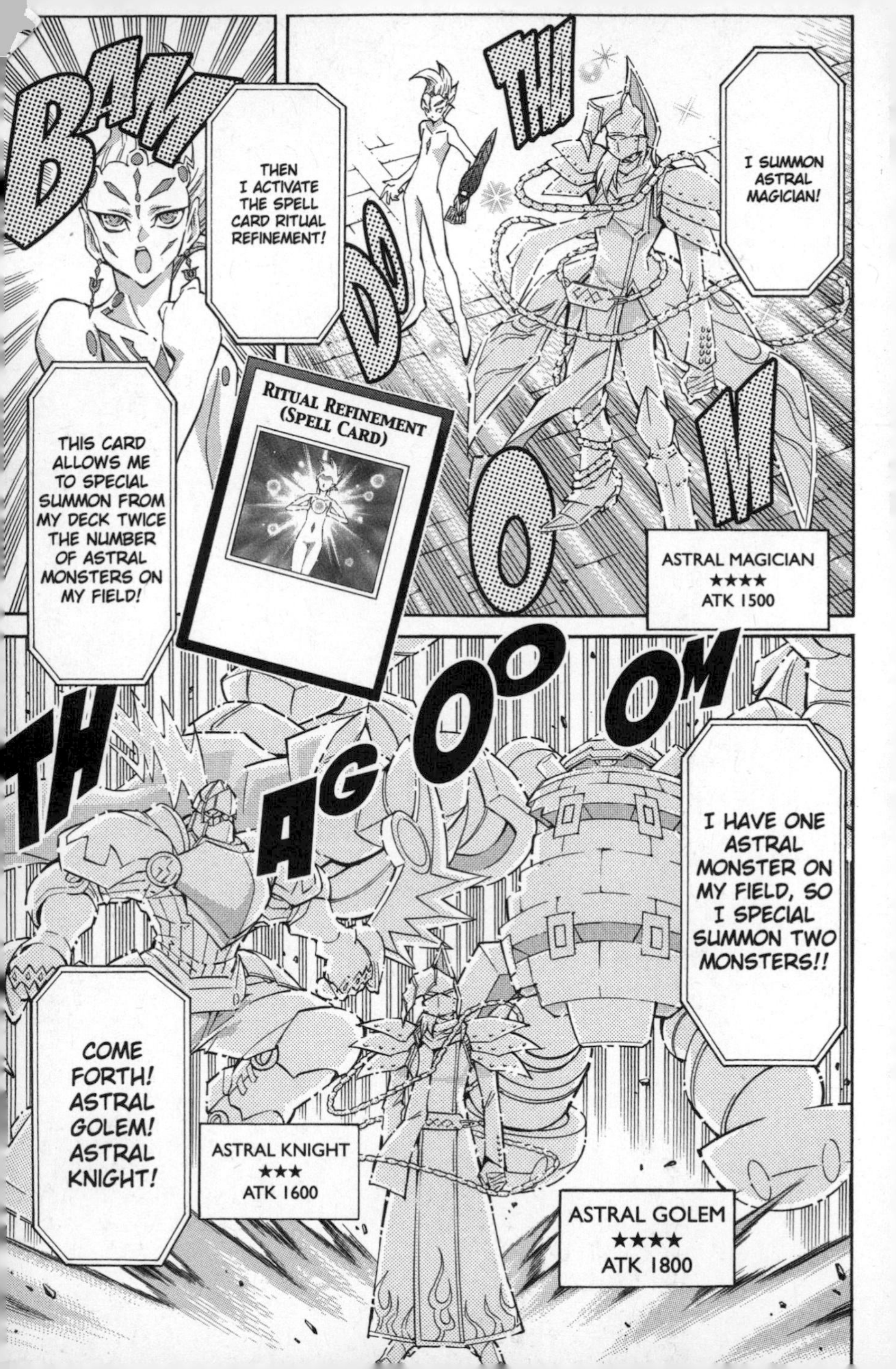
I SUMMON ASTRAL MAGICIAN!
ASTRAL MAGICIAN
★★★★
ATK 1500
BAM
THEN I ACTIVATE THE SPELL CARD RITUAL REFINEMENT!
RITUAL REFINEMENT (SPELL CARD)
THIS CARD ALLOWS ME TO SPECIAL SUMMON FROM MY DECK TWICE THE NUMBER OF ASTRAL MONSTERS ON MY FIELD!
I HAVE ONE ASTRAL MONSTER ON MY FIELD, SO I SPECIAL SUMMON TWO MONSTERS!!
COME FORTH! ASTRAL GOLEM! ASTRAL KNIGHT!
ASTRAL KNIGHT
★★★
ATK 1600
ASTRAL GOLEM
★★★★
ATK 1800

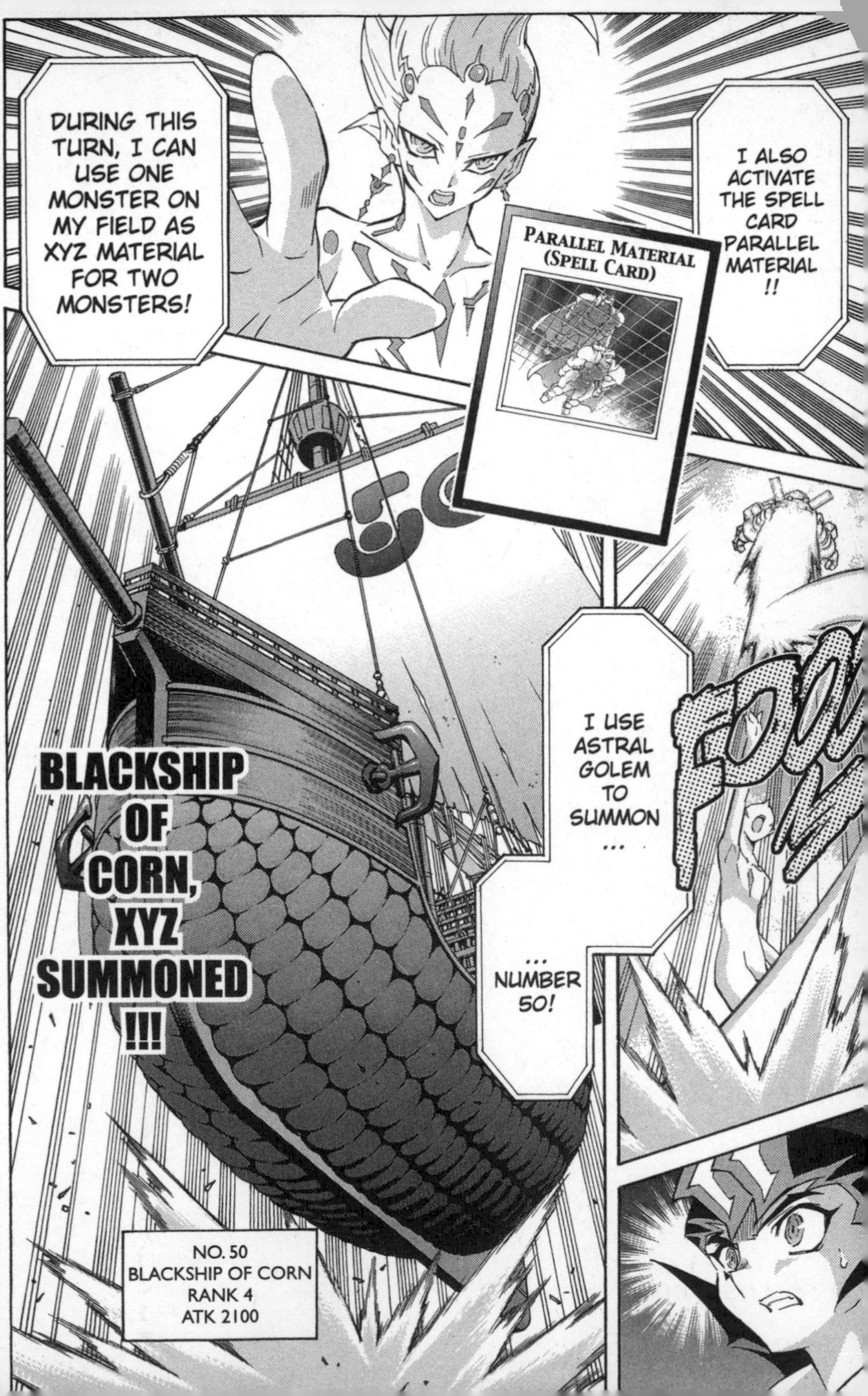
I ALSO ACTIVATE THE SPELL CARD PARALLEL MATERIAL !!
DURING THIS TURN, I CAN USE ONE MONSTER ON MY FIELD AS XYZ MATERIAL FOR TWO MONSTERS!
PARALLEL MATERIAL
(SPELL CARD)
I USE ASTRAL GOLEM TO SUMMON ...
... NUMBER 50!
BLACKSHIP OF CORN, XYZ SUMMONED !!!
NO. 50
BLACKSHIP OF CORN
RANK 4
ATK 2100

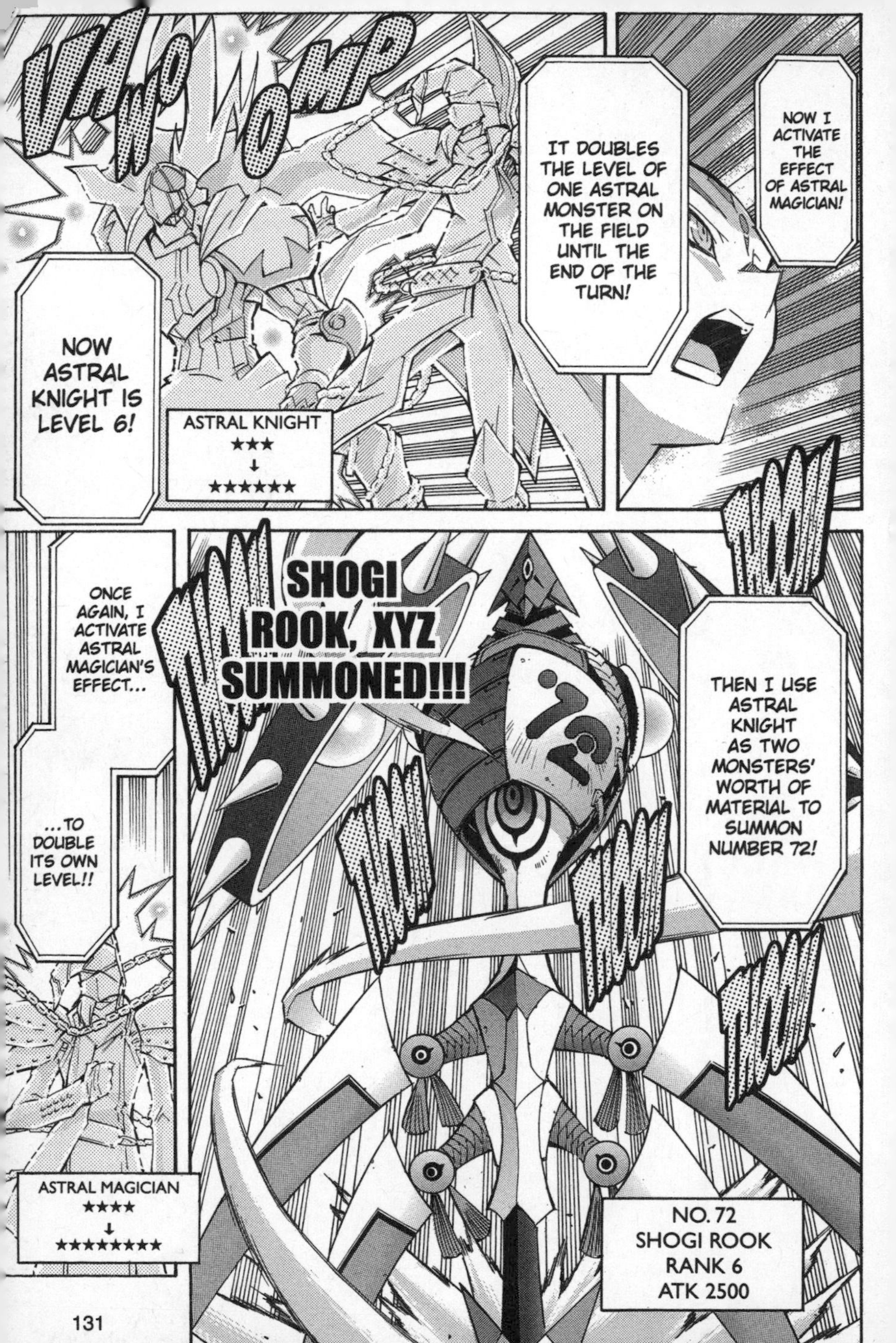
NOW I ACTIVATE THE EFFECT OF ASTRAL MAGICIAN!
IT DOUBLES THE LEVEL OF ONE ASTRAL MONSTER ON THE FIELD UNTIL THE END OF THE TURN!
VAWOOMP
NOW ASTRAL KNIGHT IS LEVEL 6!
ASTRAL KNIGHT ★★★ ↓ ★★★★★★
THEN I USE ASTRAL KNIGHT AS TWO MONSTERS' WORTH OF MATERIAL TO SUMMON NUMBER 72!
SHOGI ROOK, XYZ SUMMONED!!!
NO. 72 SHOGI ROOK RANK 6 ATK 2500
ONCE AGAIN, I ACTIVATE ASTRAL MAGICIAN'S EFFECT...
...TO DOUBLE ITS OWN LEVEL!!
ASTRAL MAGICIAN ★★★★ ↓ ★★★★★★★★

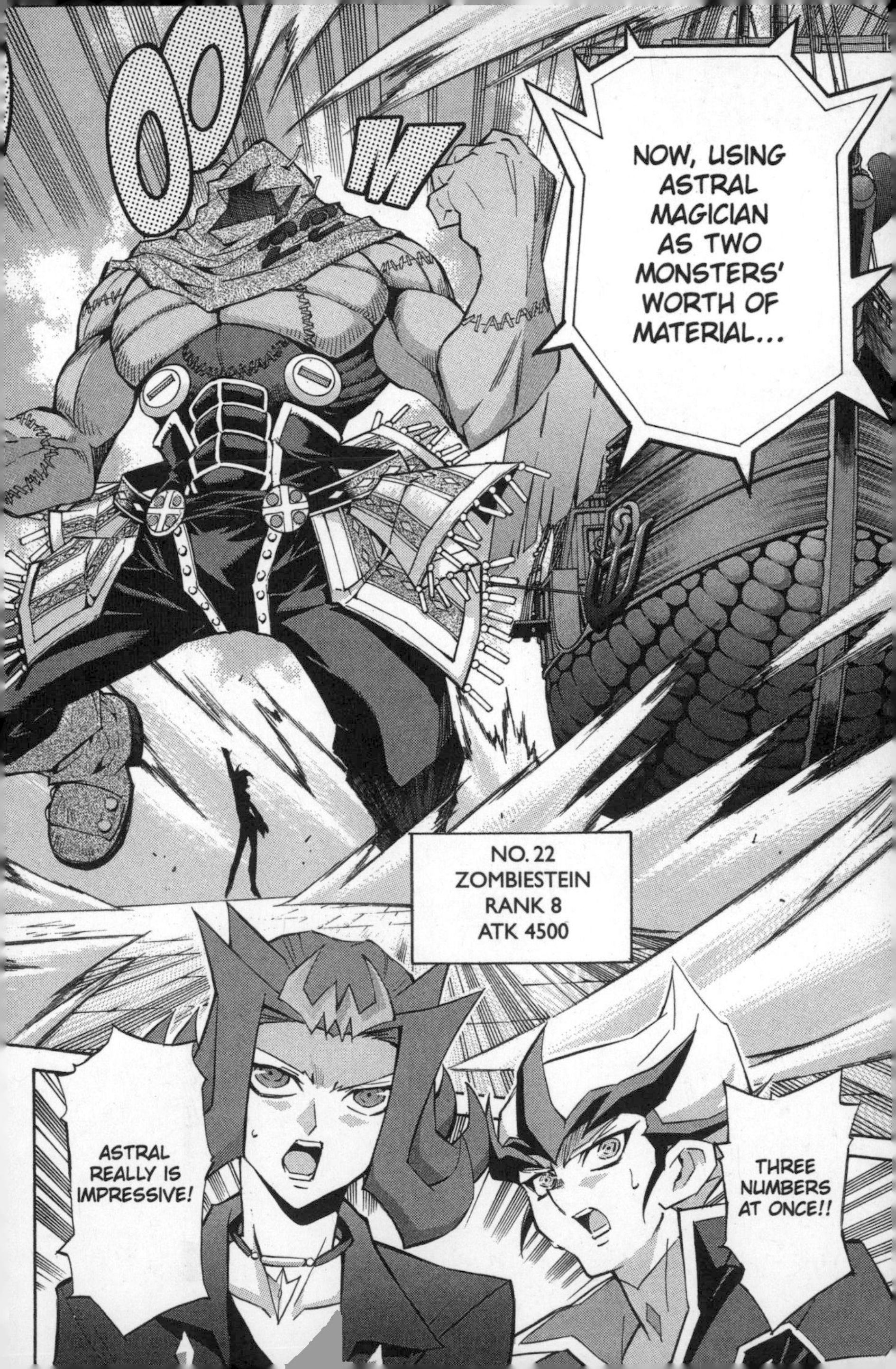
NOW, USING ASTRAL MAGICIAN AS TWO MONSTERS' WORTH OF MATERIAL...
OOOM
NO. 22 ZOMBIESTEIN RANK 8 ATK 4500
THREE NUMBERS AT ONCE!!
ASTRAL REALLY IS IMPRESSIVE!

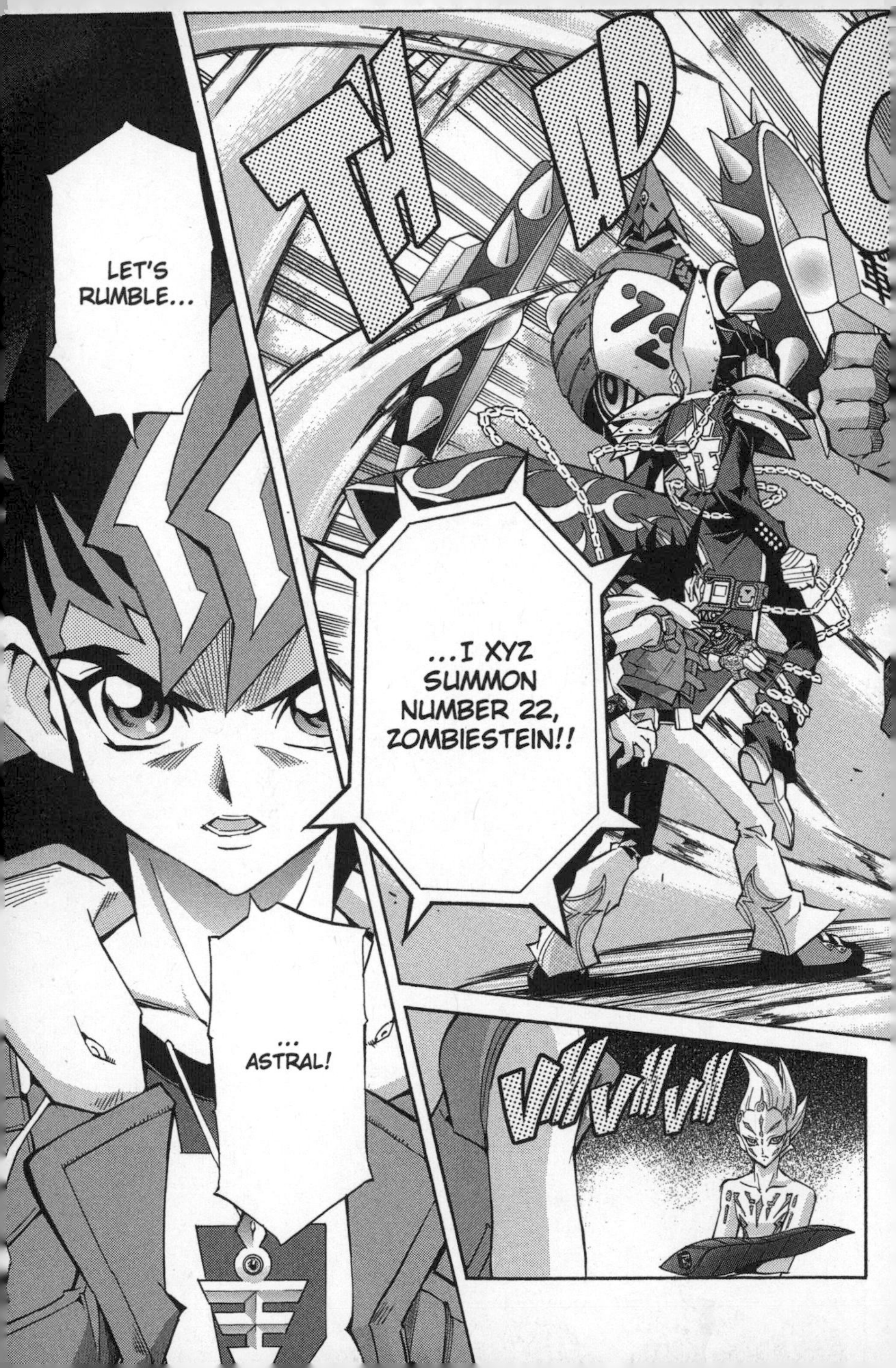
THUD
...I XYZ SUMMON NUMBER 22, ZOMBIESTEIN!!
LET'S RUMBLE...
... ASTRAL!

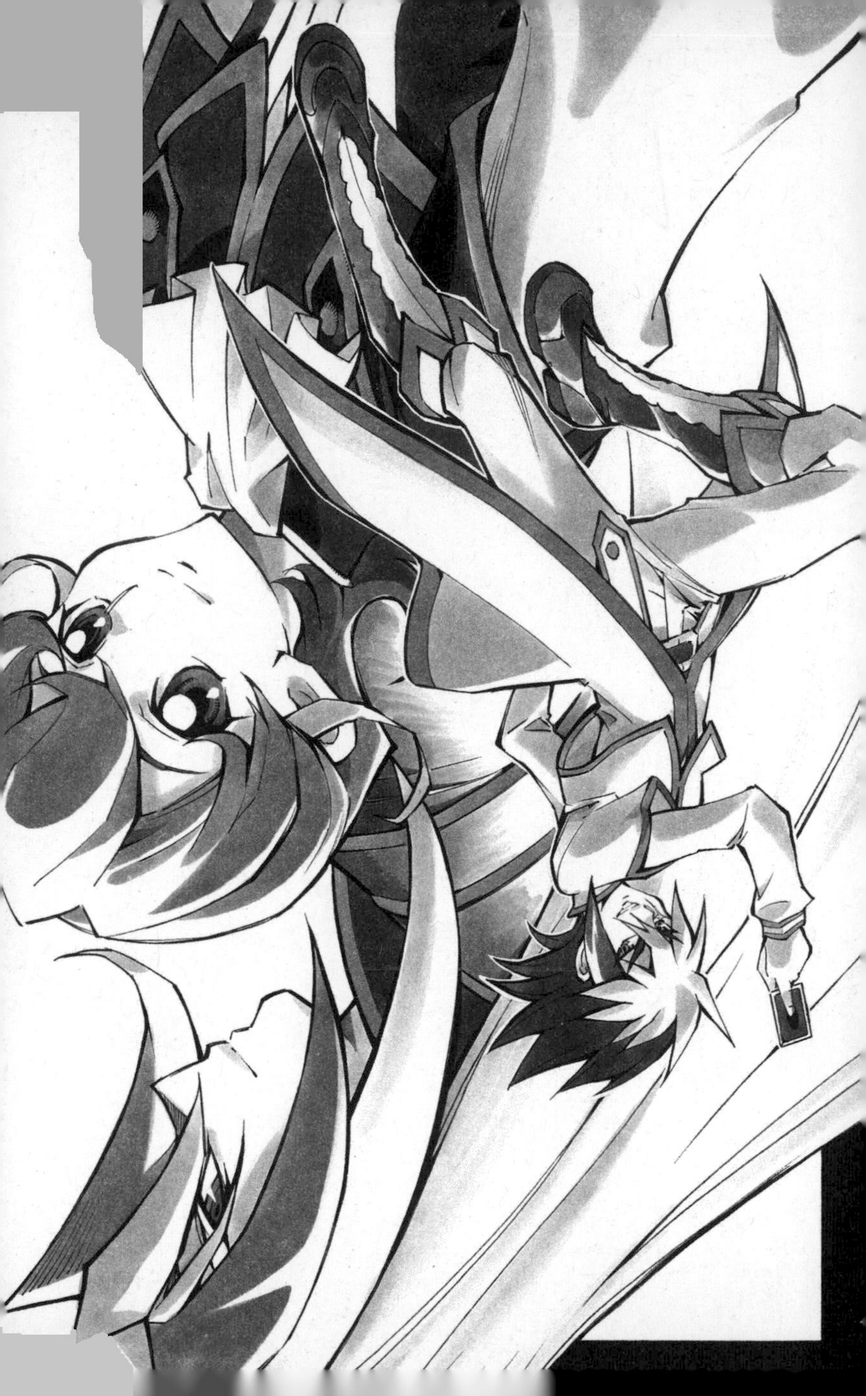

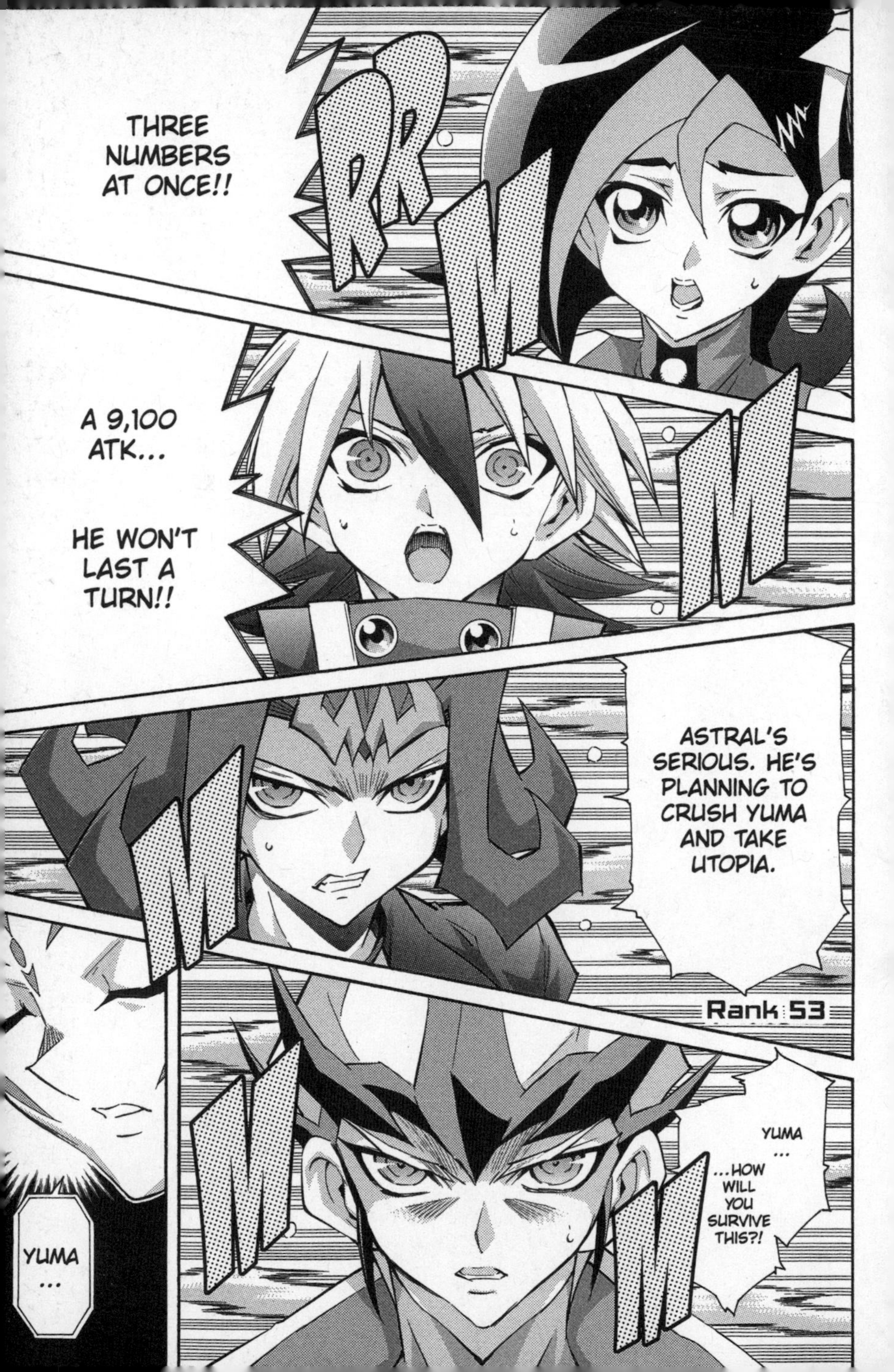
RRMM
THREE NUMBERS AT ONCE!!
MM
A 9,100 ATK...
HE WON'T LAST A TURN!!
MM
ASTRAL'S SERIOUS. HE'S PLANNING TO CRUSH YUMA AND TAKE UTOPIA.
MM
YUMA ...
...HOW WILL YOU SURVIVE THIS?!
YUMA ...

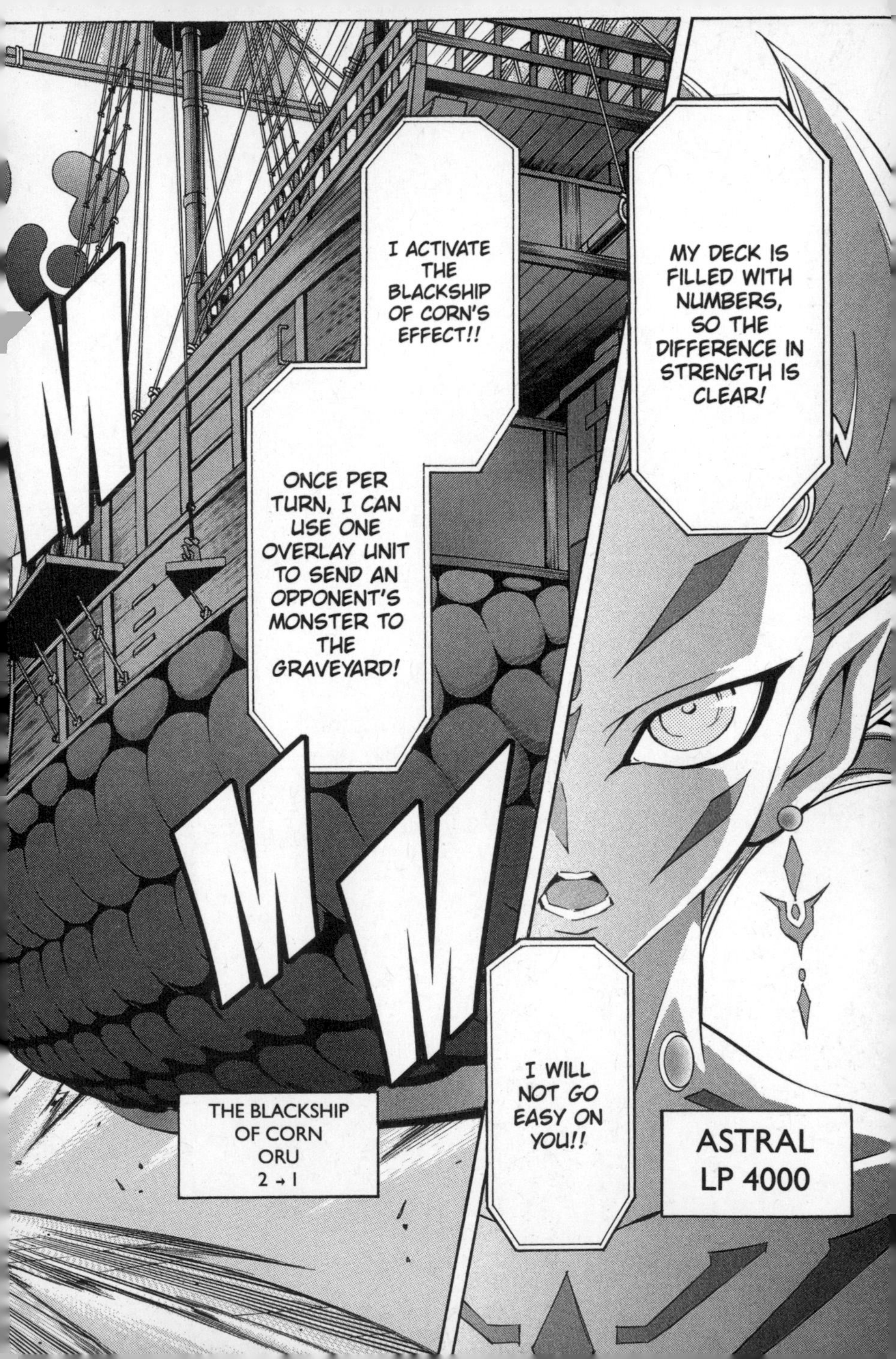
MY DECK IS FILLED WITH NUMBERS, SO THE DIFFERENCE IN STRENGTH IS CLEAR!
I ACTIVATE THE BLACKSHIP OF CORN'S EFFECT!!
ONCE PER TURN, I CAN USE ONE OVERLAY UNIT TO SEND AN OPPONENT'S MONSTER TO THE GRAVEYARD!
MMM
ASTRAL LP 4000
I WILL NOT GO EASY ON YOU!!
THE BLACKSHIP OF CORN ORU 2 → 1

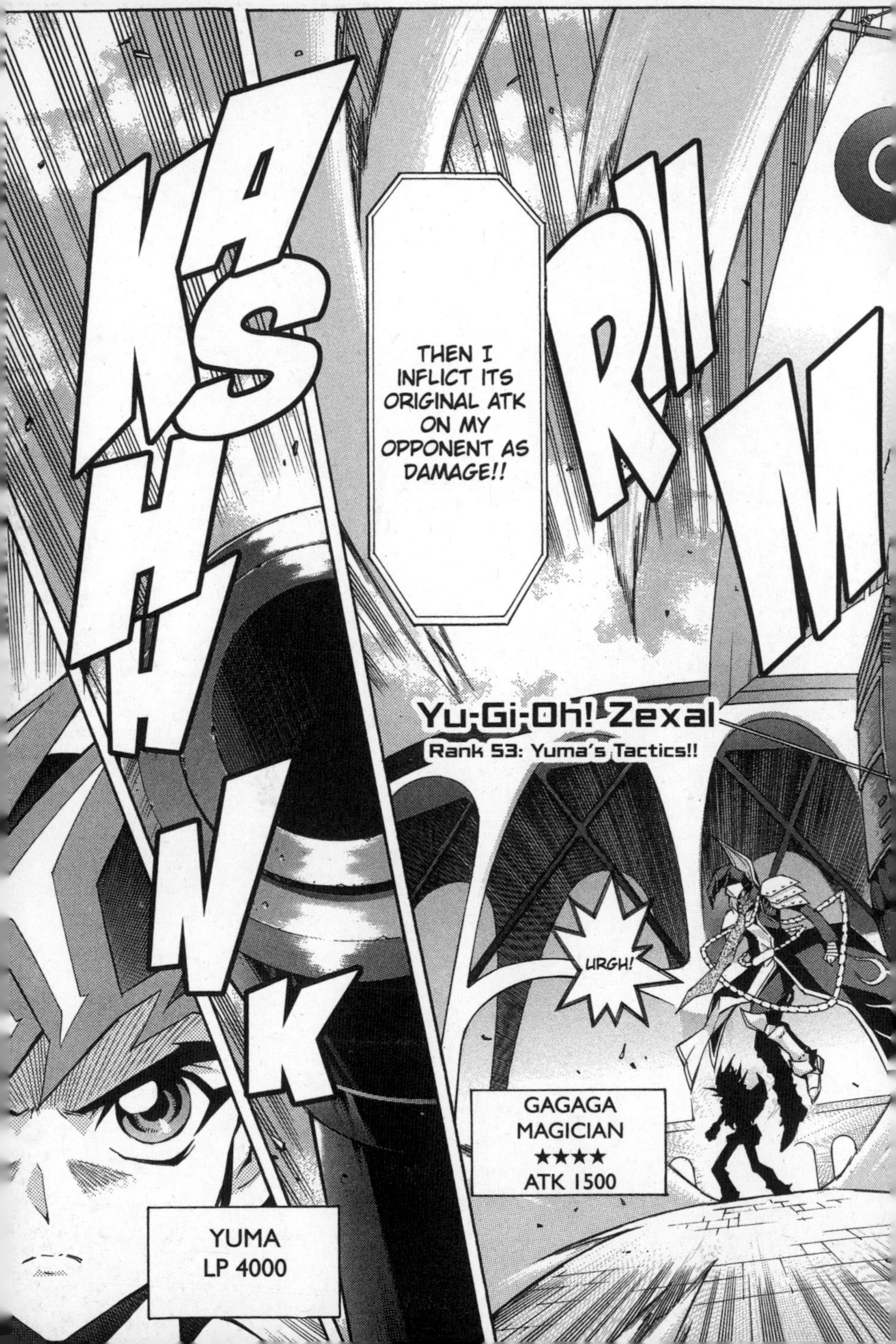
THEN I INFLICT ITS ORIGINAL ATK ON MY OPPONENT AS DAMAGE!!
Yu-Gi-Oh! Zexal
Rank 53: Yuma's Tactics!!
URGH!
GAGAGA MAGICIAN ★★★★ ATK 1500
YUMA LP 4000

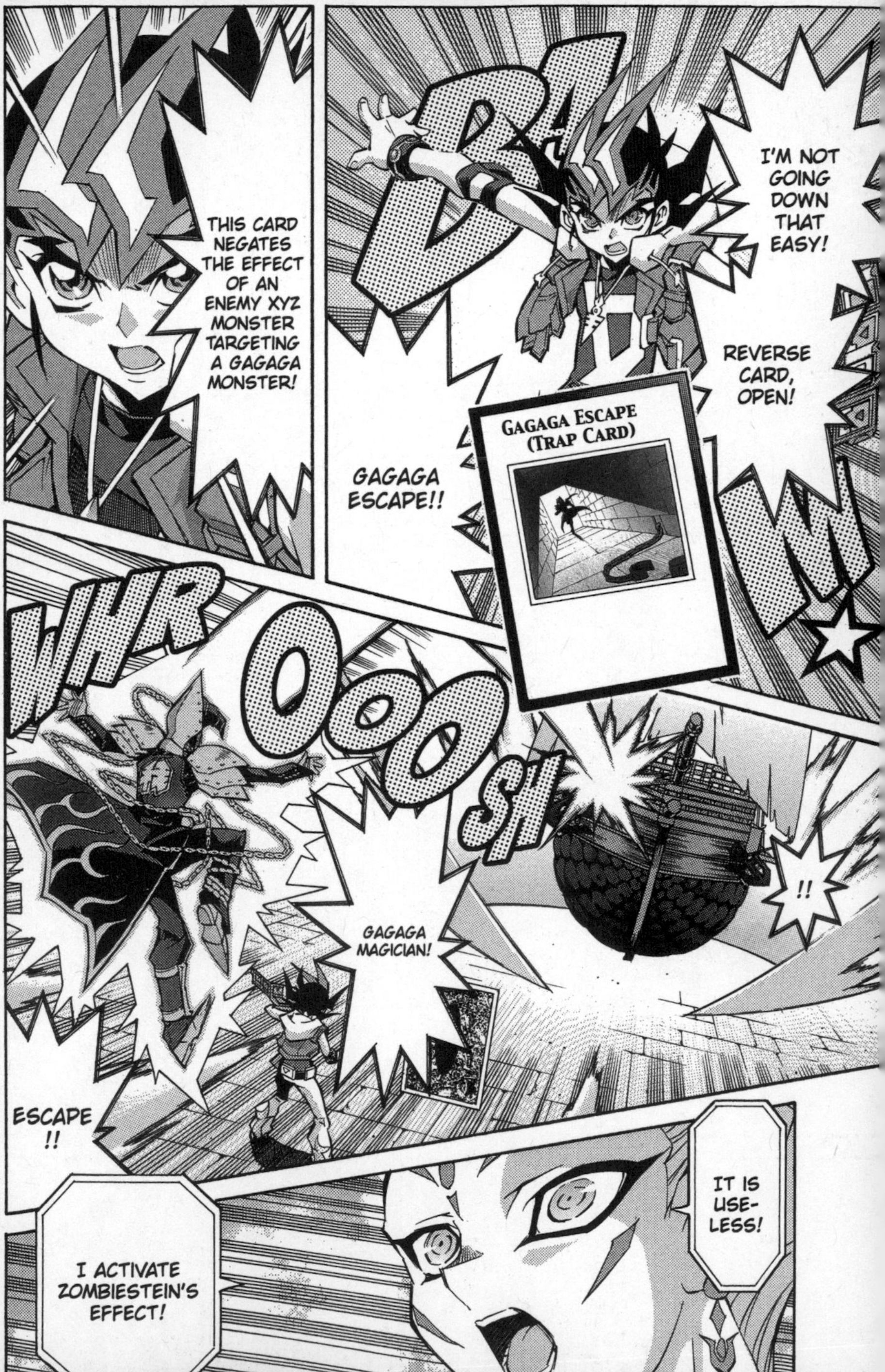
I'M NOT GOING DOWN THAT EASY!
BAM
REVERSE CARD, OPEN!
GAGAGA ESCAPE (TRAP CARD)
GAGAGA ESCAPE!!
THIS CARD NEGATES THE EFFECT OF AN ENEMY XYZ MONSTER TARGETING A GAGAGA MONSTER!
!!
WHROOOSH
GAGAGA MAGICIAN!
ESCAPE !!
IT IS USE-LESS!
I ACTIVATE ZOMBIESTEIN'S EFFECT!

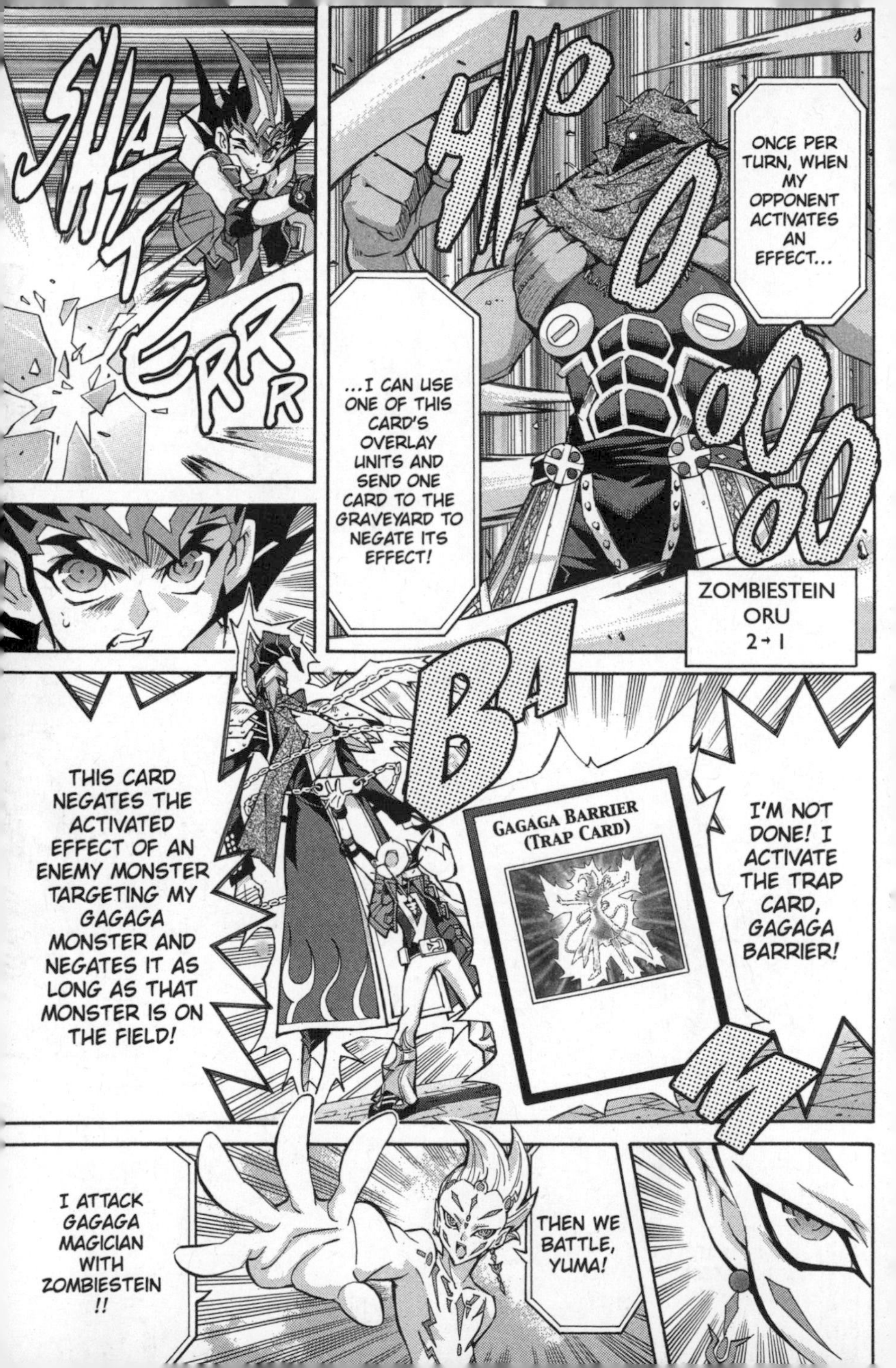
WHOOOOOOO
ONCE PER TURN, WHEN MY OPPONENT ACTIVATES AN EFFECT...
...I CAN USE ONE OF THIS CARD'S OVERLAY UNITS AND SEND ONE CARD TO THE GRAVEYARD TO NEGATE ITS EFFECT!
ZOMBIESTEIN ORU 2→1
SHATTERRR
BAM
I'M NOT DONE! I ACTIVATE THE TRAP CARD, GAGAGA BARRIER!
GAGAGA BARRIER (TRAP CARD)
THIS CARD NEGATES THE ACTIVATED EFFECT OF AN ENEMY MONSTER TARGETING MY GAGAGA MONSTER AND NEGATES IT AS LONG AS THAT MONSTER IS ON THE FIELD!
THEN WE BATTLE, YUMA!
I ATTACK GAGAGA MAGICIAN WITH ZOMBIESTEIN !!

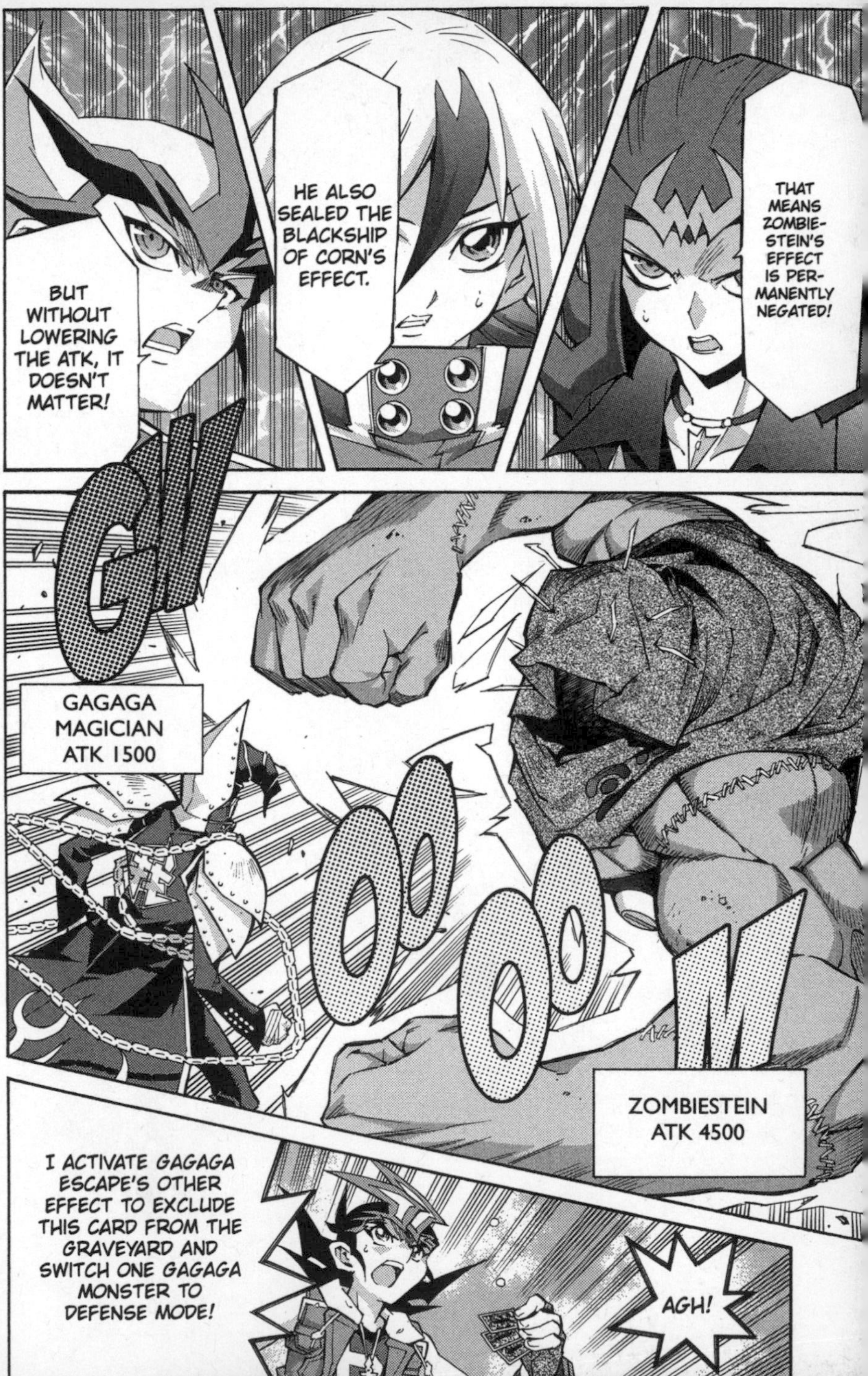
THAT MEANS ZOMBIE-STEIN'S EFFECT IS PER-MANENTLY NEGATED!
HE ALSO SEALED THE BLACKSHIP OF CORN'S EFFECT.
BUT WITHOUT LOWERING THE ATK, IT DOESN'T MATTER!
ZOMBIESTEIN ATK 4500
GWOOOOOM
GAGAGA MAGICIAN ATK 1500
AGH!
I ACTIVATE GAGAGA ESCAPE'S OTHER EFFECT TO EXCLUDE THIS CARD FROM THE GRAVEYARD AND SWITCH ONE GAGAGA MONSTER TO DEFENSE MODE!

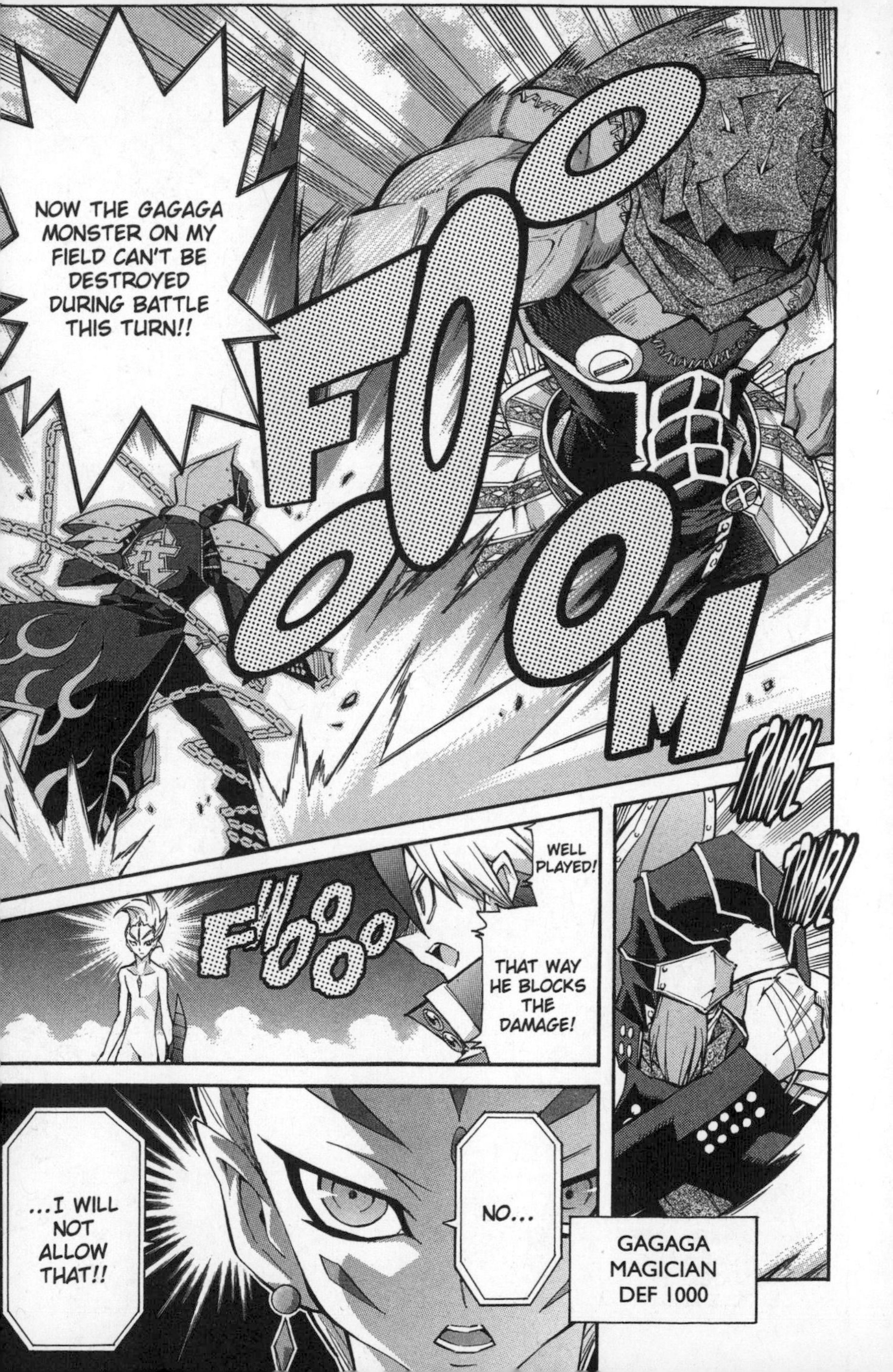
NOW THE GAGAGA MONSTER ON MY FIELD CAN'T BE DESTROYED DURING BATTLE THIS TURN!!
FOOOOM
GAGAGA MAGICIAN DEF 1000
WELL PLAYED!
THAT WAY HE BLOCKS THE DAMAGE!
NO...
...I WILL NOT ALLOW THAT!!

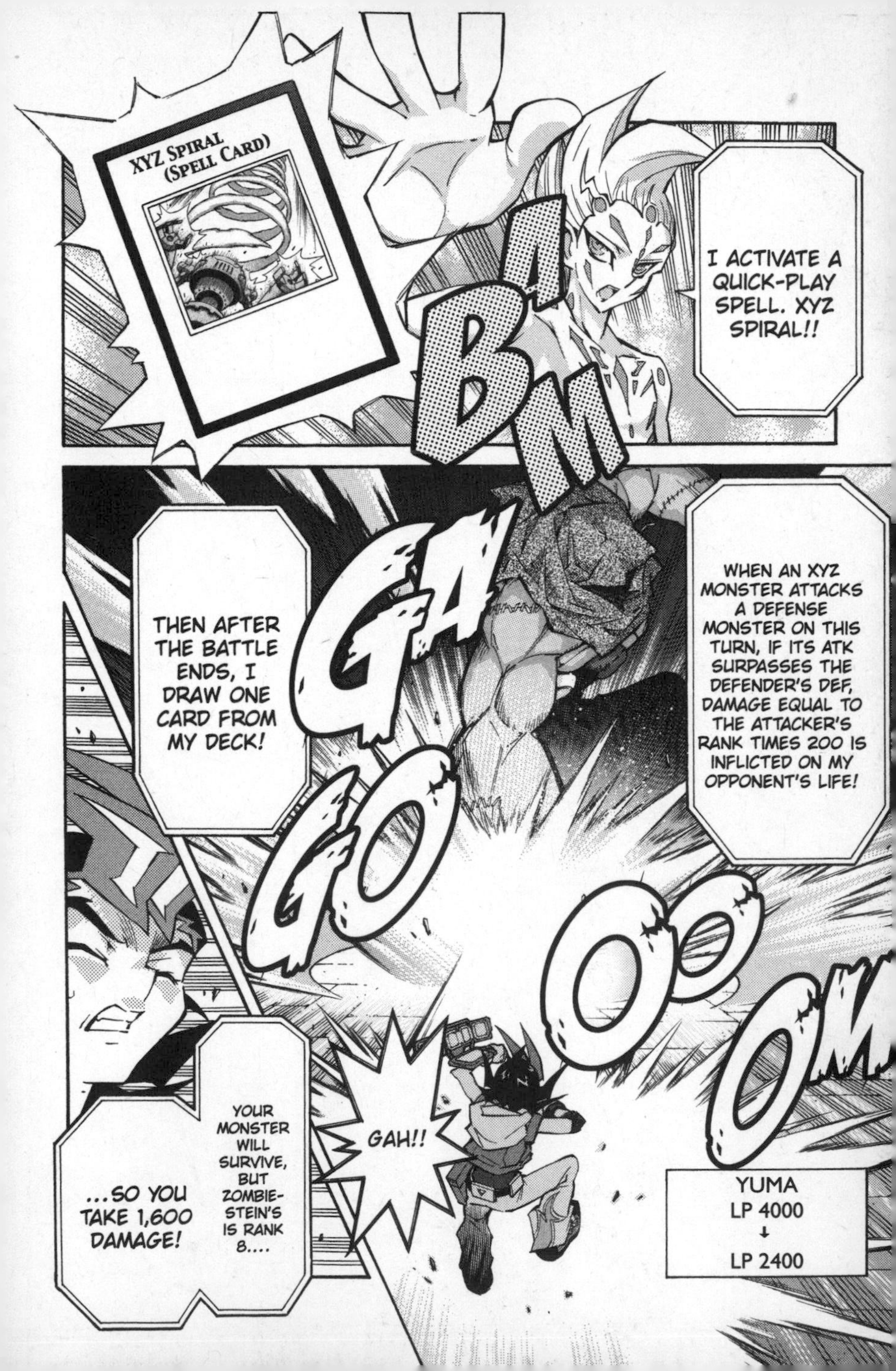
I ACTIVATE A QUICK-PLAY SPELL. XYZ SPIRAL!!
BAM
XYZ SPIRAL (SPELL CARD)
WHEN AN XYZ MONSTER ATTACKS A DEFENSE MONSTER ON THIS TURN, IF ITS ATK SURPASSES THE DEFENDER'S DEF, DAMAGE EQUAL TO THE ATTACKER'S RANK TIMES 200 IS INFLICTED ON MY OPPONENT'S LIFE!
THEN AFTER THE BATTLE ENDS, I DRAW ONE CARD FROM MY DECK!
GAGOOOOM
YUMA LP 4000 ↓ LP 2400
GAH!!
YOUR MONSTER WILL SURVIVE, BUT ZOMBIE-STEIN'S IS RANK 8....
...SO YOU TAKE 1,600 DAMAGE!

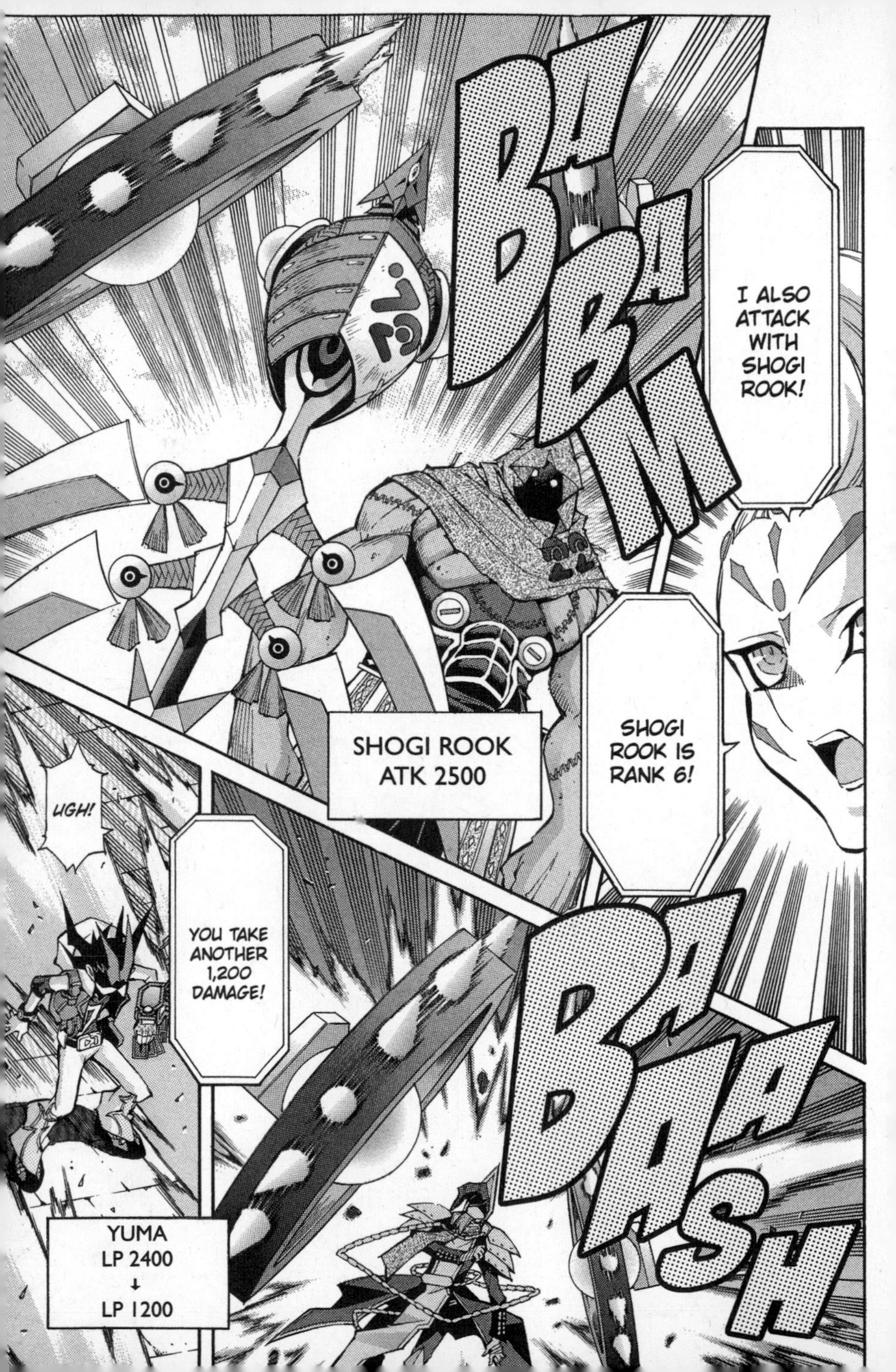
I ALSO ATTACK WITH SHOGI ROOK!
BA-BA-BAM
SHOGI ROOK IS RANK 6!
SHOGI ROOK ATK 2500
BA-BA-BASH
YOU TAKE ANOTHER 1,200 DAMAGE!
UGH!
YUMA LP 2400 ↓ LP 1200

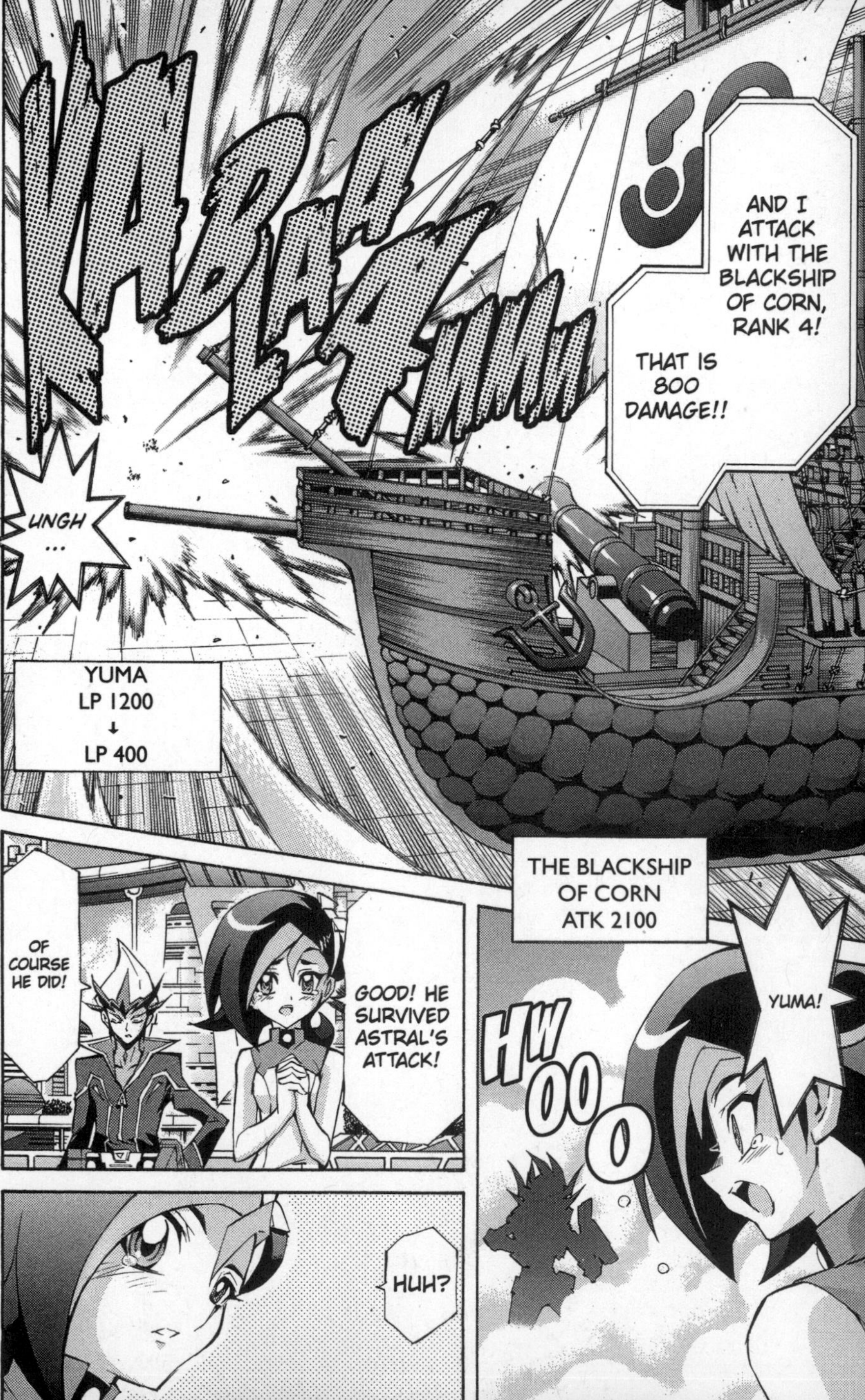
AND I ATTACK WITH THE BLACKSHIP OF CORN, RANK 4!
THAT IS 800 DAMAGE!!
KABAAAMMMM
UNGH ...
YUMA
LP 1200
↓
LP 400
THE BLACKSHIP OF CORN
ATK 2100
YUMA!
HWOOO
GOOD! HE SURVIVED ASTRAL'S ATTACK!
OF COURSE HE DID!
HUH?

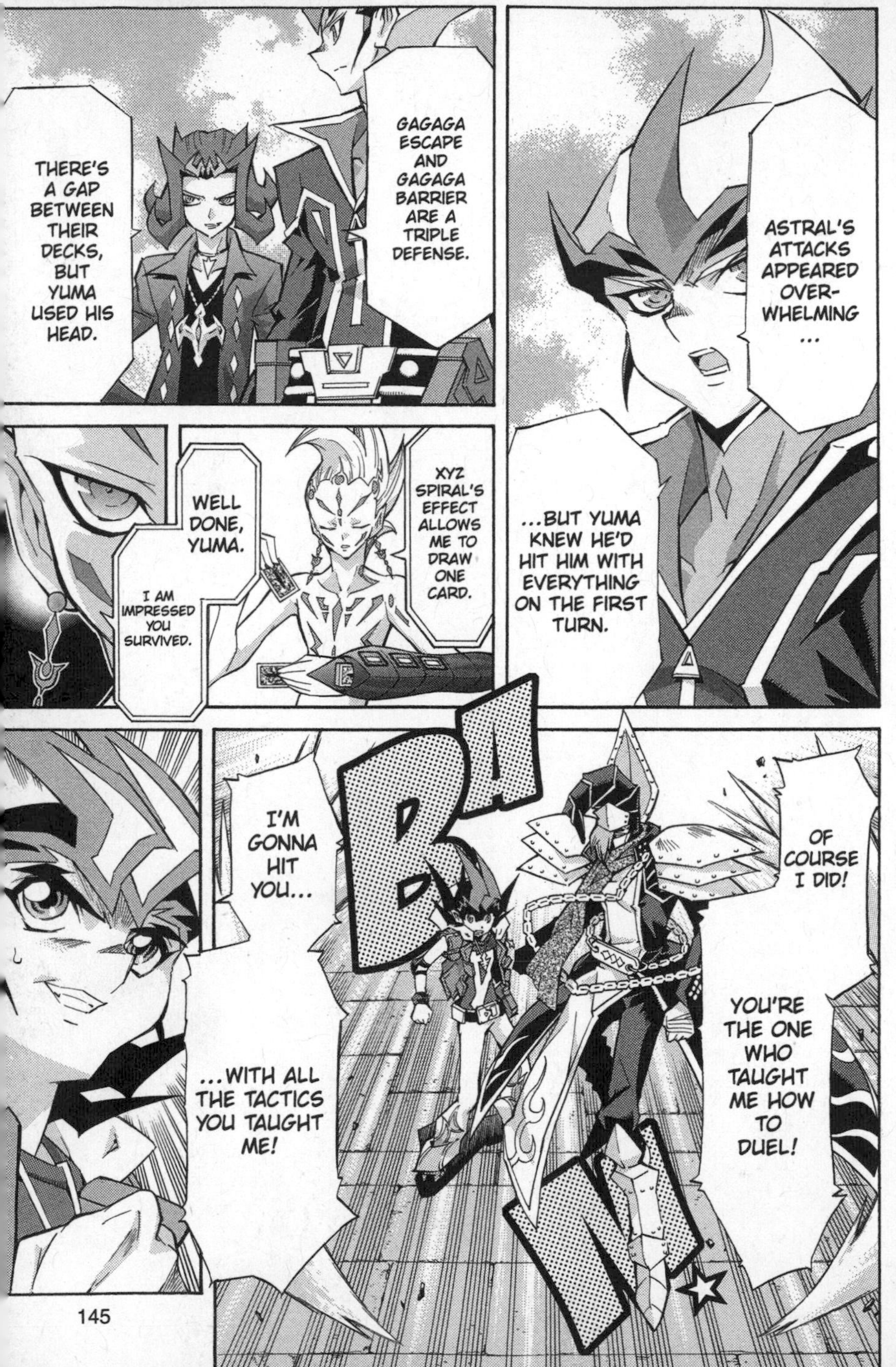
ASTRAL'S ATTACKS APPEARED OVER-WHELMING...
...BUT YUMA KNEW HE'D HIT HIM WITH EVERYTHING ON THE FIRST TURN.
GAGAGA ESCAPE AND GAGAGA BARRIER ARE A TRIPLE DEFENSE.
THERE'S A GAP BETWEEN THEIR DECKS, BUT YUMA USED HIS HEAD.
XYZ SPIRAL'S EFFECT ALLOWS ME TO DRAW ONE CARD.
WELL DONE, YUMA.
I AM IMPRESSED YOU SURVIVED.
OF COURSE I DID!
YOU'RE THE ONE WHO TAUGHT ME HOW TO DUEL!
BAM
I'M GONNA HIT YOU...
...WITH ALL THE TACTICS YOU TAUGHT ME!

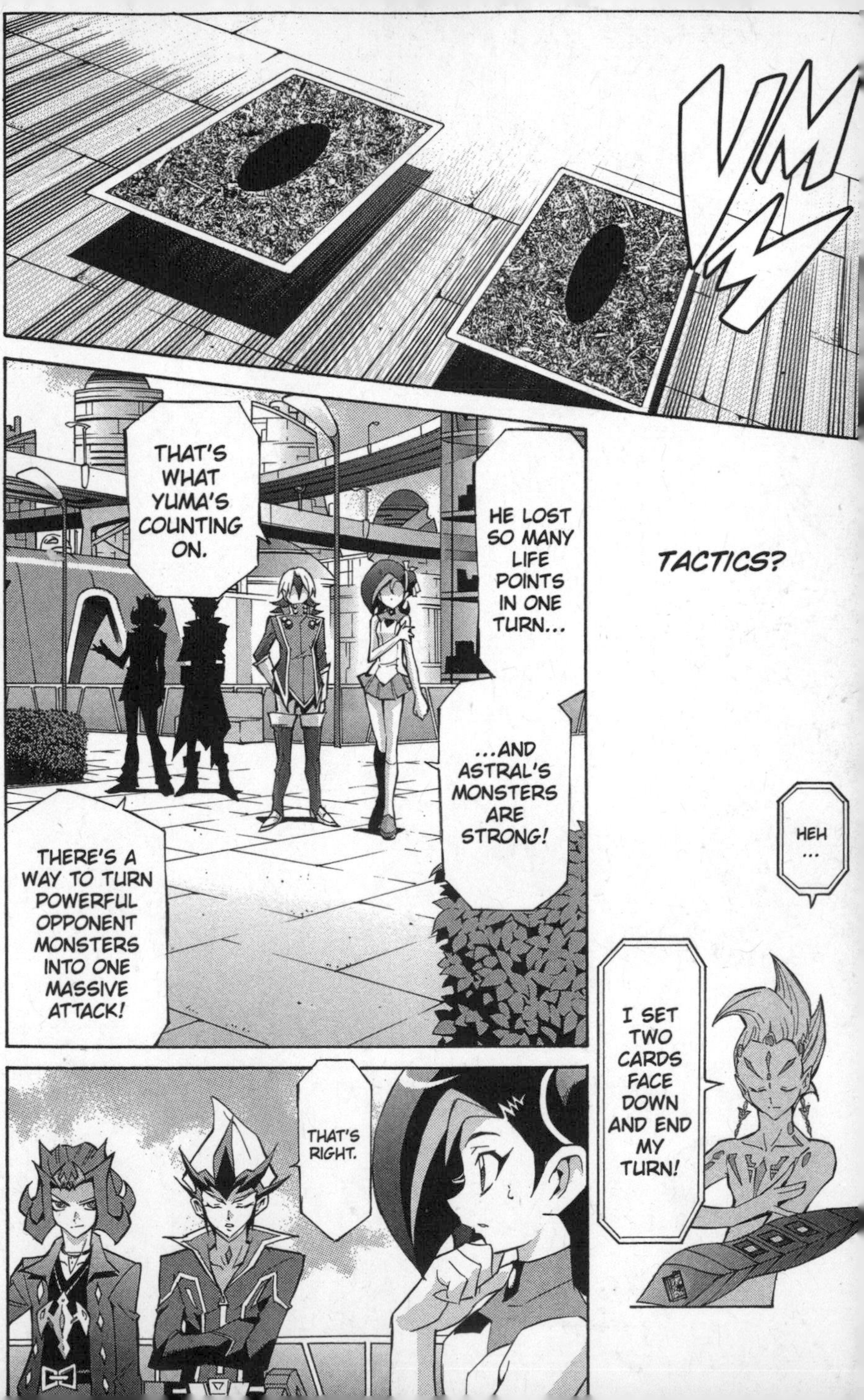
VMM
TACTICS?
HEH ...
I SET TWO CARDS FACE DOWN AND END MY TURN!
HE LOST SO MANY LIFE POINTS IN ONE TURN...
...AND ASTRAL'S MONSTERS ARE STRONG!
THAT'S WHAT YUMA'S COUNTING ON.
THERE'S A WAY TO TURN POWERFUL OPPONENT MONSTERS INTO ONE MASSIVE ATTACK!
THAT'S RIGHT.

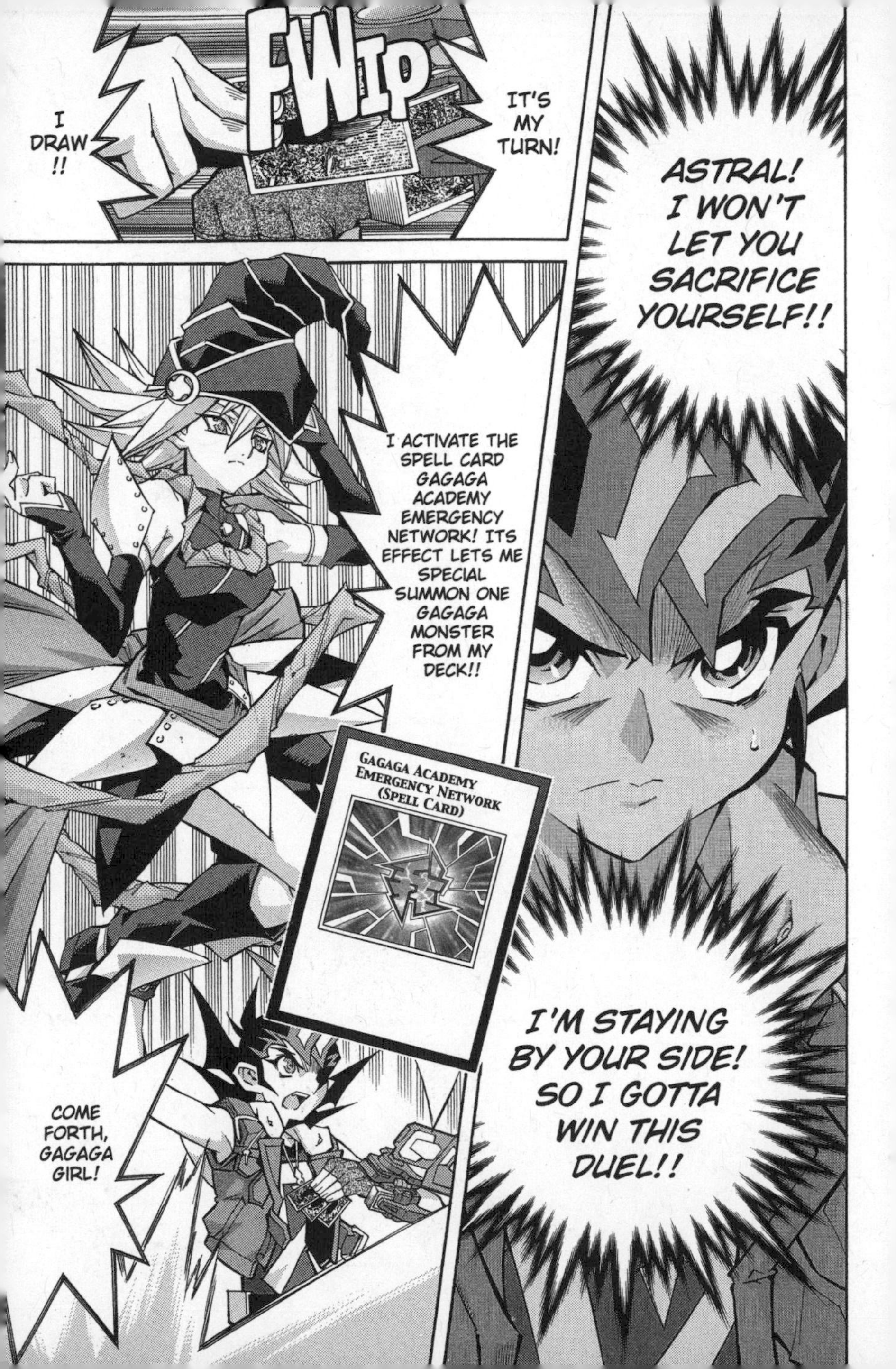
ASTRAL! I WON'T LET YOU SACRIFICE YOURSELF!!
I'M STAYING BY YOUR SIDE! SO I GOTTA WIN THIS DUEL!!
IT'S MY TURN!
FWIP
I DRAW!!
I ACTIVATE THE SPELL CARD GAGAGA ACADEMY EMERGENCY NETWORK! ITS EFFECT LETS ME SPECIAL SUMMON ONE GAGAGA MONSTER FROM MY DECK!!
GAGAGA ACADEMY EMERGENCY NETWORK (SPELL CARD)
COME FORTH, GAGAGA GIRL!

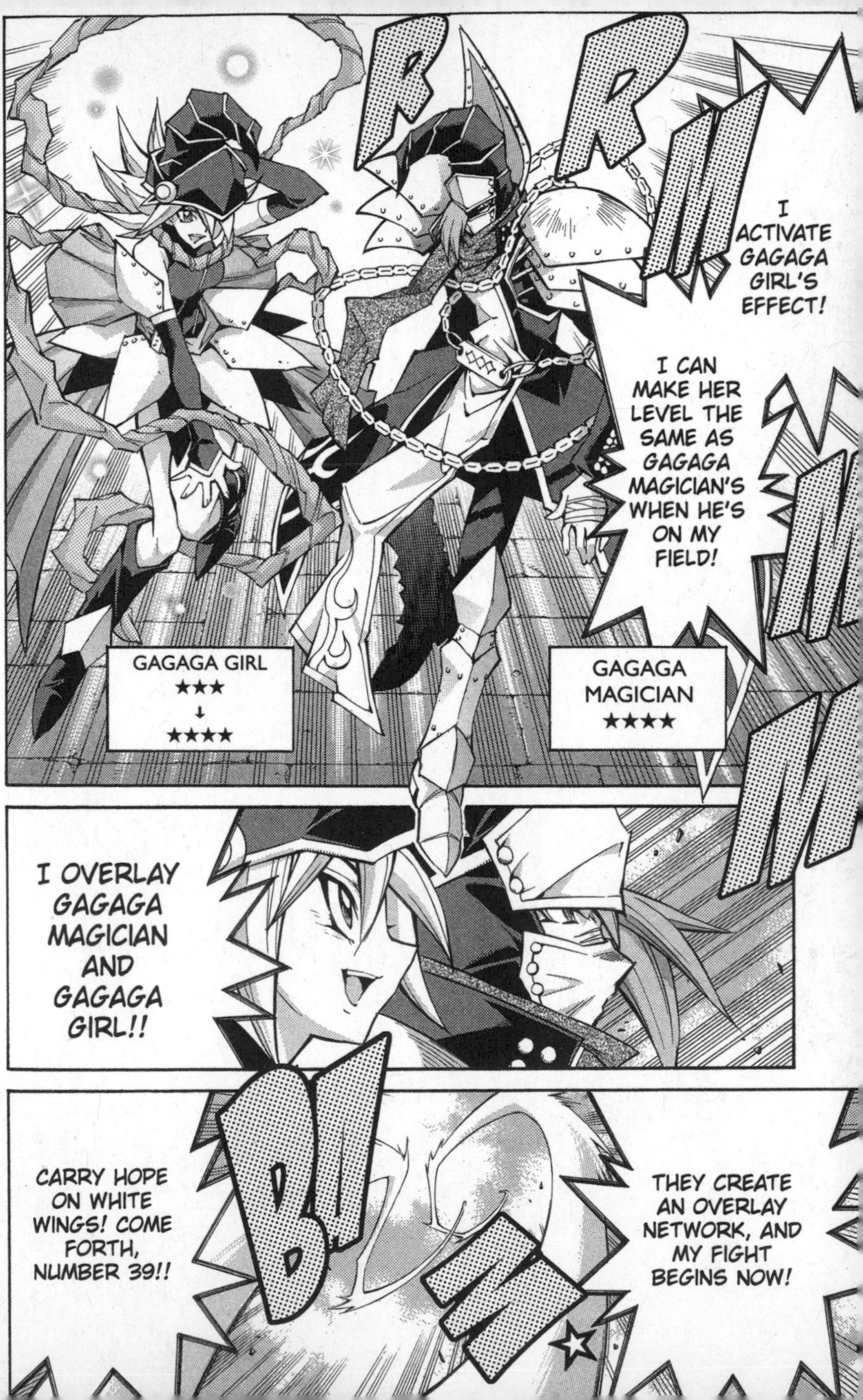
I ACTIVATE GAGAGA GIRL'S EFFECT!
I CAN MAKE HER LEVEL THE SAME AS GAGAGA MAGICIAN'S WHEN HE'S ON MY FIELD!
GAGAGA MAGICIAN ★★★★
GAGAGA GIRL ★★★ ↓ ★★★★
I OVERLAY GAGAGA MAGICIAN AND GAGAGA GIRL!!
THEY CREATE AN OVERLAY NETWORK, AND MY FIGHT BEGINS NOW!
CARRY HOPE ON WHITE WINGS! COME FORTH, NUMBER 39!!

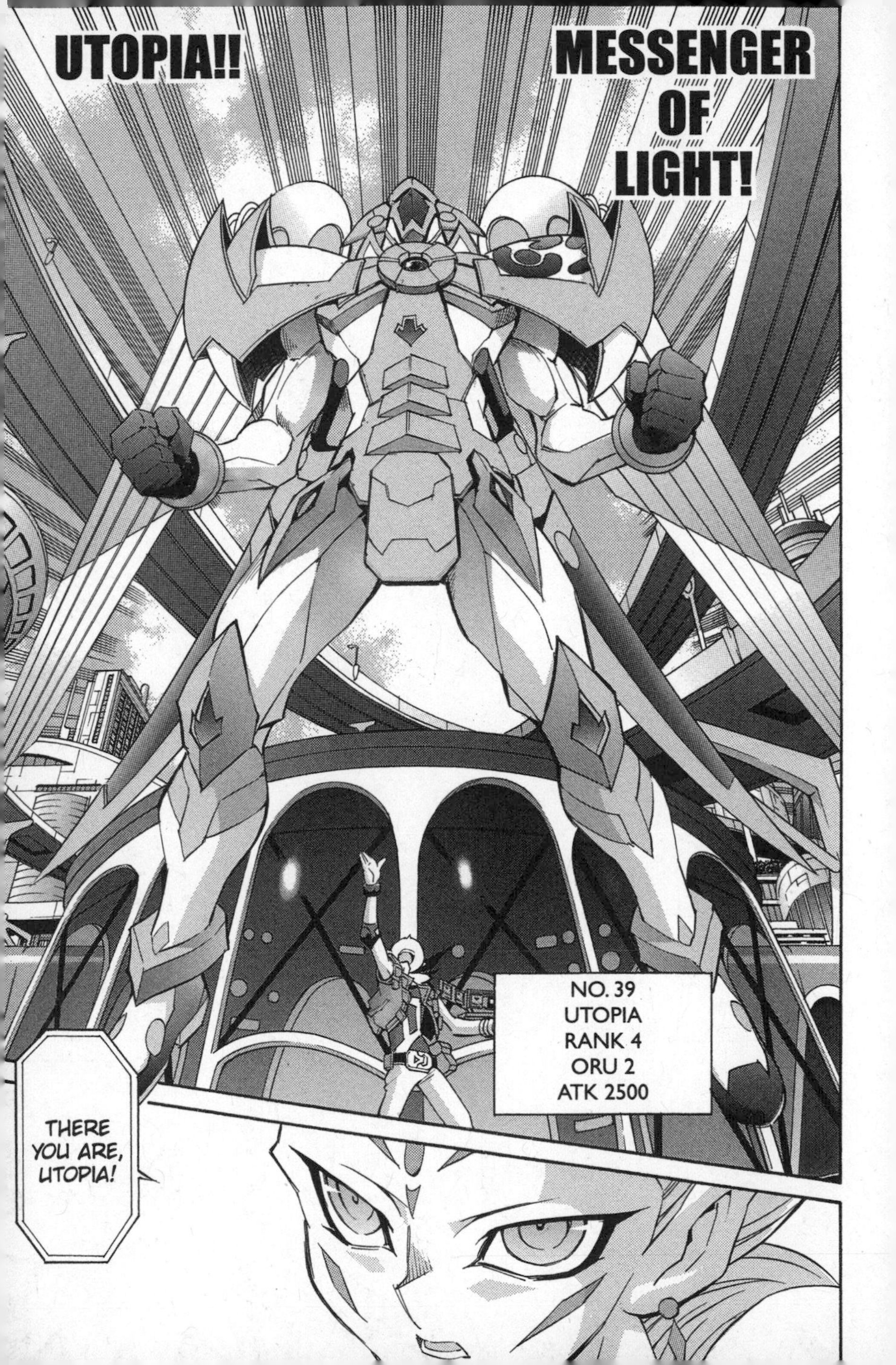
MESSENGER OF LIGHT!
UTOPIA!!
NO. 39 UTOPIA RANK 4 ORU 2 ATK 2500
THERE YOU ARE, UTOPIA!

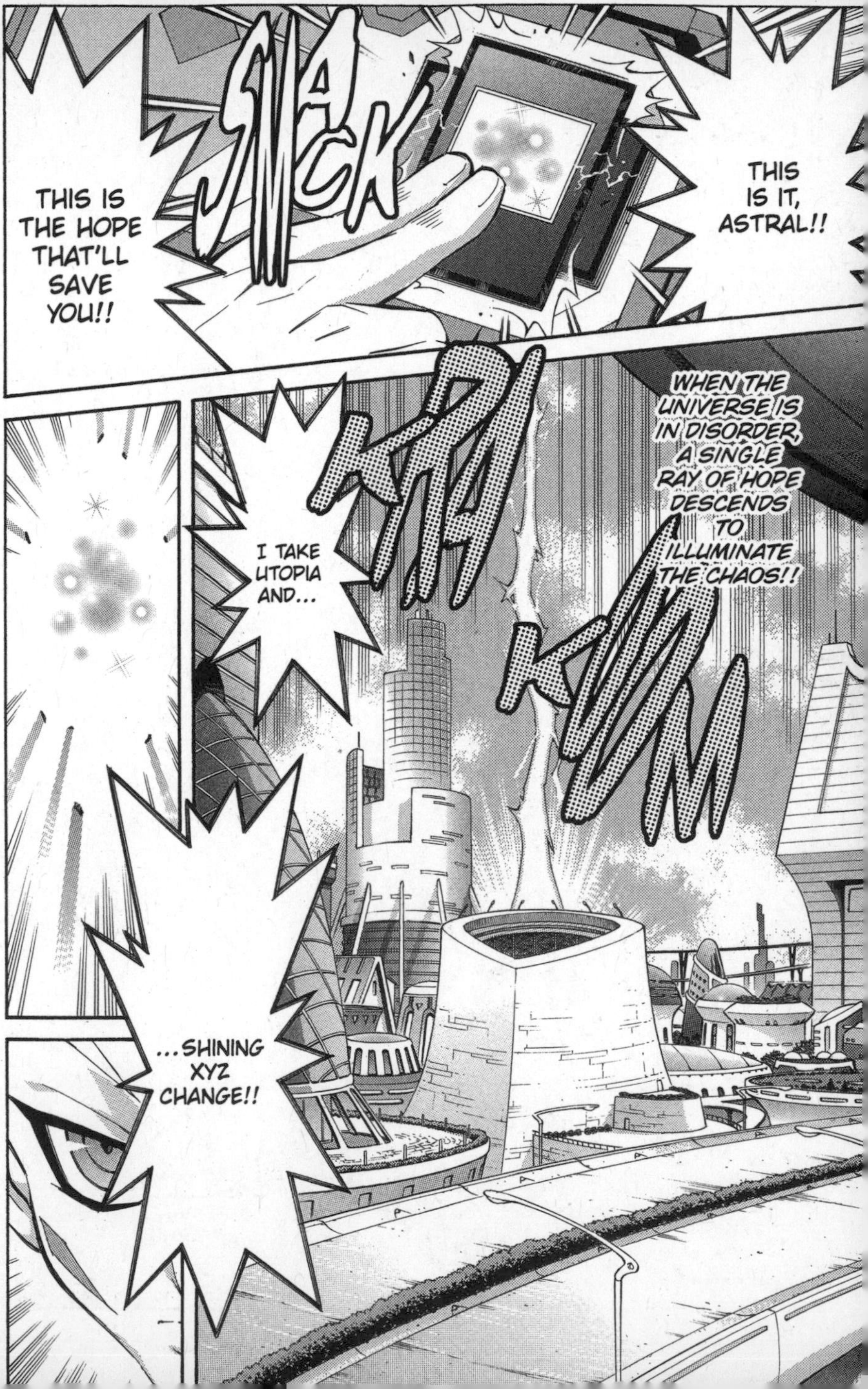
THIS IS IT, ASTRAL!!
SNACK
THIS IS THE HOPE THAT'LL SAVE YOU!!
WHEN THE UNIVERSE IS IN DISORDER, A SINGLE RAY OF HOPE DESCENDS TO ILLUMINATE THE CHAOS!!
I TAKE UTOPIA AND...
...SHINING XYZ CHANGE!!

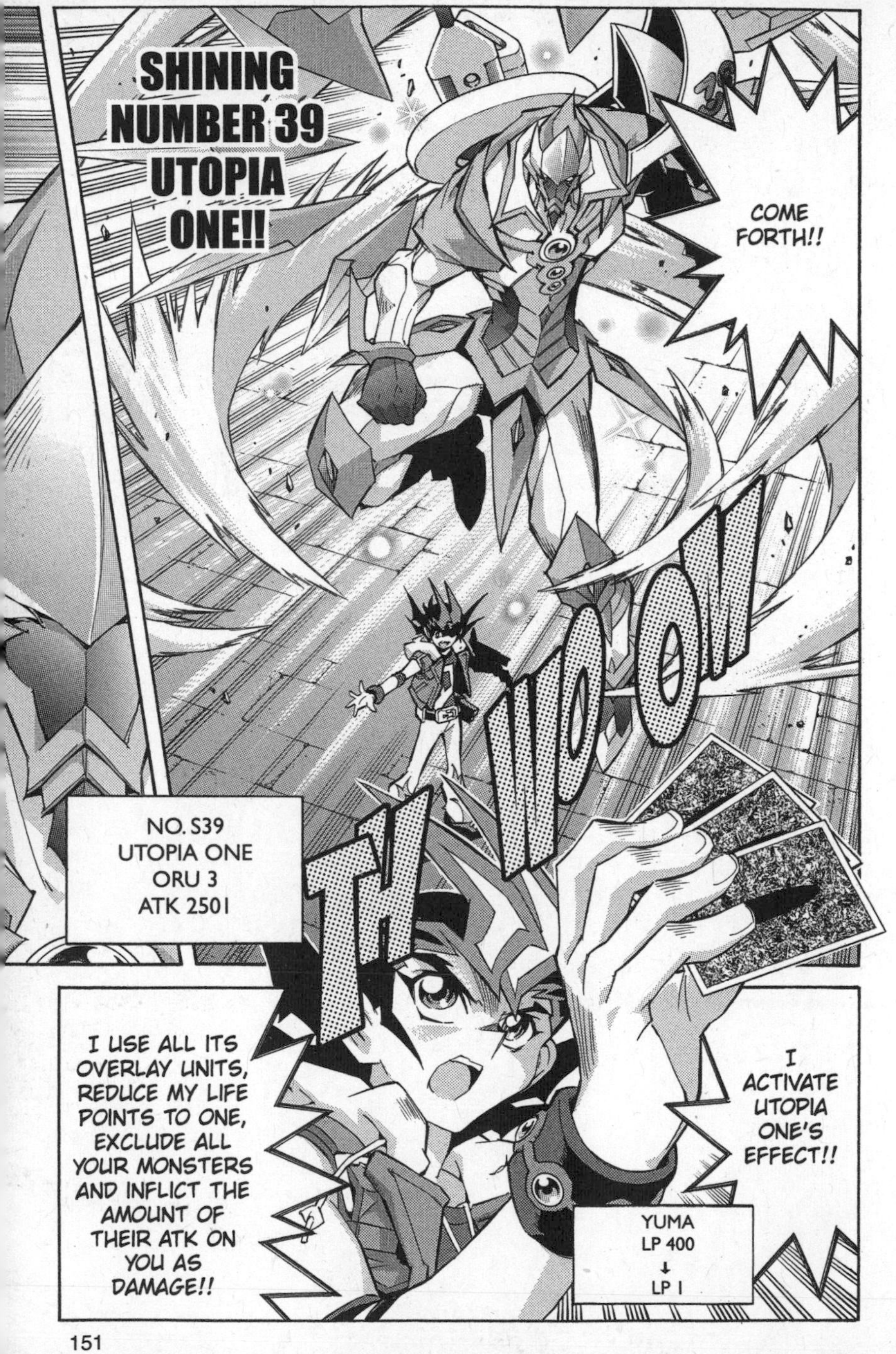
COME FORTH!!
SHINING NUMBER 39 UTOPIA ONE!!
THWOO-OM
NO. S39 UTOPIA ONE ORU 3 ATK 2501
I ACTIVATE UTOPIA ONE'S EFFECT!!
YUMA LP 400 ↓ LP 1
I USE ALL ITS OVERLAY UNITS, REDUCE MY LIFE POINTS TO ONE, EXCLUDE ALL YOUR MONSTERS AND INFLICT THE AMOUNT OF THEIR ATK ON YOU AS DAMAGE!!

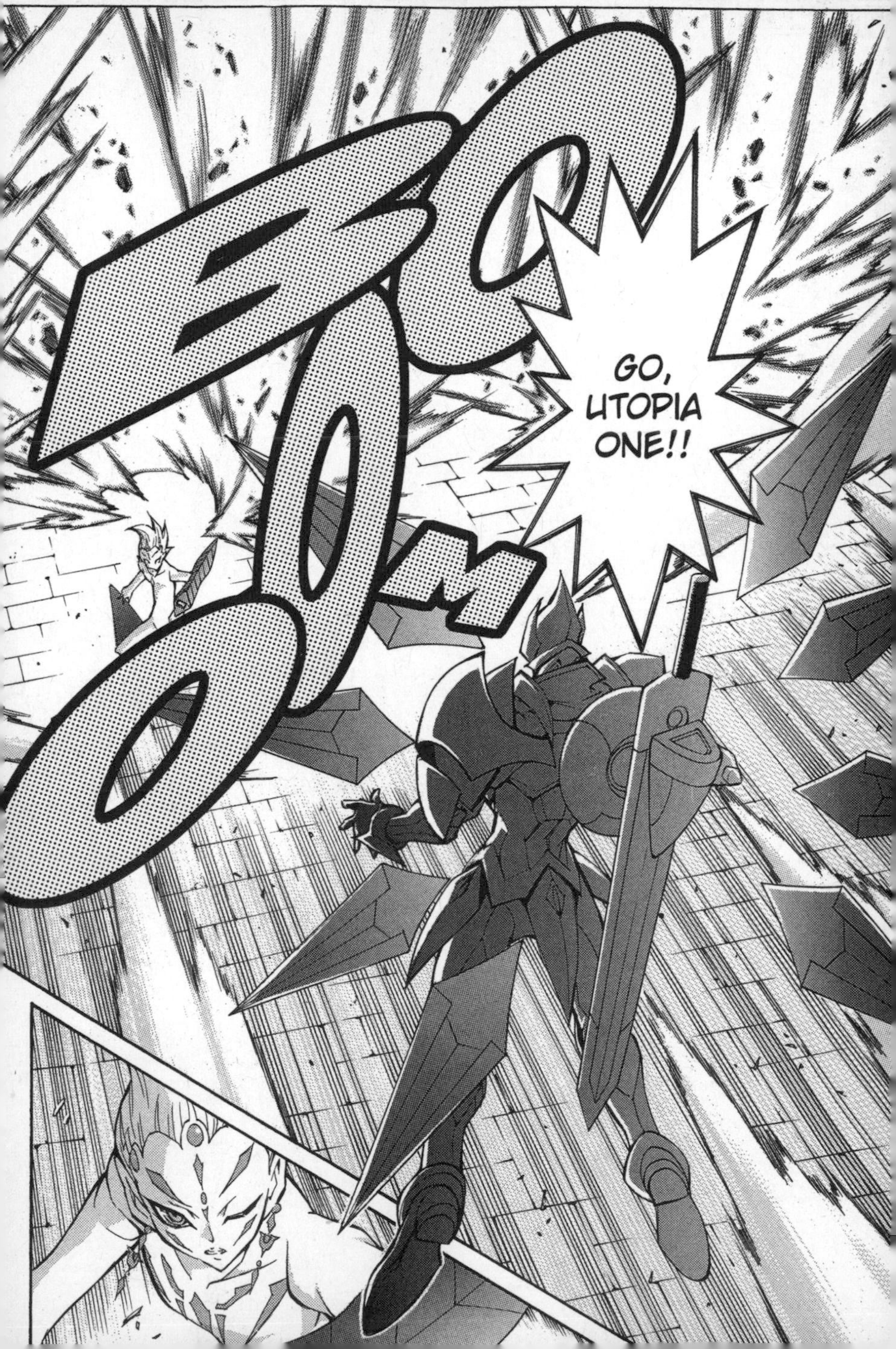
GO, UTOPIA ONE!!

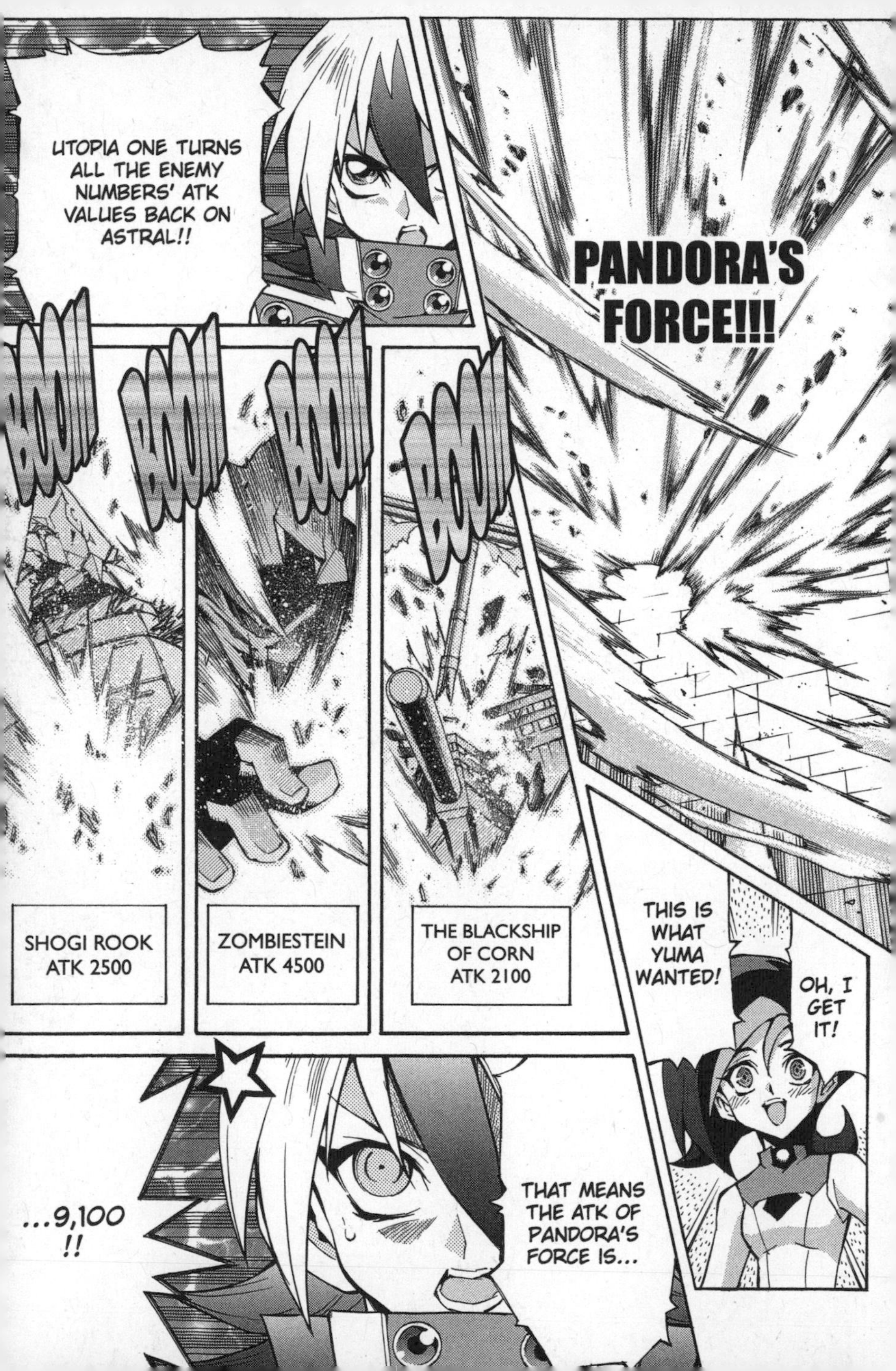
PANDORA'S FORCE!!!
UTOPIA ONE TURNS ALL THE ENEMY NUMBERS' ATK VALUES BACK ON ASTRAL!!
BOOM!!
THE BLACKSHIP OF CORN ATK 2100
BOOM!!
BOOM!!
ZOMBIESTEIN ATK 4500
BOOM!!
SHOGI ROOK ATK 2500
THIS IS WHAT YUMA WANTED!
OH, I GET IT!
THAT MEANS THE ATK OF PANDORA'S FORCE IS...
...9,100 !!

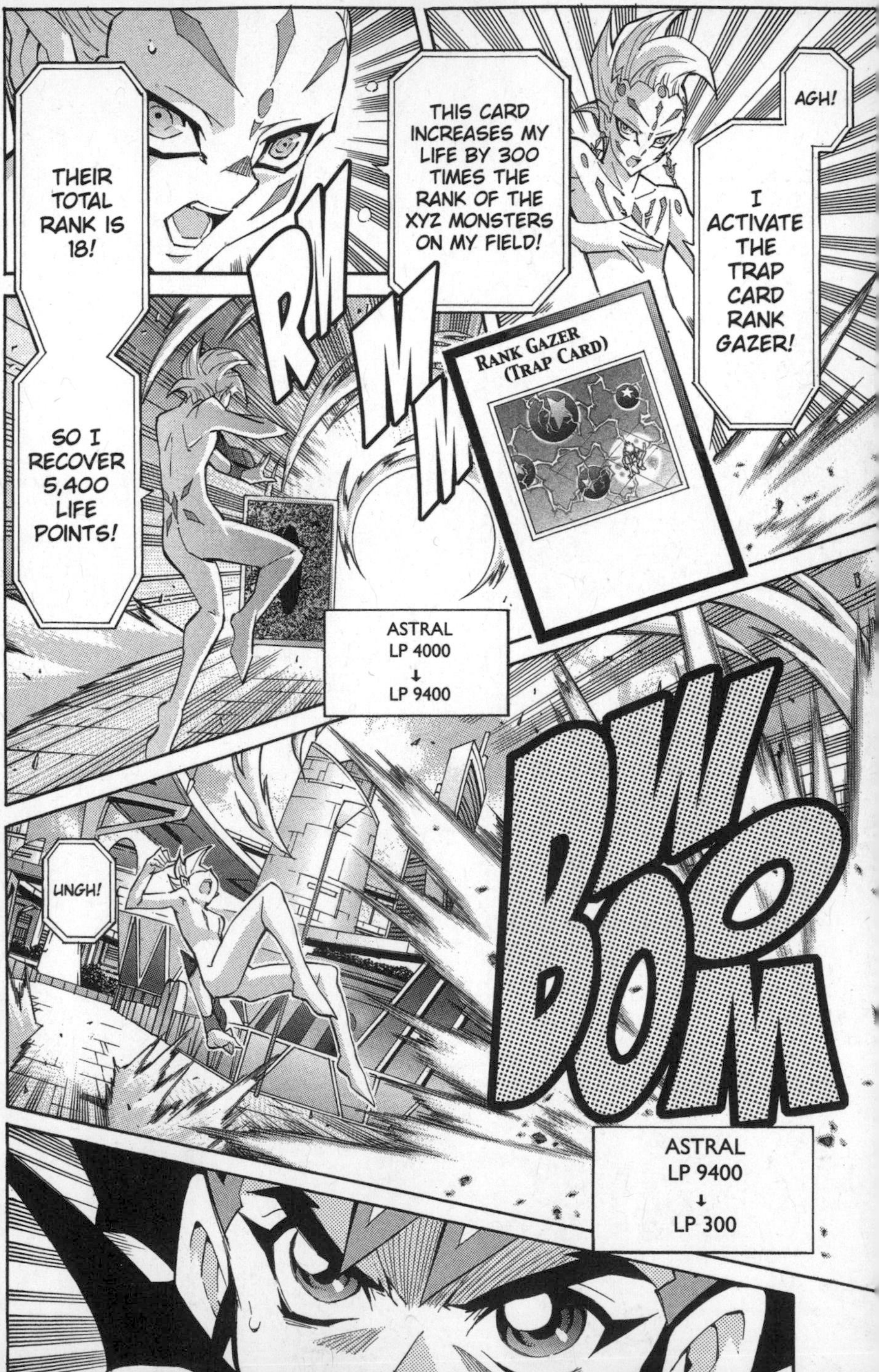
AGH!
I ACTIVATE THE TRAP CARD RANK GAZER!
THIS CARD INCREASES MY LIFE BY 300 TIMES THE RANK OF THE XYZ MONSTERS ON MY FIELD!
THEIR TOTAL RANK IS 18!
RANK GAZER (TRAP CARD)
RMMM
SO I RECOVER 5,400 LIFE POINTS!
ASTRAL LP 4000 ↓ LP 9400
BOOM
UNGH!
ASTRAL LP 9400 ↓ LP 300

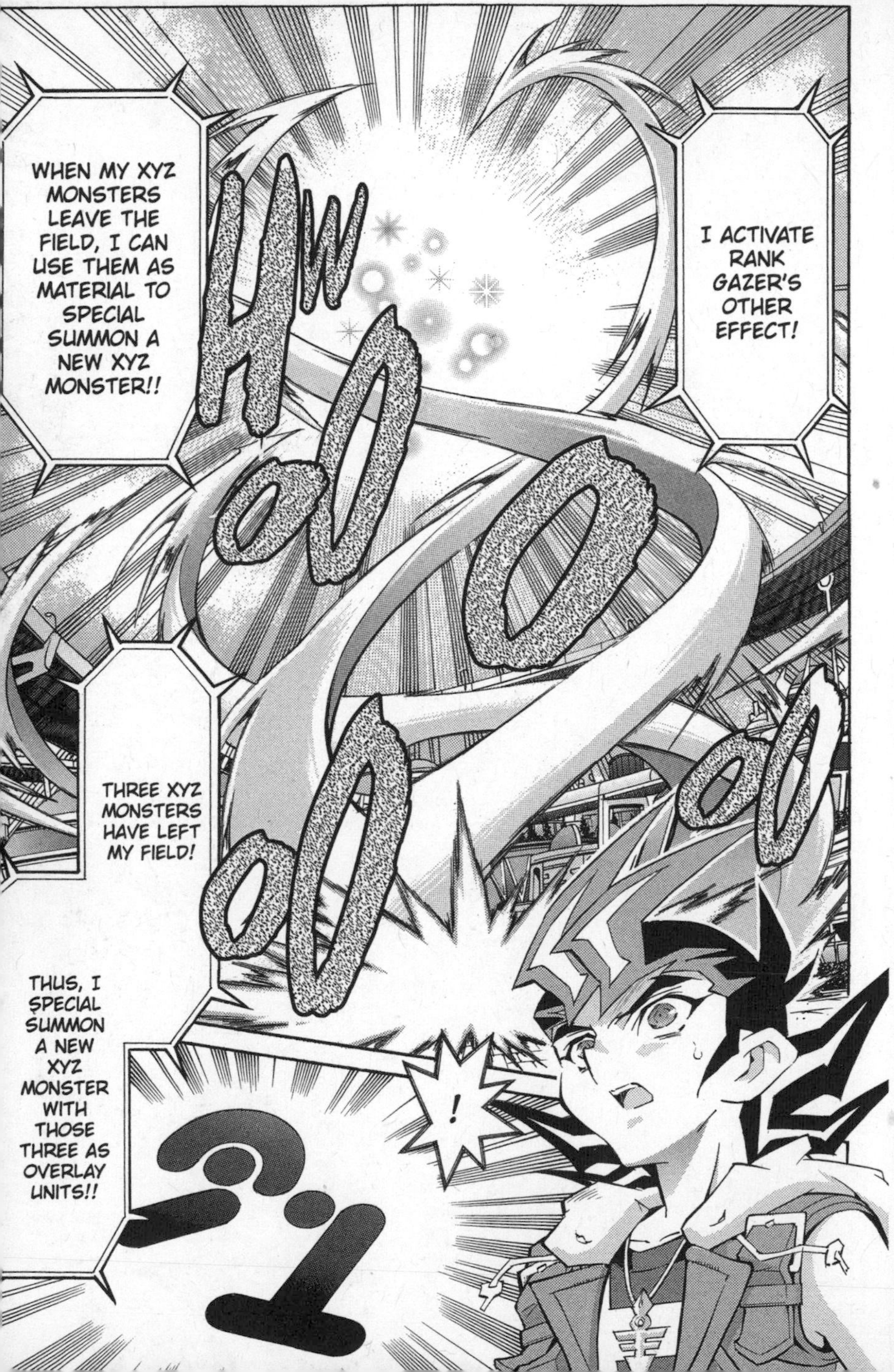
I ACTIVATE RANK GAZER'S OTHER EFFECT!
WHEN MY XYZ MONSTERS LEAVE THE FIELD, I CAN USE THEM AS MATERIAL TO SPECIAL SUMMON A NEW XYZ MONSTER!!
HWOOOOOOO
THREE XYZ MONSTERS HAVE LEFT MY FIELD!
!
THUS, I SPECIAL SUMMON A NEW XYZ MONSTER WITH THOSE THREE AS OVERLAY UNITS!!
?!

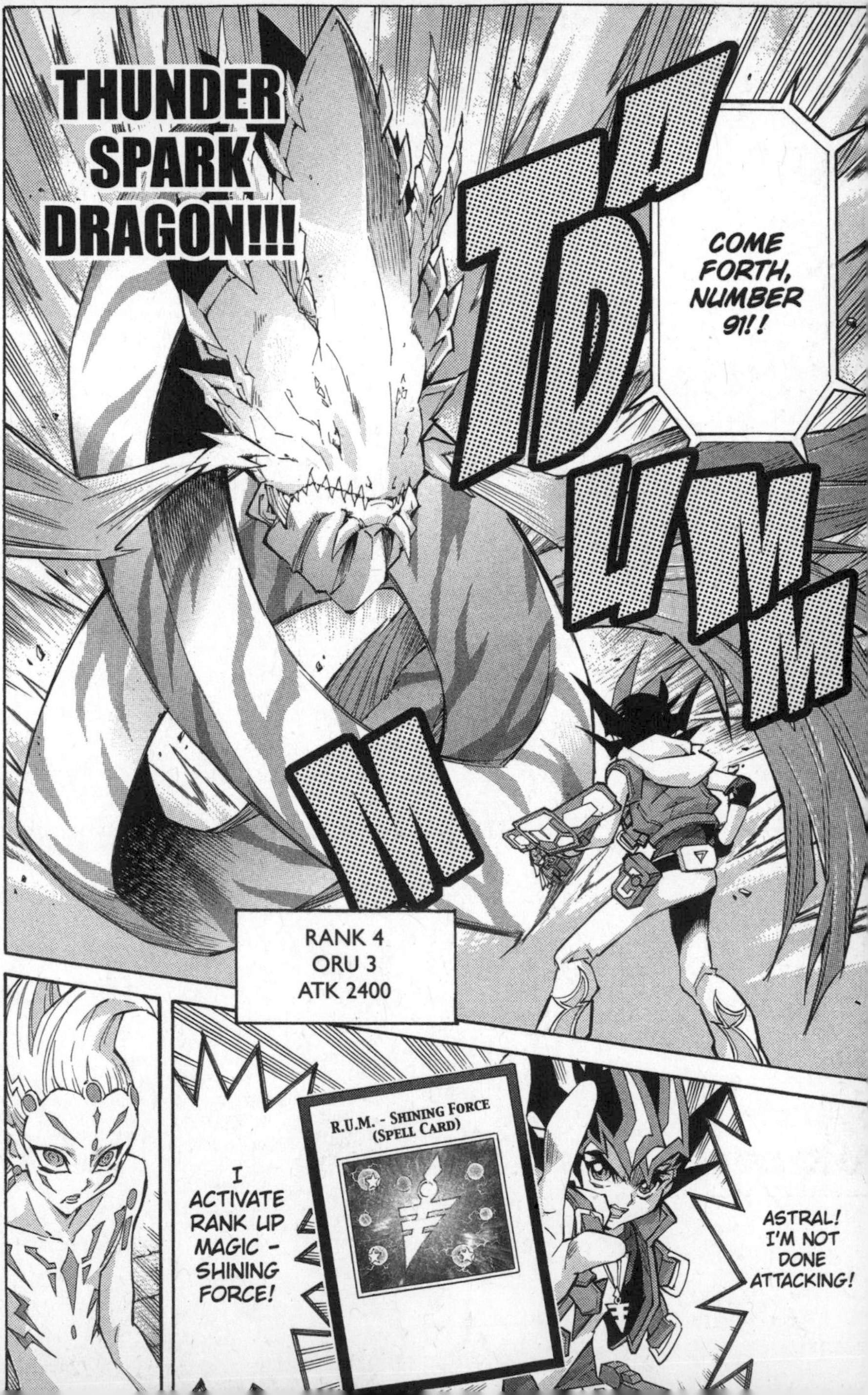
COME FORTH, NUMBER 91!!
TDAWMM
THUNDER SPARK DRAGON!!!
RANK 4
ORU 3
ATK 2400
ASTRAL! I'M NOT DONE ATTACKING!
R.U.M. - SHINING FORCE
(SPELL CARD)
I ACTIVATE RANK UP MAGIC - SHINING FORCE!

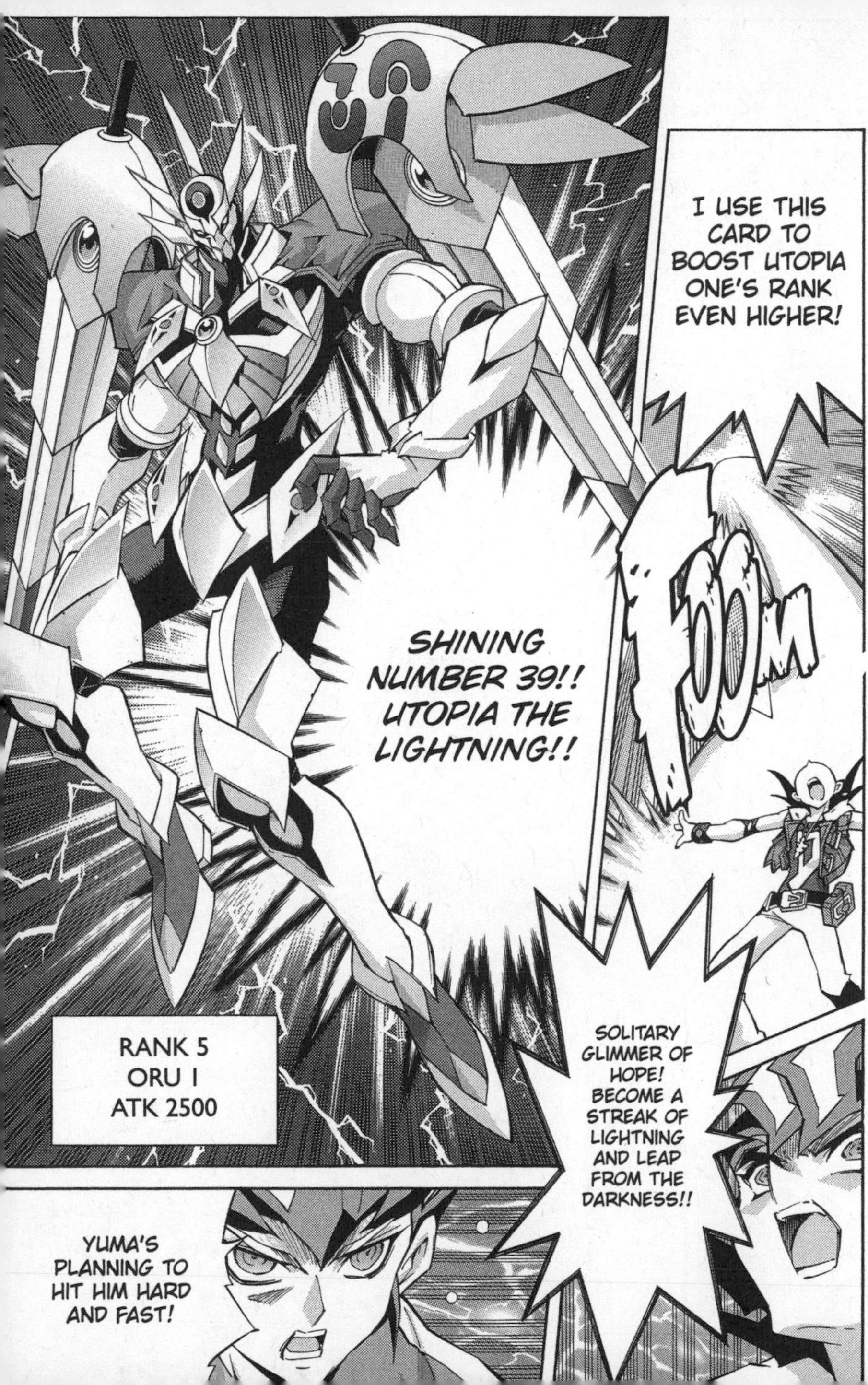
I USE THIS CARD TO BOOST UTOPIA ONE'S RANK EVEN HIGHER!
BOOM
SHINING NUMBER 39!! UTOPIA THE LIGHTNING!!
SOLITARY GLIMMER OF HOPE! BECOME A STREAK OF LIGHTNING AND LEAP FROM THE DARKNESS!!
RANK 5
ORU 1
ATK 2500
YUMA'S PLANNING TO HIT HIM HARD AND FAST!

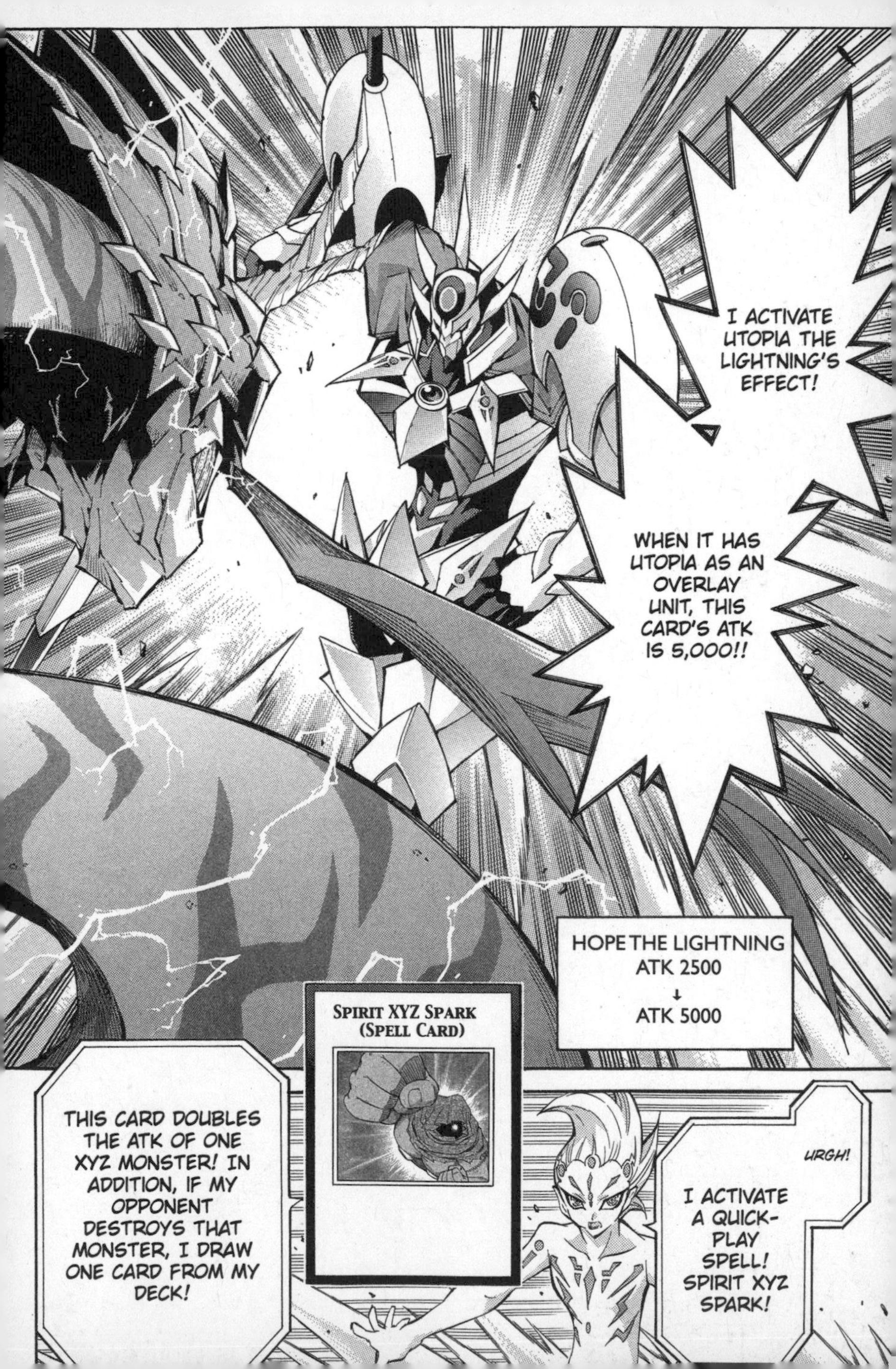
I ACTIVATE UTOPIA THE LIGHTNING'S EFFECT!
WHEN IT HAS UTOPIA AS AN OVERLAY UNIT, THIS CARD'S ATK IS 5,000!!
HOPE THE LIGHTNING ATK 2500 ↓ ATK 5000
URGH!
I ACTIVATE A QUICK-PLAY SPELL! SPIRIT XYZ SPARK!
SPIRIT XYZ SPARK (SPELL CARD)
THIS CARD DOUBLES THE ATK OF ONE XYZ MONSTER! IN ADDITION, IF MY OPPONENT DESTROYS THAT MONSTER, I DRAW ONE CARD FROM MY DECK!

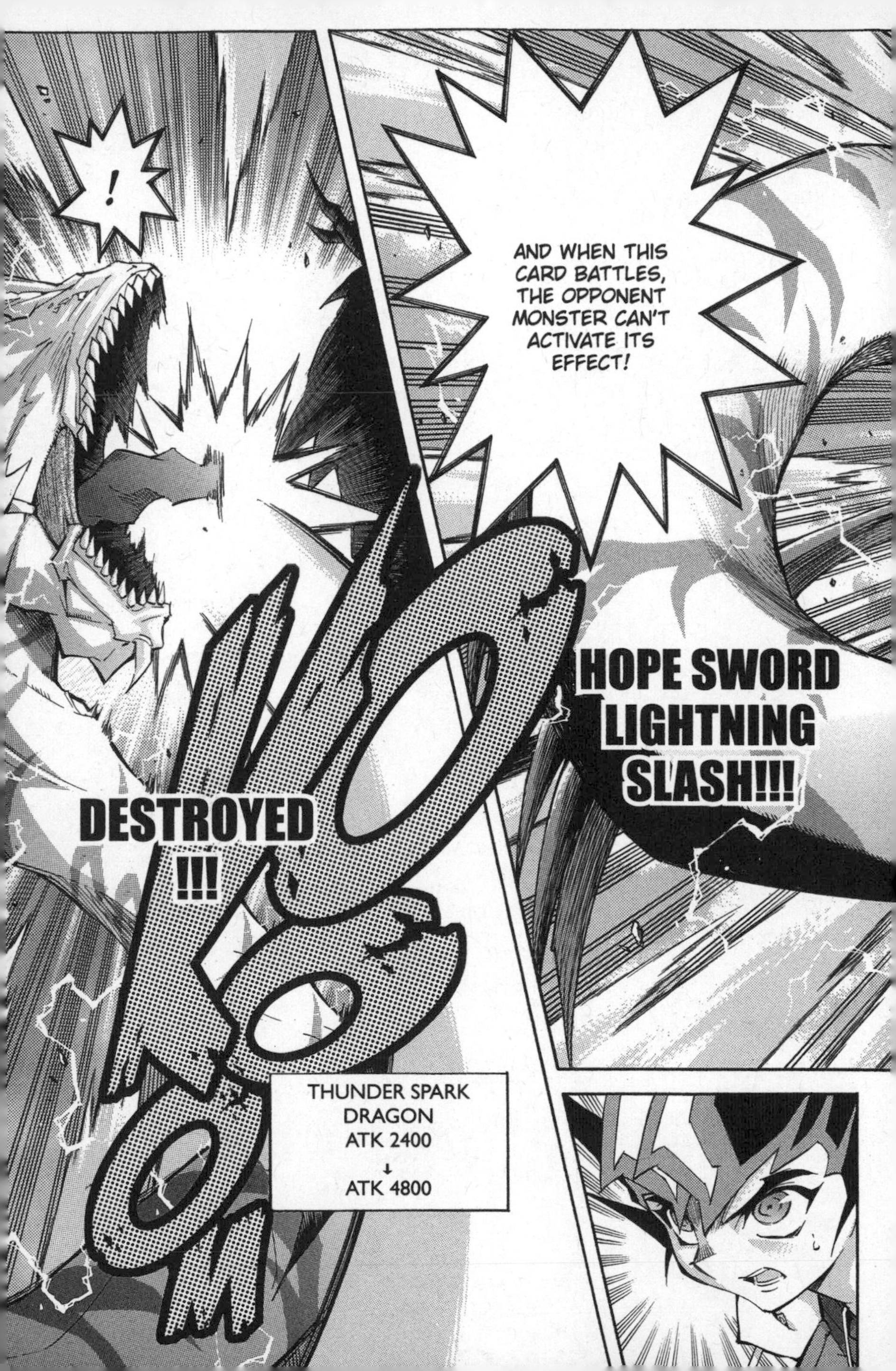
AND WHEN THIS CARD BATTLES, THE OPPONENT MONSTER CAN'T ACTIVATE ITS EFFECT!
HOPE SWORD LIGHTNING SLASH!!!
!
DESTROYED !!!
THUNDER SPARK DRAGON ATK 2400 ↓ ATK 4800

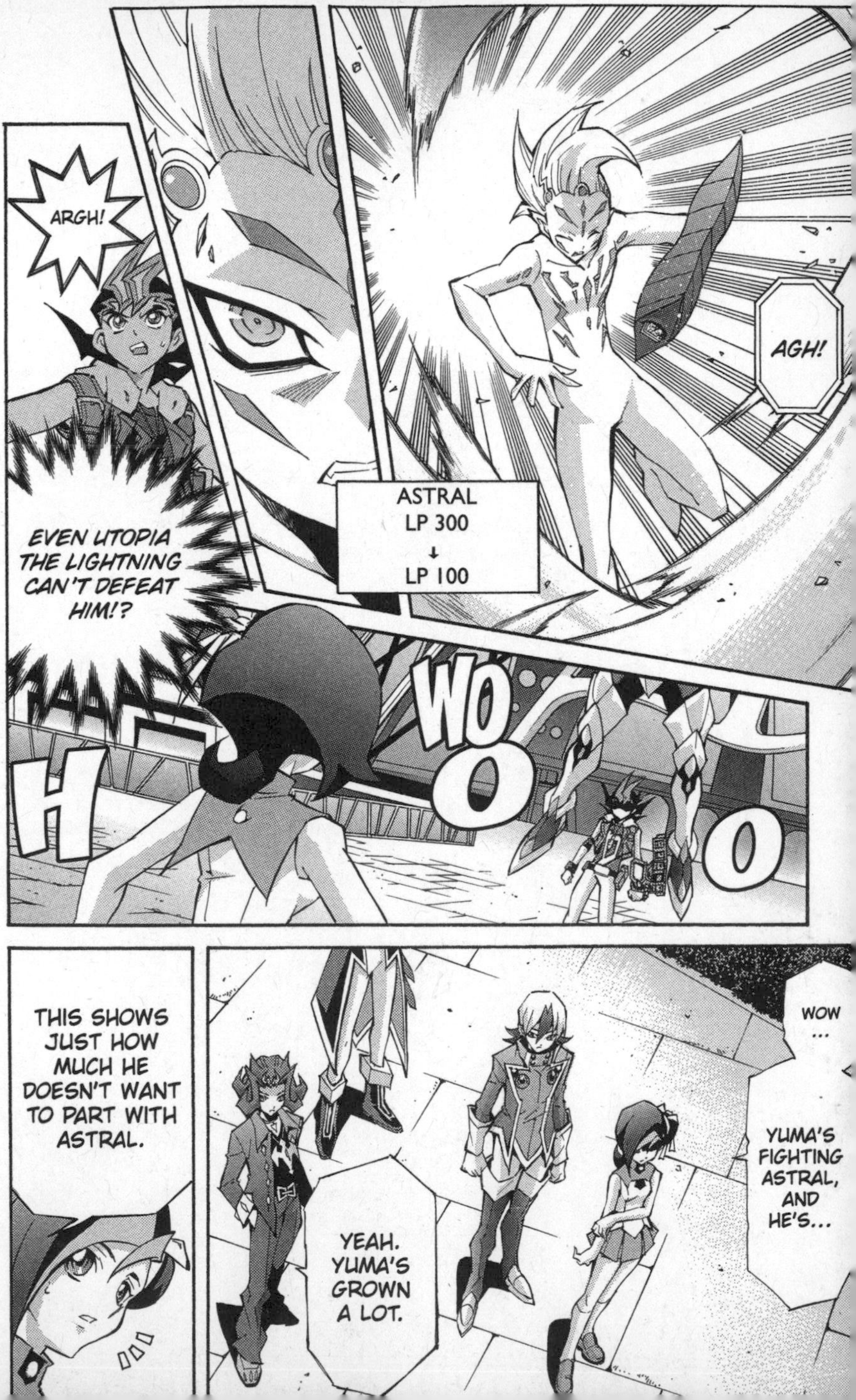
AGH!
ASTRAL
LP 300
↓
LP 100
ARGH!
EVEN UTOPIA THE LIGHTNING CAN'T DEFEAT HIM!?
WOOOH
WOW…
YUMA'S FIGHTING ASTRAL, AND HE'S…
YEAH. YUMA'S GROWN A LOT.
THIS SHOWS JUST HOW MUCH HE DOESN'T WANT TO PART WITH ASTRAL.

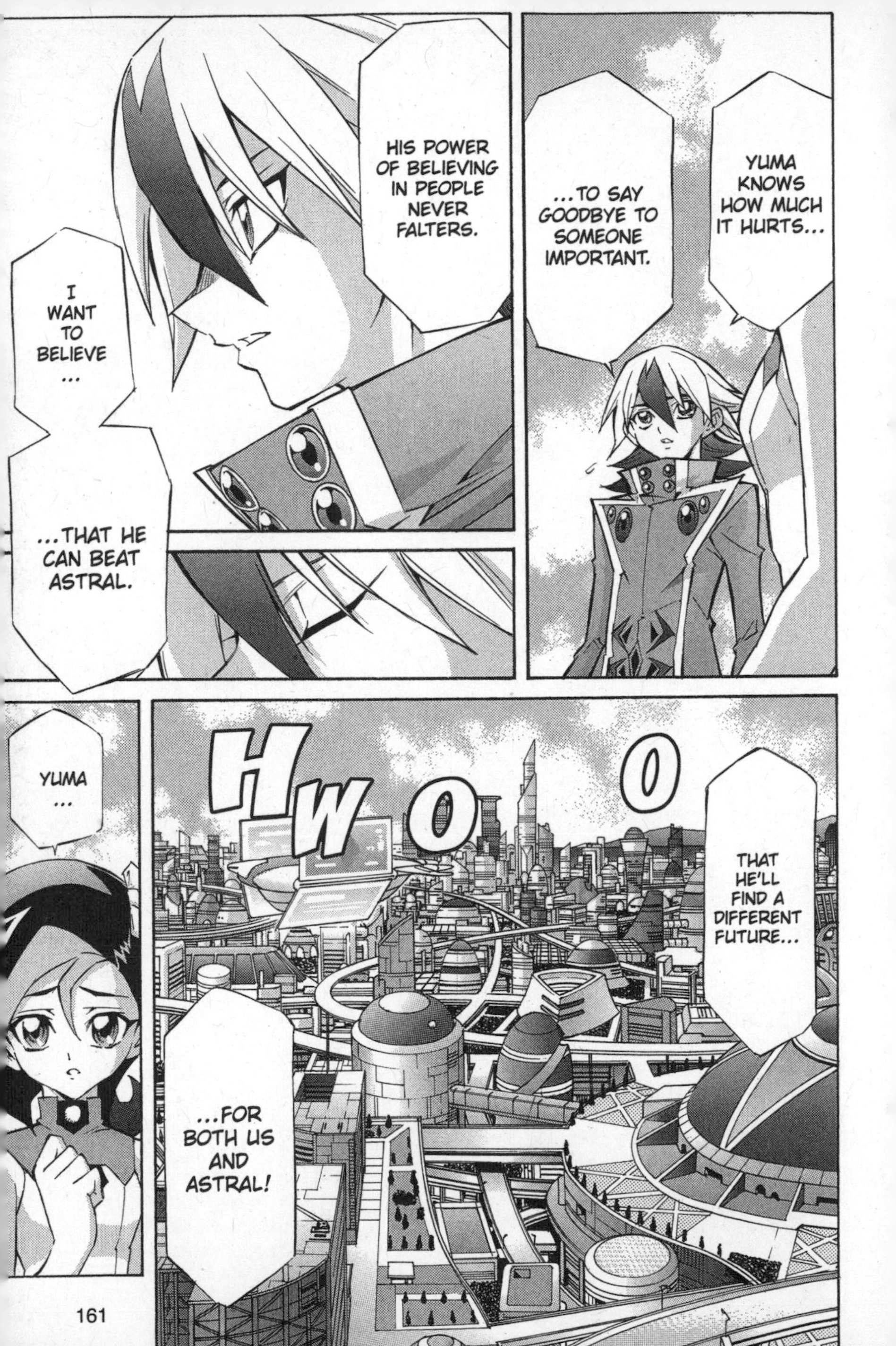
YUMA KNOWS HOW MUCH IT HURTS...
...TO SAY GOODBYE TO SOMEONE IMPORTANT.
HIS POWER OF BELIEVING IN PEOPLE NEVER FALTERS.
I WANT TO BELIEVE ...
...THAT HE CAN BEAT ASTRAL.
THAT HE'LL FIND A DIFFERENT FUTURE...
HWOO
...FOR BOTH US AND ASTRAL!
YUMA ...

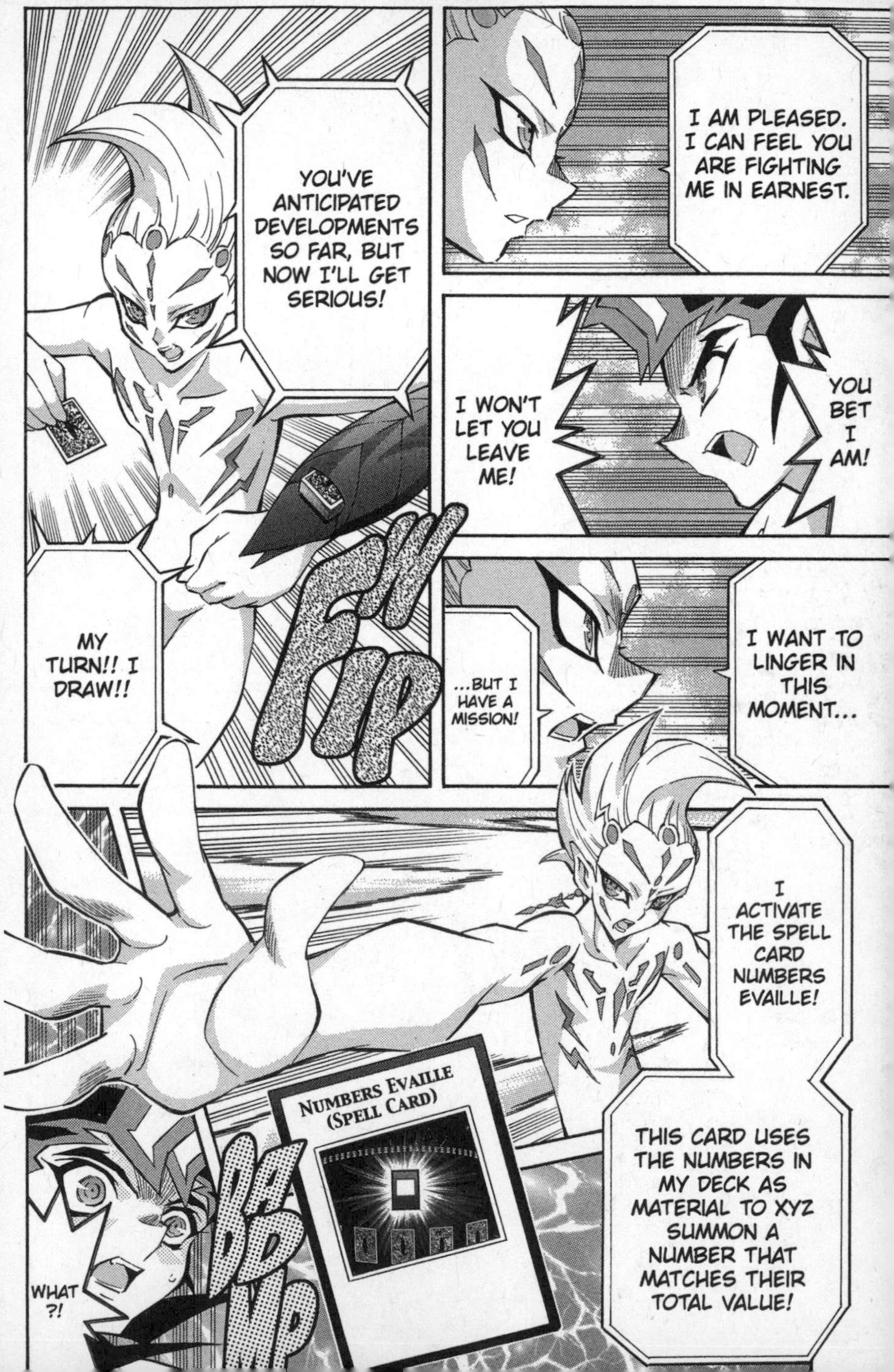
I AM PLEASED. I CAN FEEL YOU ARE FIGHTING ME IN EARNEST.
YOU BET I AM!
I WON'T LET YOU LEAVE ME!
I WANT TO LINGER IN THIS MOMENT...
...BUT I HAVE A MISSION!
YOU'VE ANTICIPATED DEVELOPMENTS SO FAR, BUT NOW I'LL GET SERIOUS!
MY TURN!! I DRAW!!
I ACTIVATE THE SPELL CARD NUMBERS EVAILLE!
THIS CARD USES THE NUMBERS IN MY DECK AS MATERIAL TO XYZ SUMMON A NUMBER THAT MATCHES THEIR TOTAL VALUE!
NUMBERS EVAILLE (SPELL CARD)
WHAT ?!

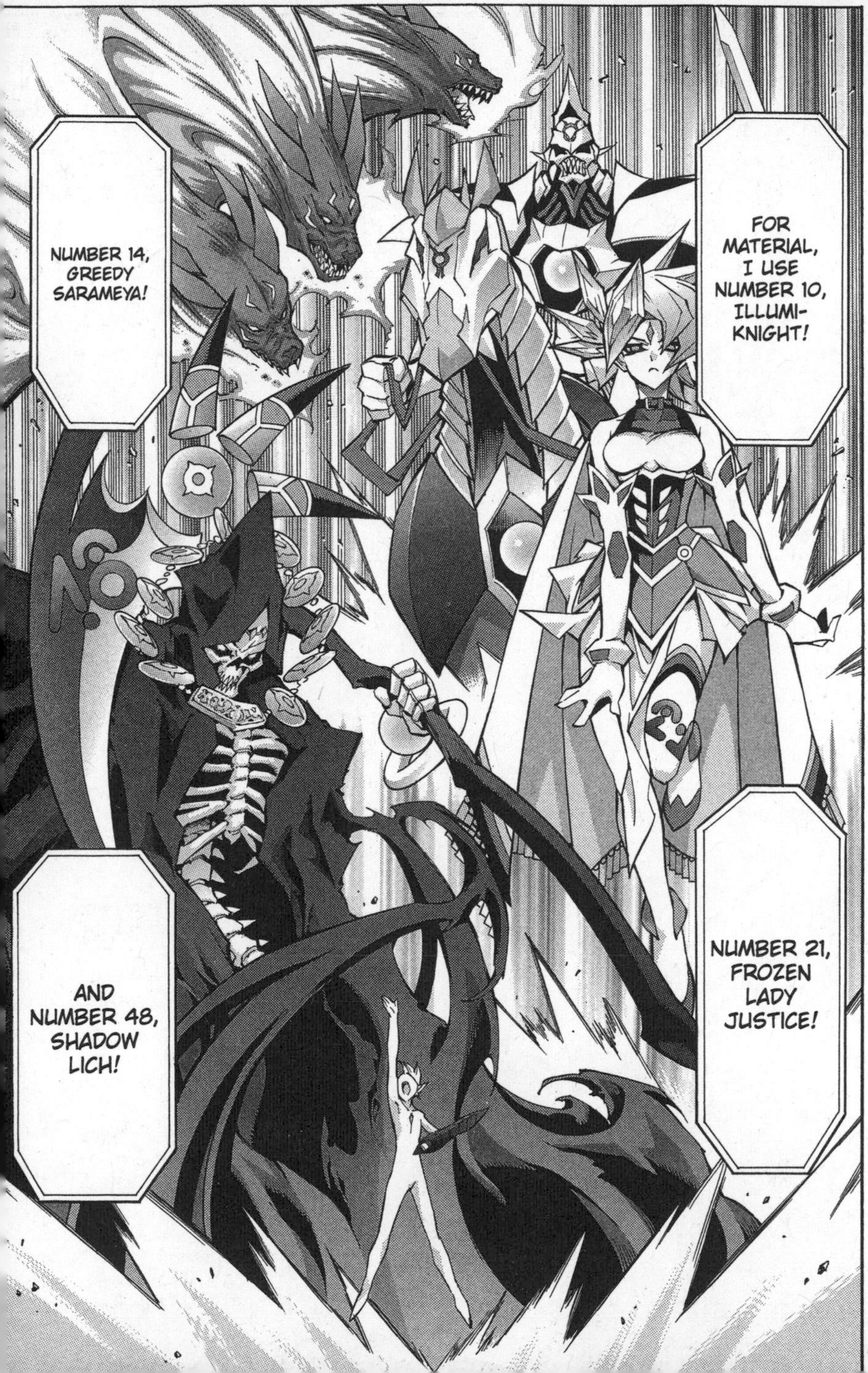
FOR MATERIAL, I USE NUMBER 10, ILLUMI-KNIGHT!
NUMBER 14, GREEDY SARAMEYA!
NUMBER 21, FROZEN LADY JUSTICE!
AND NUMBER 48, SHADOW LICH!

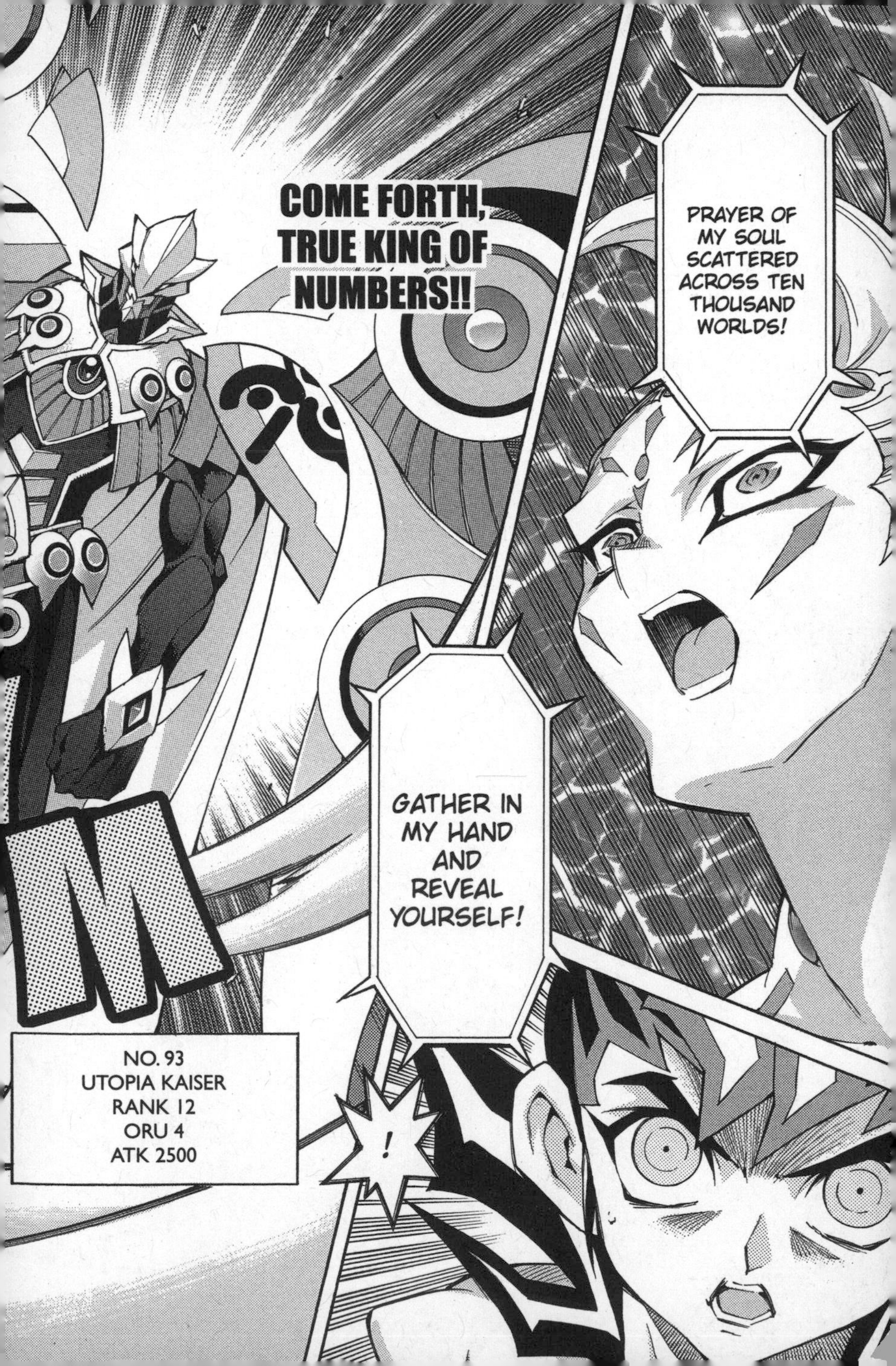
PRAYER OF MY SOUL SCATTERED ACROSS TEN THOUSAND WORLDS!
GATHER IN MY HAND AND REVEAL YOURSELF!
COME FORTH, TRUE KING OF NUMBERS!!
M
NO. 93
UTOPIA KAISER
RANK 12
ORU 4
ATK 2500
!

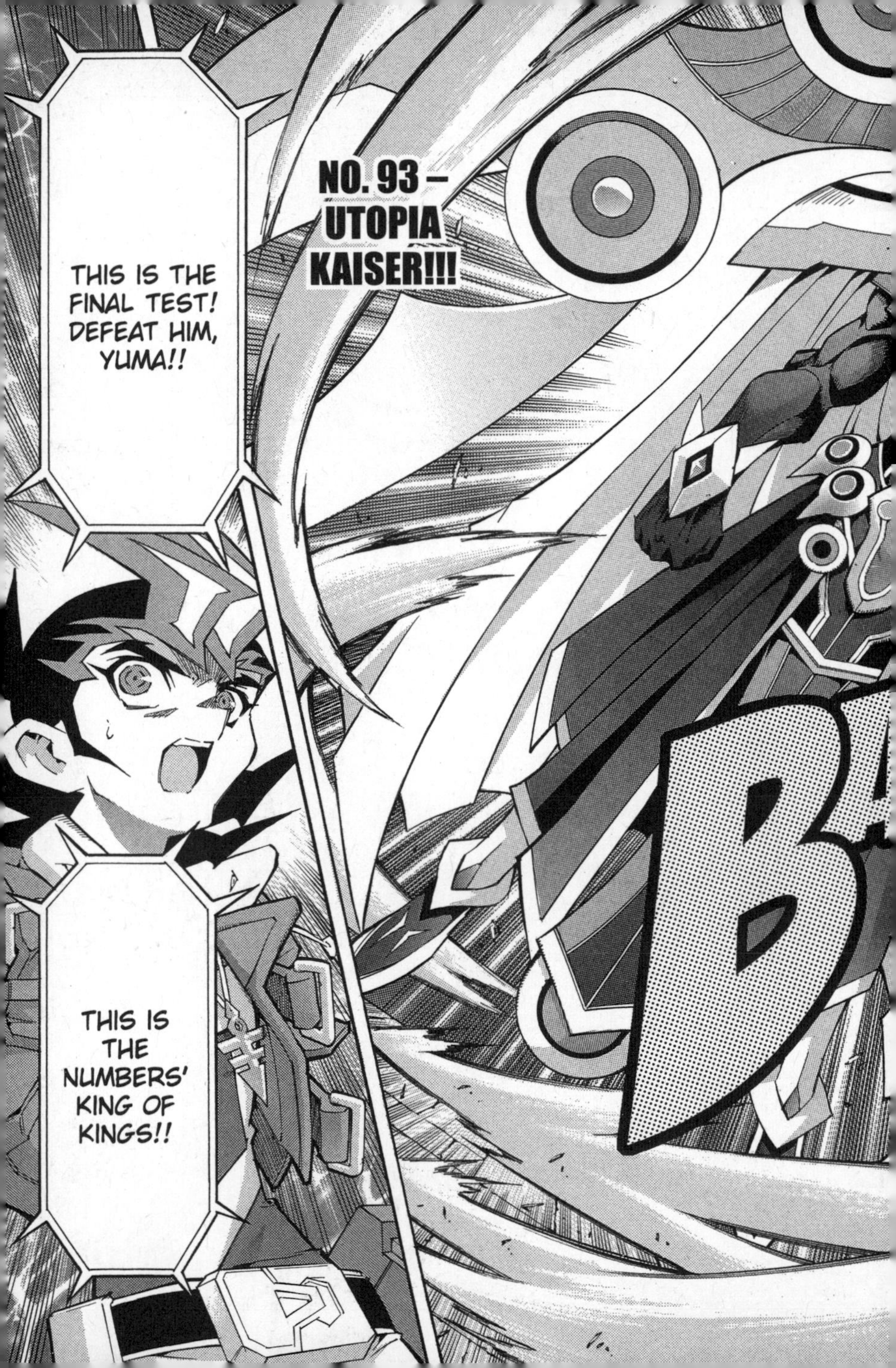
NO. 93 – UTOPIA KAISER!!!
THIS IS THE FINAL TEST! DEFEAT HIM, YUMA!!
B
THIS IS THE NUMBERS' KING OF KINGS!!

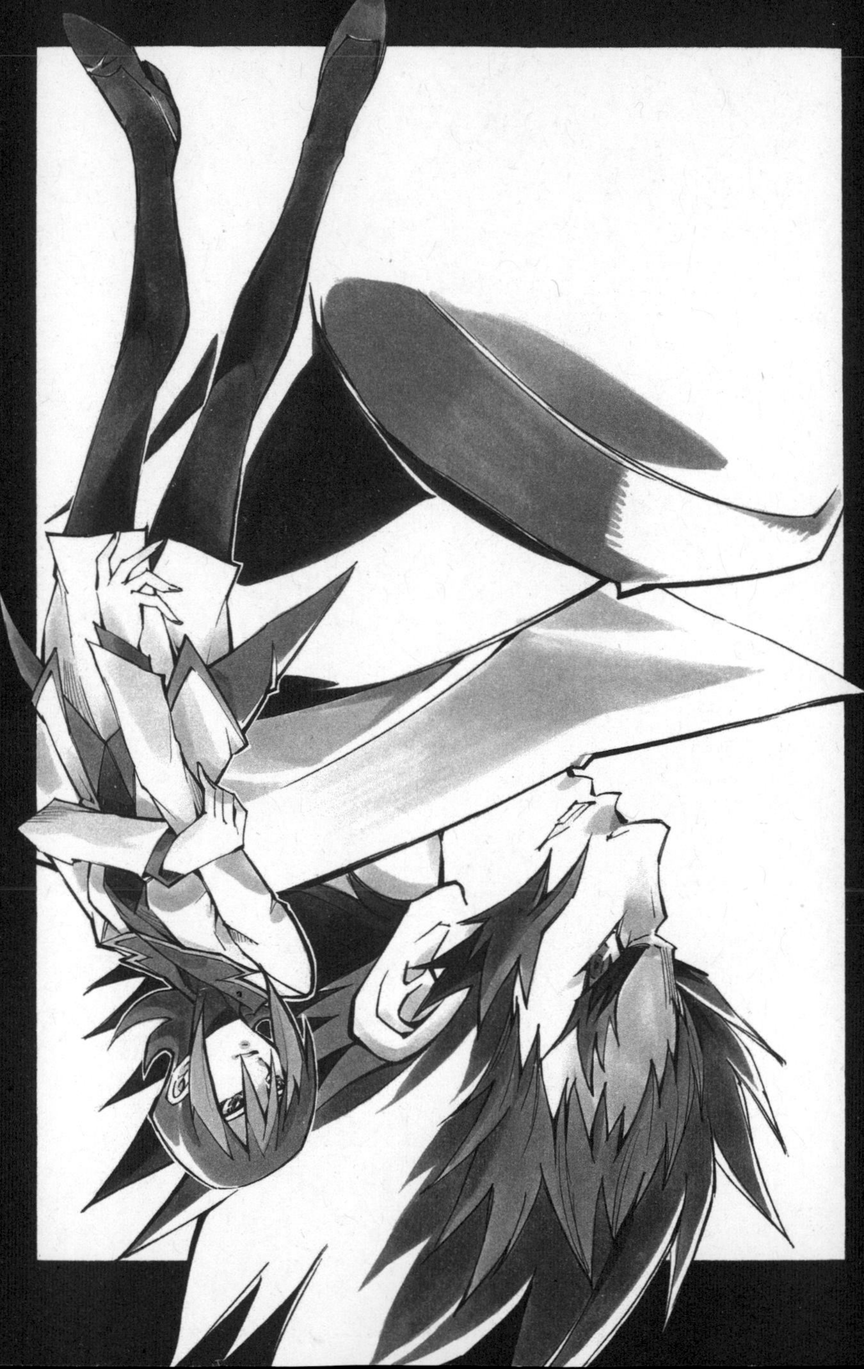

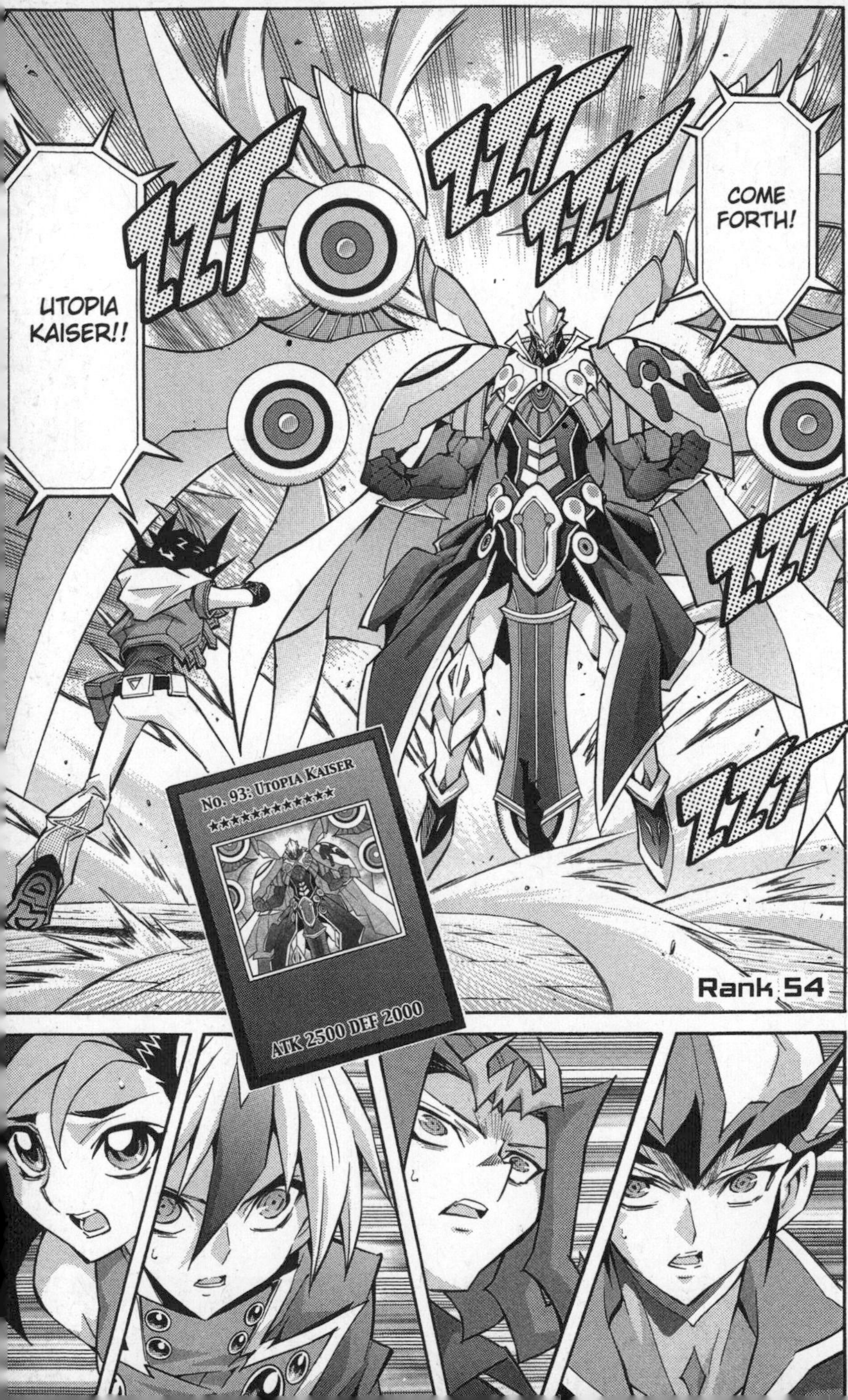
COME FORTH!
ZZZT
ZZZT
ZZZT
UTOPIA KAISER!!
ZZZT
ZZZT
No. 93: Utopia Kaiser
ATK 2500 DEF 2000
Rank 54

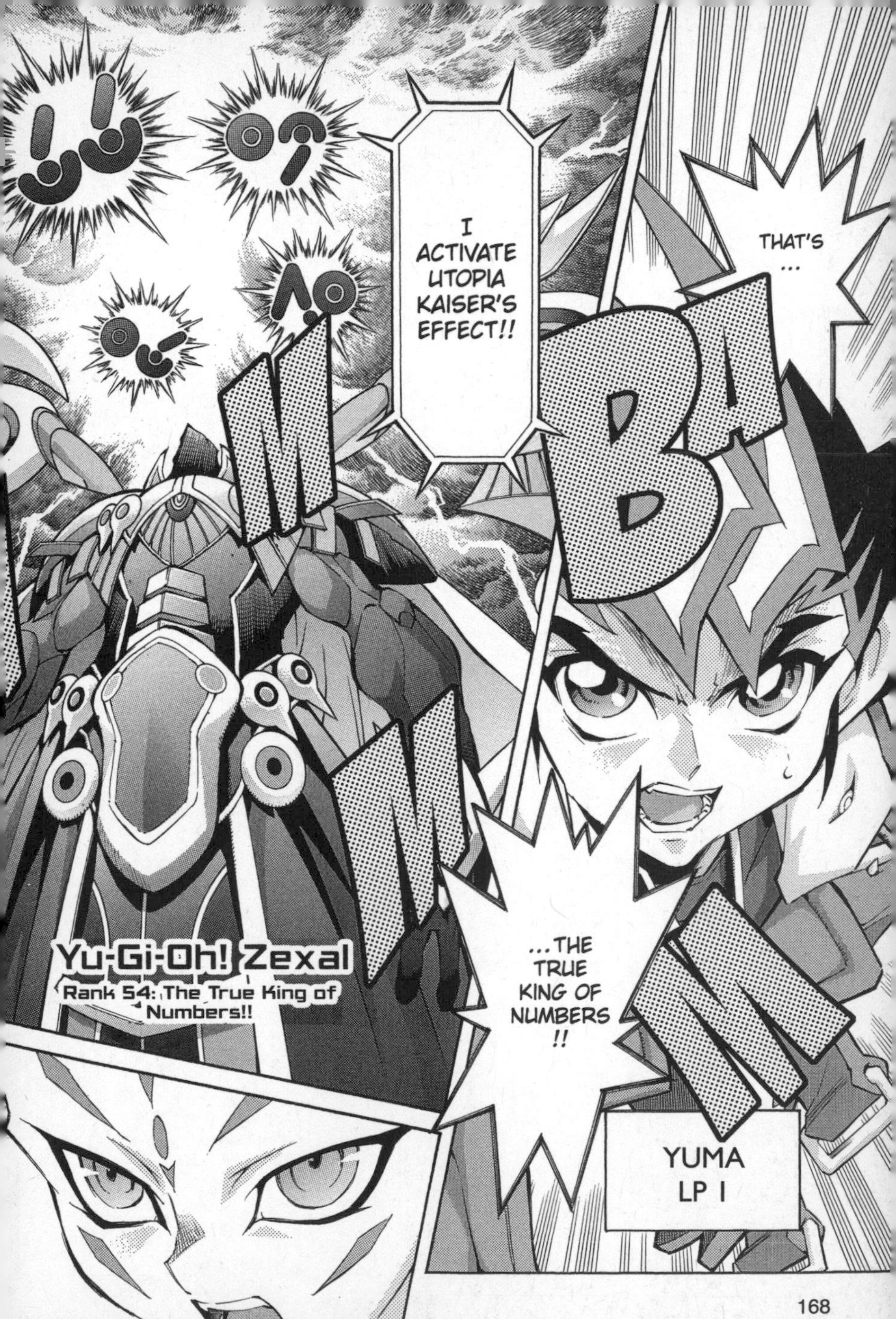
THAT'S ...
I ACTIVATE UTOPIA KAISER'S EFFECT!!
BAMM
...THE TRUE KING OF NUMBERS !!
YUMA LP 1
Yu-Gi-Oh! Zexal
Rank 54: The True King of Numbers!!

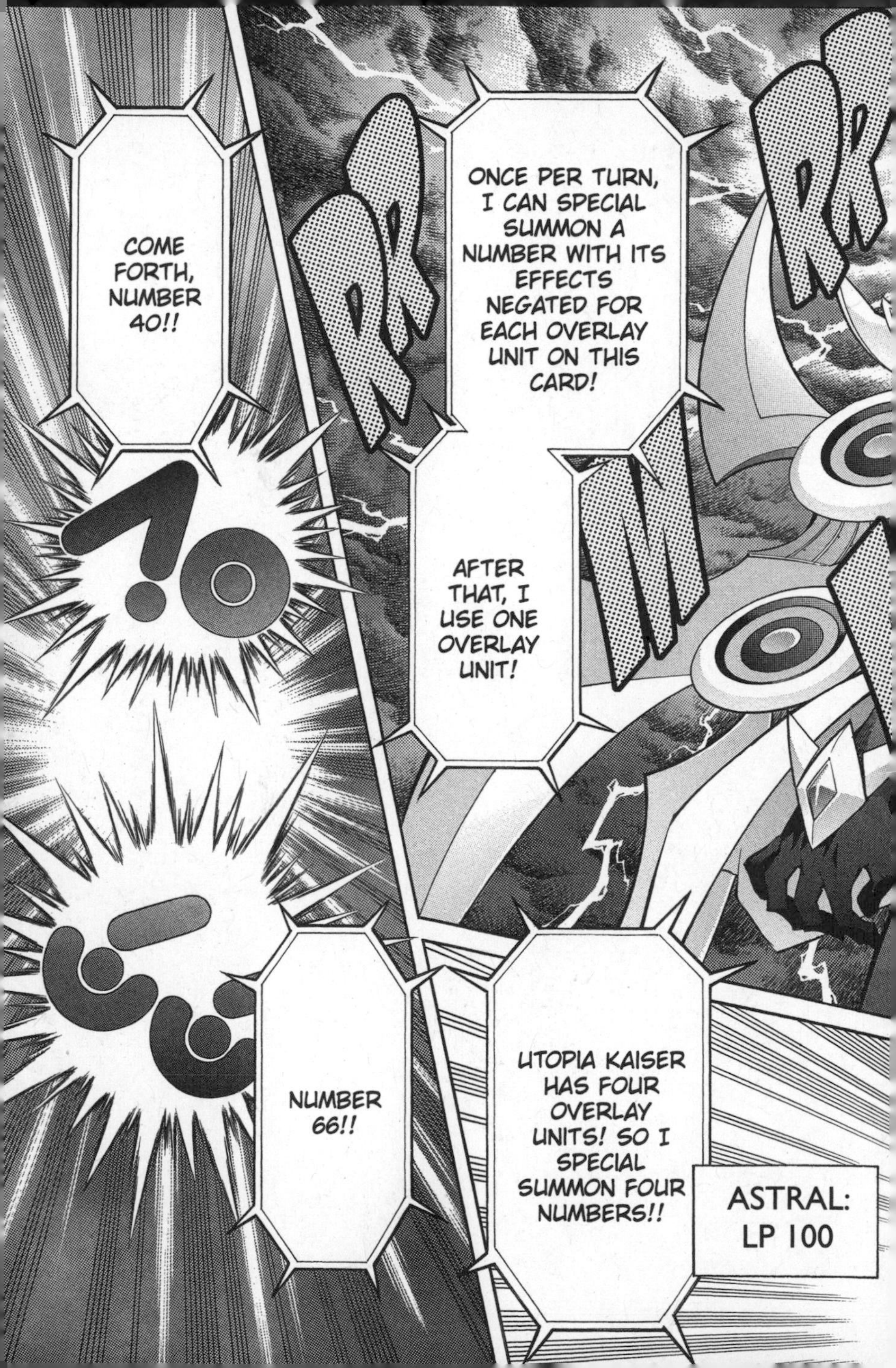
ONCE PER TURN, I CAN SPECIAL SUMMON A NUMBER WITH ITS EFFECTS NEGATED FOR EACH OVERLAY UNIT ON THIS CARD!
AFTER THAT, I USE ONE OVERLAY UNIT!
UTOPIA KAISER HAS FOUR OVERLAY UNITS! SO I SPECIAL SUMMON FOUR NUMBERS!!
ASTRAL: LP 100
COME FORTH, NUMBER 40!!
NUMBER 66!!

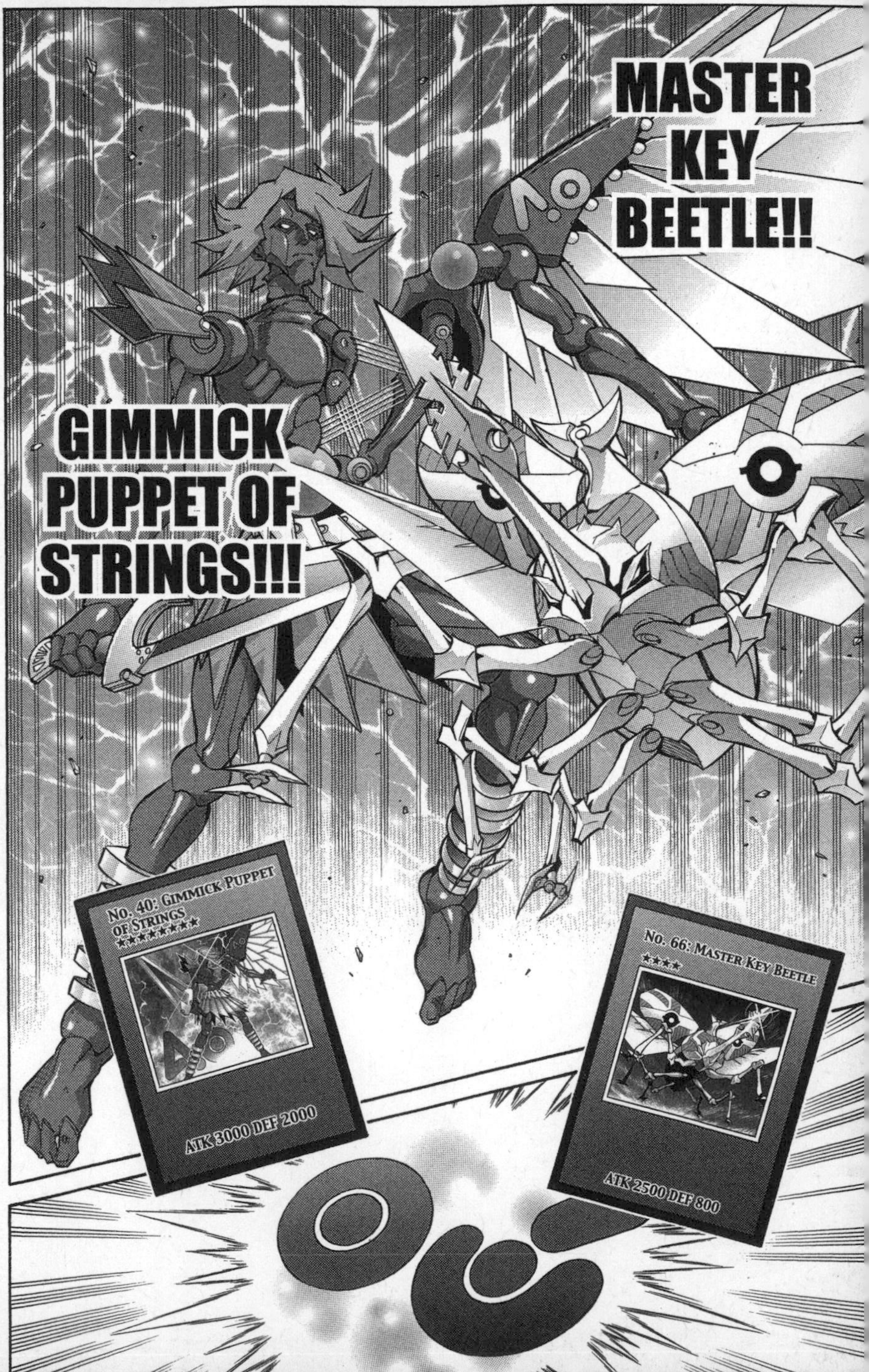
MASTER KEY BEETLE!!
GIMMICK PUPPET OF STRINGS!!!
No. 66: Master Key Beetle
ATK 2500 DEF 800
No. 40: Gimmick Puppet of Strings
ATK 3000 DEF 2000

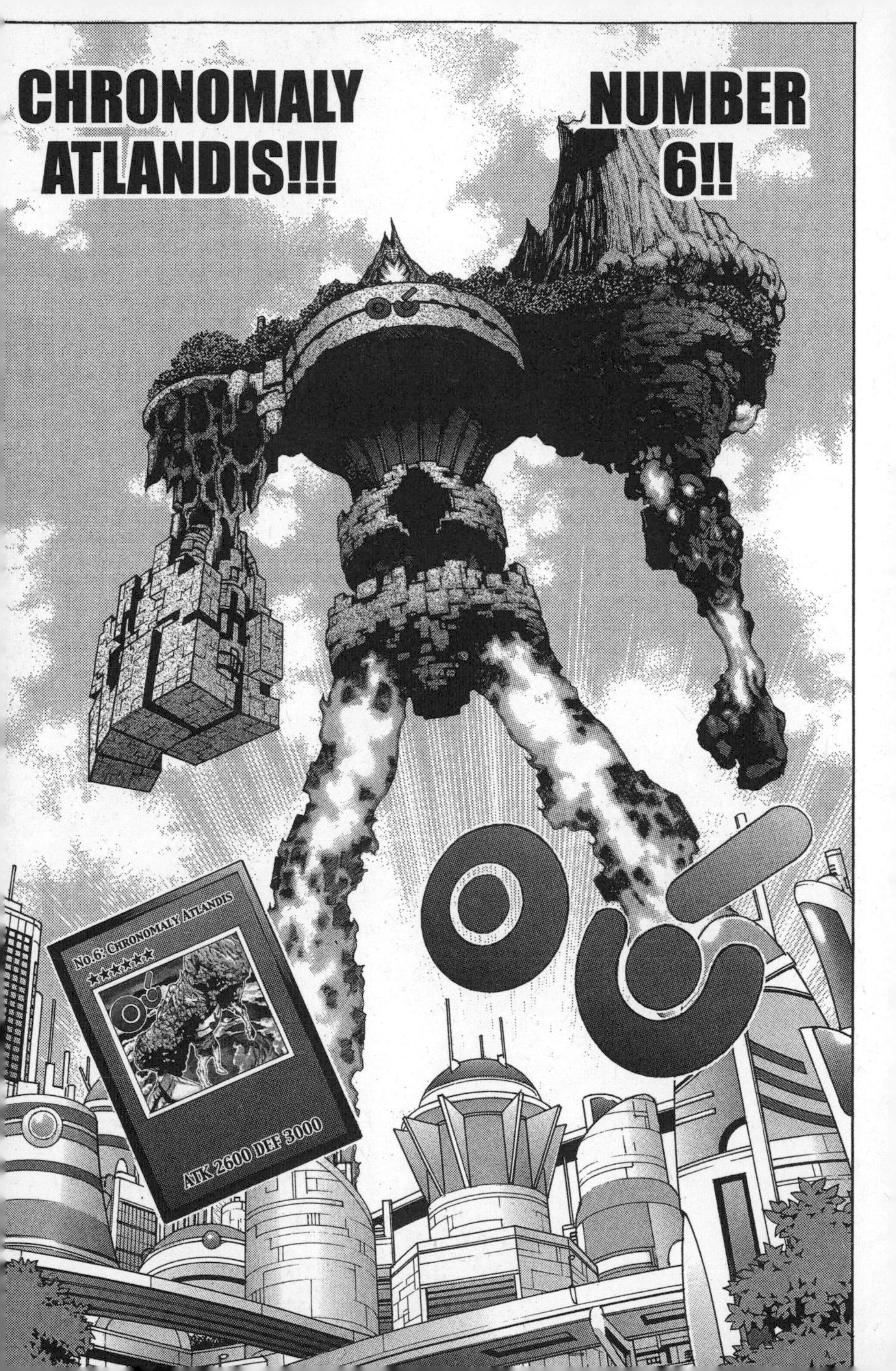
NUMBER 6!!
CHRONOMALY ATLANDIS!!!
No.6: Chronomaly Atlandis
ATK 2600 DEF 3000

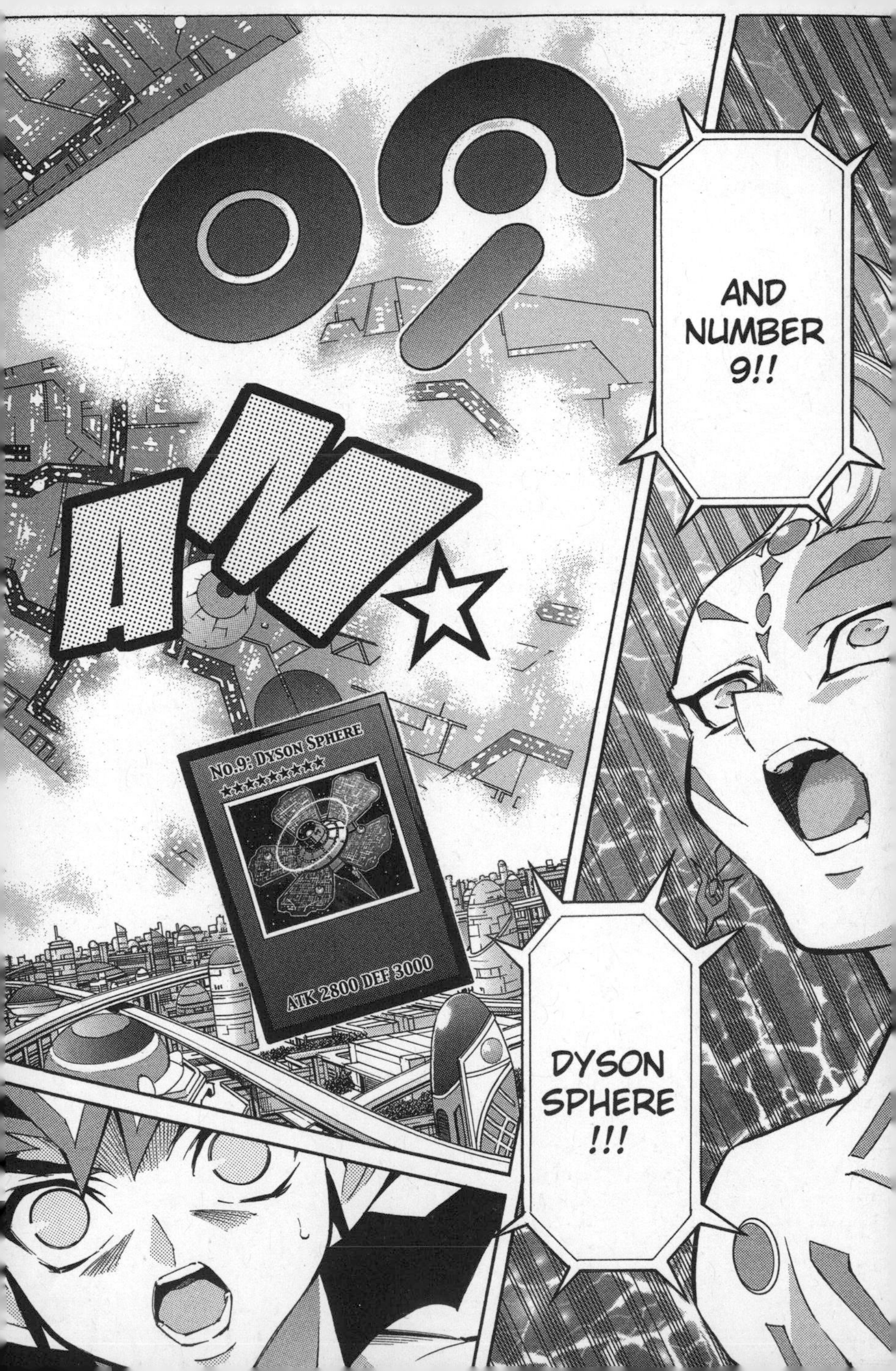
AND NUMBER 9!!
DYSON SPHERE !!!
No.9: DYSON SPHERE
ATK 2800 DEF 3000

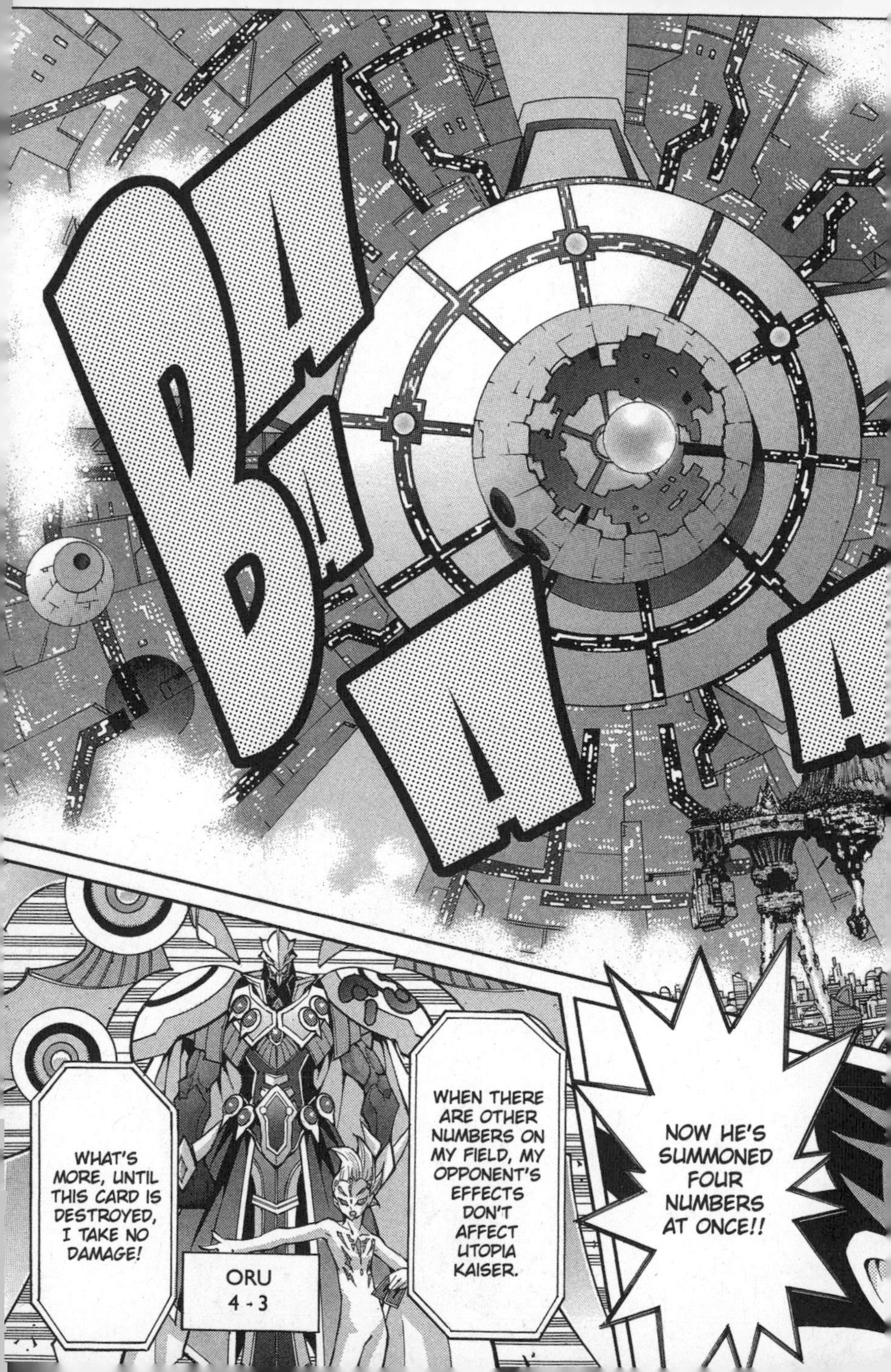
NOW HE'S SUMMONED FOUR NUMBERS AT ONCE!!
WHEN THERE ARE OTHER NUMBERS ON MY FIELD, MY OPPONENT'S EFFECTS DON'T AFFECT UTOPIA KAISER.
ORU 4 → 3
WHAT'S MORE, UNTIL THIS CARD IS DESTROYED, I TAKE NO DAMAGE!

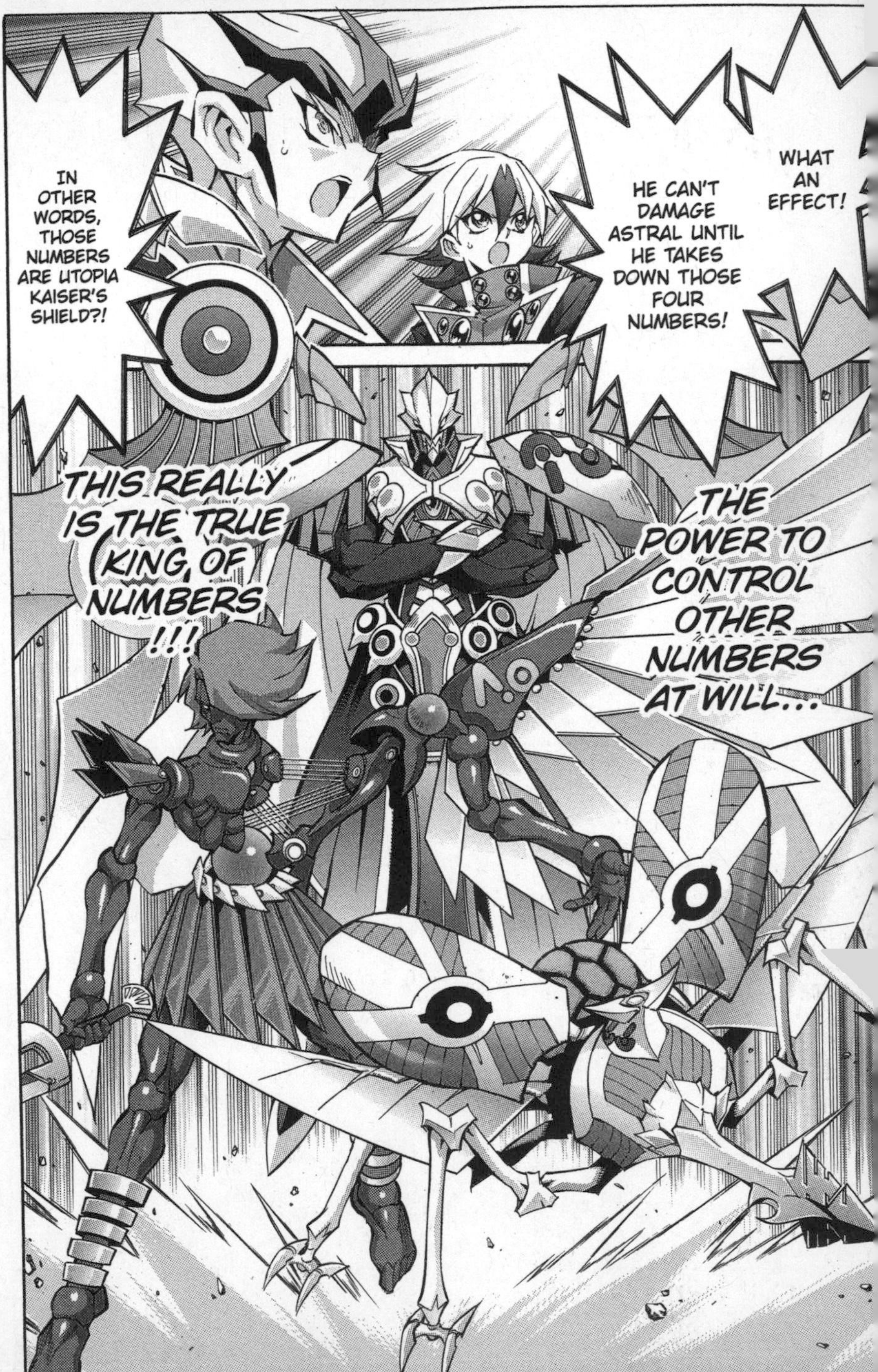
WHAT AN EFFECT!
HE CAN'T DAMAGE ASTRAL UNTIL HE TAKES DOWN THOSE FOUR NUMBERS!
IN OTHER WORDS, THOSE NUMBERS ARE UTOPIA KAISER'S SHIELD?!
THE POWER TO CONTROL OTHER NUMBERS AT WILL...
THIS REALLY IS THE TRUE KING OF NUMBERS!!!

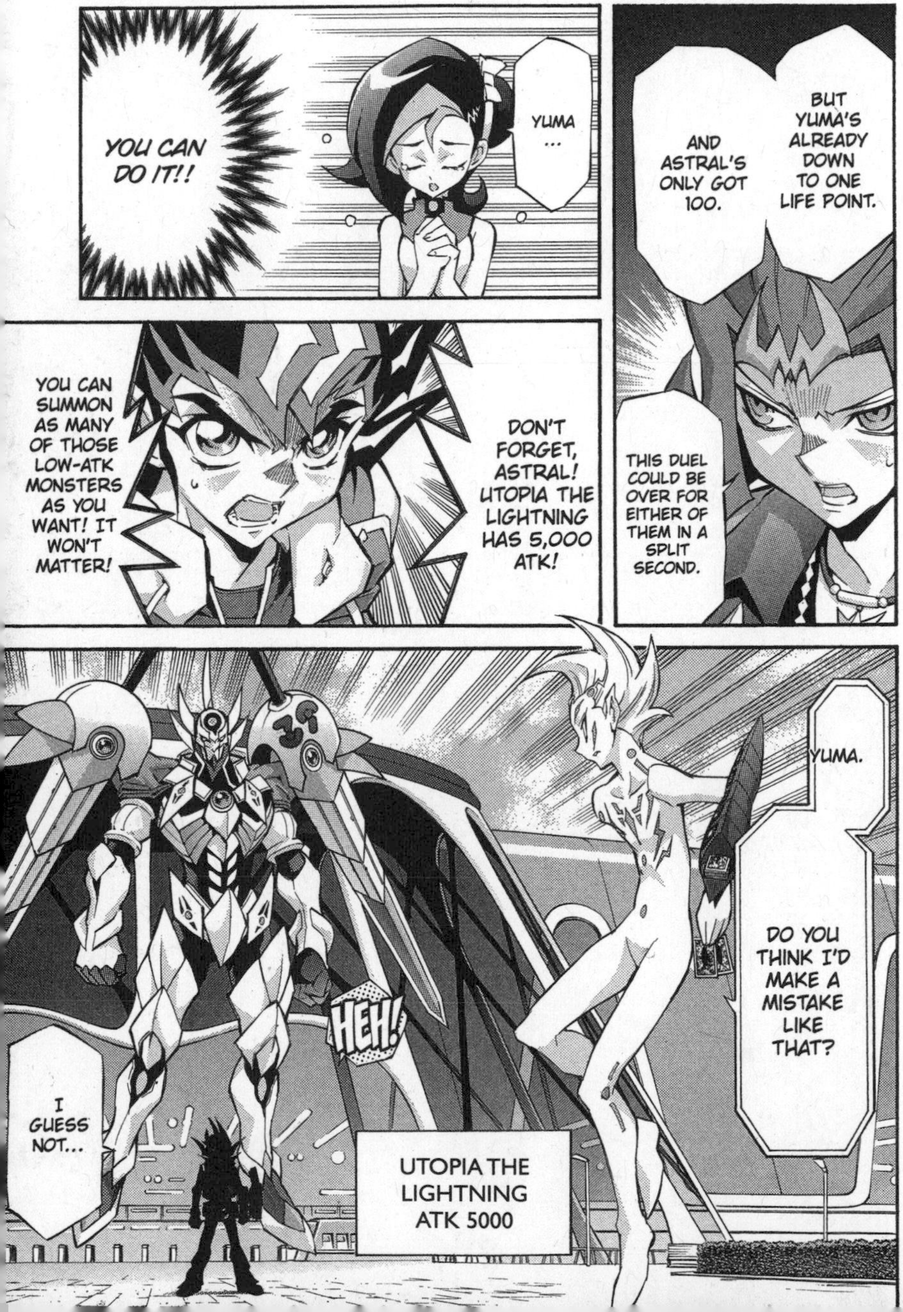
BUT YUMA'S ALREADY DOWN TO ONE LIFE POINT.
AND ASTRAL'S ONLY GOT 100.
THIS DUEL COULD BE OVER FOR EITHER OF THEM IN A SPLIT SECOND.
YUMA ...
YOU CAN DO IT!!
DON'T FORGET, ASTRAL! UTOPIA THE LIGHTNING HAS 5,000 ATK!
YOU CAN SUMMON AS MANY OF THOSE LOW-ATK MONSTERS AS YOU WANT! IT WON'T MATTER!
YUMA.
DO YOU THINK I'D MAKE A MISTAKE LIKE THAT?
HEH!
UTOPIA THE LIGHTNING ATK 5000
I GUESS NOT...

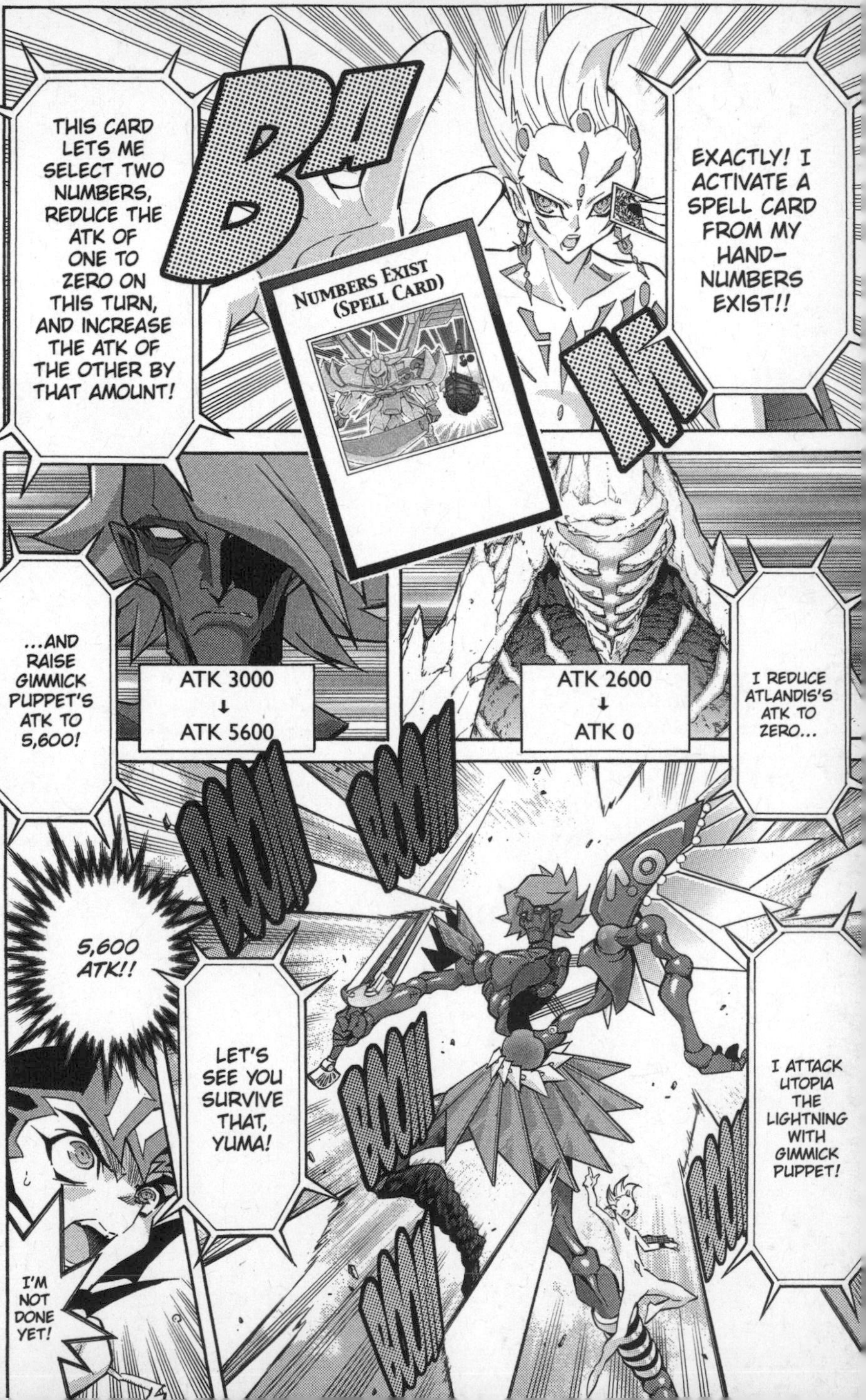
EXACTLY! I ACTIVATE A SPELL CARD FROM MY HAND-NUMBERS EXIST!!
BA
THIS CARD LETS ME SELECT TWO NUMBERS, REDUCE THE ATK OF ONE TO ZERO ON THIS TURN, AND INCREASE THE ATK OF THE OTHER BY THAT AMOUNT!
NUMBERS EXIST (SPELL CARD)
I REDUCE ATLANDIS'S ATK TO ZERO...
ATK 2600 ↓ ATK 0
ATK 3000 ↓ ATK 5600
...AND RAISE GIMMICK PUPPET'S ATK TO 5,600!
I ATTACK UTOPIA THE LIGHTNING WITH GIMMICK PUPPET!
LET'S SEE YOU SURVIVE THAT, YUMA!
5,600 ATK!!
I'M NOT DONE YET!

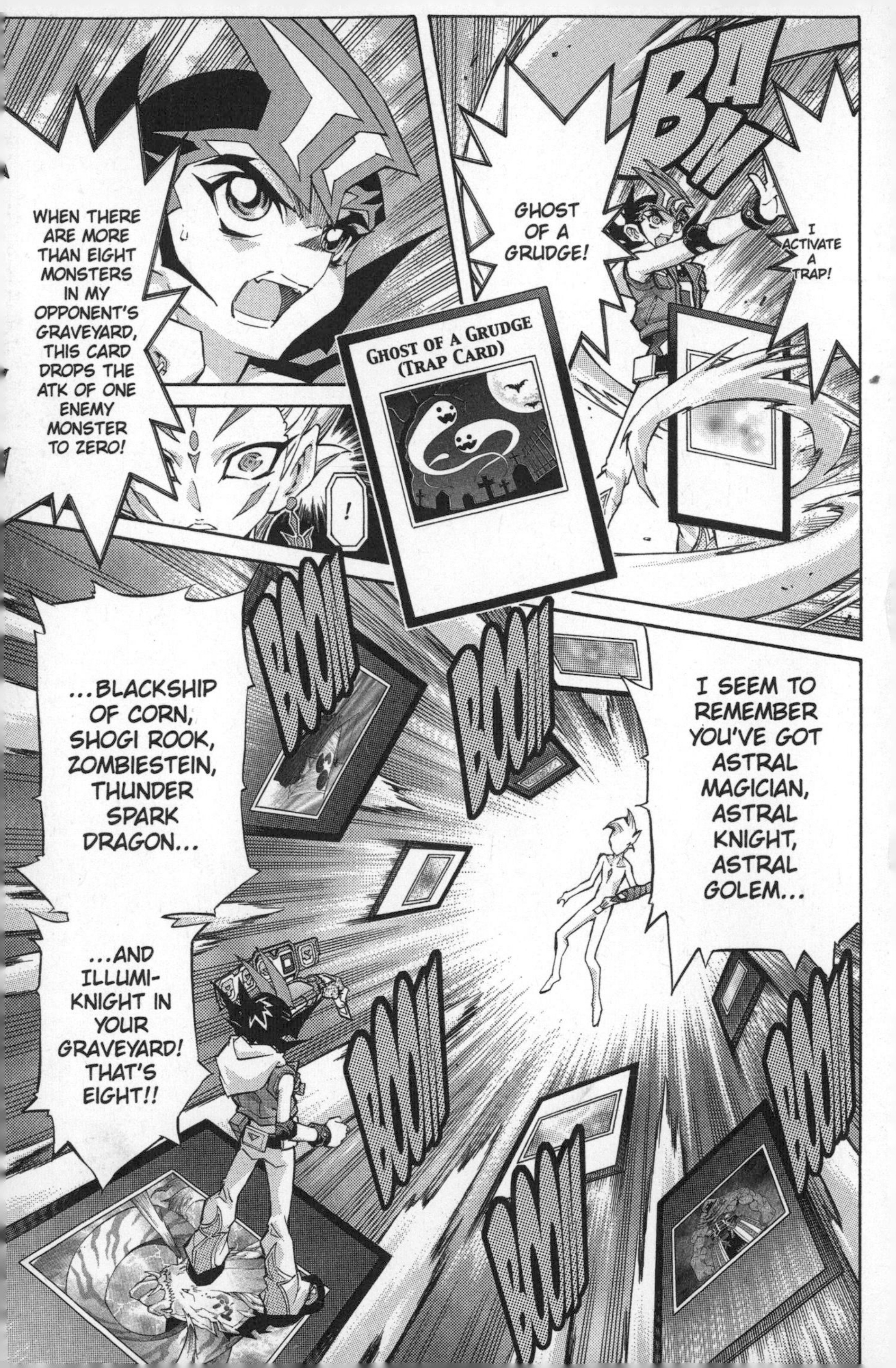
BAM
I ACTIVATE A TRAP!
GHOST OF A GRUDGE!
WHEN THERE ARE MORE THAN EIGHT MONSTERS IN MY OPPONENT'S GRAVEYARD, THIS CARD DROPS THE ATK OF ONE ENEMY MONSTER TO ZERO!
GHOST OF A GRUDGE (TRAP CARD)
!
I SEEM TO REMEMBER YOU'VE GOT ASTRAL MAGICIAN, ASTRAL KNIGHT, ASTRAL GOLEM...
...BLACKSHIP OF CORN, SHOGI ROOK, ZOMBIESTEIN, THUNDER SPARK DRAGON...
...AND ILLUMI-KNIGHT IN YOUR GRAVEYARD! THAT'S EIGHT!!

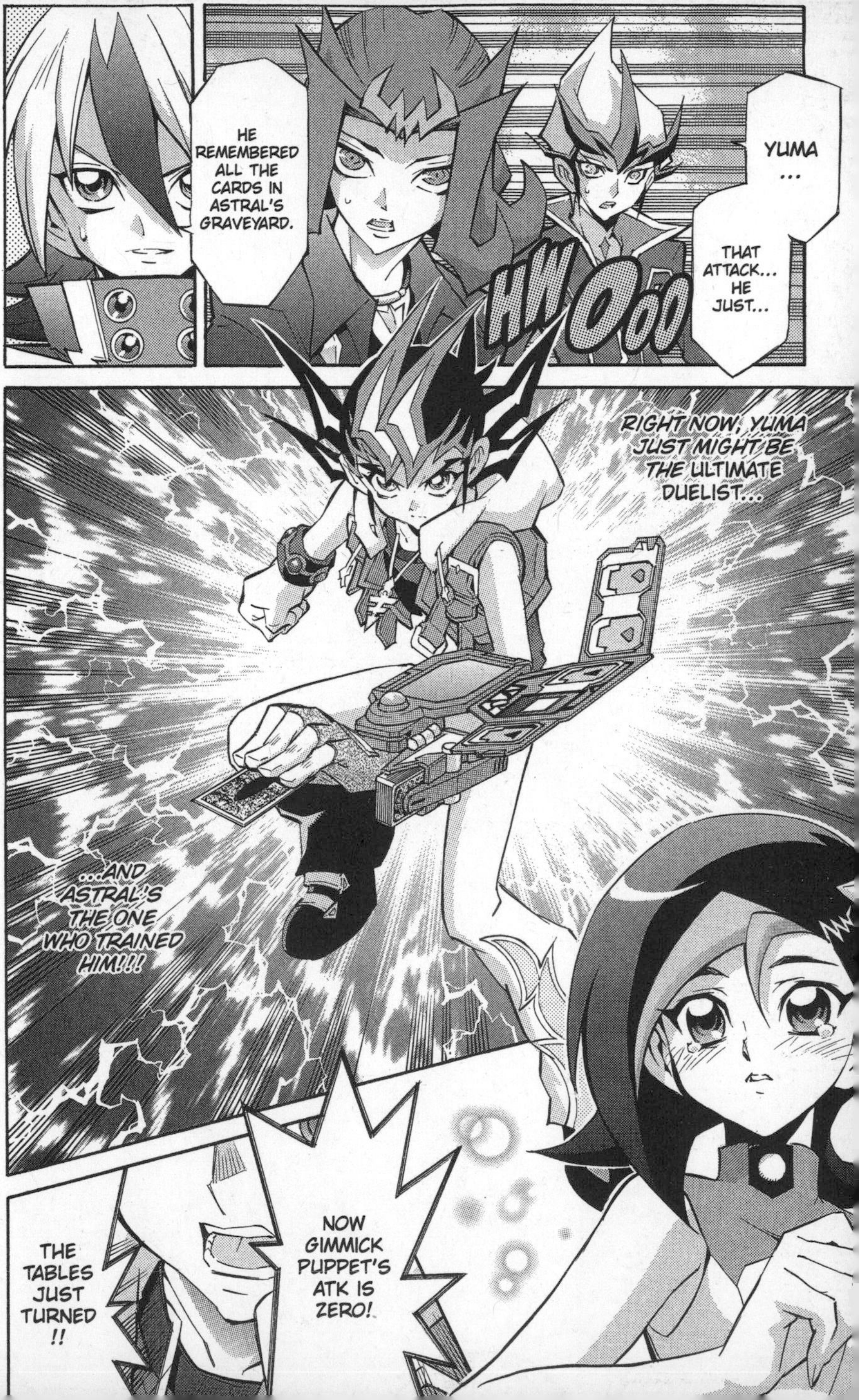
YUMA
...
THAT ATTACK... HE JUST...
HWOOO
HE REMEMBERED ALL THE CARDS IN ASTRAL'S GRAVEYARD.
RIGHT NOW, YUMA JUST MIGHT BE THE ULTIMATE DUELIST...
...AND ASTRAL'S THE ONE WHO TRAINED HIM!!!
NOW GIMMICK PUPPET'S ATK IS ZERO!
THE TABLES JUST TURNED !!

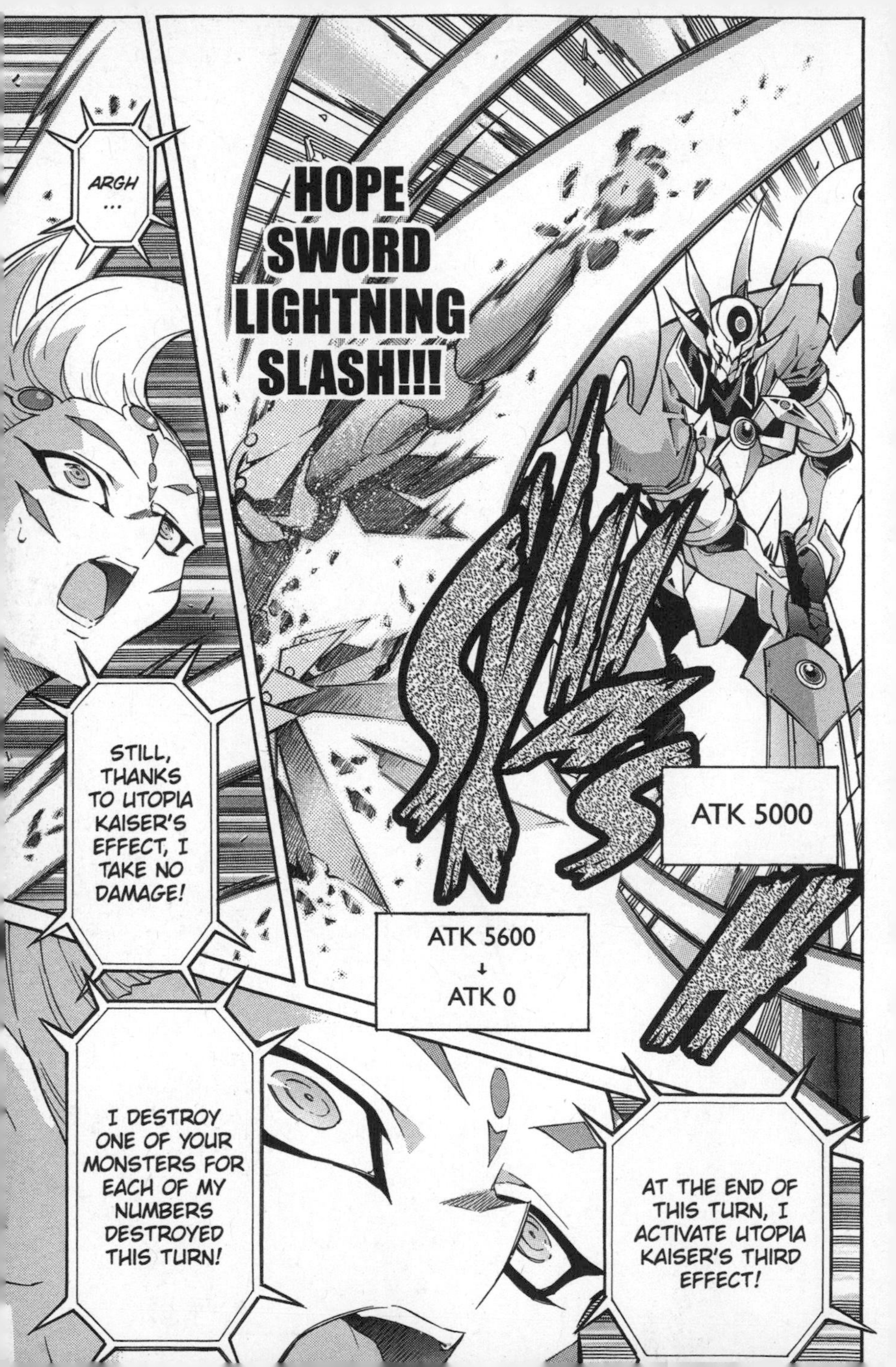
HOPE SWORD LIGHTNING SLASH!!!
ATK 5000
ATK 5600 ↓ ATK 0
ARGH ...
STILL, THANKS TO UTOPIA KAISER'S EFFECT, I TAKE NO DAMAGE!
AT THE END OF THIS TURN, I ACTIVATE UTOPIA KAISER'S THIRD EFFECT!
I DESTROY ONE OF YOUR MONSTERS FOR EACH OF MY NUMBERS DESTROYED THIS TURN!

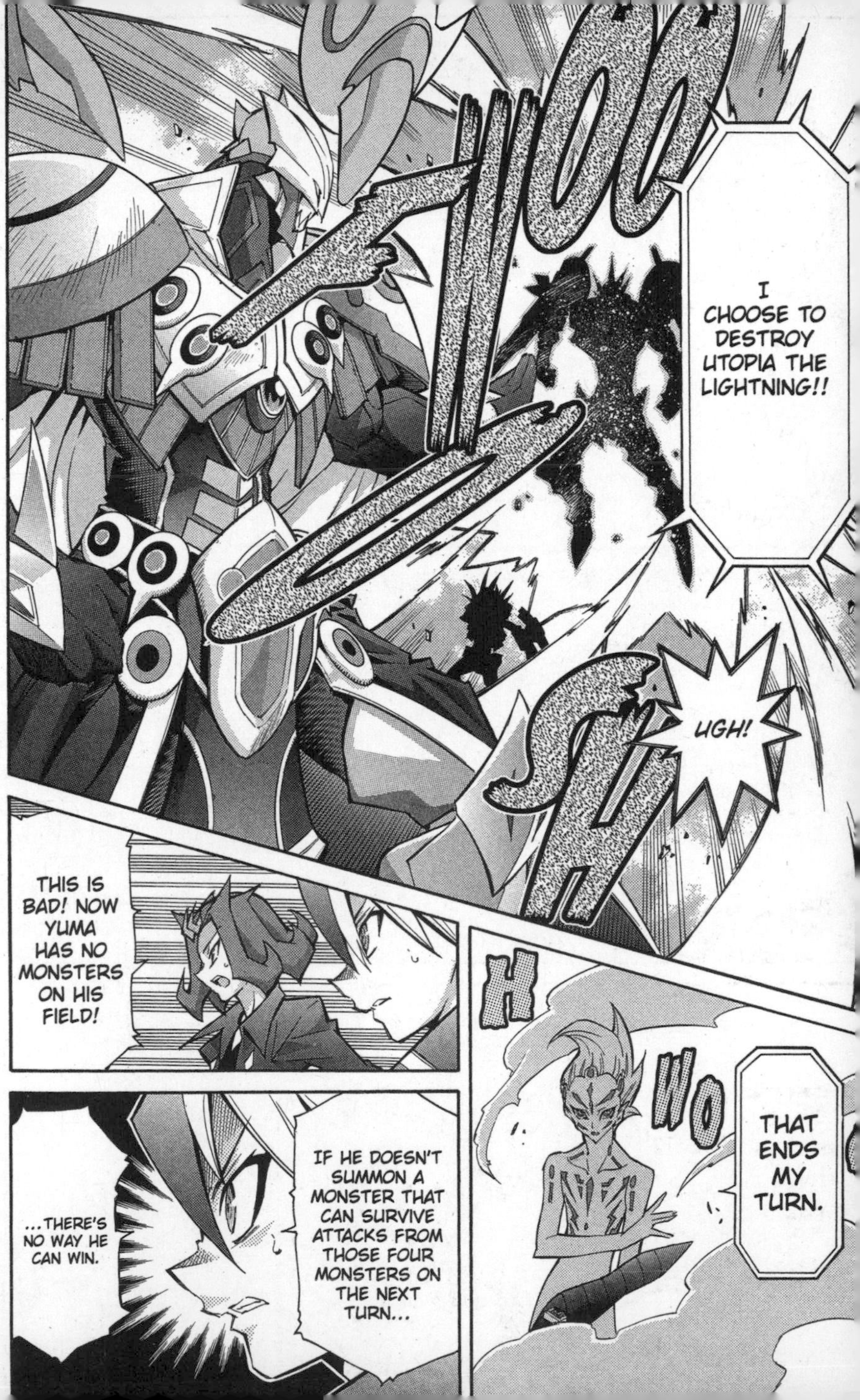
I CHOOSE TO DESTROY UTOPIA THE LIGHTNING!!
UGH!
THAT ENDS MY TURN.
THIS IS BAD! NOW YUMA HAS NO MONSTERS ON HIS FIELD!
IF HE DOESN'T SUMMON A MONSTER THAT CAN SURVIVE ATTACKS FROM THOSE FOUR MONSTERS ON THE NEXT TURN...
...THERE'S NO WAY HE CAN WIN.

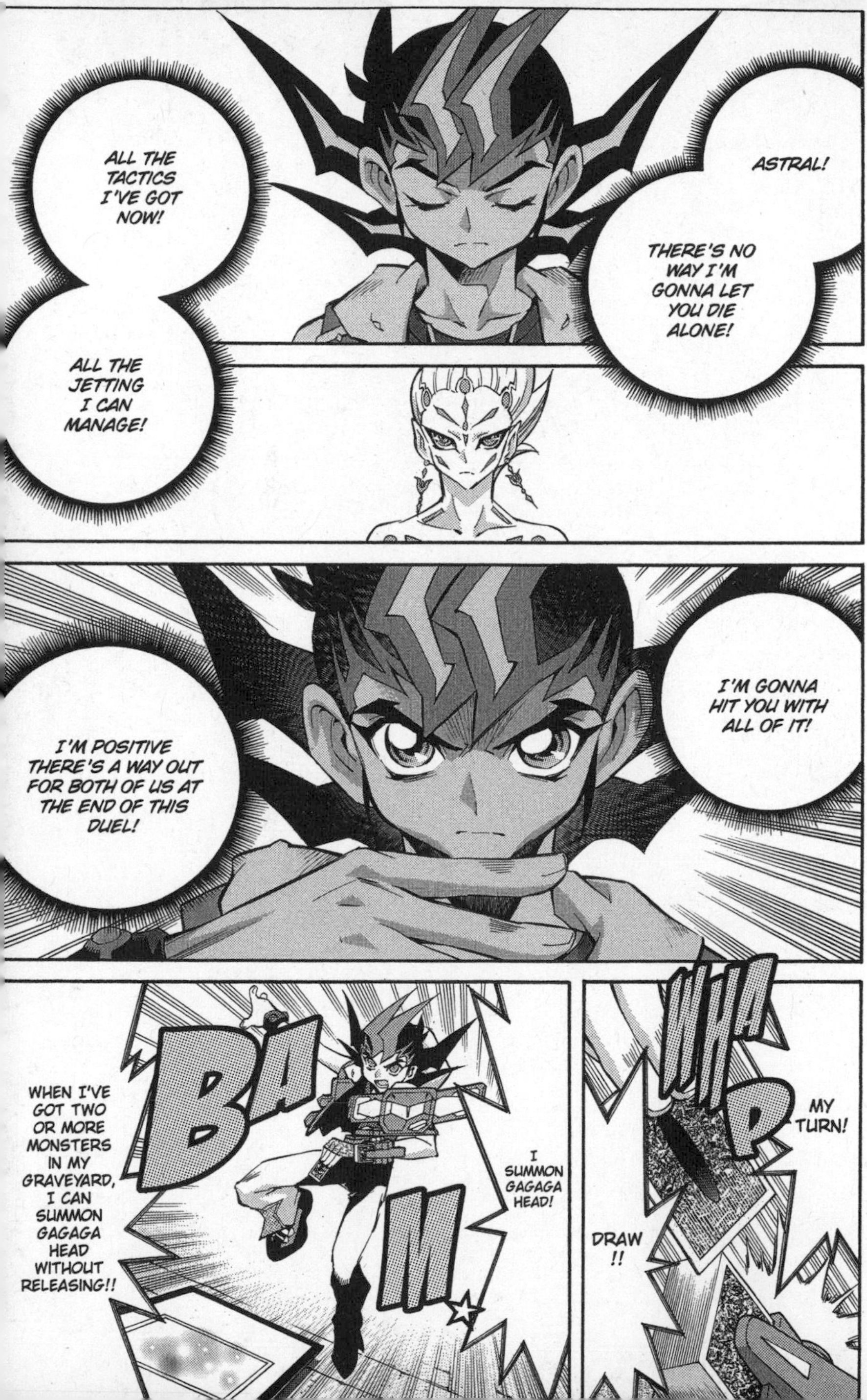
ASTRAL!
THERE'S NO WAY I'M GONNA LET YOU DIE ALONE!
ALL THE TACTICS I'VE GOT NOW!
ALL THE JETTING I CAN MANAGE!
I'M GONNA HIT YOU WITH ALL OF IT!
I'M POSITIVE THERE'S A WAY OUT FOR BOTH OF US AT THE END OF THIS DUEL!
WHAP
MY TURN!
DRAW !!
I SUMMON GAGAGA HEAD!
BAM
WHEN I'VE GOT TWO OR MORE MONSTERS IN MY GRAVEYARD, I CAN SUMMON GAGAGA HEAD WITHOUT RELEASING!!

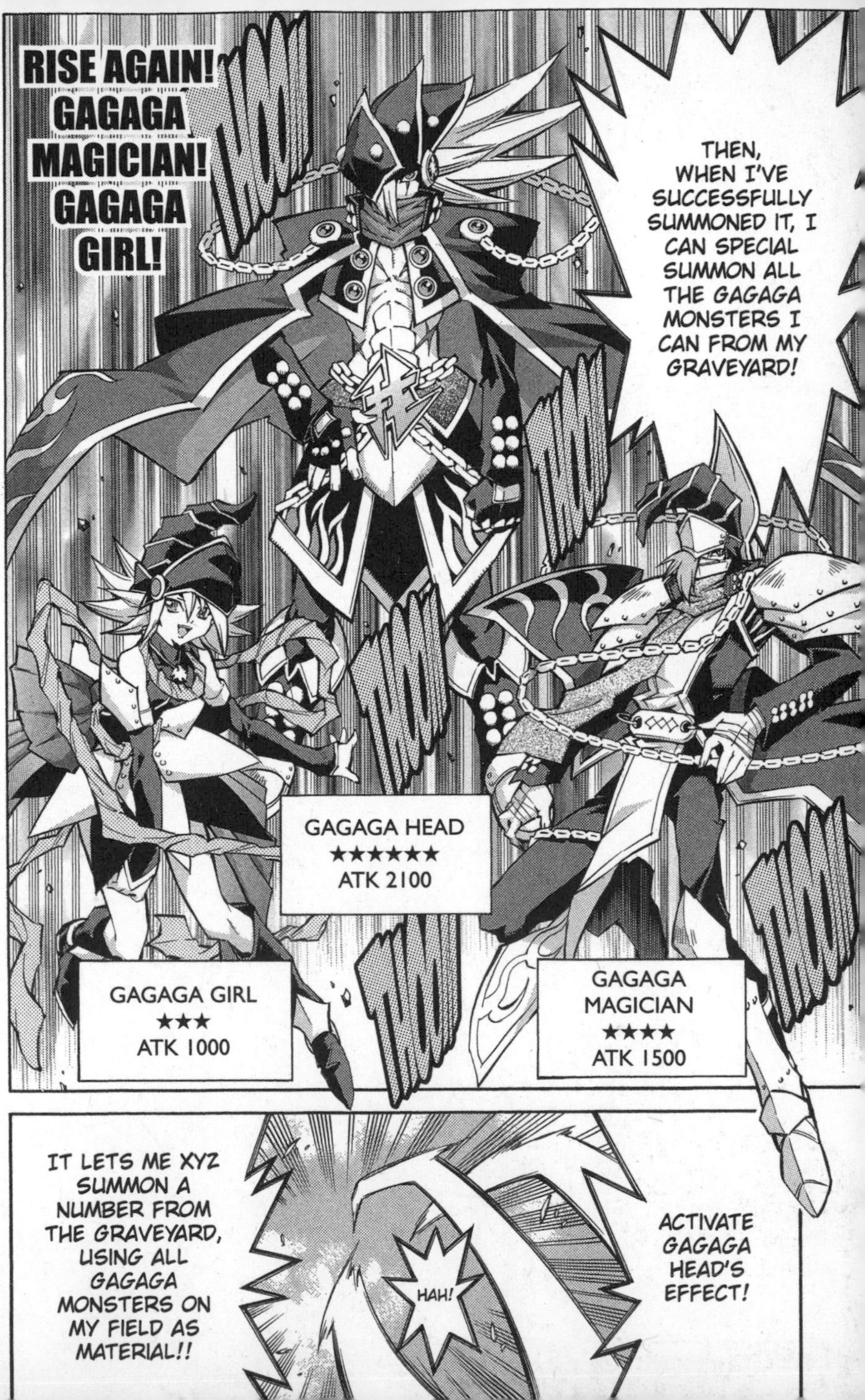
THEN, WHEN I'VE SUCCESSFULLY SUMMONED IT, I CAN SPECIAL SUMMON ALL THE GAGAGA MONSTERS I CAN FROM MY GRAVEYARD!
RISE AGAIN! GAGAGA MAGICIAN! GAGAGA GIRL!
GAGAGA HEAD ★★★★★★ ATK 2100
GAGAGA MAGICIAN ★★★★ ATK 1500
GAGAGA GIRL ★★★ ATK 1000
ACTIVATE GAGAGA HEAD'S EFFECT!
HAH!
IT LETS ME XYZ SUMMON A NUMBER FROM THE GRAVEYARD, USING ALL GAGAGA MONSTERS ON MY FIELD AS MATERIAL!!

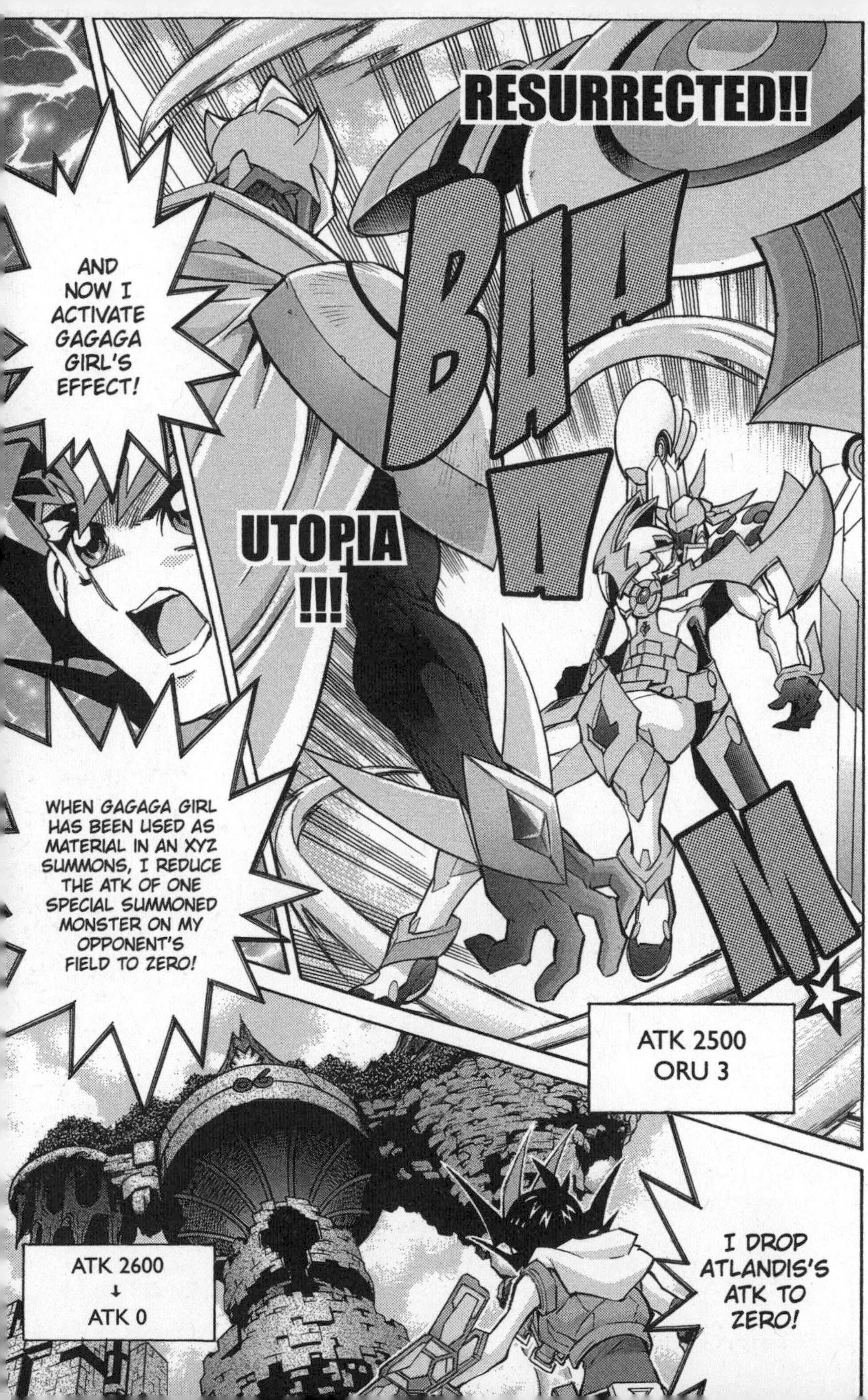
RESURRECTED!!
BAAAM
UTOPIA!!!
AND NOW I ACTIVATE GAGAGA GIRL'S EFFECT!
WHEN GAGAGA GIRL HAS BEEN USED AS MATERIAL IN AN XYZ SUMMONS, I REDUCE THE ATK OF ONE SPECIAL SUMMONED MONSTER ON MY OPPONENT'S FIELD TO ZERO!
ATK 2500
ORU 3
I DROP ATLANDIS'S ATK TO ZERO!
ATK 2600
↓
ATK 0

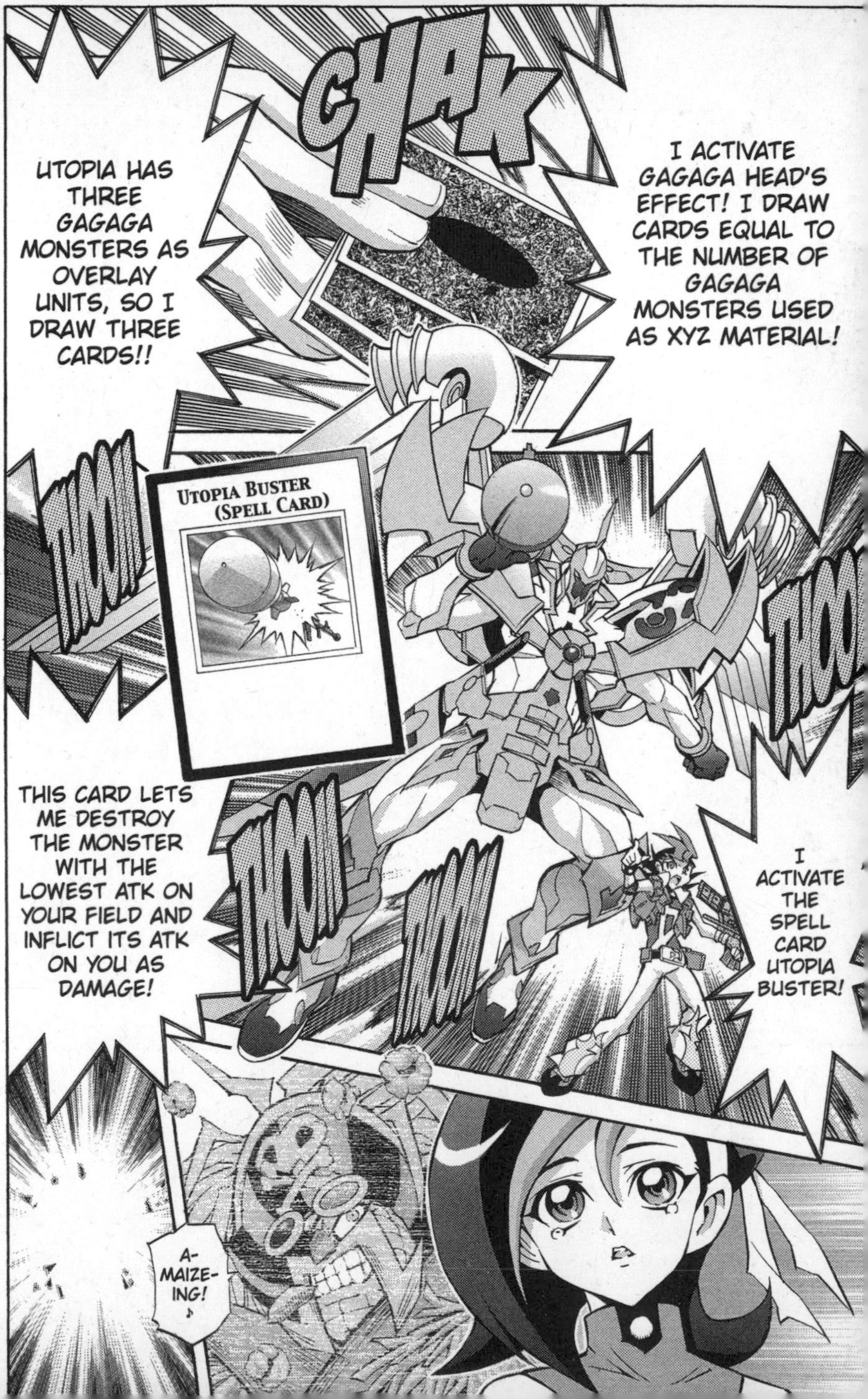
I ACTIVATE GAGAGA HEAD'S EFFECT! I DRAW CARDS EQUAL TO THE NUMBER OF GAGAGA MONSTERS USED AS XYZ MATERIAL!
CHAK
UTOPIA HAS THREE GAGAGA MONSTERS AS OVERLAY UNITS, SO I DRAW THREE CARDS!!
THOOM
UTOPIA BUSTER (SPELL CARD)
THOOM
I ACTIVATE THE SPELL CARD UTOPIA BUSTER!
THIS CARD LETS ME DESTROY THE MONSTER WITH THE LOWEST ATK ON YOUR FIELD AND INFLICT ITS ATK ON YOU AS DAMAGE!
THOOM
THOOM
A-MAIZE-ING! ♪

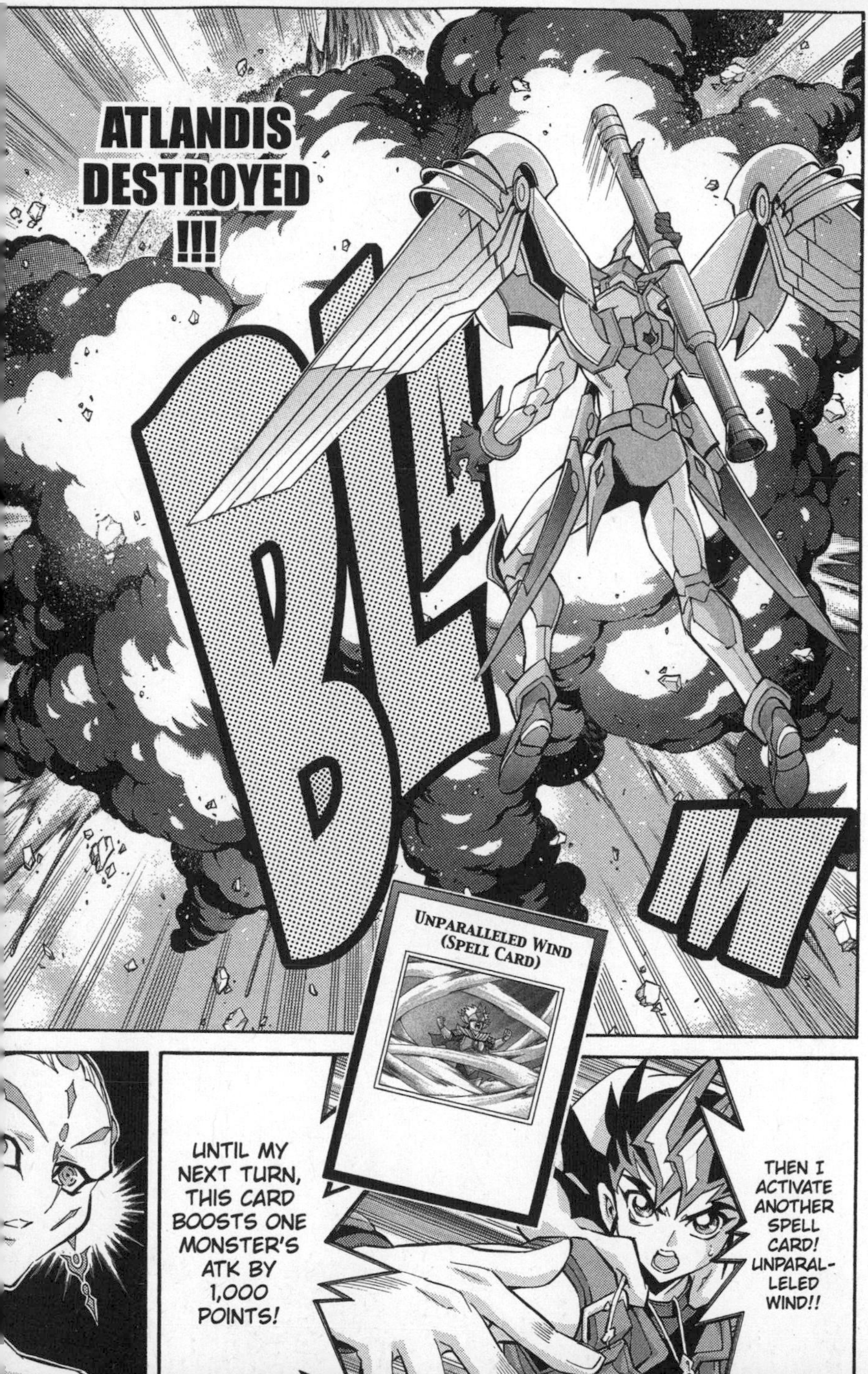
ATLANDIS DESTROYED !!!
BLM
Unparalleled Wind (Spell Card)
THEN I ACTIVATE ANOTHER SPELL CARD! UNPARAL-LELED WIND!!
UNTIL MY NEXT TURN, THIS CARD BOOSTS ONE MONSTER'S ATK BY 1,000 POINTS!

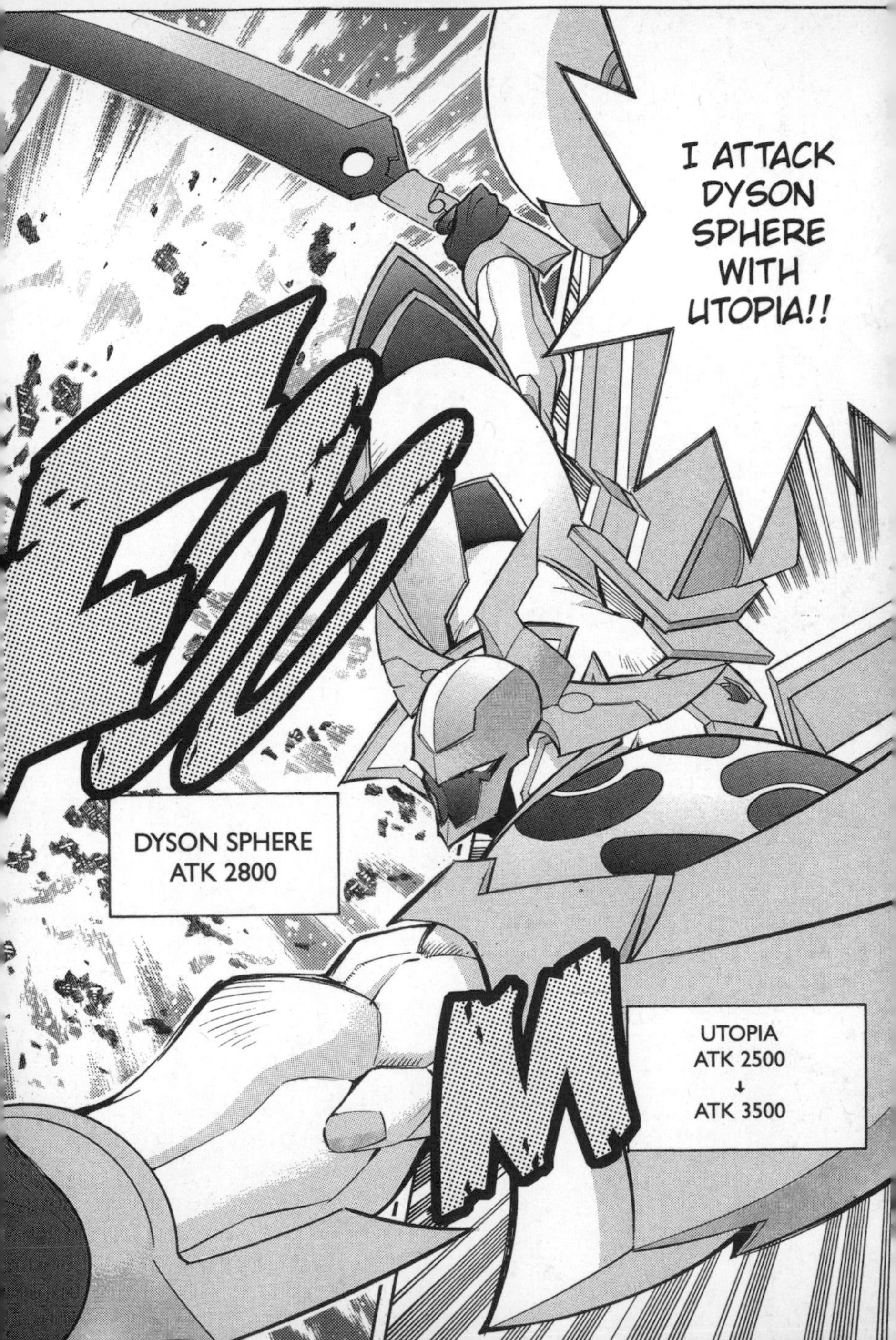
I ATTACK DYSON SPHERE WITH UTOPIA!!
DYSON SPHERE ATK 2800
UTOPIA ATK 2500 ↓ ATK 3500

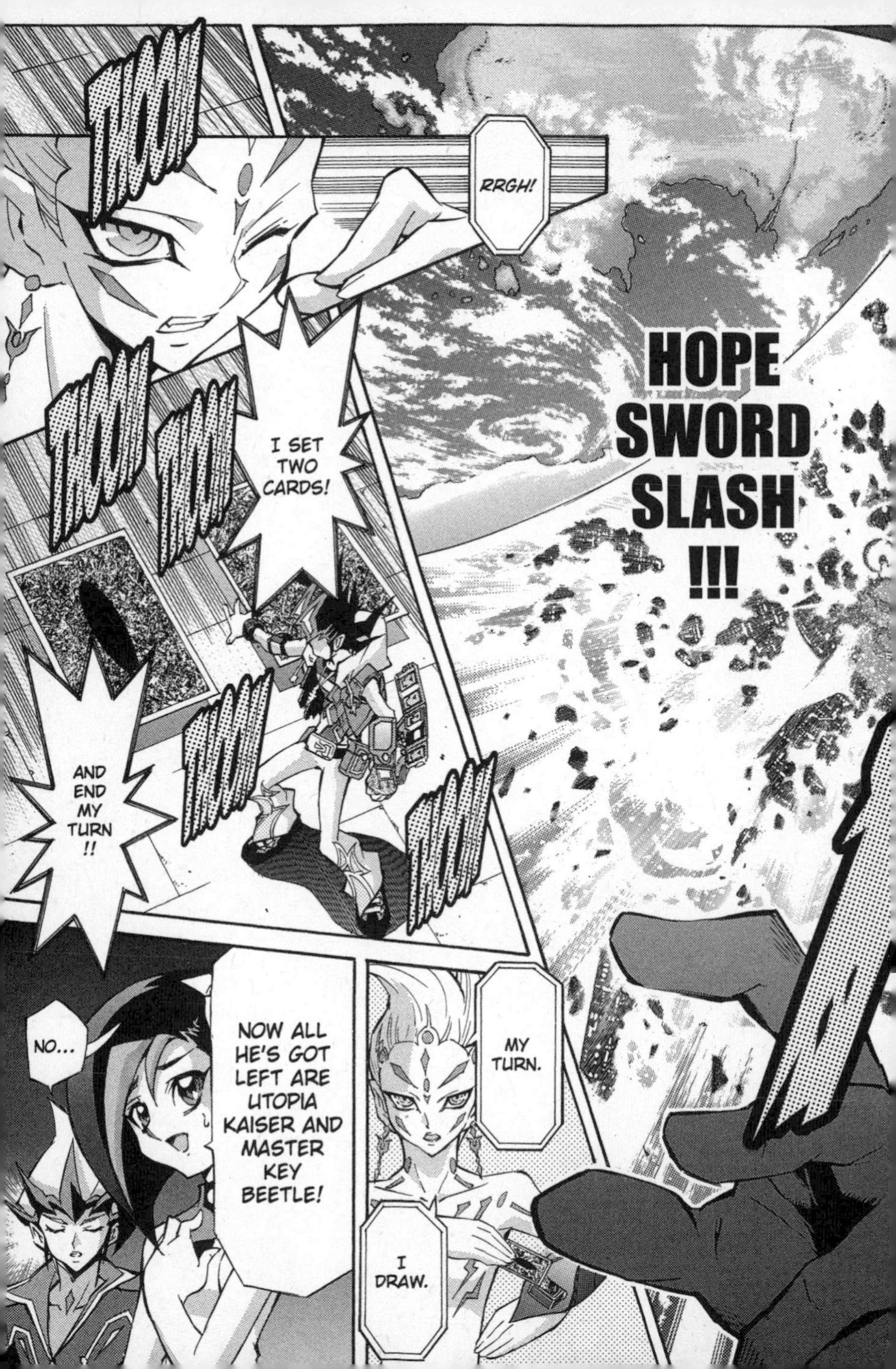
HOPE SWORD SLASH !!!
RRGH!
I SET TWO CARDS!
AND END MY TURN !!
MY TURN.
I DRAW.
NOW ALL HE'S GOT LEFT ARE UTOPIA KAISER AND MASTER KEY BEETLE!
NO...

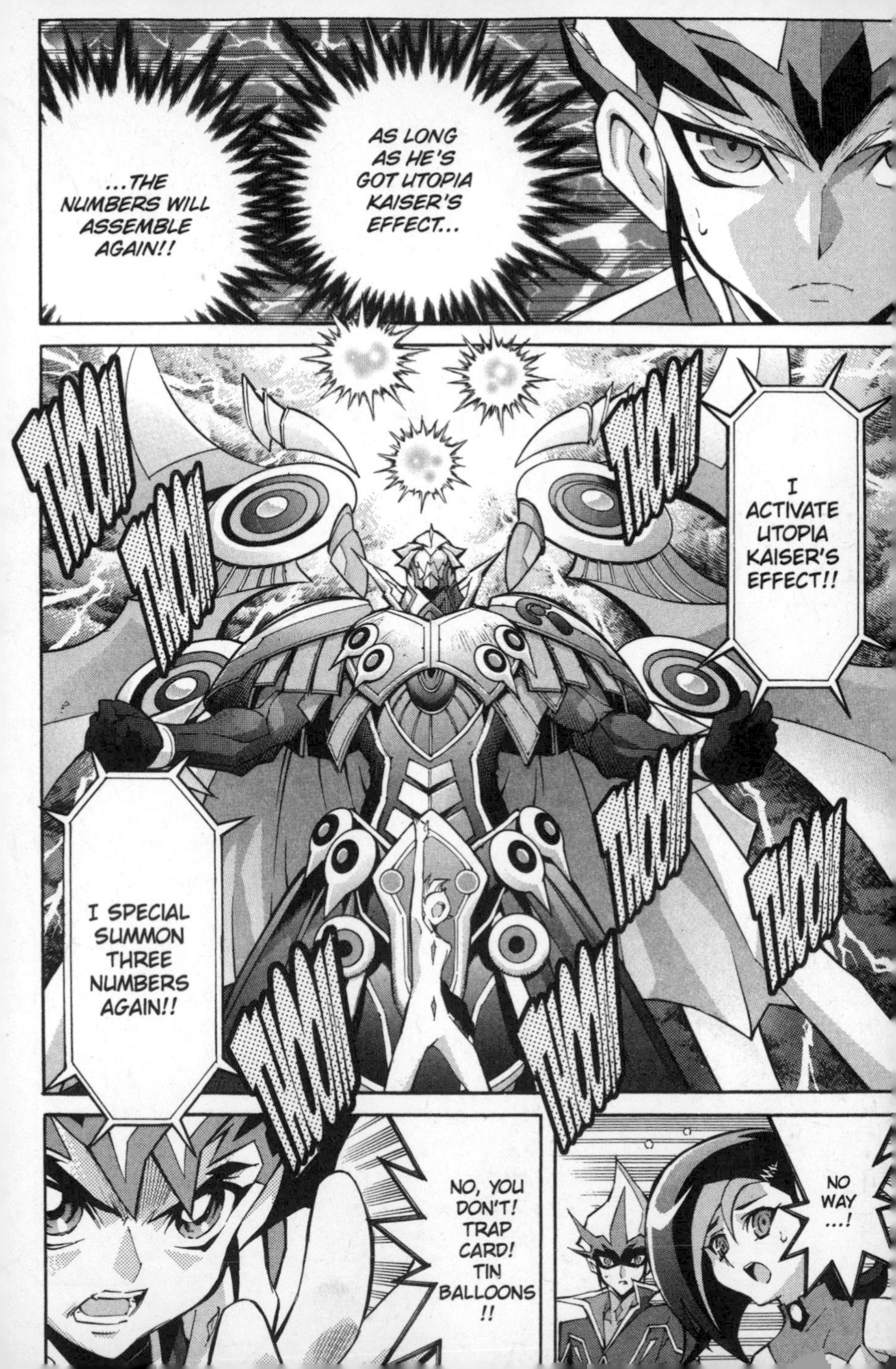
AS LONG AS HE'S GOT UTOPIA KAISER'S EFFECT...
...THE NUMBERS WILL ASSEMBLE AGAIN!!
I ACTIVATE UTOPIA KAISER'S EFFECT!!
THOOM
THOOM
THOOM
THOOM
I SPECIAL SUMMON THREE NUMBERS AGAIN!!
THOOM
THOOM
THOOM
THOOM
NO WAY ...!
NO, YOU DON'T! TRAP CARD! TIN BALLOONS !!

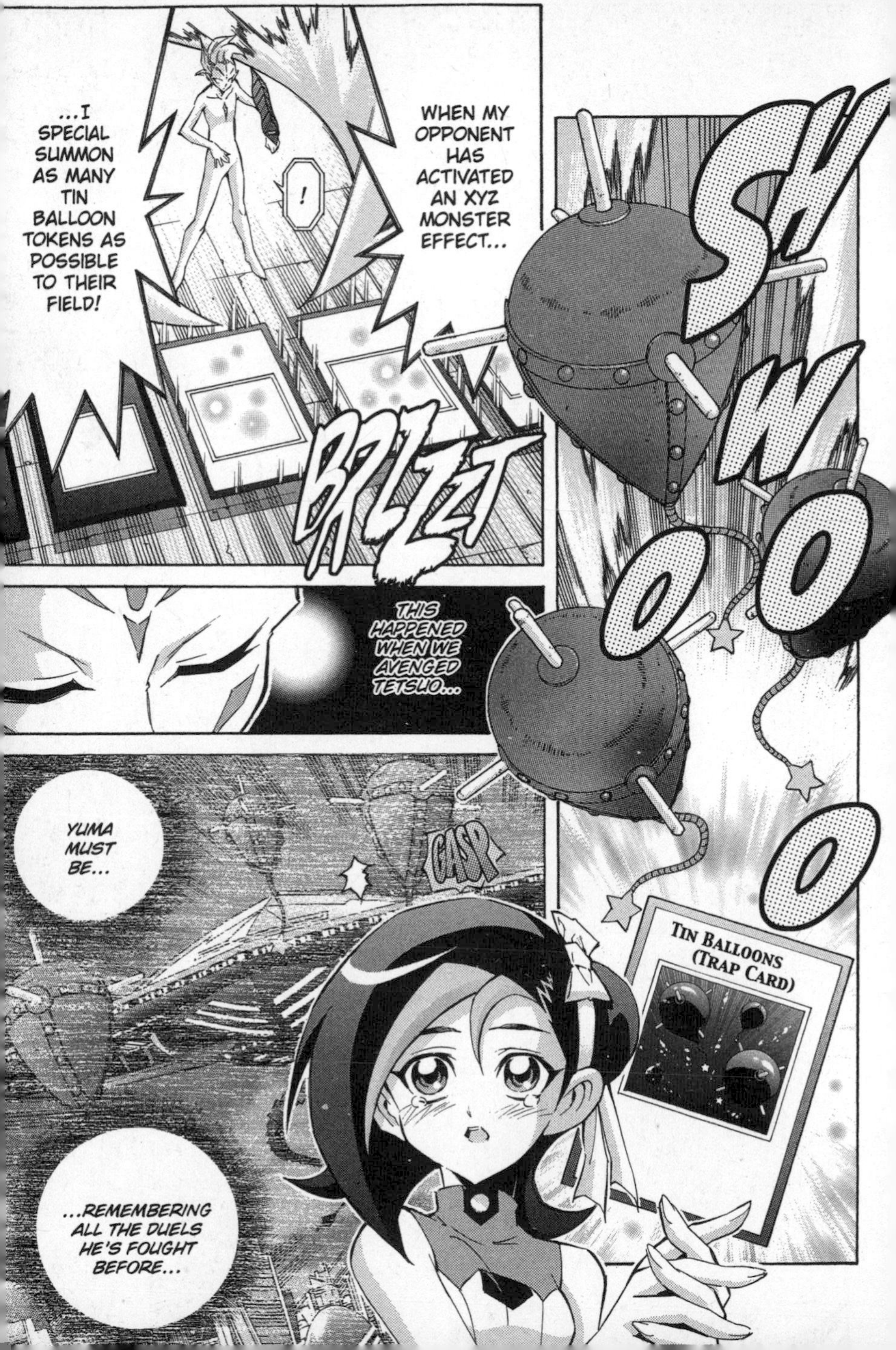
SHWOOOO
TIN BALLOONS (TRAP CARD)
WHEN MY OPPONENT HAS ACTIVATED AN XYZ MONSTER EFFECT...
!
...I SPECIAL SUMMON AS MANY TIN BALLOON TOKENS AS POSSIBLE TO THEIR FIELD!
BRZZZT
THIS HAPPENED WHEN WE AVENGED TETSUO...
GASP
YUMA MUST BE...
...REMEMBERING ALL THE DUELS HE'S FOUGHT BEFORE...

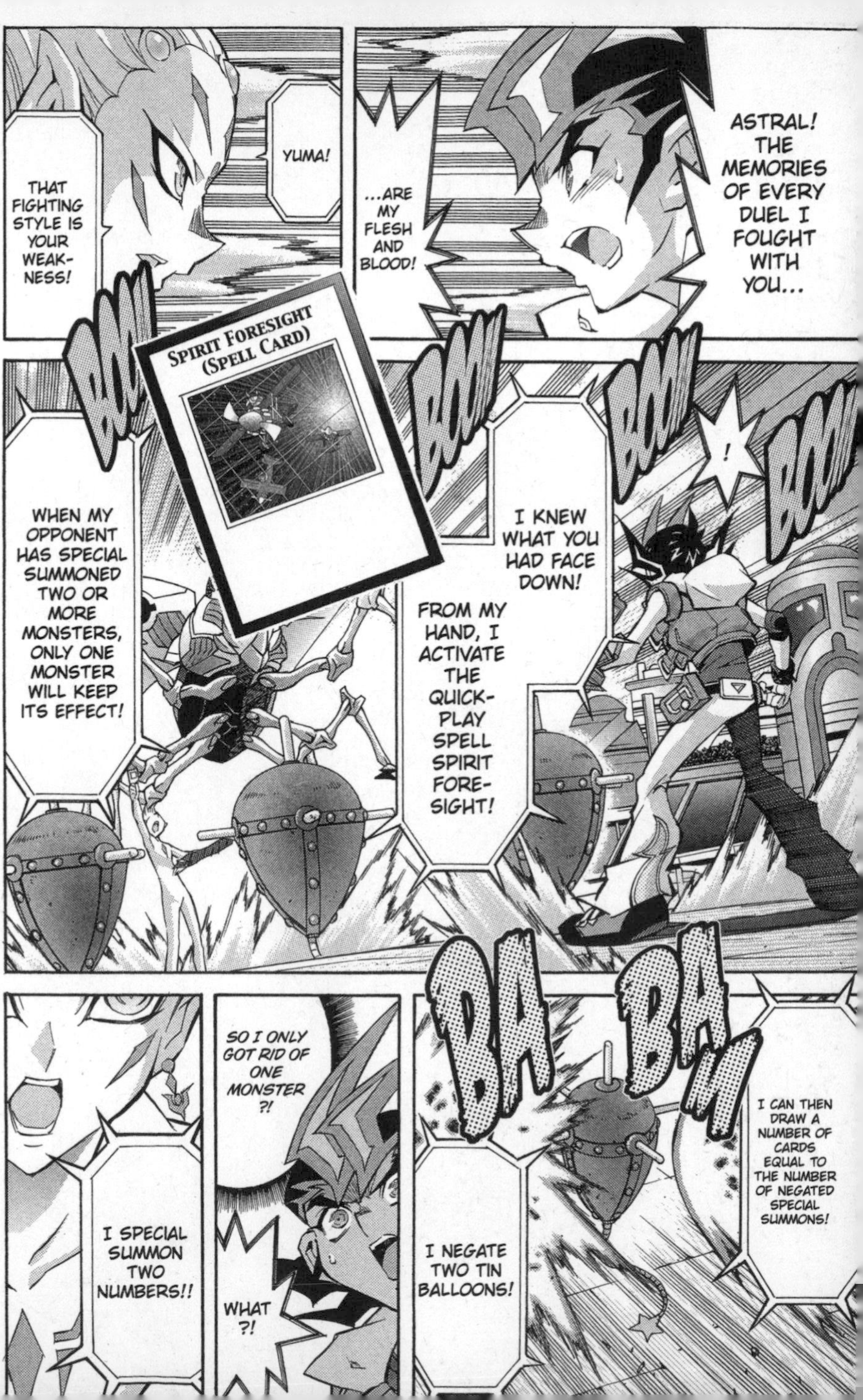

ASTRAL! THE MEMORIES OF EVERY DUEL I FOUGHT WITH YOU...
...ARE MY FLESH AND BLOOD!
YUMA!
THAT FIGHTING STYLE IS YOUR WEAK-NESS!
BOOM
BOOM
!
I KNEW WHAT YOU HAD FACE DOWN!
FROM MY HAND, I ACTIVATE THE QUICK-PLAY SPELL SPIRIT FORE-SIGHT!
BOOM
BOOM
SPIRIT FORESIGHT (SPELL CARD)
WHEN MY OPPONENT HAS SPECIAL SUMMONED TWO OR MORE MONSTERS, ONLY ONE MONSTER WILL KEEP ITS EFFECT!
BA BAM
I CAN THEN DRAW A NUMBER OF CARDS EQUAL TO THE NUMBER OF NEGATED SPECIAL SUMMONS!
I NEGATE TWO TIN BALLOONS!
SO I ONLY GOT RID OF ONE MONSTER ?!
WHAT ?!
I SPECIAL SUMMON TWO NUMBERS!!

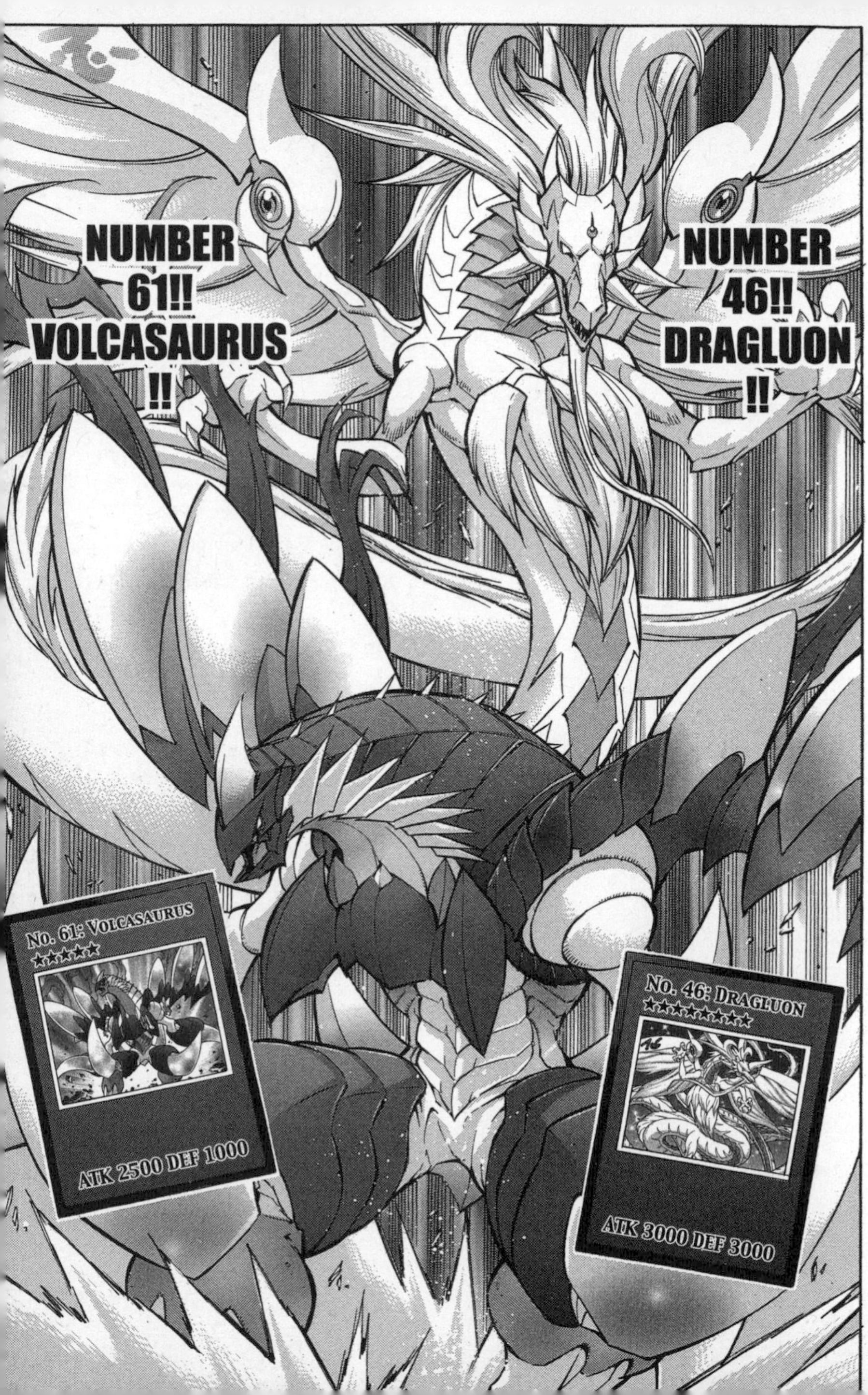
NUMBER 46!! DRAGLUON !!
NUMBER 61!! VOLCASAURUS !!
No. 61: VOLCASAURUS
ATK 2500 DEF 1000
No. 46: DRAGLUON
ATK 3000 DEF 3000

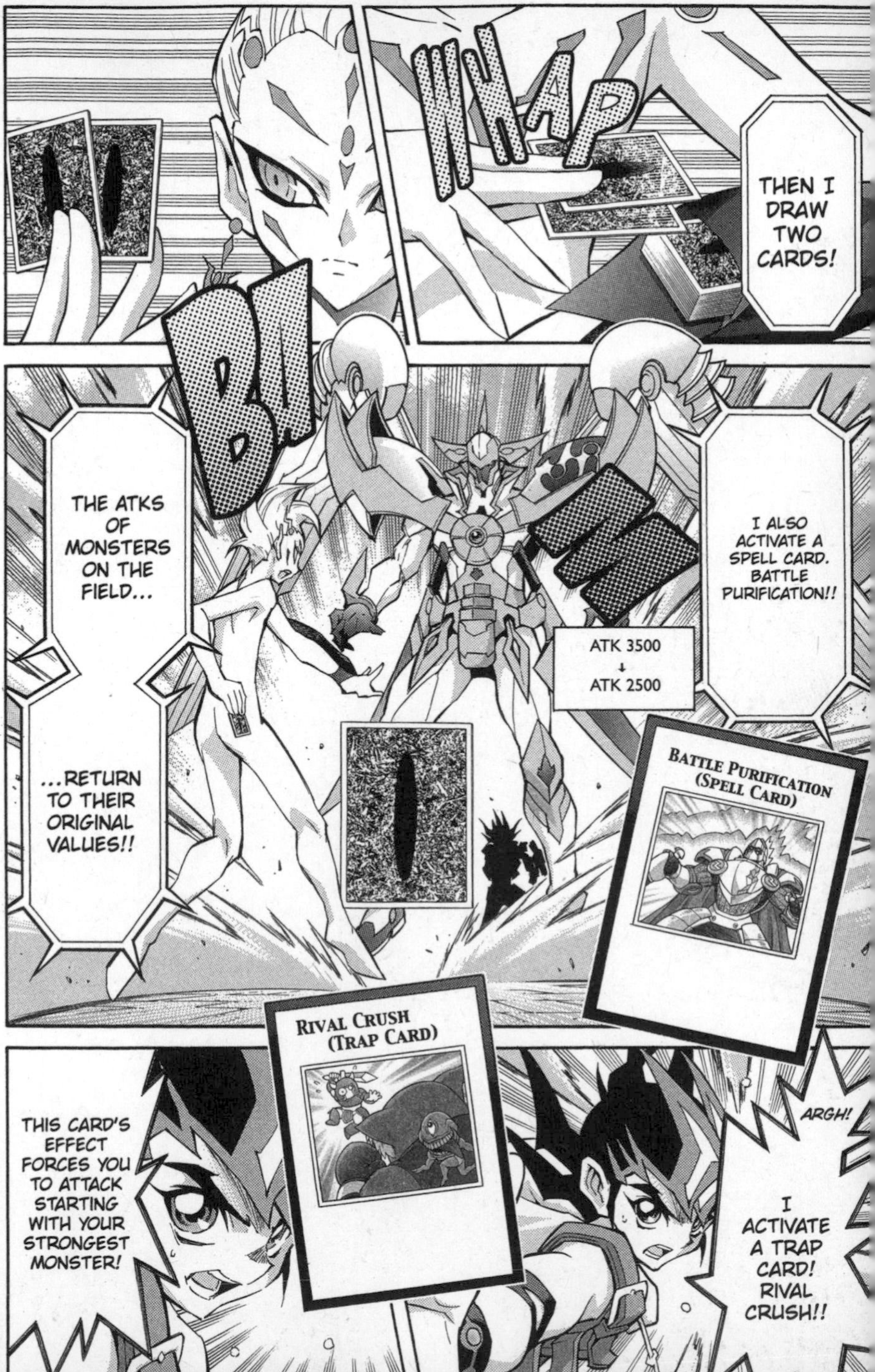
THEN I DRAW TWO CARDS!
WHAP
BA
I ALSO ACTIVATE A SPELL CARD. BATTLE PURIFICATION!!
ATK 3500
↓
ATK 2500
BATTLE PURIFICATION (SPELL CARD)
THE ATKS OF MONSTERS ON THE FIELD...
...RETURN TO THEIR ORIGINAL VALUES!!
ARGH!
I ACTIVATE A TRAP CARD! RIVAL CRUSH!!
RIVAL CRUSH (TRAP CARD)
THIS CARD'S EFFECT FORCES YOU TO ATTACK STARTING WITH YOUR STRONGEST MONSTER!

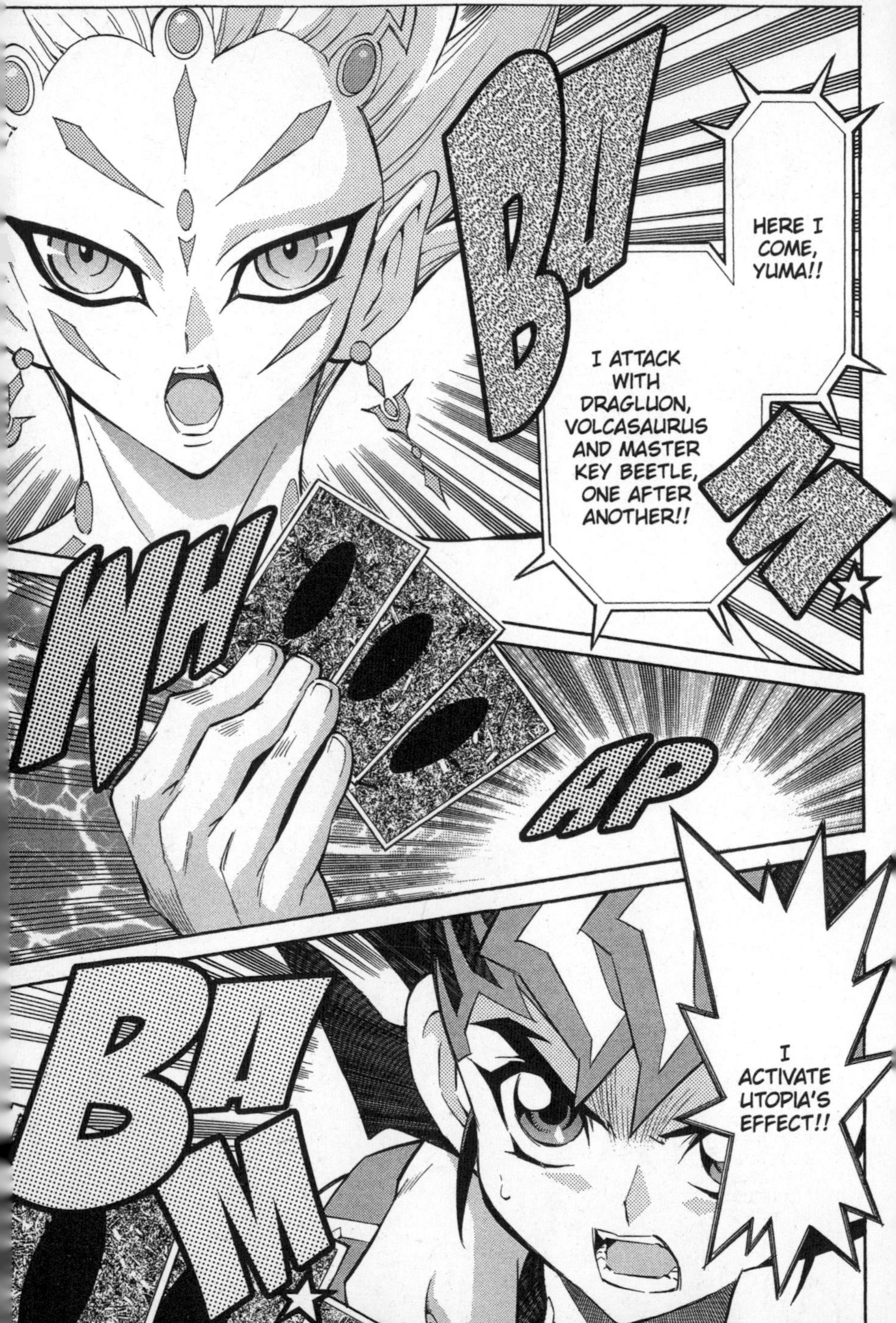
HERE I COME, YUMA!!
I ATTACK WITH DRAGLUON, VOLCASAURUS AND MASTER KEY BEETLE, ONE AFTER ANOTHER!!
BAM
WHAP
I ACTIVATE UTOPIA'S EFFECT!!
BAM

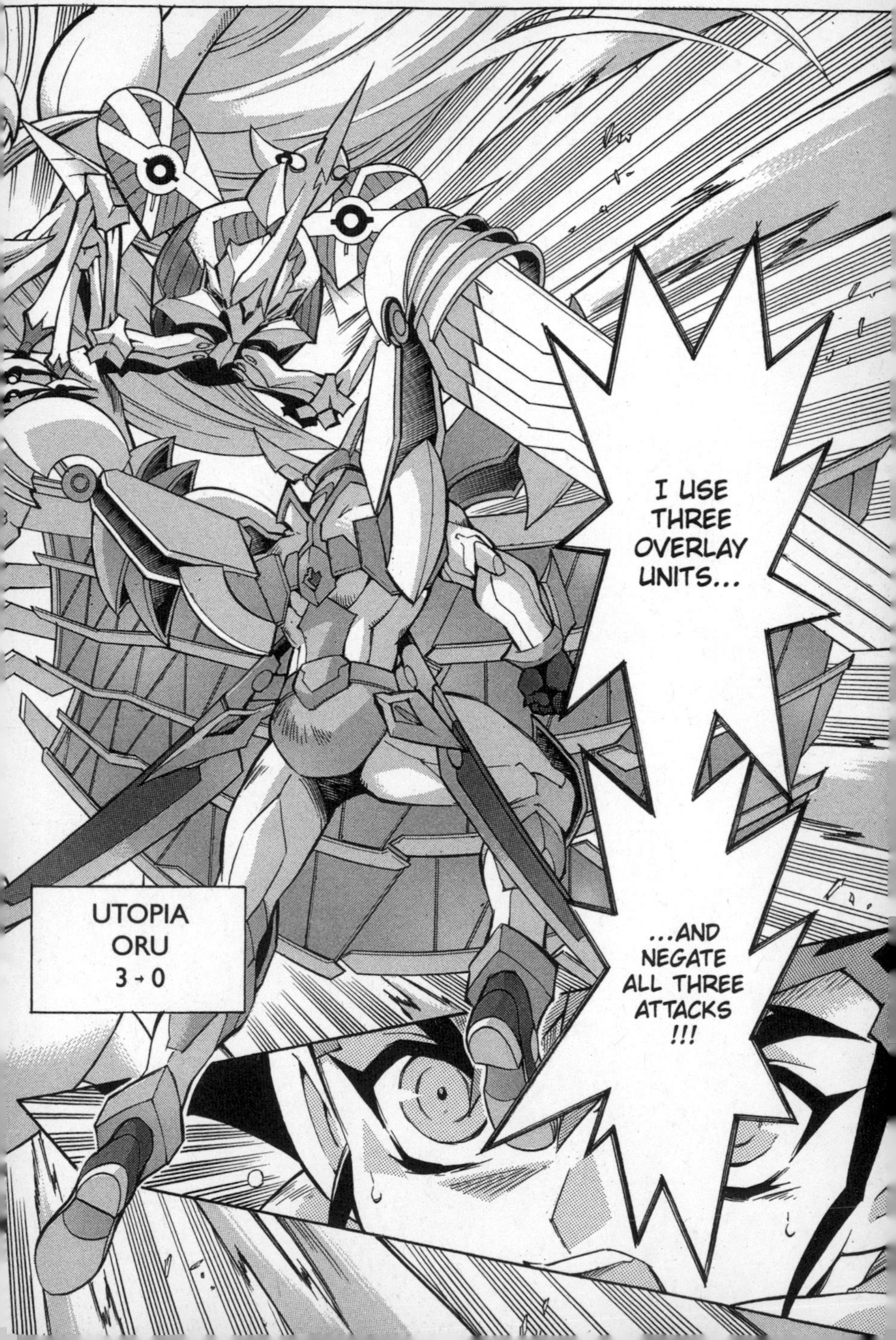
I USE THREE OVERLAY UNITS...
...AND NEGATE ALL THREE ATTACKS !!!
UTOPIA ORU 3 → 0

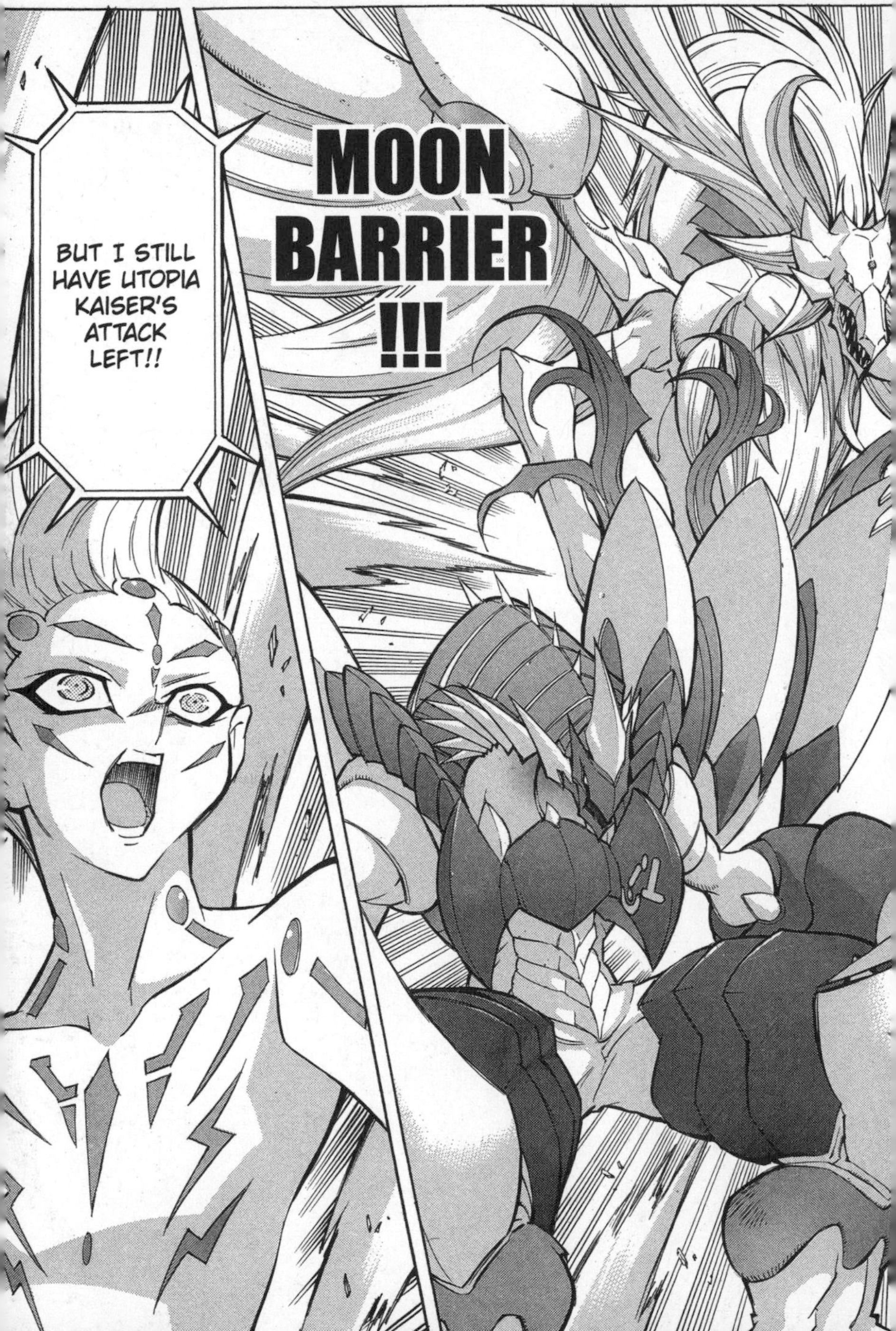
MOON BARRIER !!!
BUT I STILL HAVE UTOPIA KAISER'S ATTACK LEFT!!

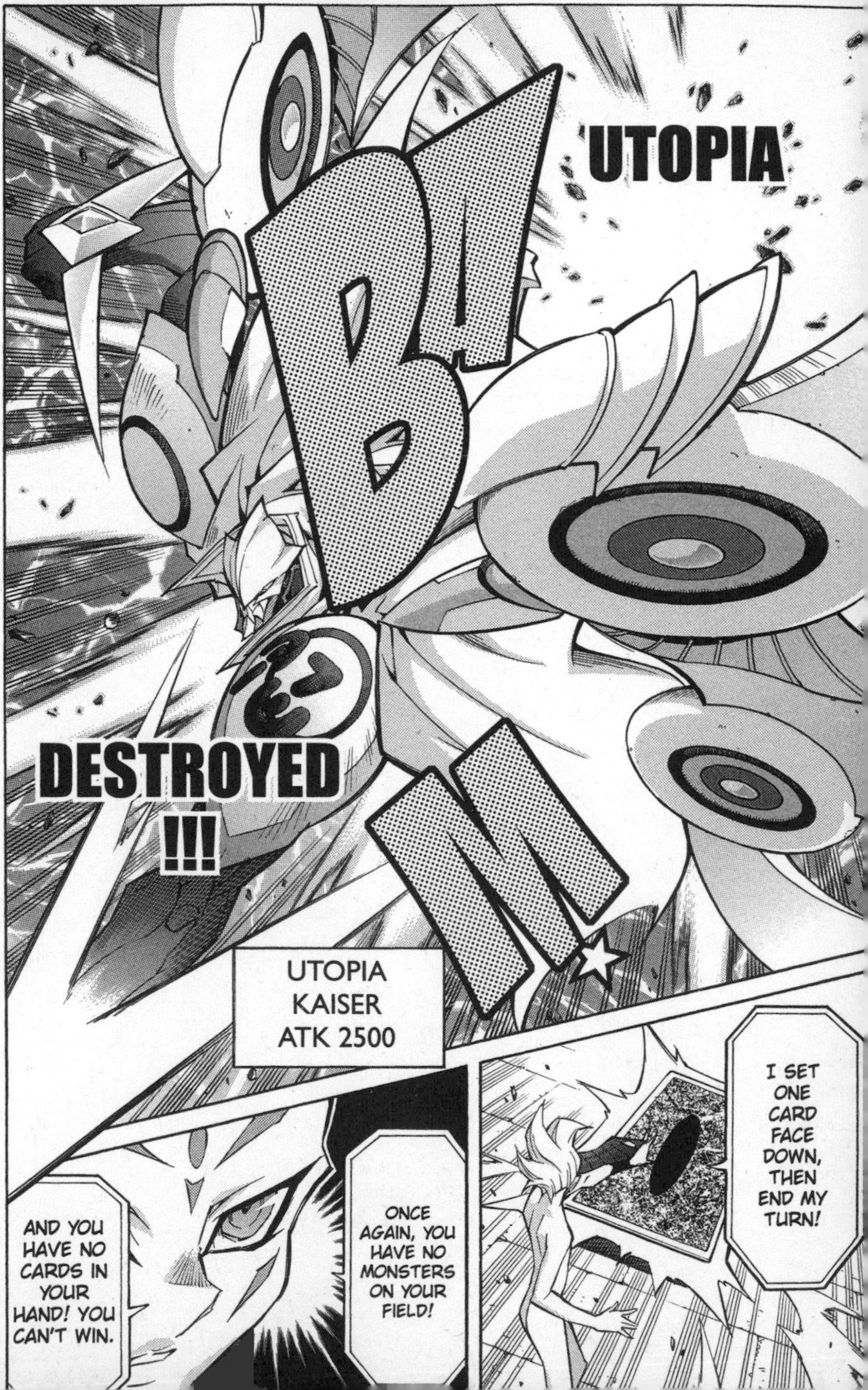
UTOPIA
BAM!
DESTROYED !!!
UTOPIA KAISER ATK 2500
I SET ONE CARD FACE DOWN, THEN END MY TURN!
ONCE AGAIN, YOU HAVE NO MONSTERS ON YOUR FIELD!
AND YOU HAVE NO CARDS IN YOUR HAND! YOU CAN'T WIN.

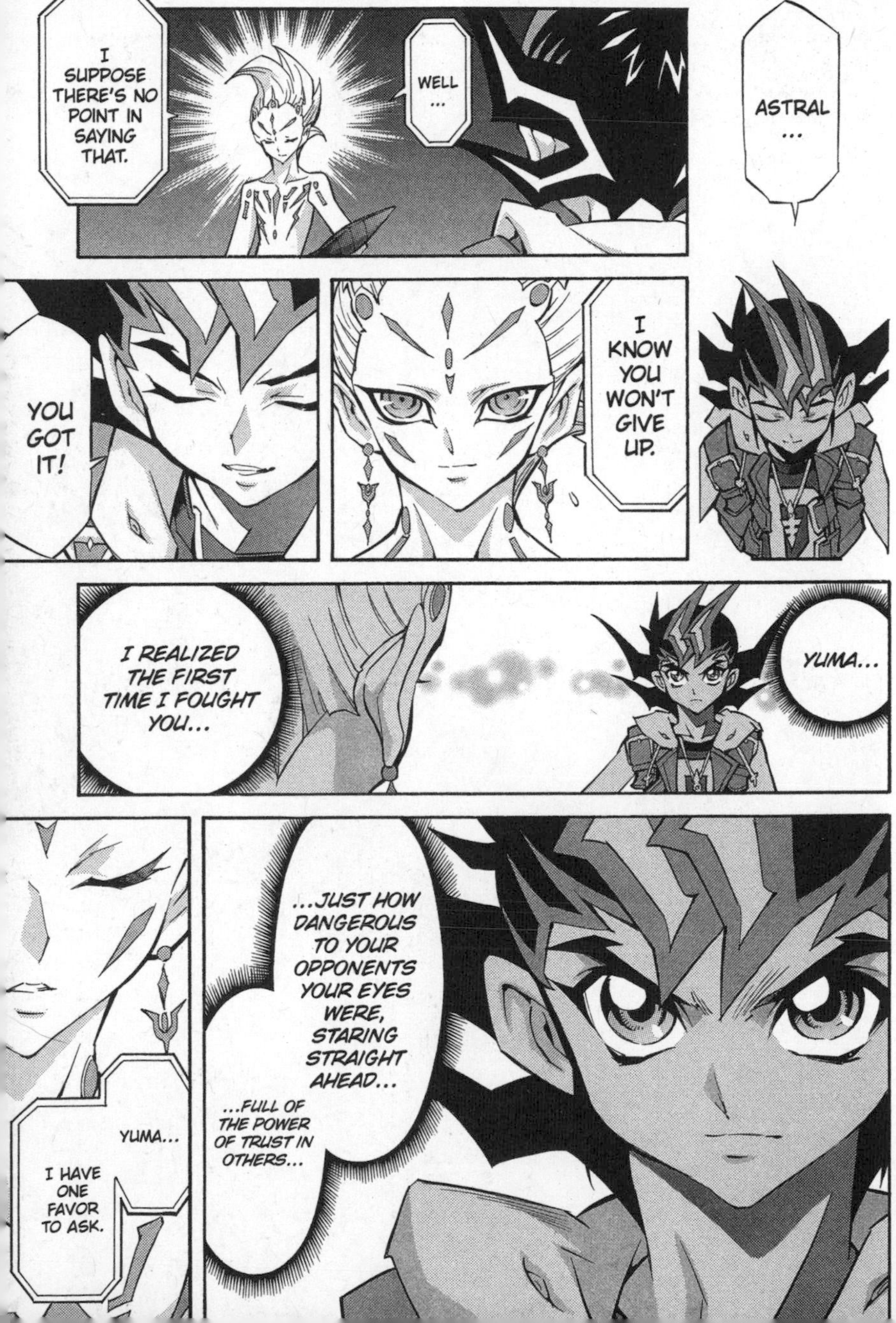
ASTRAL ...
WELL ...
I SUPPOSE THERE'S NO POINT IN SAYING THAT.
I KNOW YOU WON'T GIVE UP.
YOU GOT IT!
YUMA...
I REALIZED THE FIRST TIME I FOUGHT YOU...
...JUST HOW DANGEROUS TO YOUR OPPONENTS YOUR EYES WERE, STARING STRAIGHT AHEAD...
...FULL OF THE POWER OF TRUST IN OTHERS...
YUMA...
I HAVE ONE FAVOR TO ASK.

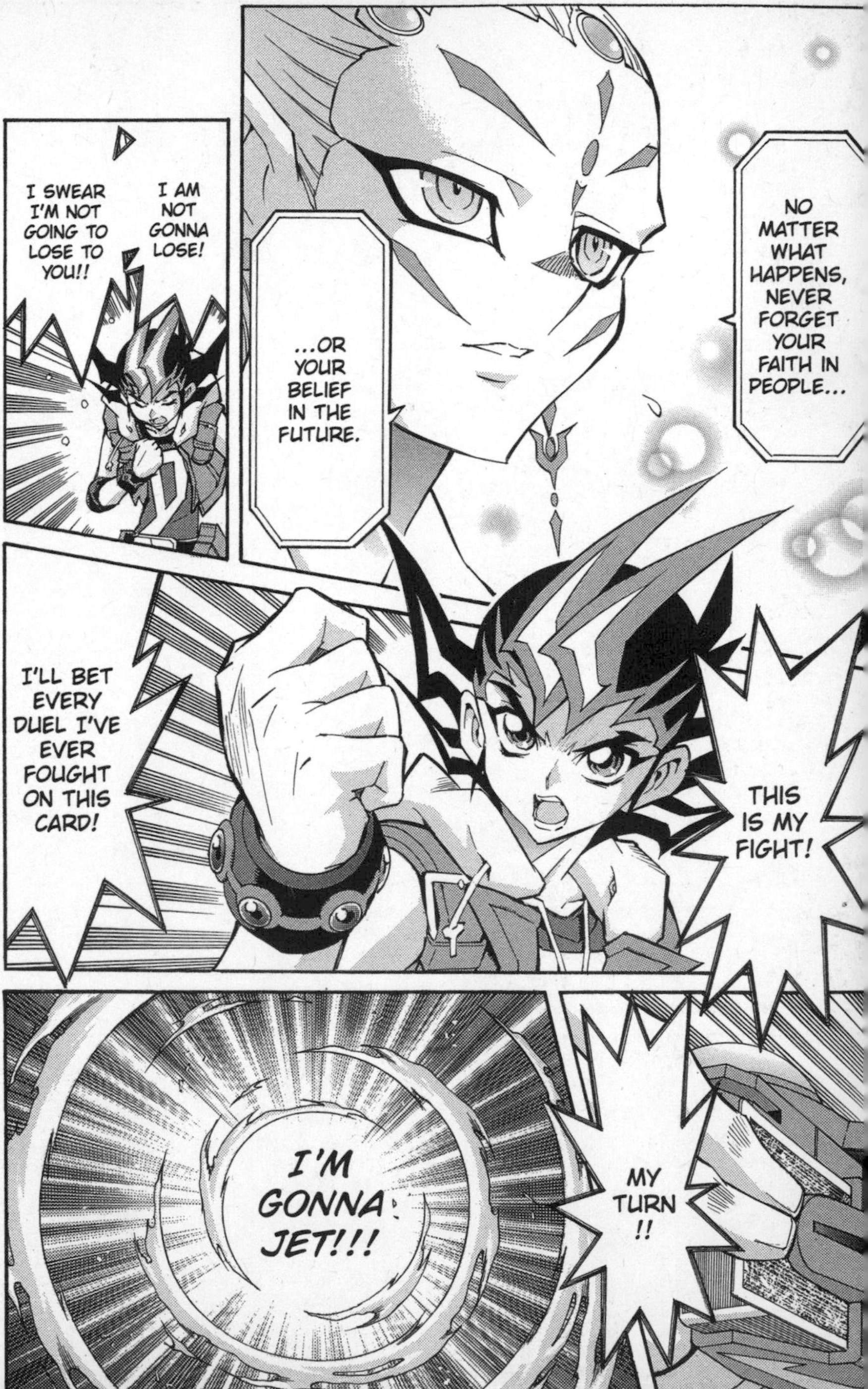
NO MATTER WHAT HAPPENS, NEVER FORGET YOUR FAITH IN PEOPLE...
...OR YOUR BELIEF IN THE FUTURE.
I AM NOT GONNA LOSE!
I SWEAR I'M NOT GOING TO LOSE TO YOU!!
THIS IS MY FIGHT!
I'LL BET EVERY DUEL I'VE EVER FOUGHT ON THIS CARD!
MY TURN !!
I'M GONNA JET!!!

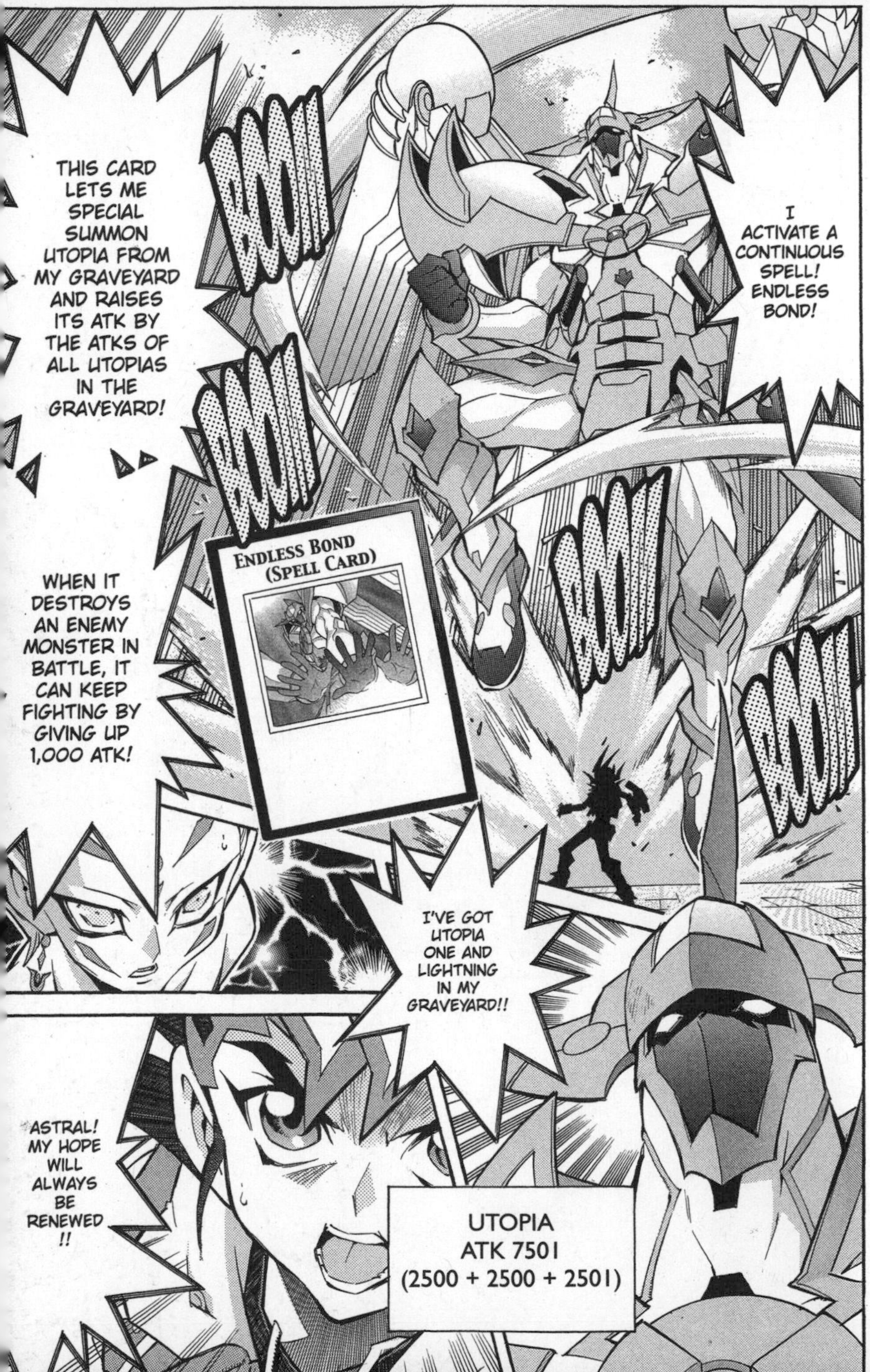

I ACTIVATE A CONTINUOUS SPELL! ENDLESS BOND!
BOOM
BOOM
THIS CARD LETS ME SPECIAL SUMMON UTOPIA FROM MY GRAVEYARD AND RAISES ITS ATK BY THE ATKS OF ALL UTOPIAS IN THE GRAVEYARD!
BOOM
BOOM
ENDLESS BOND (SPELL CARD)
WHEN IT DESTROYS AN ENEMY MONSTER IN BATTLE, IT CAN KEEP FIGHTING BY GIVING UP 1,000 ATK!
I'VE GOT UTOPIA ONE AND LIGHTNING IN MY GRAVEYARD!!
UTOPIA ATK 7501 (2500 + 2500 + 2501)
ASTRAL! MY HOPE WILL ALWAYS BE RENEWED !!

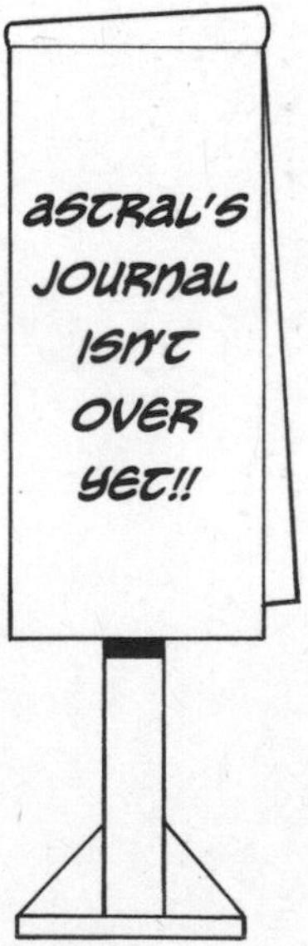
astral's journal isn't over yet!!

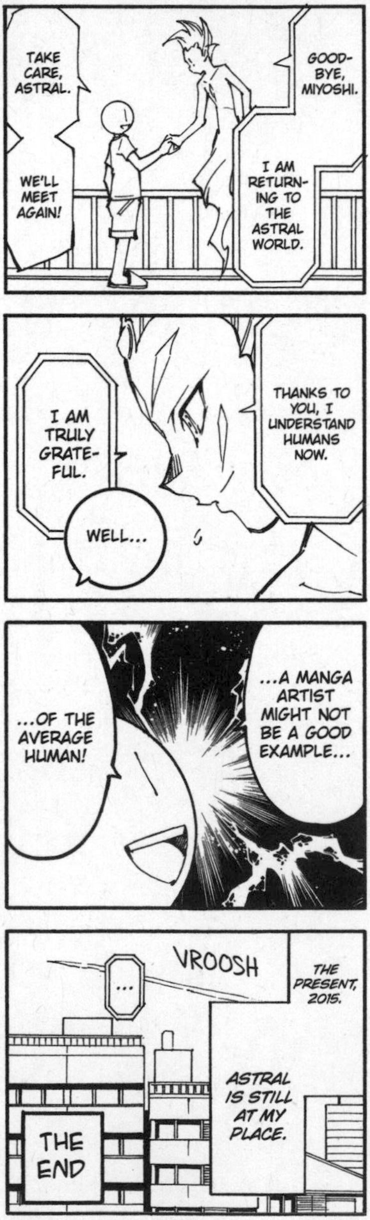
GOOD-BYE, MIYOSHI.
I AM RETURNING TO THE ASTRAL WORLD.
TAKE CARE, ASTRAL.
WE'LL MEET AGAIN!
THANKS TO YOU, I UNDERSTAND HUMANS NOW.
I AM TRULY GRATEFUL.
WELL...
...A MANGA ARTIST MIGHT NOT BE A GOOD EXAMPLE...
...OF THE AVERAGE HUMAN!
THE PRESENT, 2015.
VROOSH
...
ASTRAL IS STILL AT MY PLACE.
THE END

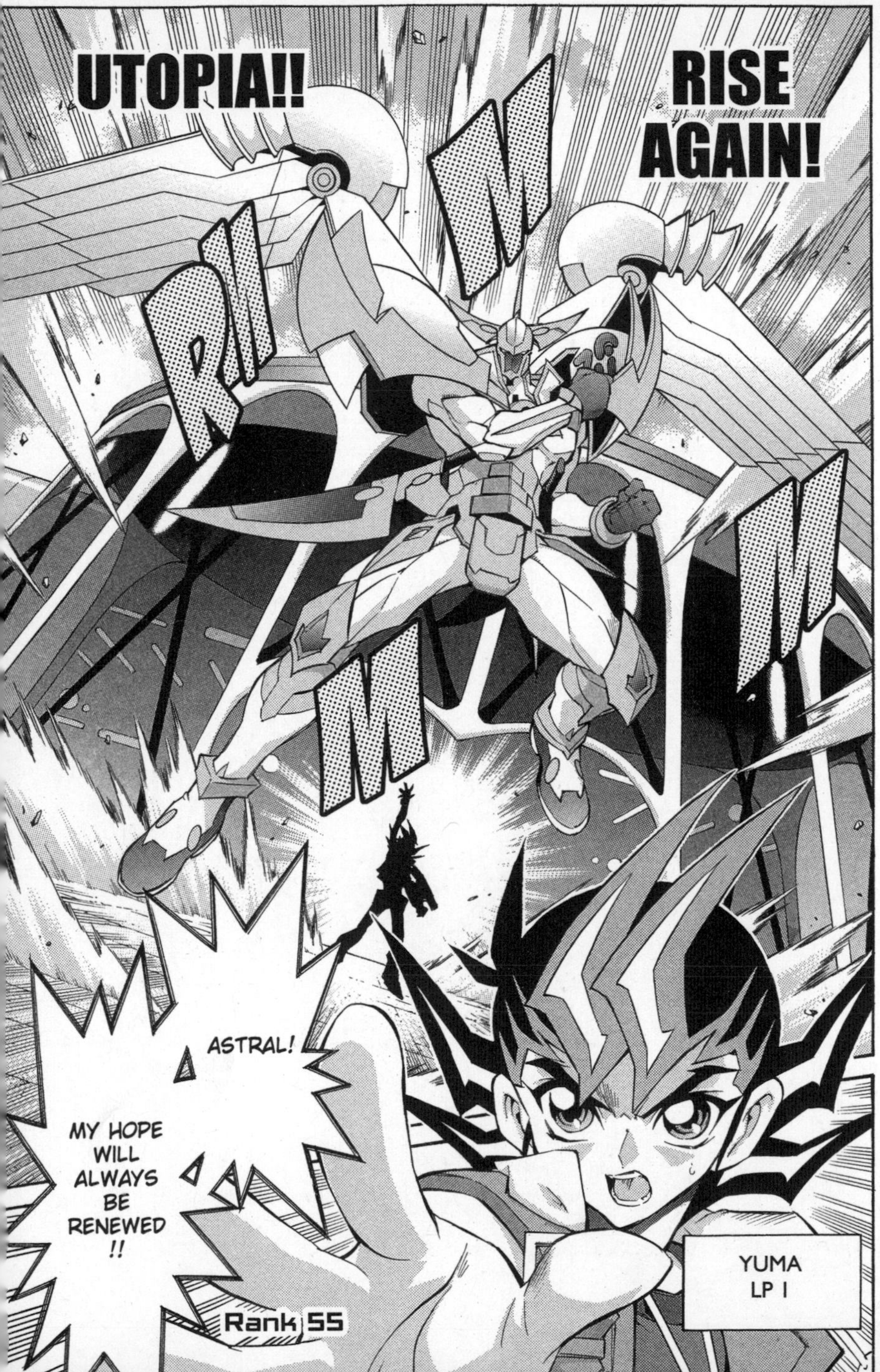
RISE AGAIN!
UTOPIA!!
RMMMMM
ASTRAL!
MY HOPE WILL ALWAYS BE RENEWED!!
YUMA
LP 1
Rank 55

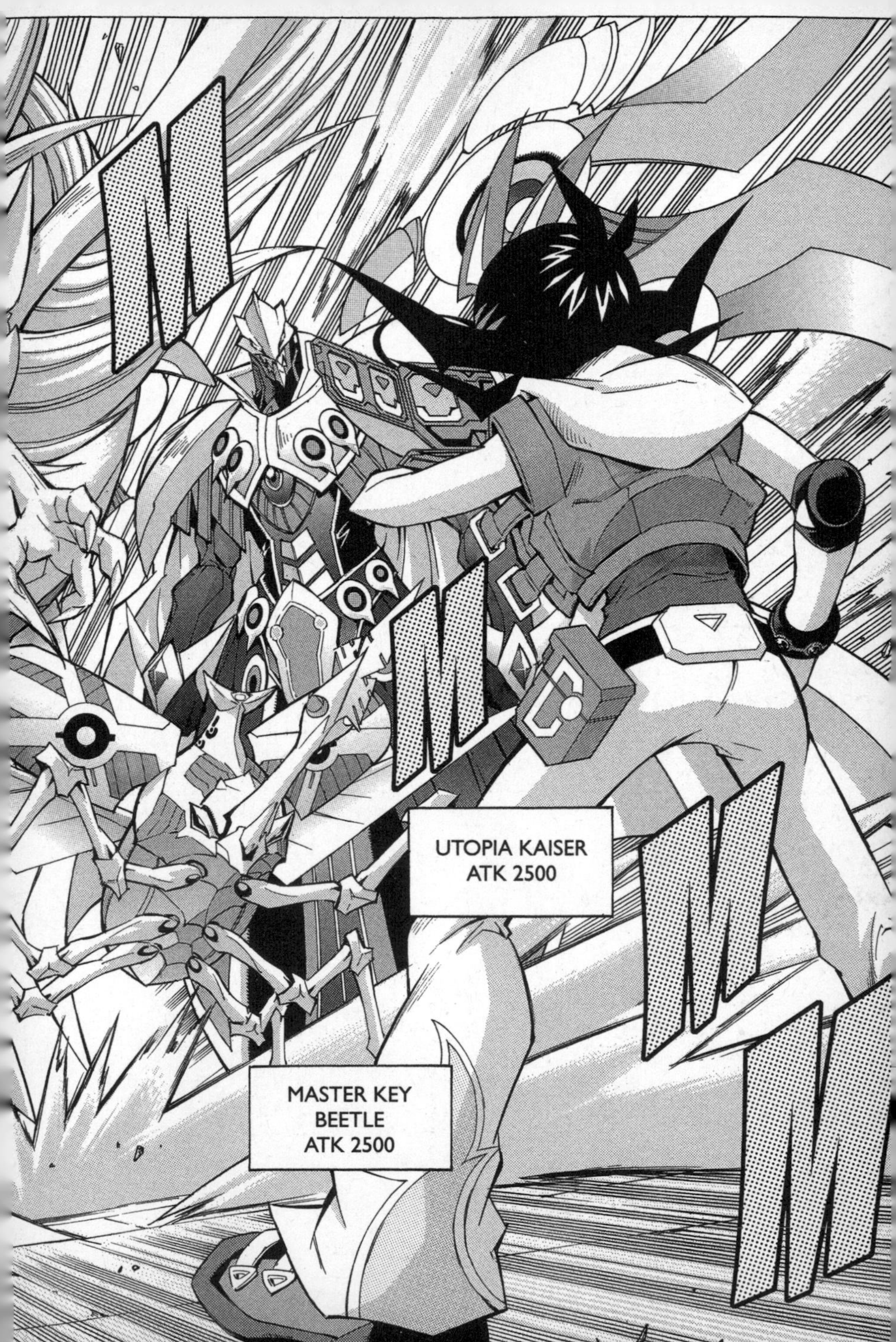
M
M
UTOPIA KAISER ATK 2500
M
M
MASTER KEY BEETLE ATK 2500

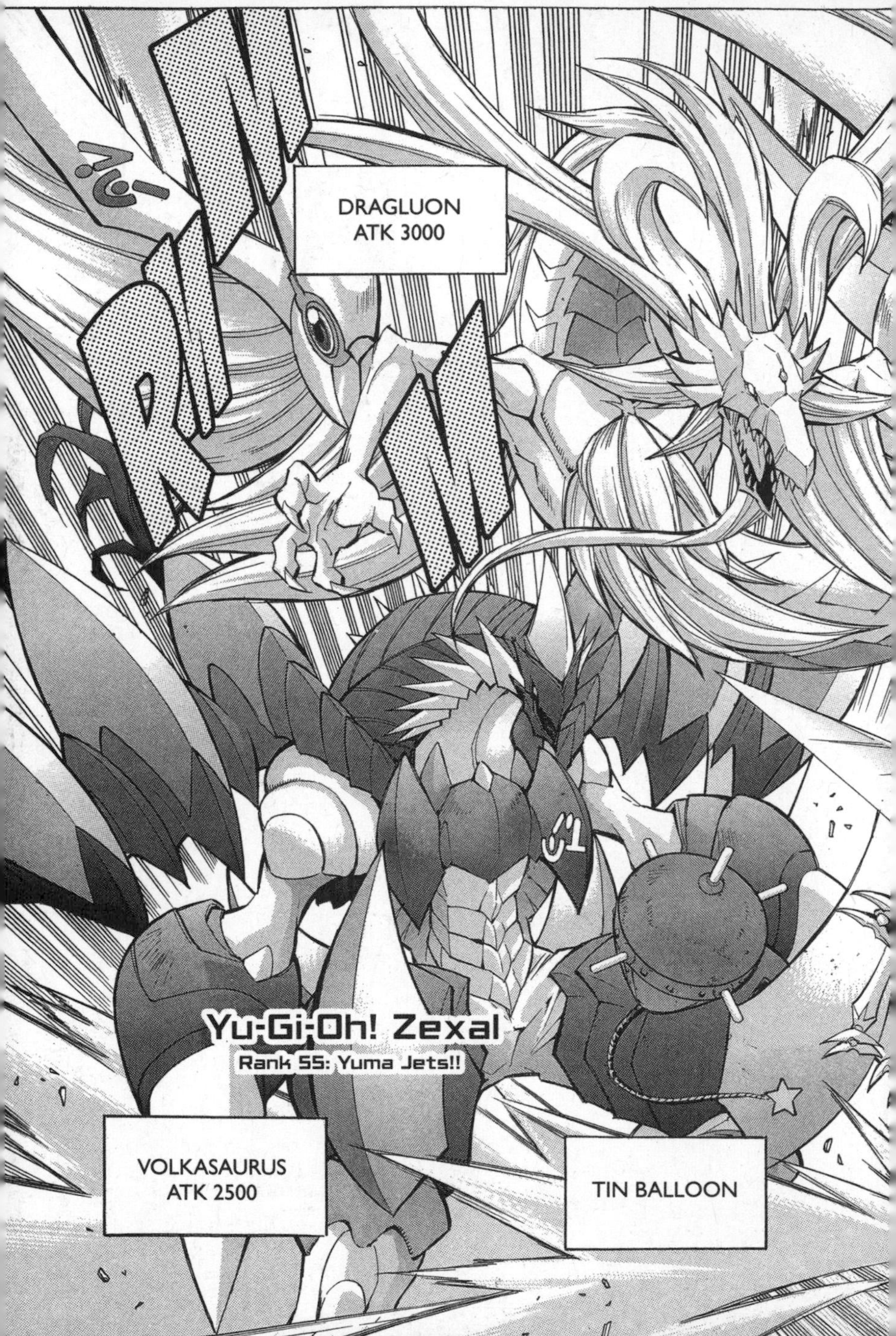
DRAGLUON
ATK 3000
Yu-Gi-Oh! Zexal
Rank 55: Yuma Jets!!
TIN BALLOON
VOLKASAURUS
ATK 2500

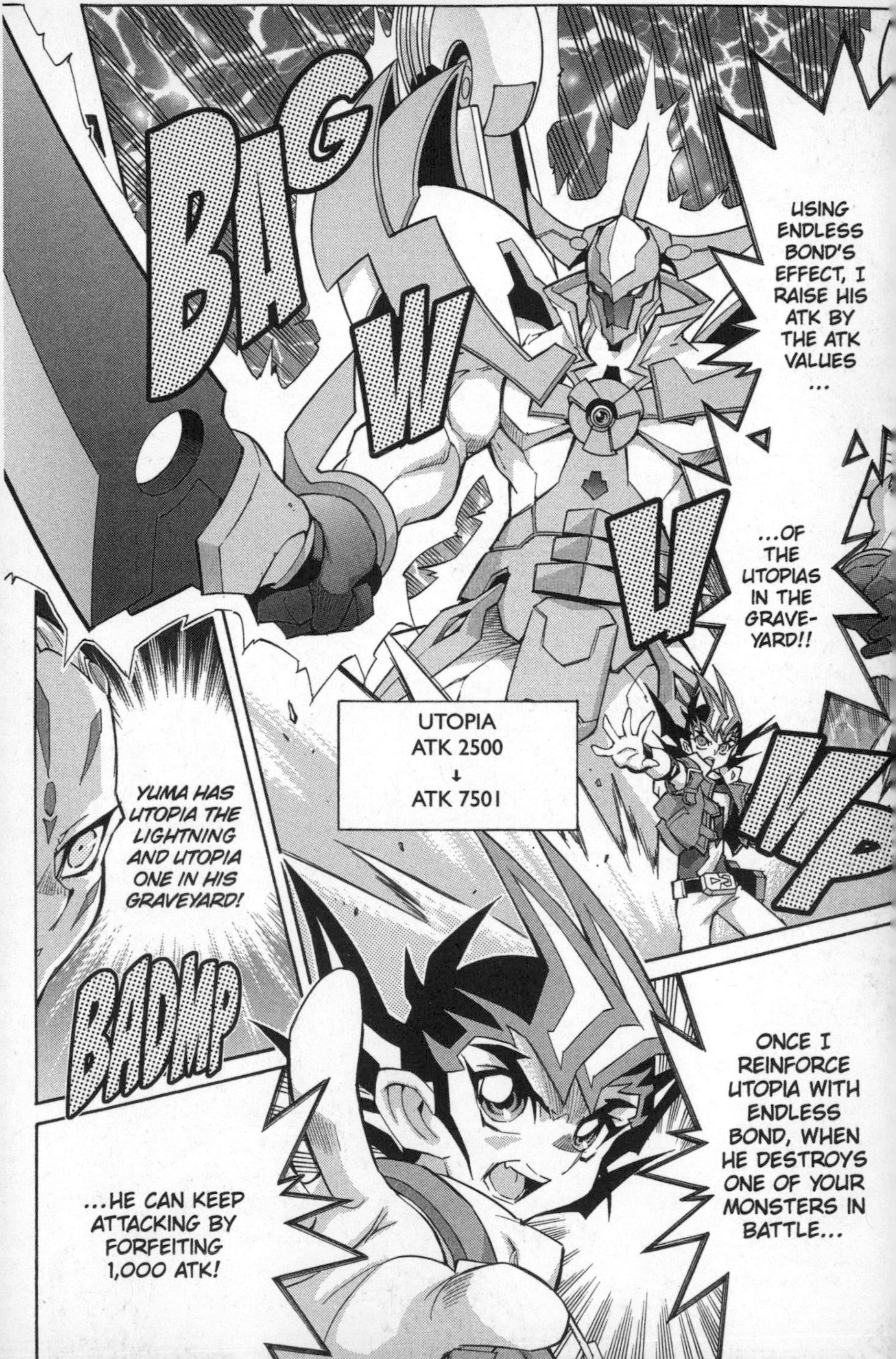
USING ENDLESS BOND'S EFFECT, I RAISE HIS ATK BY THE ATK VALUES ...
BAGWUMP
...OF THE UTOPIAS IN THE GRAVE-YARD!!
UTOPIA ATK 2500 ↓ ATK 7501
YUMA HAS UTOPIA THE LIGHTNING AND UTOPIA ONE IN HIS GRAVEYARD!
BADMP
ONCE I REINFORCE UTOPIA WITH ENDLESS BOND, WHEN HE DESTROYS ONE OF YOUR MONSTERS IN BATTLE...
...HE CAN KEEP ATTACKING BY FORFEITING 1,000 ATK!

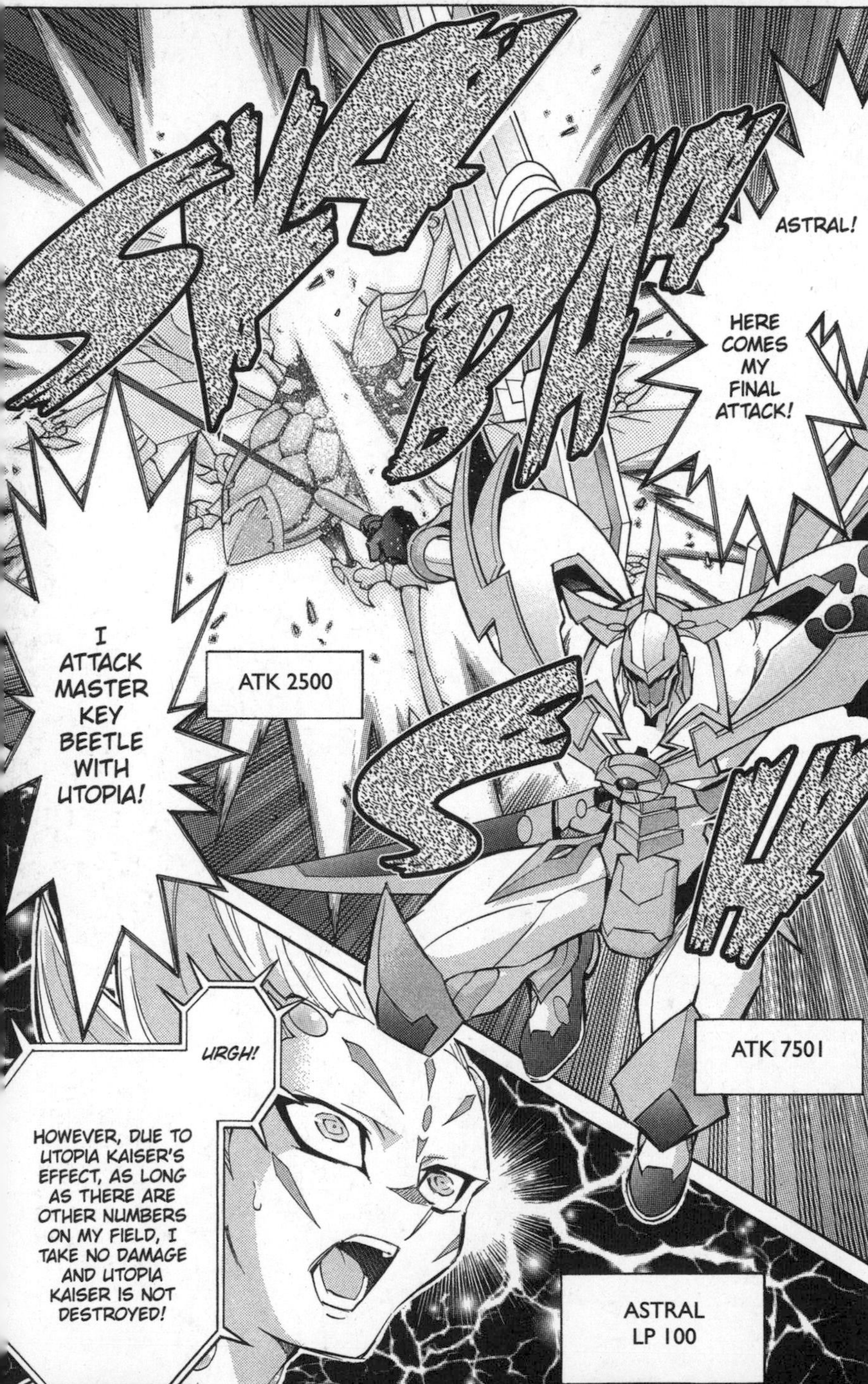
ASTRAL!
HERE COMES MY FINAL ATTACK!
SKASHH
I ATTACK MASTER KEY BEETLE WITH UTOPIA!
ATK 2500
SHH
ATK 7501
URGH!
HOWEVER, DUE TO UTOPIA KAISER'S EFFECT, AS LONG AS THERE ARE OTHER NUMBERS ON MY FIELD, I TAKE NO DAMAGE AND UTOPIA KAISER IS NOT DESTROYED!
ASTRAL LP 100

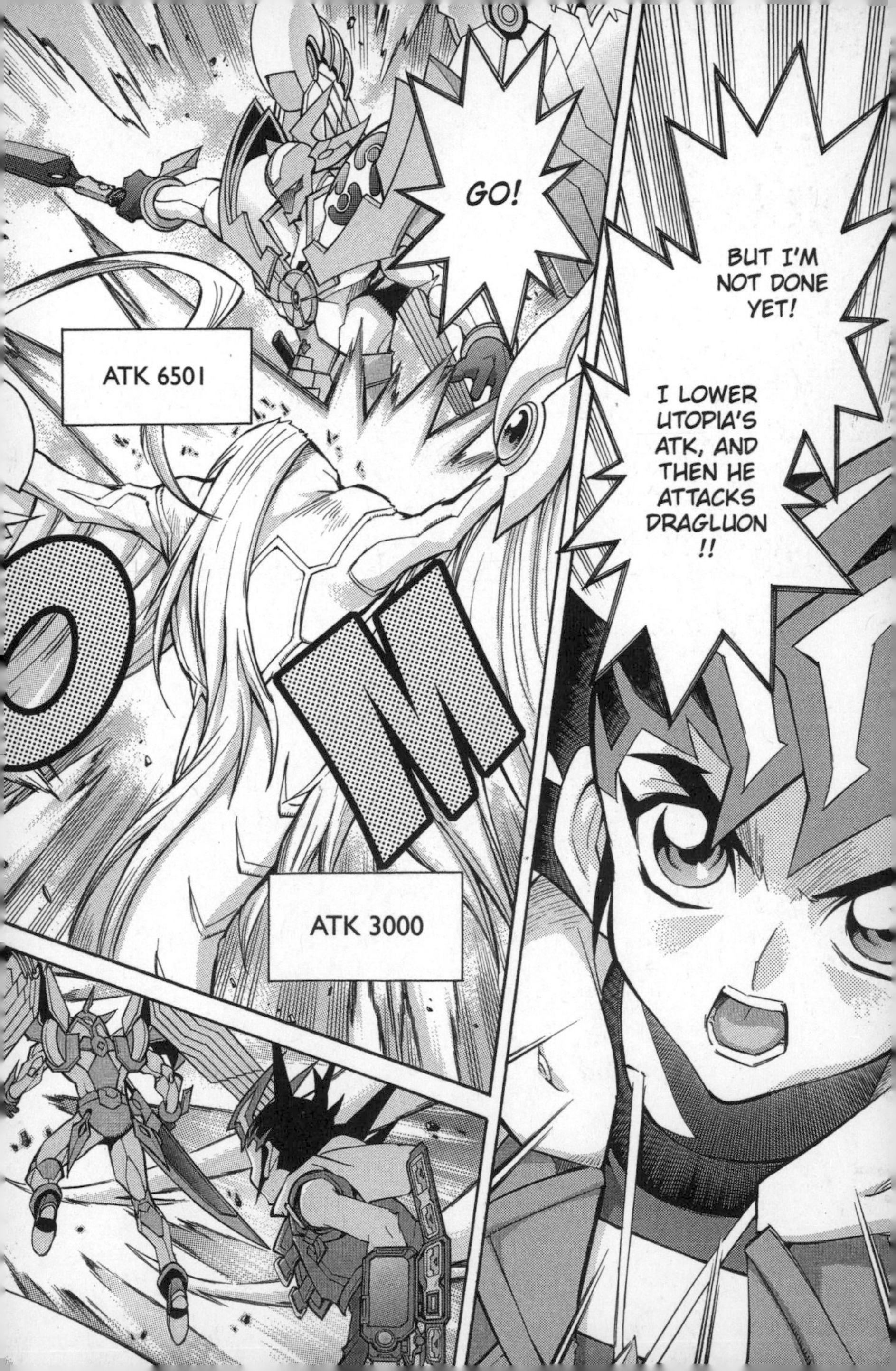
BUT I'M NOT DONE YET!
I LOWER UTOPIA'S ATK, AND THEN HE ATTACKS DRAGLUON !!
GO!
ATK 6501
ATK 3000

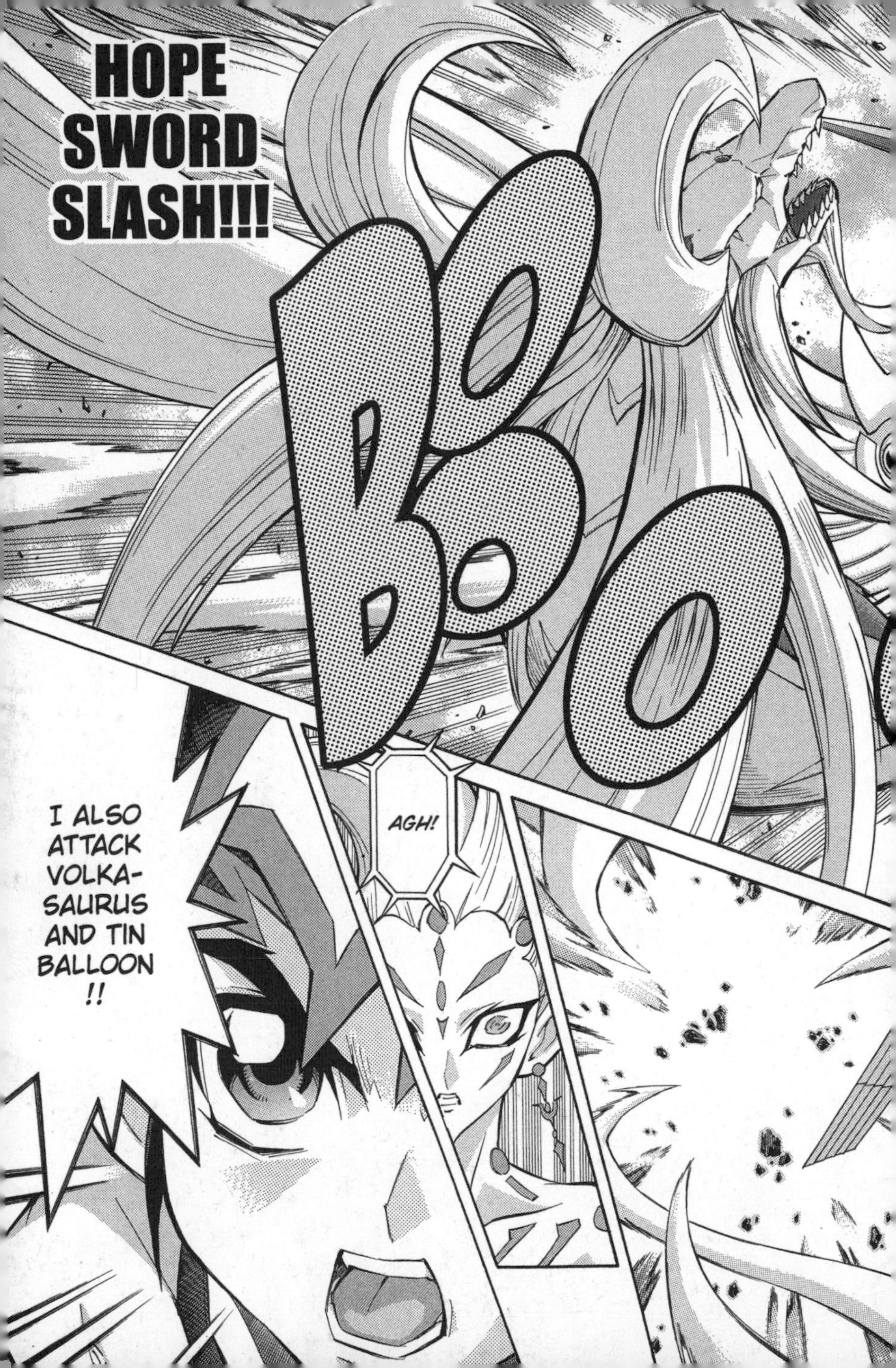
HOPE SWORD SLASH!!!
BOO
AGH!
I ALSO ATTACK VOLKA-SAURUS AND TIN BALLOON !!

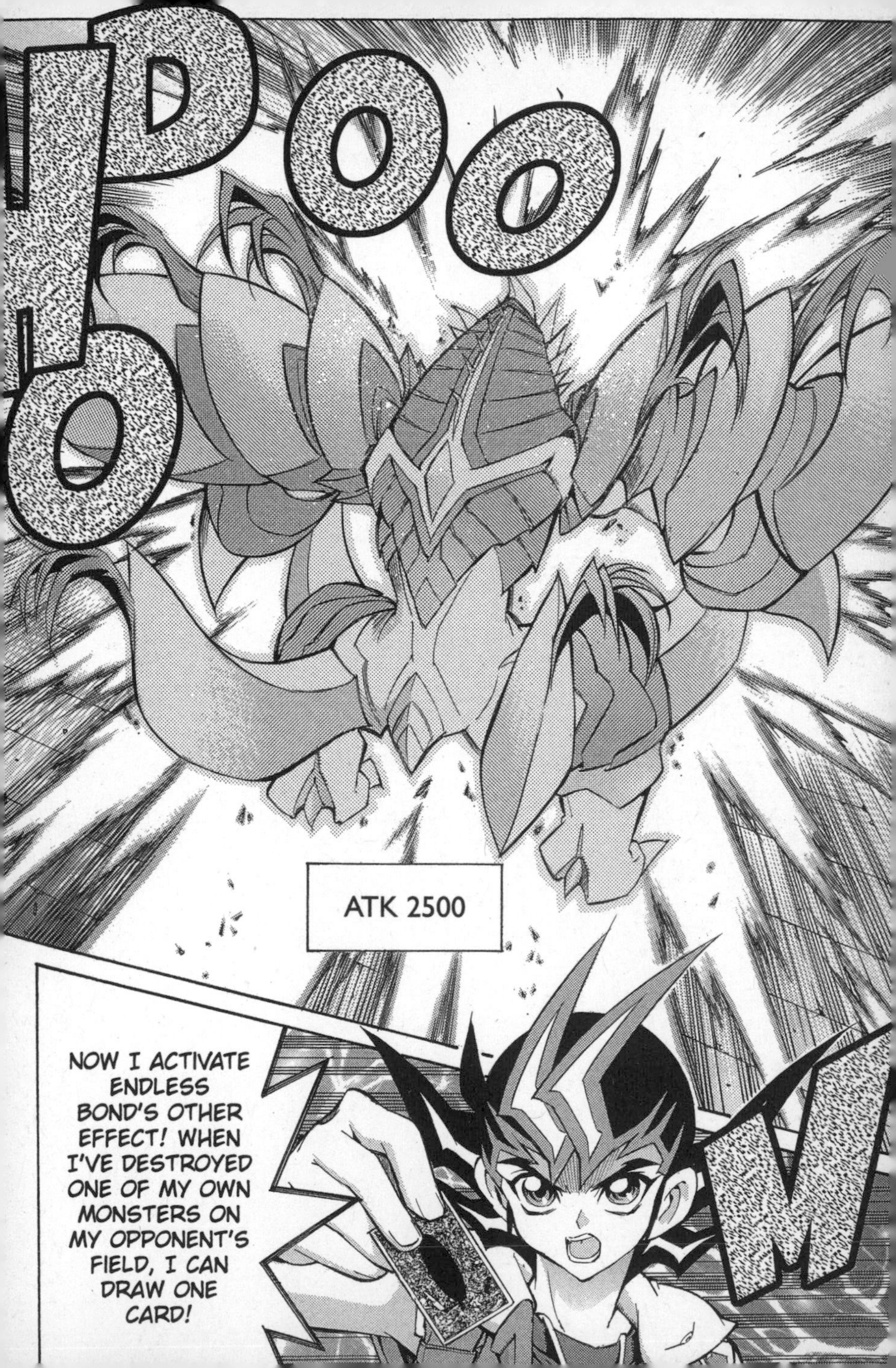
DOOOM!
ATK 2500
NOW I ACTIVATE ENDLESS BOND'S OTHER EFFECT! WHEN I'VE DESTROYED ONE OF MY OWN MONSTERS ON MY OPPONENT'S FIELD, I CAN DRAW ONE CARD!

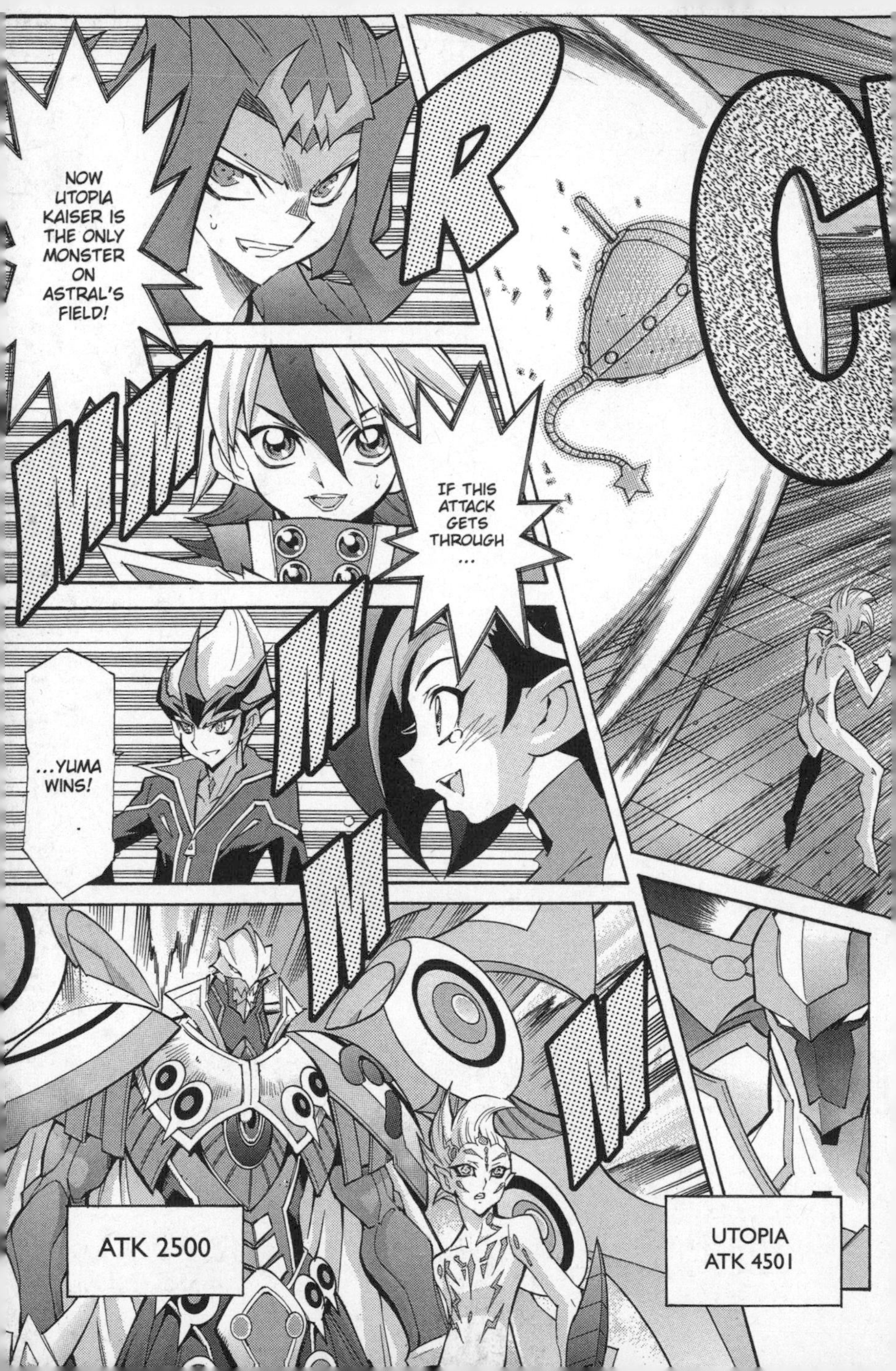
NOW UTOPIA KAISER IS THE ONLY MONSTER ON ASTRAL'S FIELD!
IF THIS ATTACK GETS THROUGH ...
...YUMA WINS!
UTOPIA ATK 4501
ATK 2500

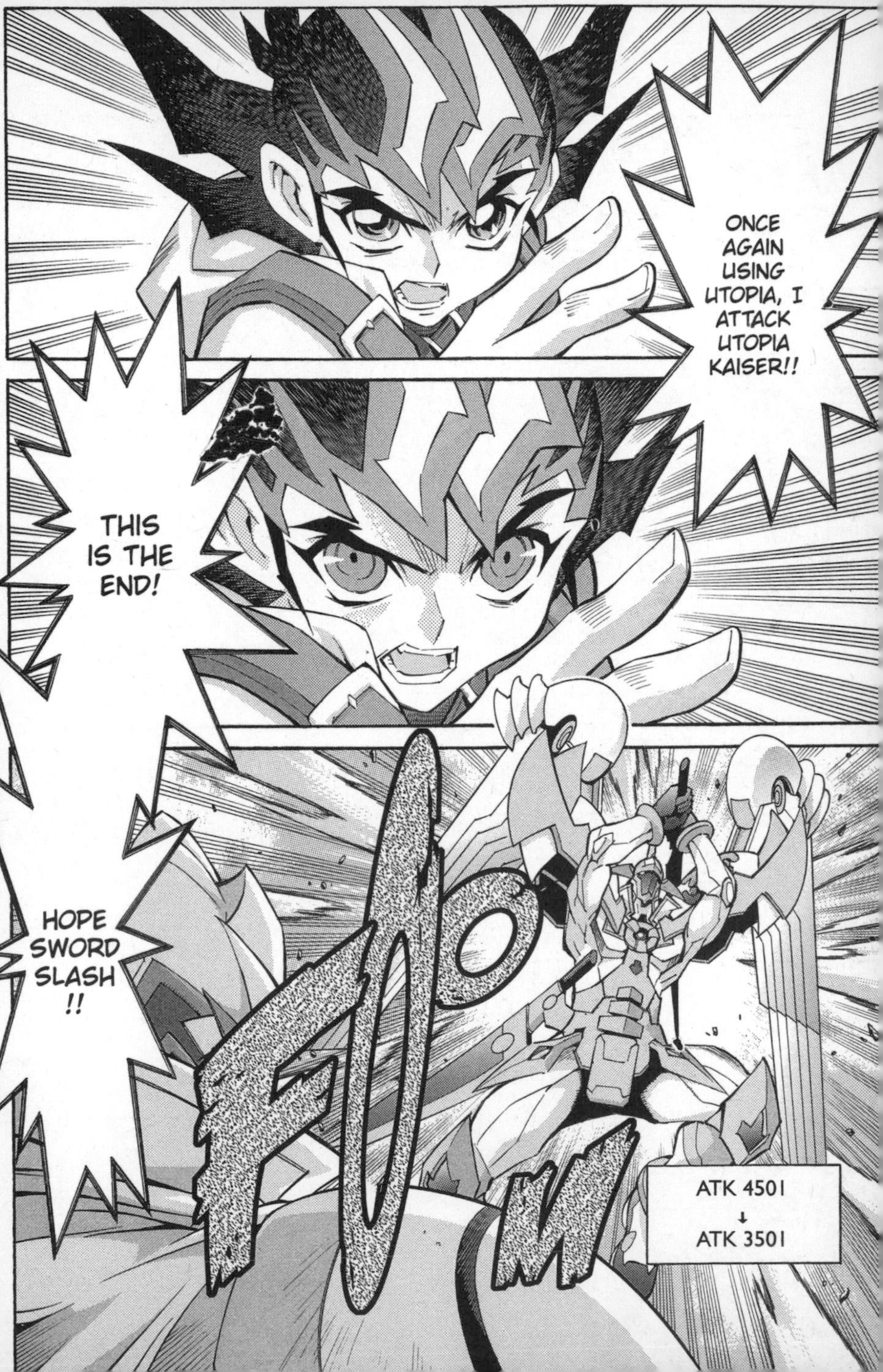
ONCE AGAIN USING UTOPIA, I ATTACK UTOPIA KAISER!!
THIS IS THE END!
HOPE SWORD SLASH !!
FOOM
ATK 4501 ↓ ATK 3501

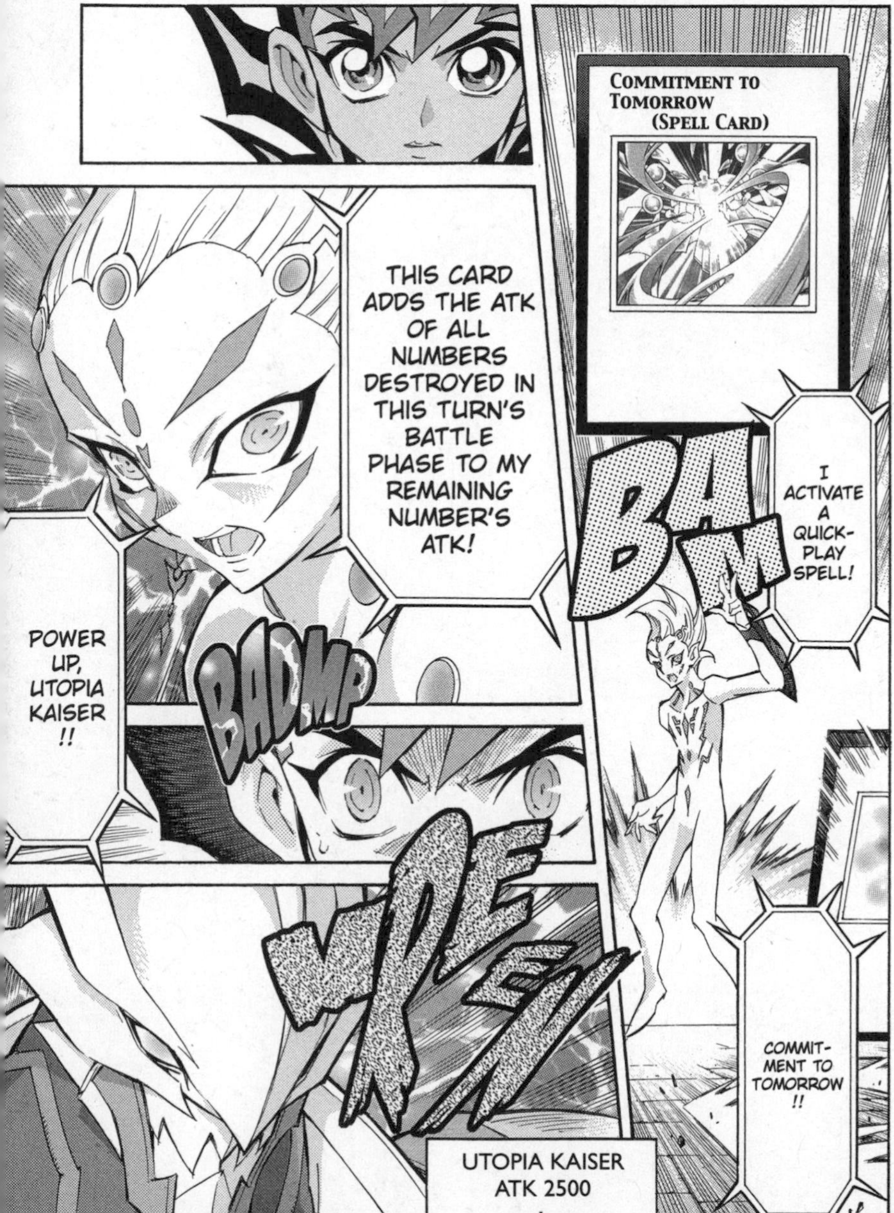
I ACTIVATE A QUICK-PLAY SPELL!
BAM
COMMITMENT TO TOMORROW (SPELL CARD)
COMMIT-MENT TO TOMORROW !!
THIS CARD ADDS THE ATK OF ALL NUMBERS DESTROYED IN THIS TURN'S BATTLE PHASE TO MY REMAINING NUMBER'S ATK!
BADMP
POWER UP, UTOPIA KAISER !!
UTOPIA KAISER ATK 2500 ↓ ATK 10500

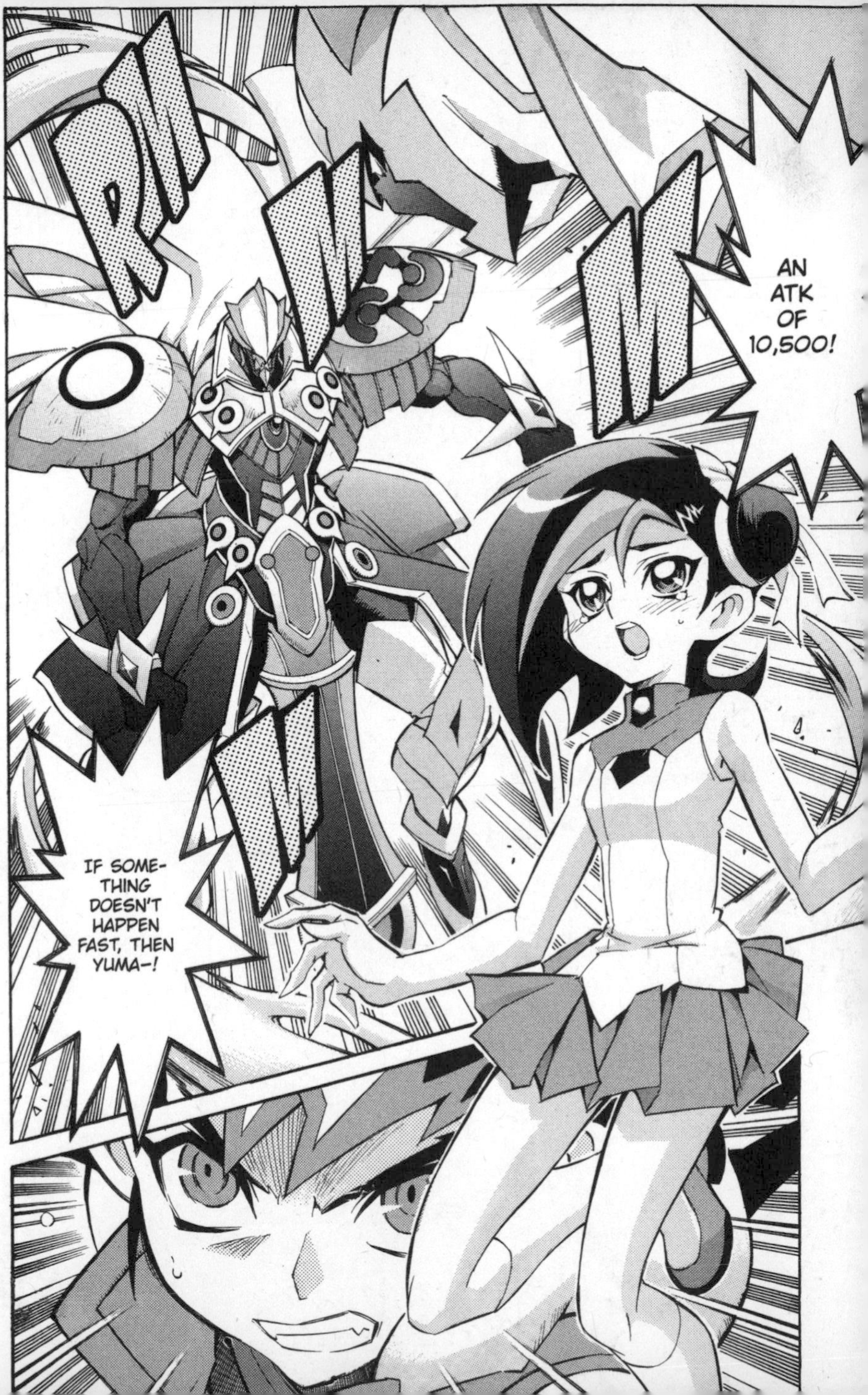
AN ATK OF 10,500!
RMMMM
IF SOME-THING DOESN'T HAPPEN FAST, THEN YUMA-!

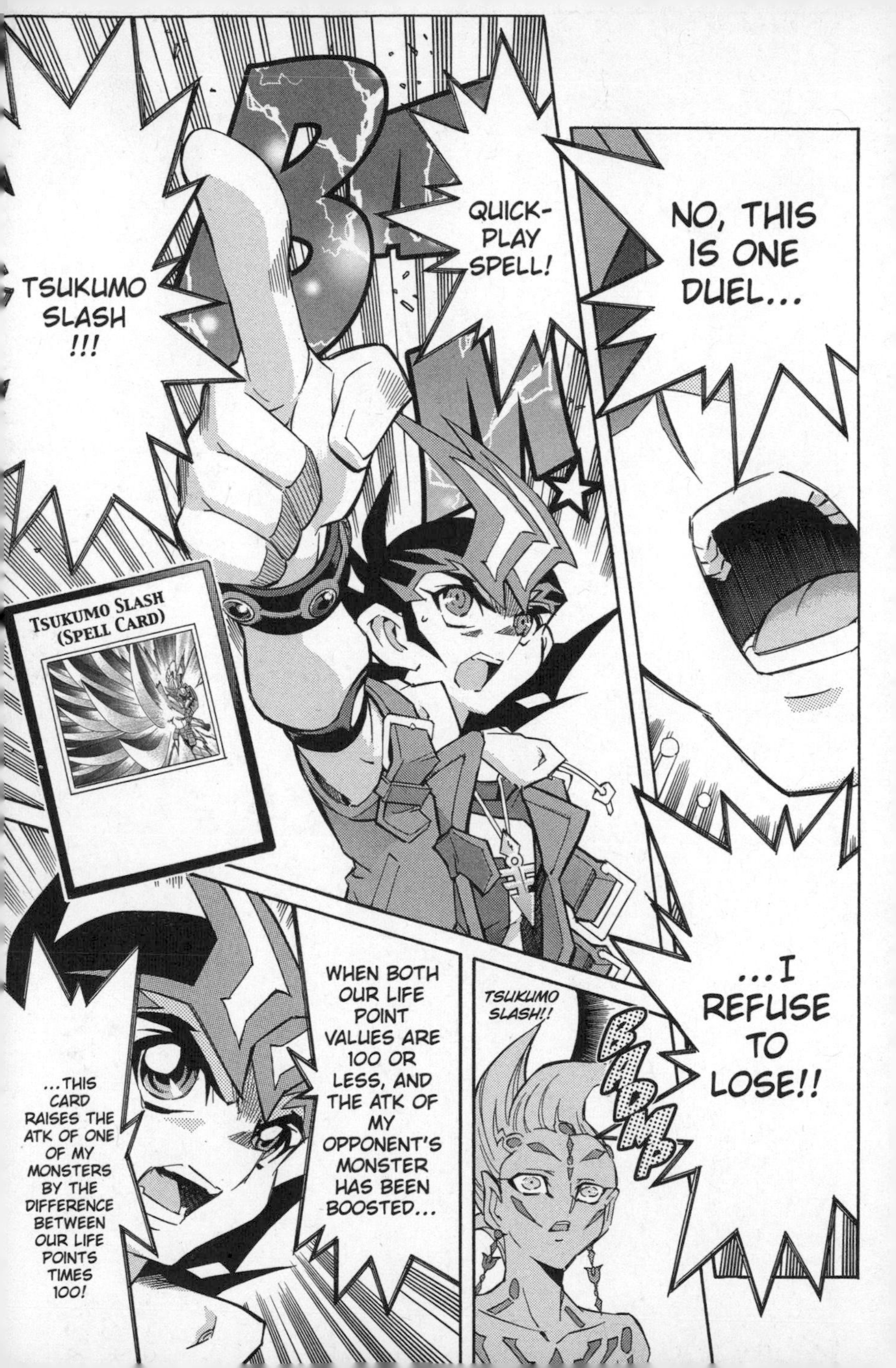
NO, THIS IS ONE DUEL...
...I REFUSE TO LOSE!!
QUICK-PLAY SPELL!
TSUKUMO SLASH !!!
TSUKUMO SLASH (SPELL CARD)
TSUKUMO SLASH!!
BADUMP
WHEN BOTH OUR LIFE POINT VALUES ARE 100 OR LESS, AND THE ATK OF MY OPPONENT'S MONSTER HAS BEEN BOOSTED...
...THIS CARD RAISES THE ATK OF ONE OF MY MONSTERS BY THE DIFFERENCE BETWEEN OUR LIFE POINTS TIMES 100!

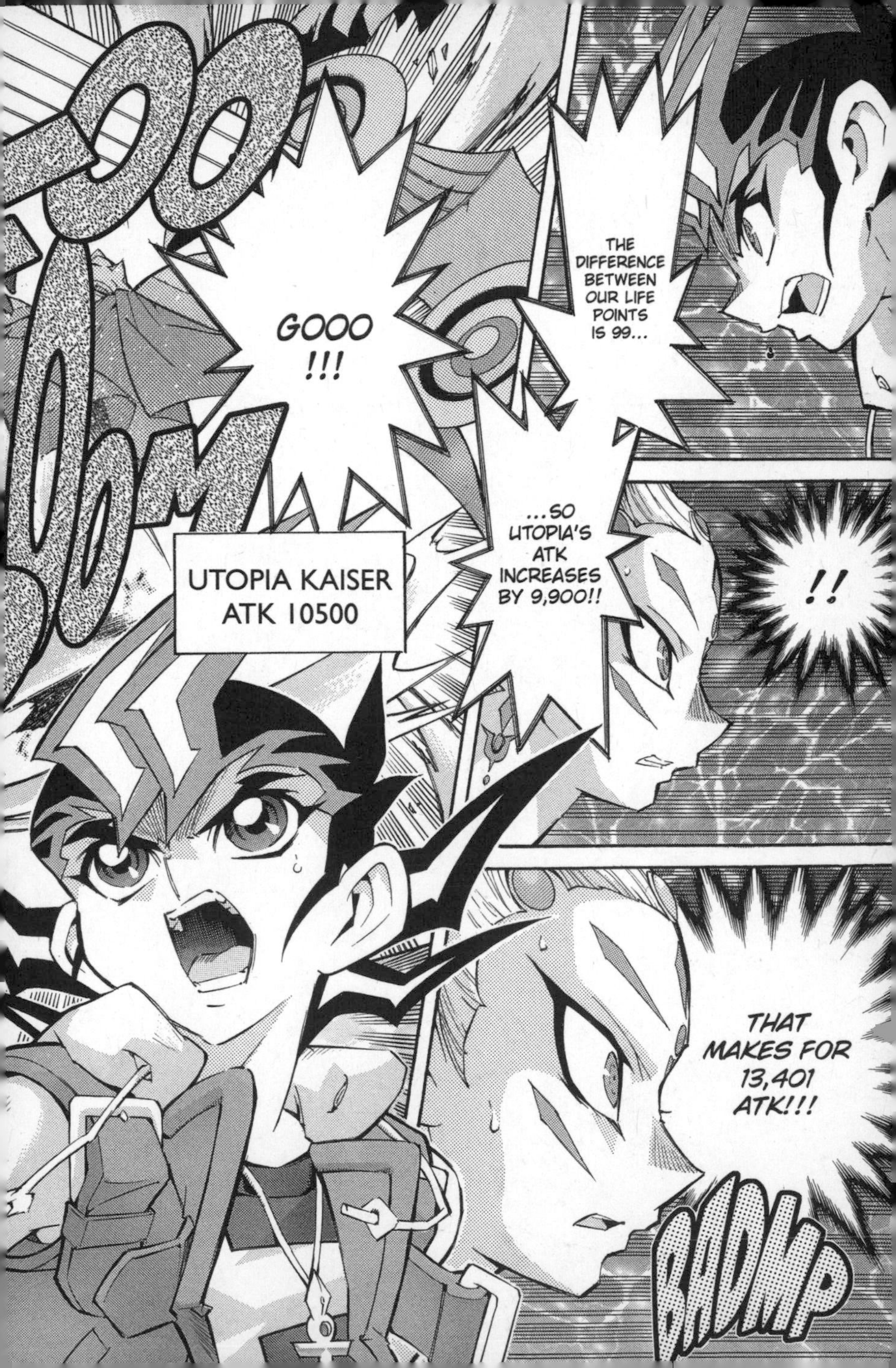
THE DIFFERENCE BETWEEN OUR LIFE POINTS IS 99...
GOOO !!!
...SO UTOPIA'S ATK INCREASES BY 9,900!!
!!
UTOPIA KAISER ATK 10500
THAT MAKES FOR 13,401 ATK!!!
BADMP

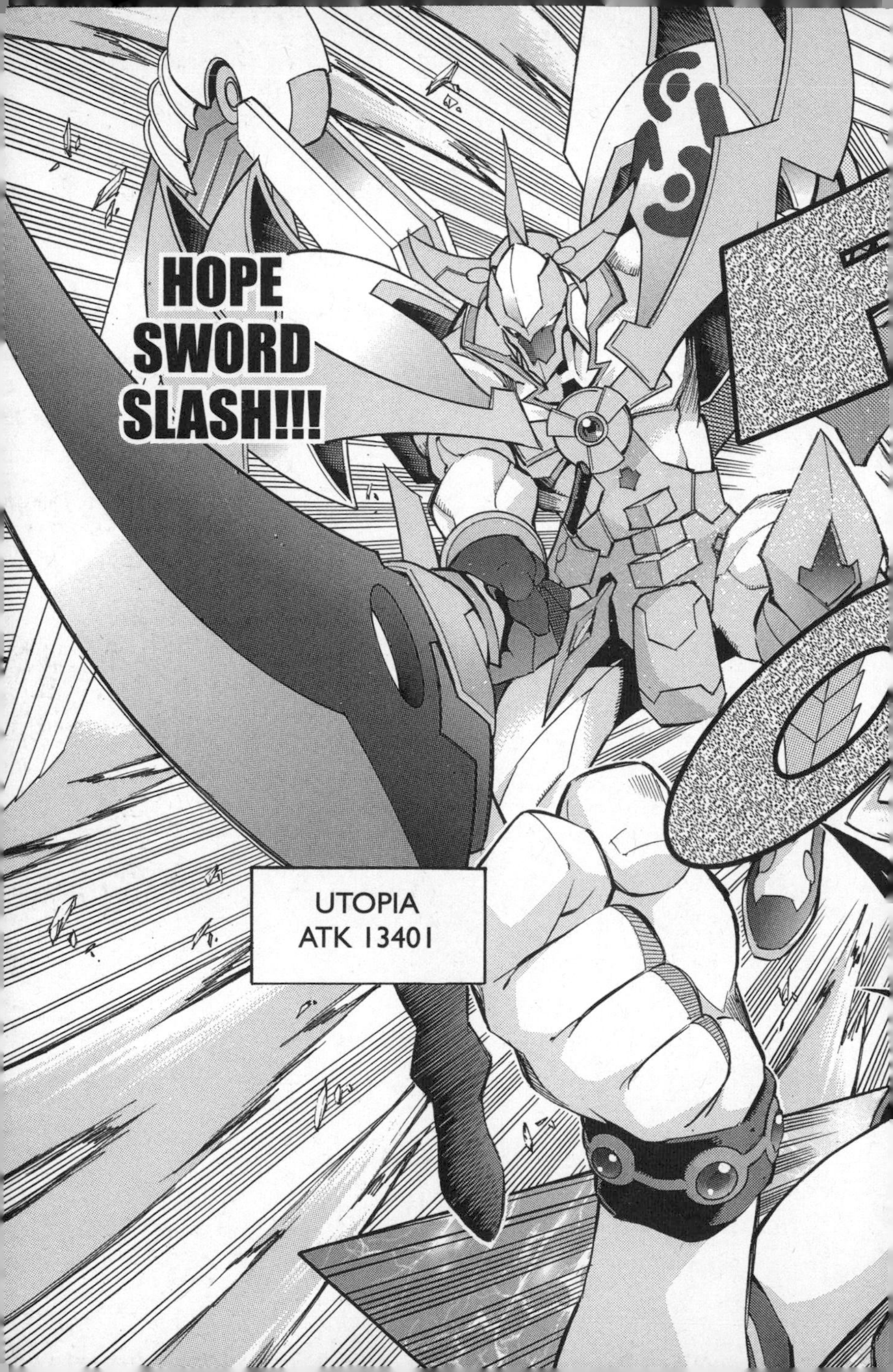
HOPE SWORD SLASH!!!
UTOPIA ATK 13401

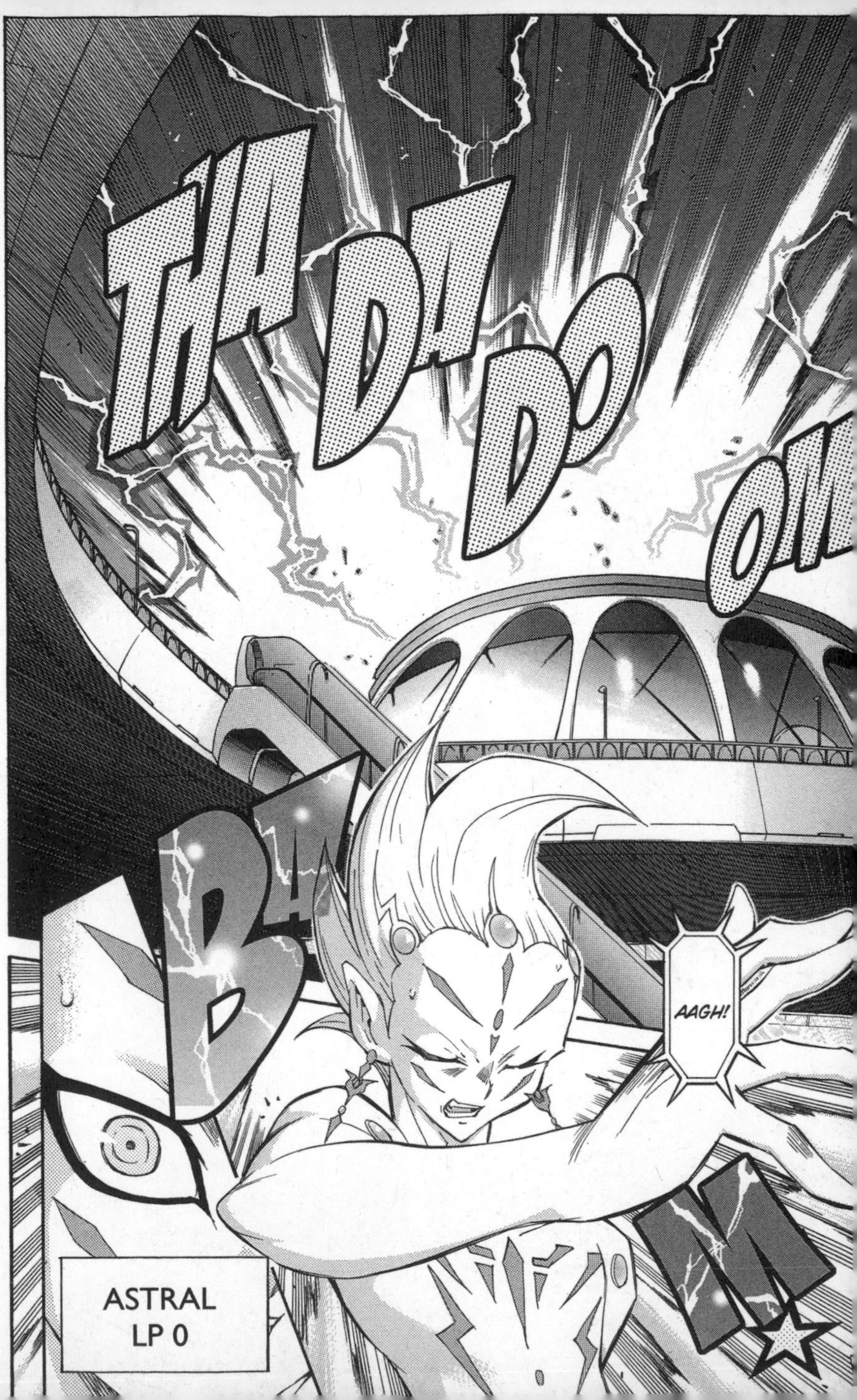
THA-DA-DO-OM
AAGH!
BAM
ASTRAL
LP 0

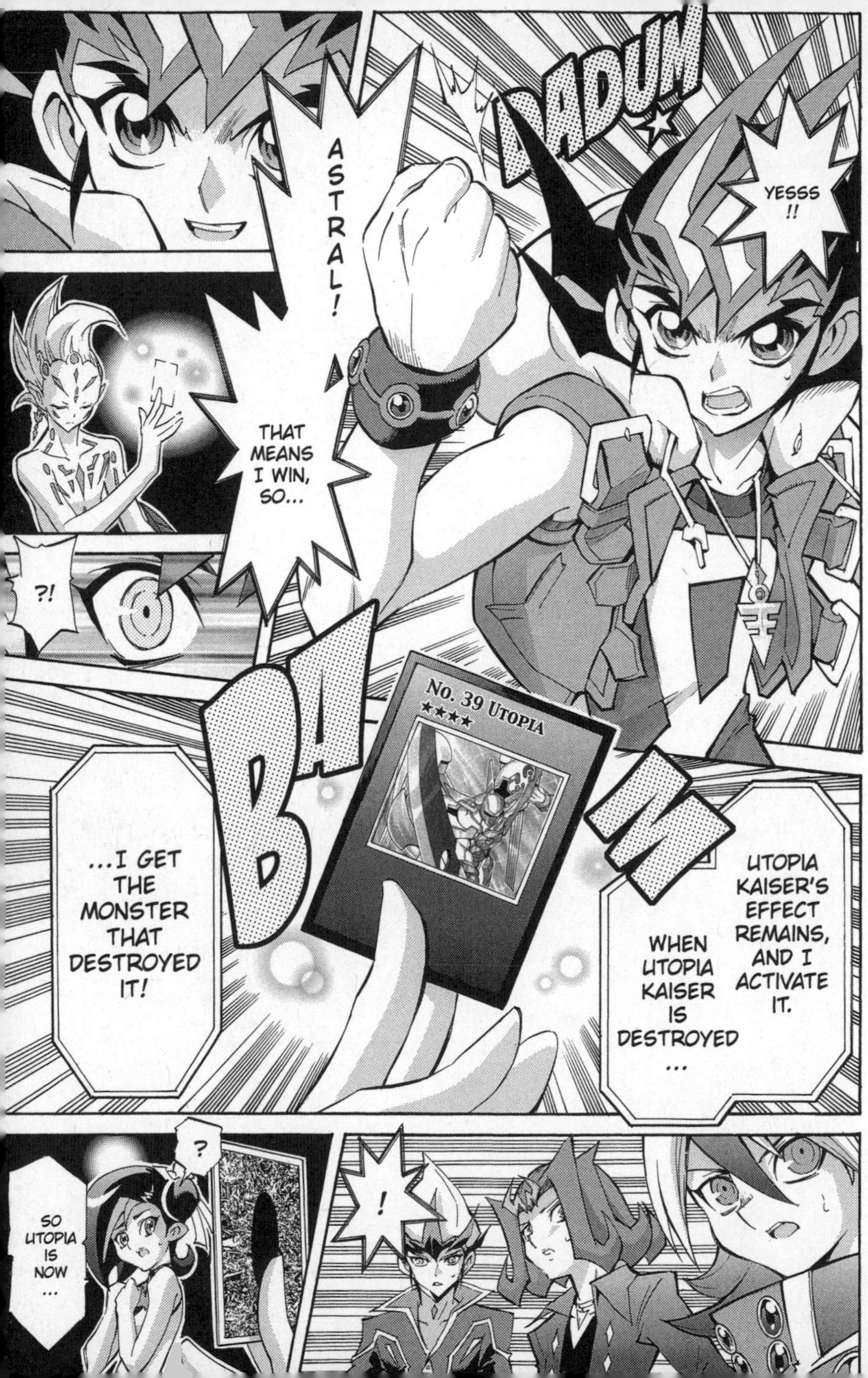
BADUM
YESSS !!
ASTRAL!
THAT MEANS I WIN, SO...
?!
BAM
UTOPIA KAISER'S EFFECT REMAINS, AND I ACTIVATE IT.
WHEN UTOPIA KAISER IS DESTROYED ...
...I GET THE MONSTER THAT DESTROYED IT!
No. 39 UTOPIA
!
?
SO UTOPIA IS NOW ...

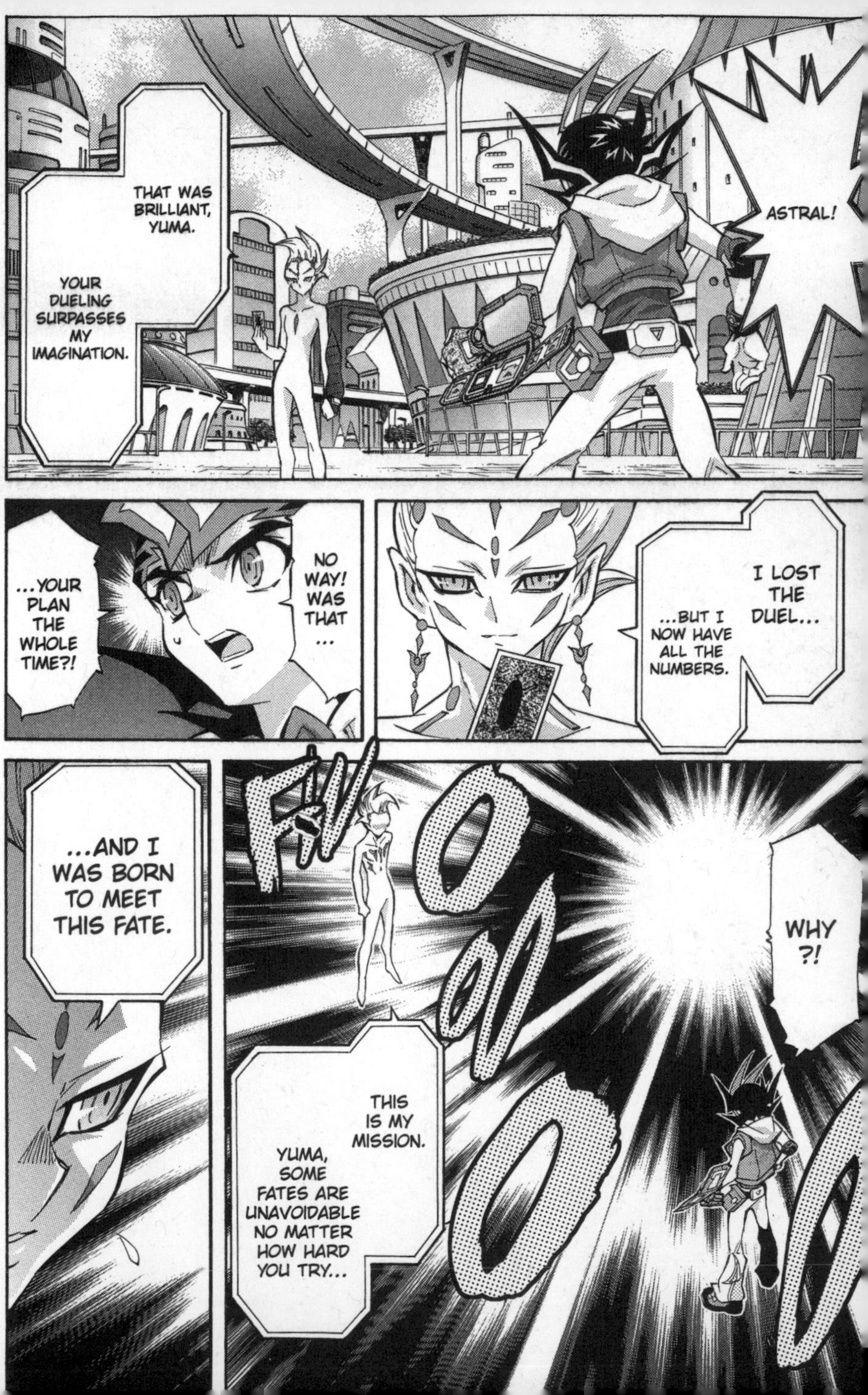
ASTRAL!
THAT WAS BRILLIANT, YUMA.
YOUR DUELING SURPASSES MY IMAGINATION.
I LOST THE DUEL...
...BUT I NOW HAVE ALL THE NUMBERS.
NO WAY! WAS THAT ...
...YOUR PLAN THE WHOLE TIME?!
WHY ?!
THIS IS MY MISSION.
YUMA, SOME FATES ARE UNAVOIDABLE NO MATTER HOW HARD YOU TRY...
...AND I WAS BORN TO MEET THIS FATE.

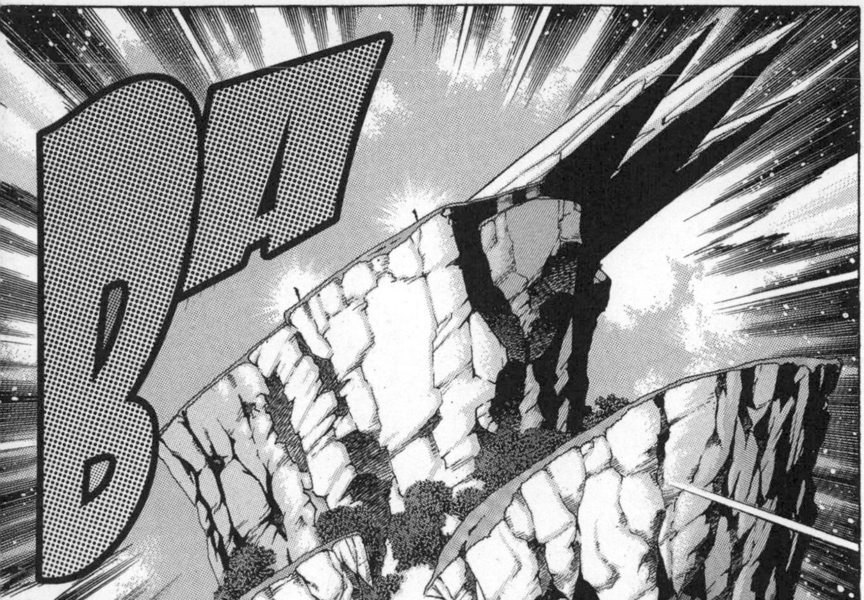
BA
M!

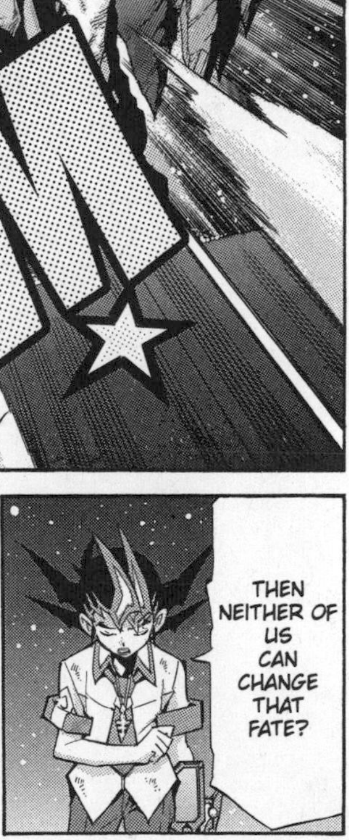
THEN NEITHER OF US CAN CHANGE THAT FATE?

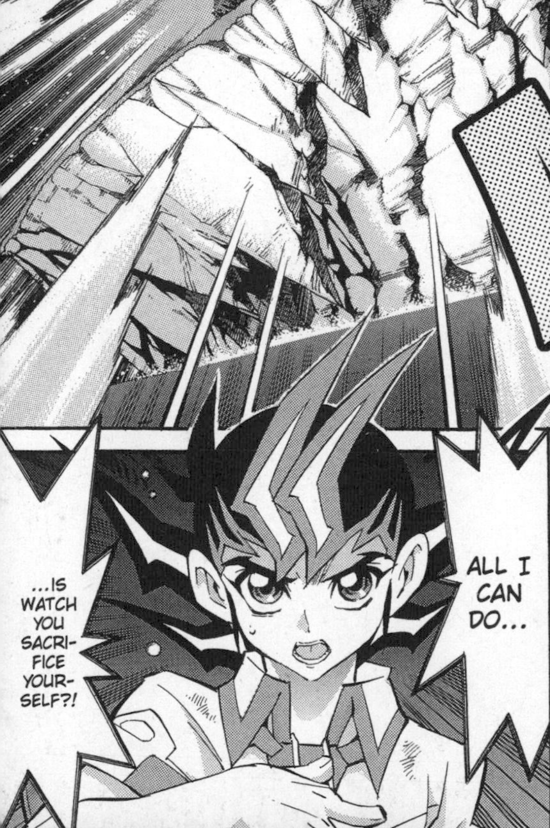
ALL I CAN DO...
...IS WATCH YOU SACRI-FICE YOUR-SELF?!

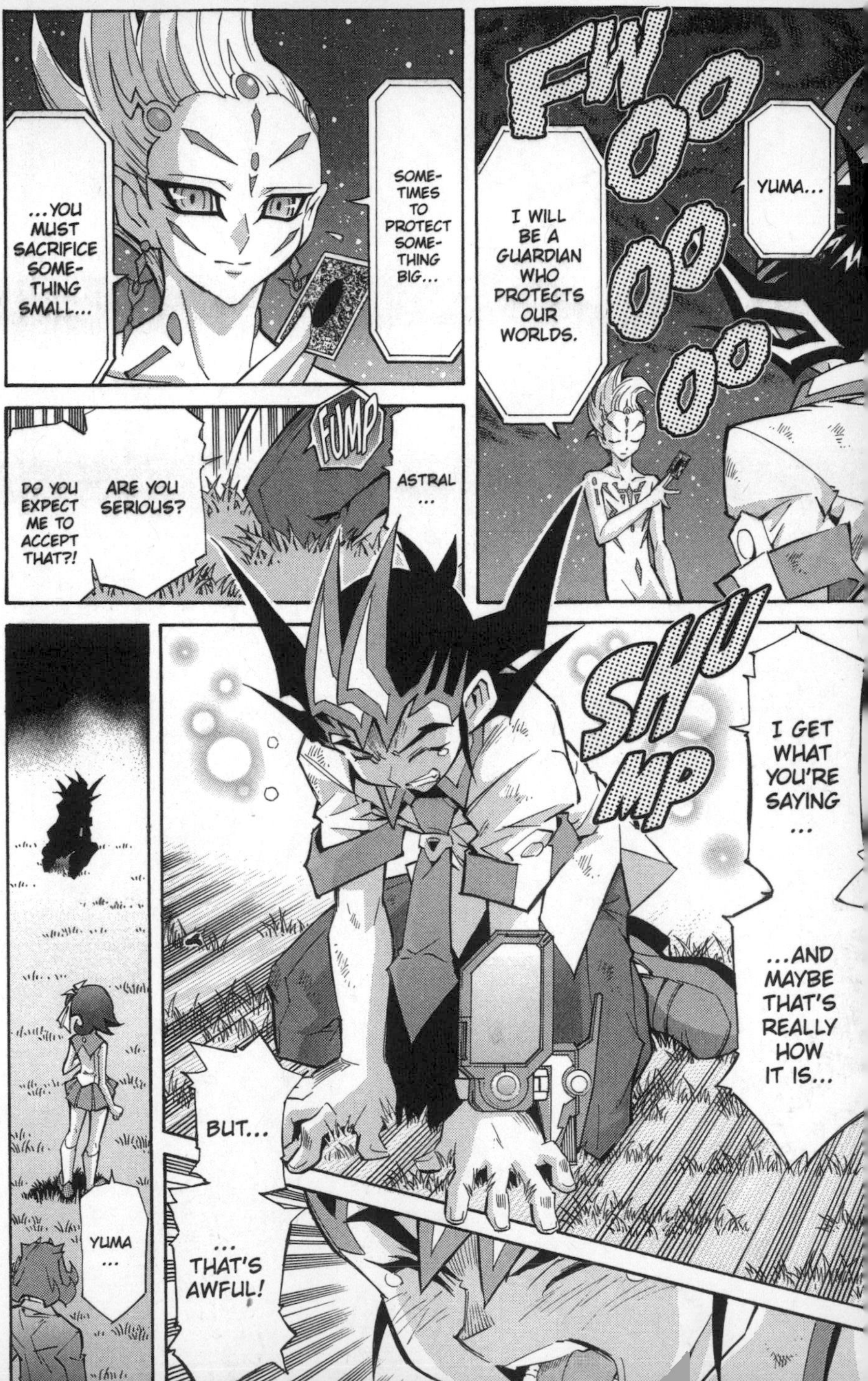
YUMA...
FWOOOOOOO
I WILL BE A GUARDIAN WHO PROTECTS OUR WORLDS.
SOMETIMES TO PROTECT SOMETHING BIG...
...YOU MUST SACRIFICE SOMETHING SMALL...
ASTRAL...
FUMP
ARE YOU SERIOUS?
DO YOU EXPECT ME TO ACCEPT THAT?!
I GET WHAT YOU'RE SAYING...
SHUMP
...AND MAYBE THAT'S REALLY HOW IT IS...
BUT...
...THAT'S AWFUL!
YUMA...

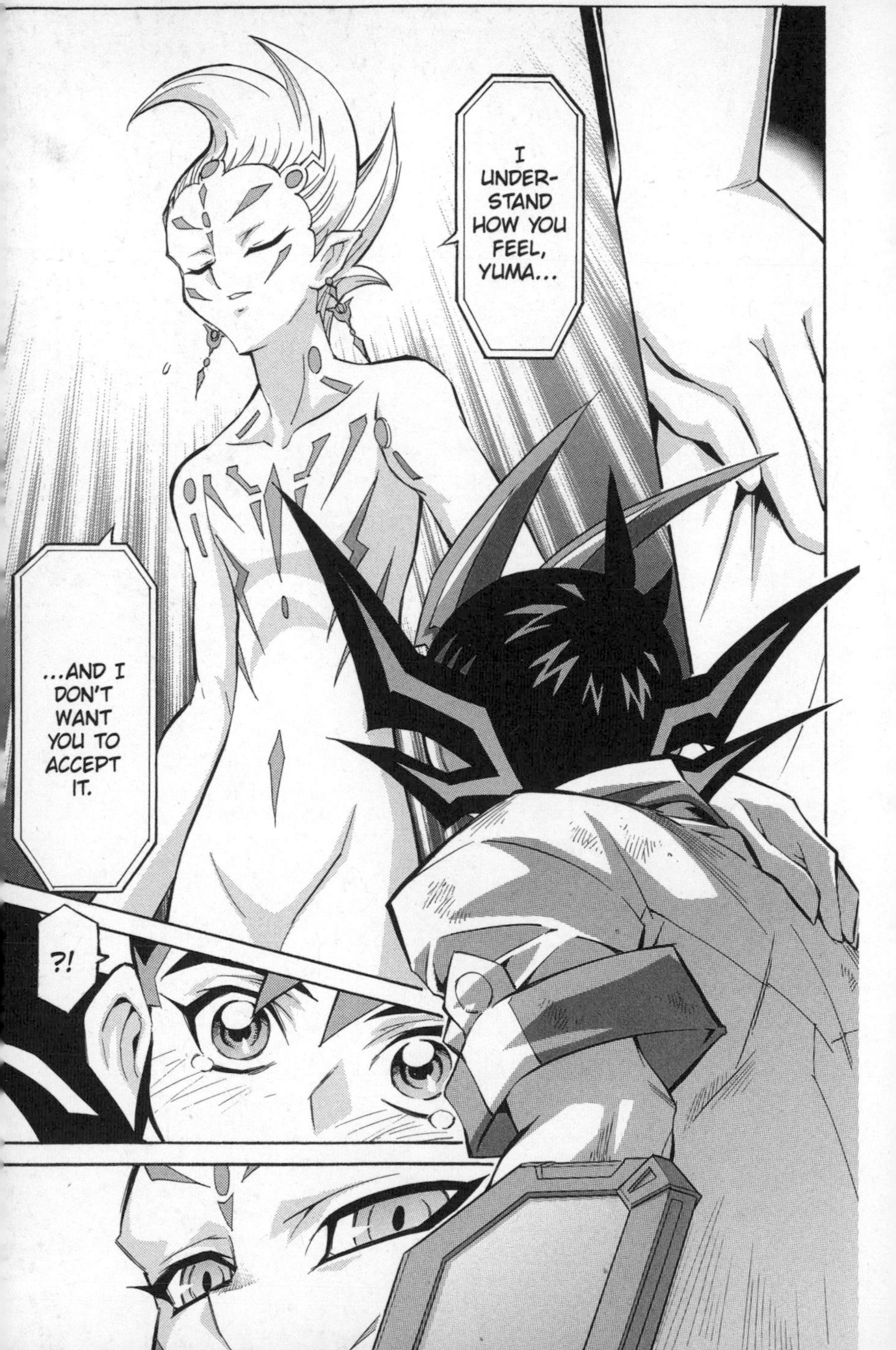
I UNDERSTAND HOW YOU FEEL, YUMA...
...AND I DON'T WANT YOU TO ACCEPT IT.
?!

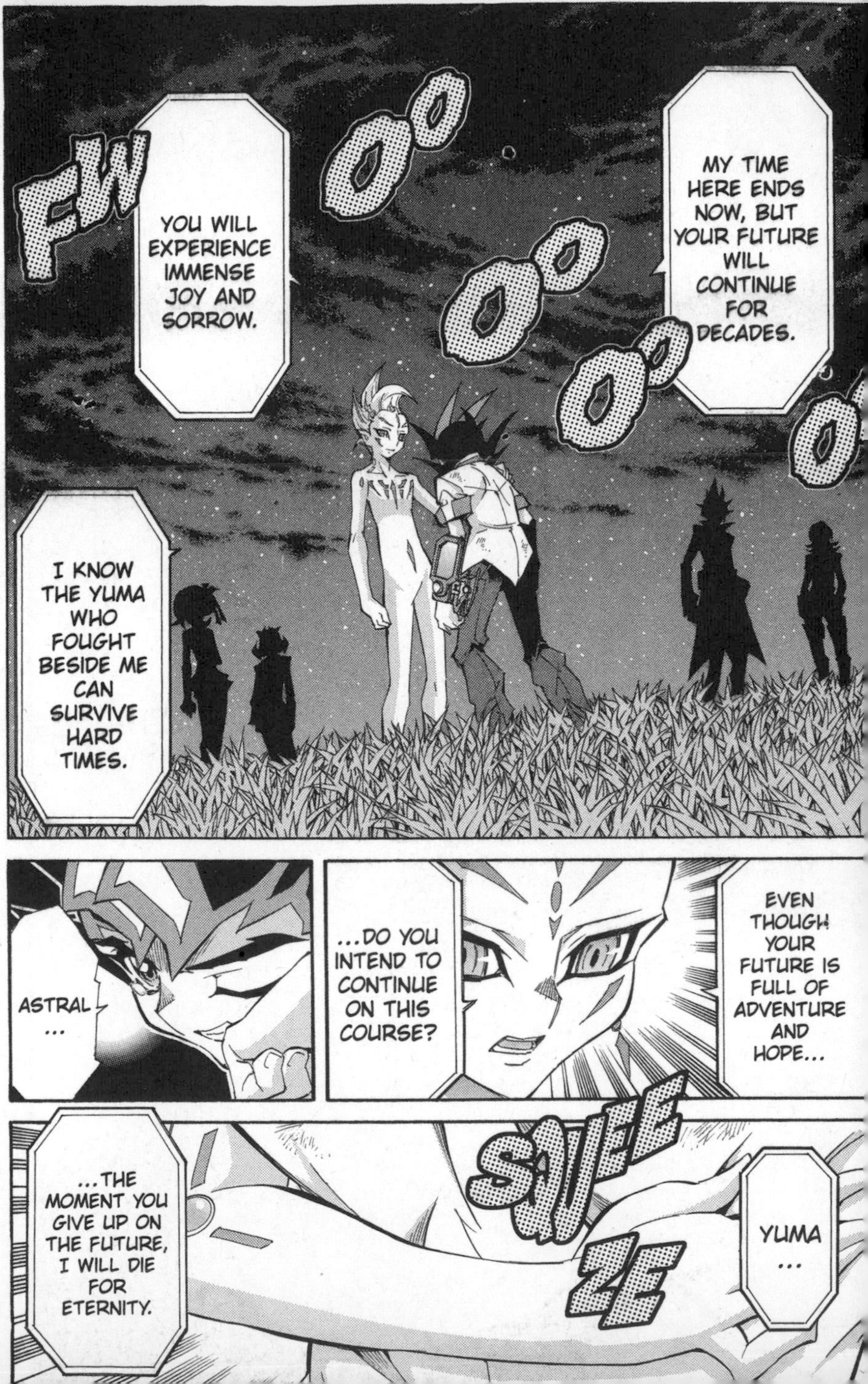
MY TIME HERE ENDS NOW, BUT YOUR FUTURE WILL CONTINUE FOR DECADES.
FWOOOOOO
YOU WILL EXPERIENCE IMMENSE JOY AND SORROW.
I KNOW THE YUMA WHO FOUGHT BESIDE ME CAN SURVIVE HARD TIMES.
EVEN THOUGH YOUR FUTURE IS FULL OF ADVENTURE AND HOPE...
...DO YOU INTEND TO CONTINUE ON THIS COURSE?
ASTRAL ...
YUMA ...
SQUEEZE
...THE MOMENT YOU GIVE UP ON THE FUTURE, I WILL DIE FOR ETERNITY.

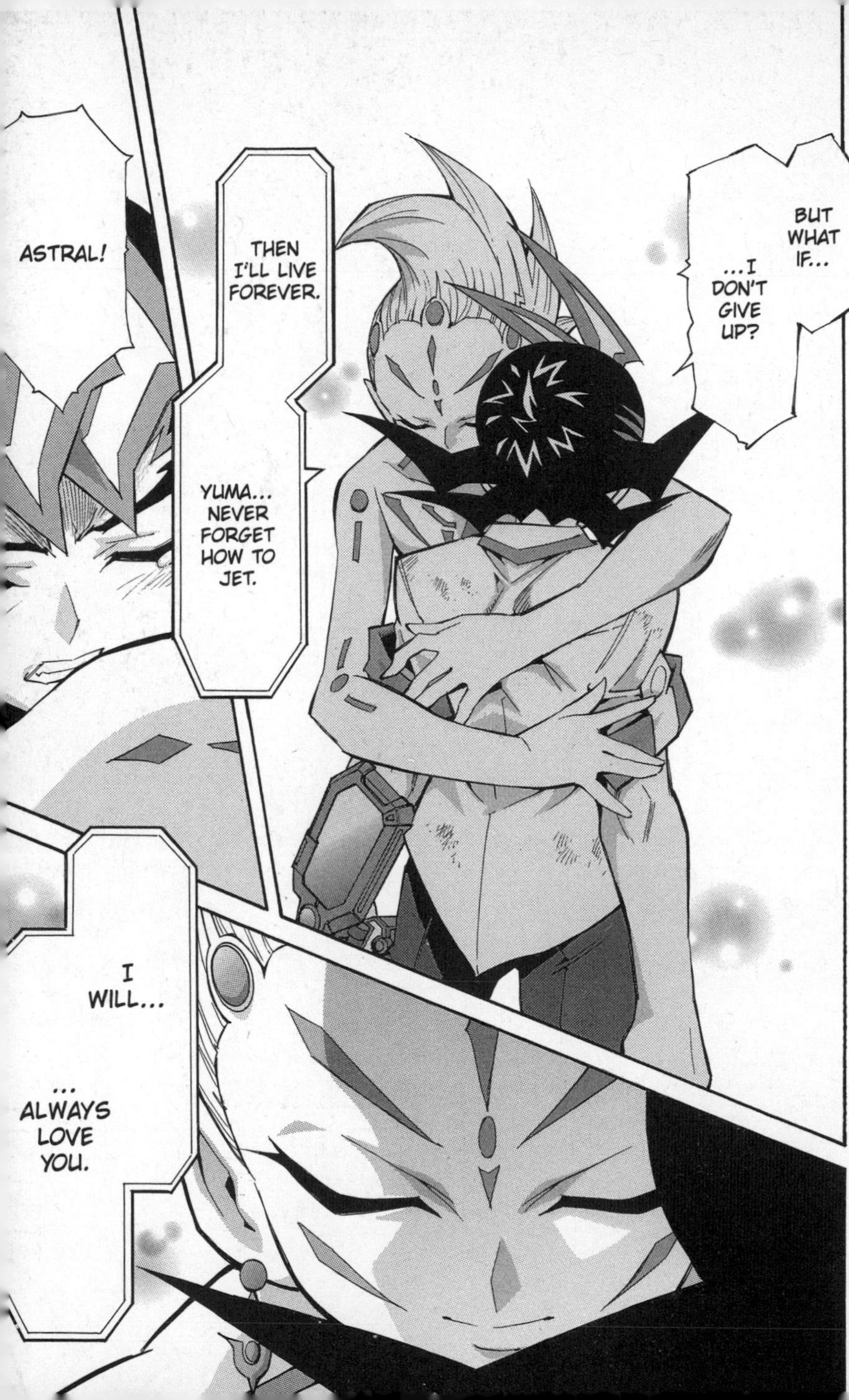
BUT WHAT IF...
...I DON'T GIVE UP?
THEN I'LL LIVE FOREVER.
ASTRAL!
YUMA... NEVER FORGET HOW TO JET.
I WILL...
...ALWAYS LOVE YOU.

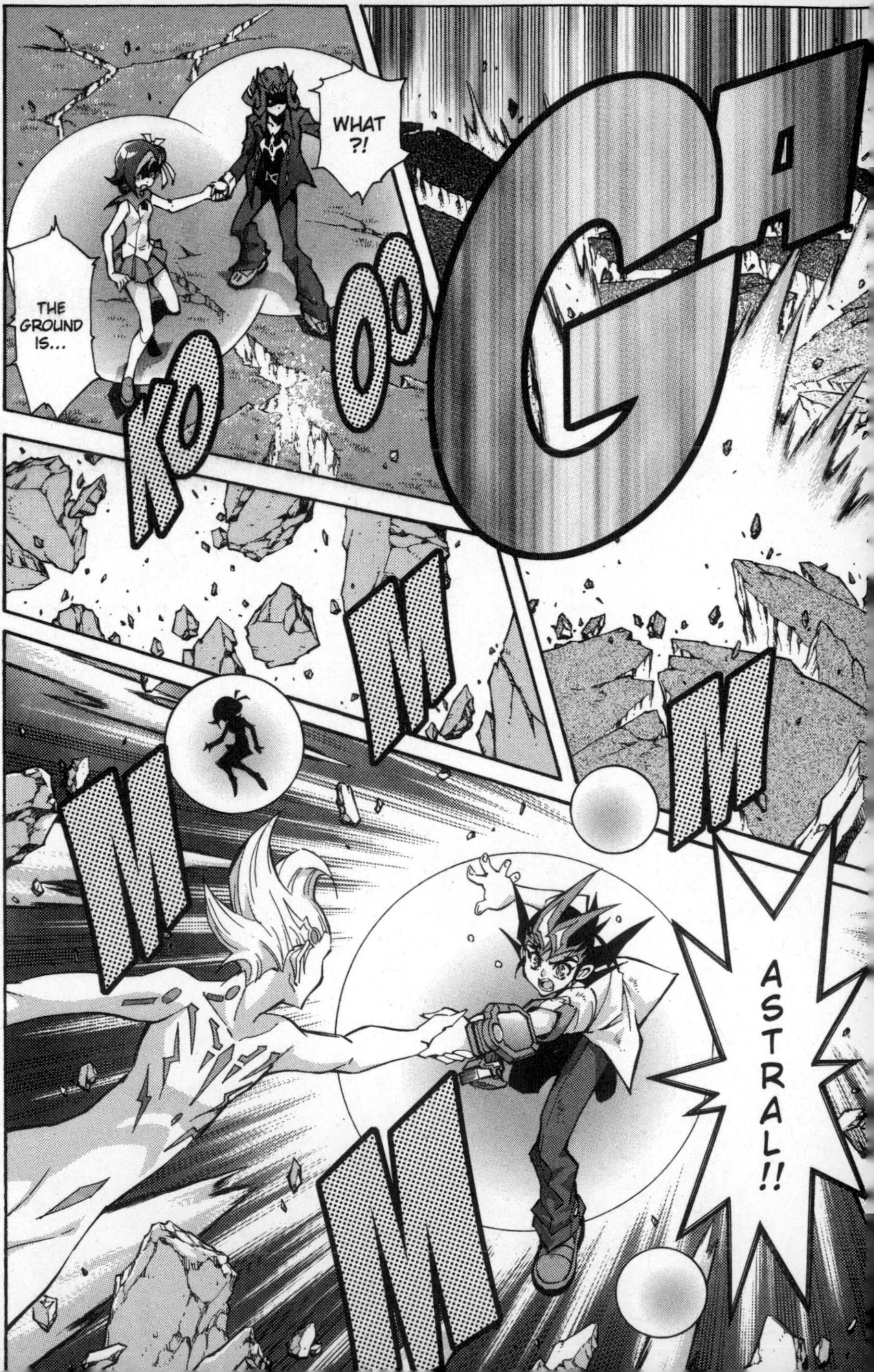
GA!
WHAT ?!
THE GROUND IS...
KOOOO
M
M
M
M
ASTRAL!!

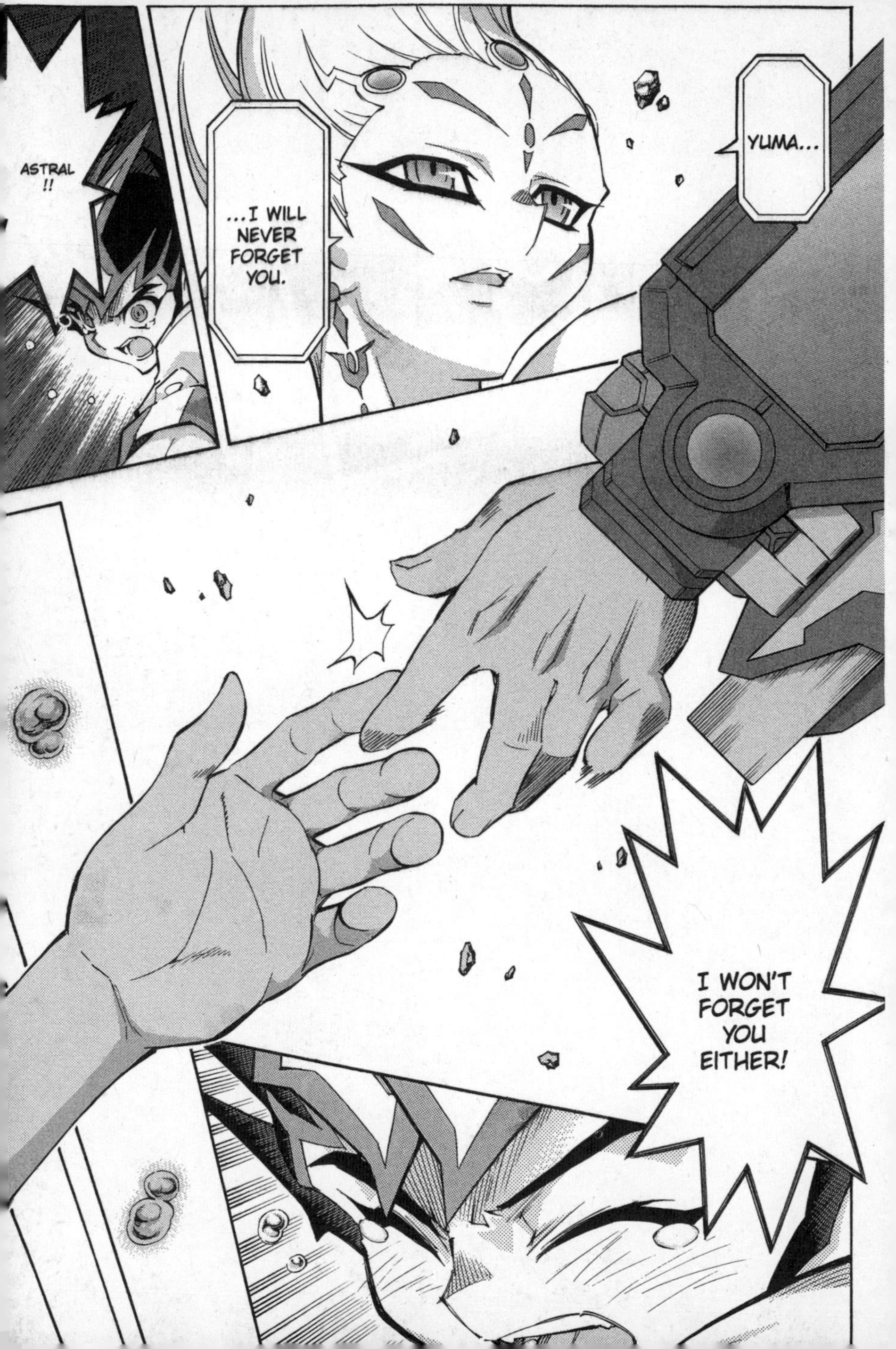
YUMA...
...I WILL NEVER FORGET YOU.
ASTRAL !!
I WON'T FORGET YOU EITHER!

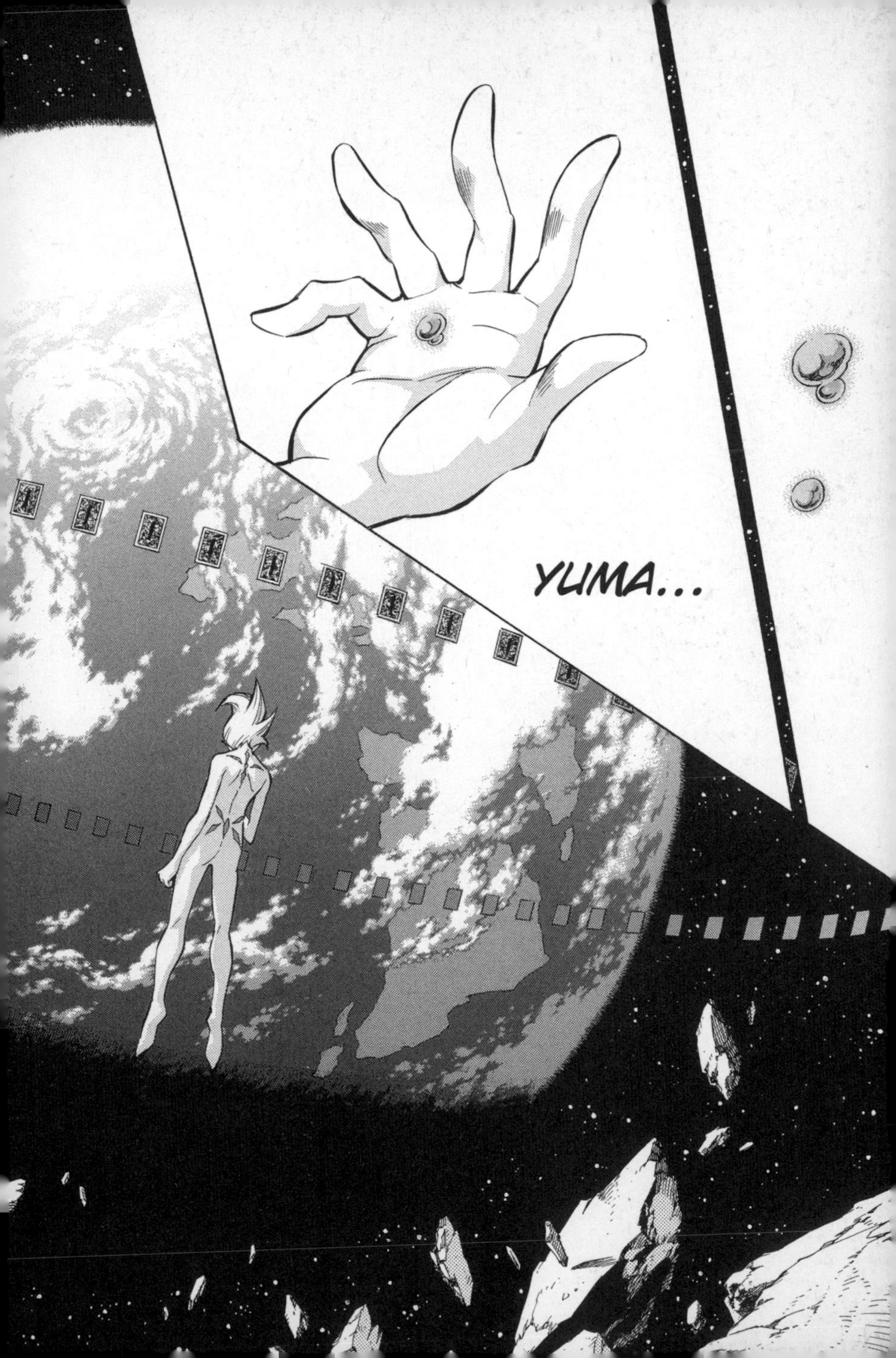
YUMA...

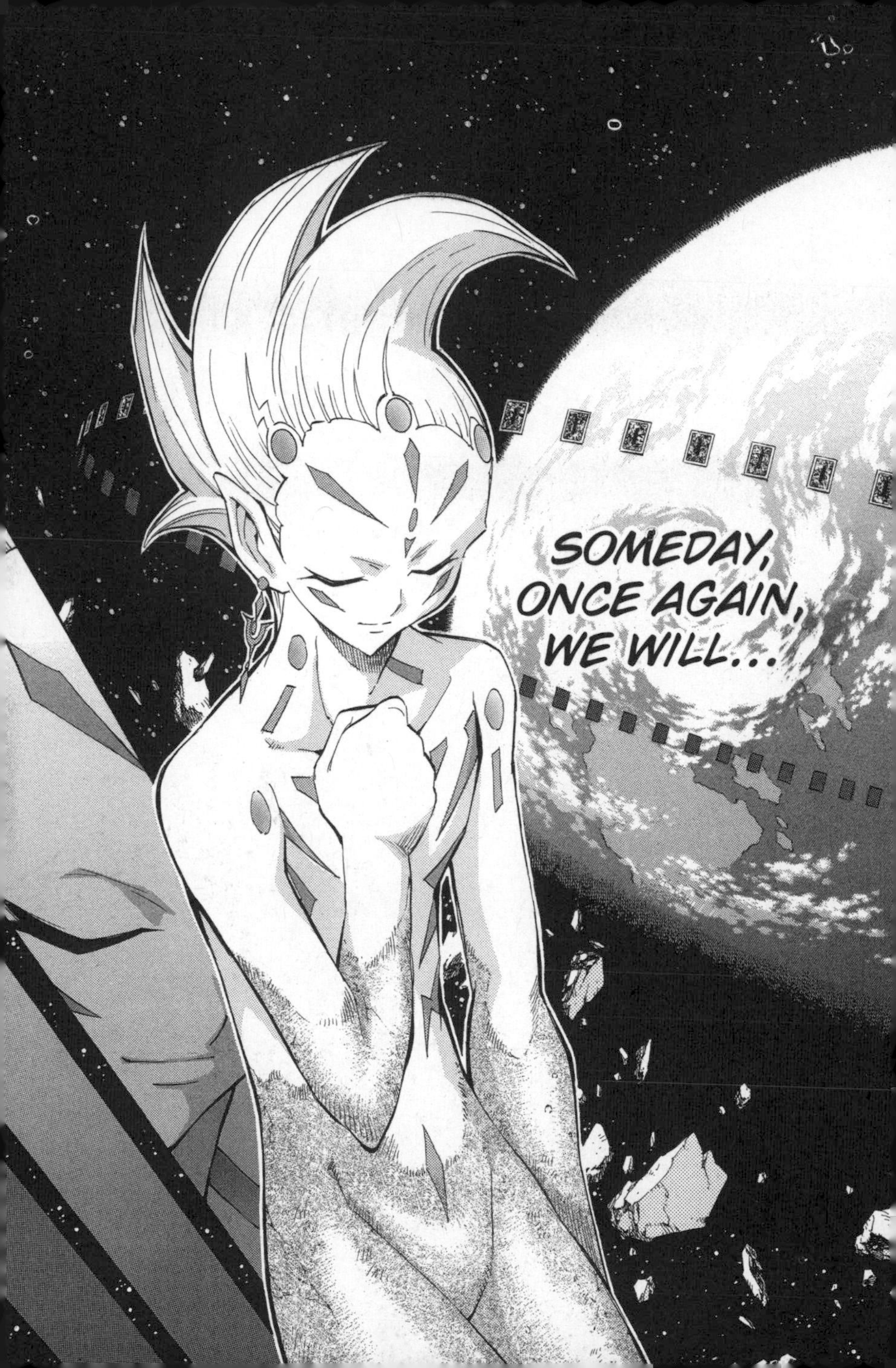
SOMEDAY, ONCE AGAIN, WE WILL...

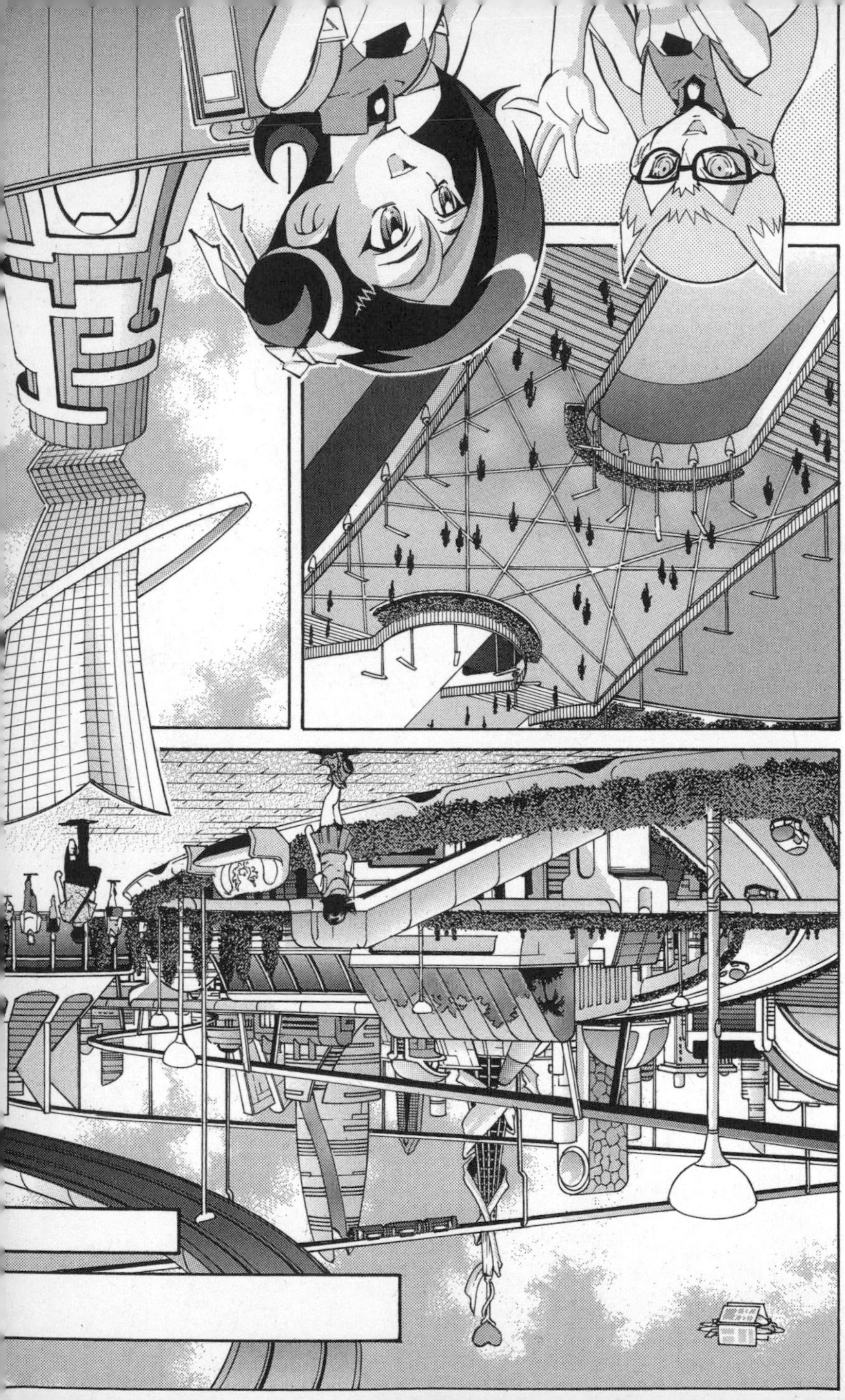

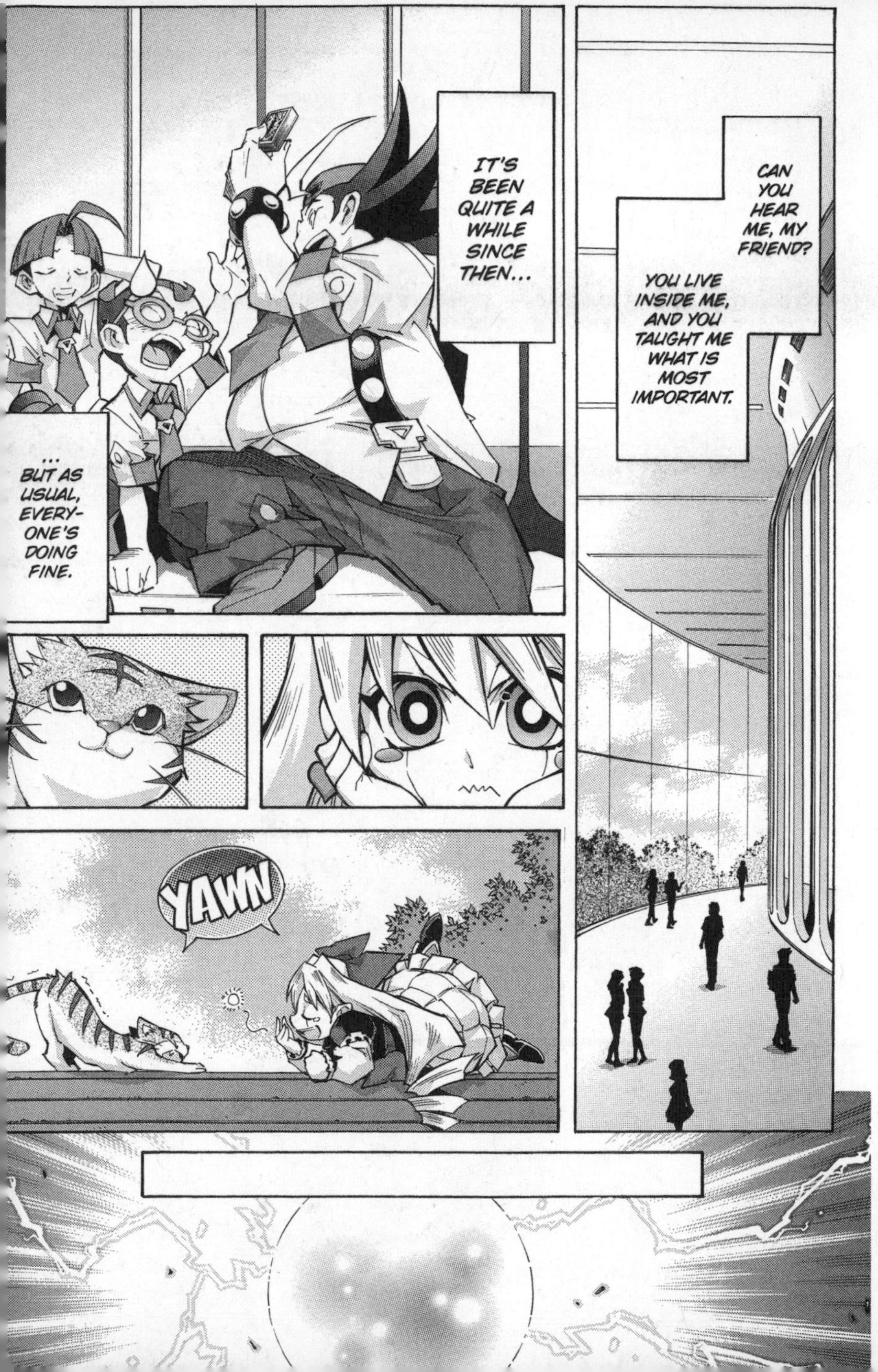
CAN YOU HEAR ME, MY FRIEND?
YOU LIVE INSIDE ME, AND YOU TAUGHT ME WHAT IS MOST IMPORTANT.
IT'S BEEN QUITE A WHILE SINCE THEN...
...BUT AS USUAL, EVERY-ONE'S DOING FINE.
YAWN

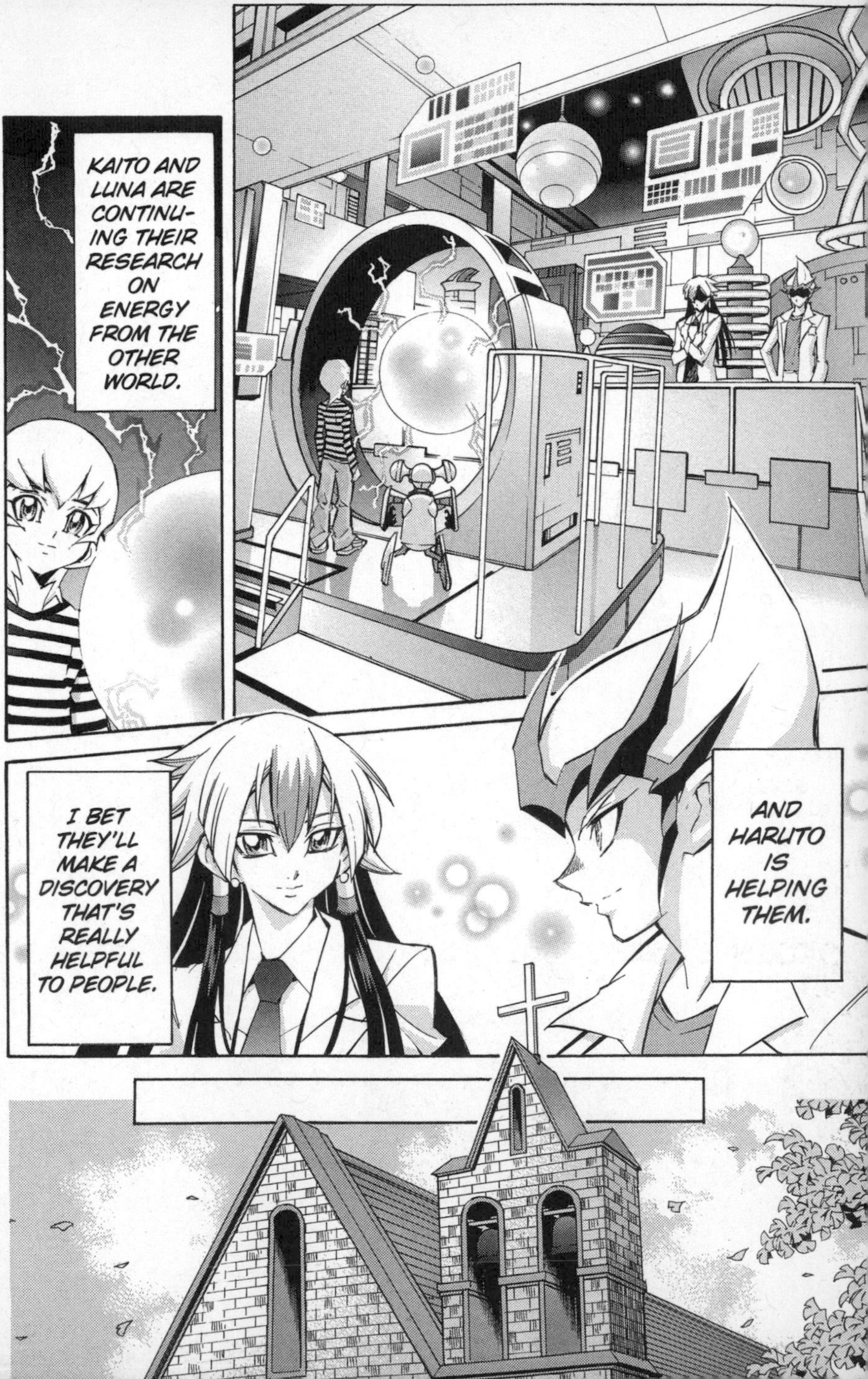
KAITO AND LUNA ARE CONTINU-ING THEIR RESEARCH ON ENERGY FROM THE OTHER WORLD.
AND HARUTO IS HELPING THEM.
I BET THEY'LL MAKE A DISCOVERY THAT'S REALLY HELPFUL TO PEOPLE.

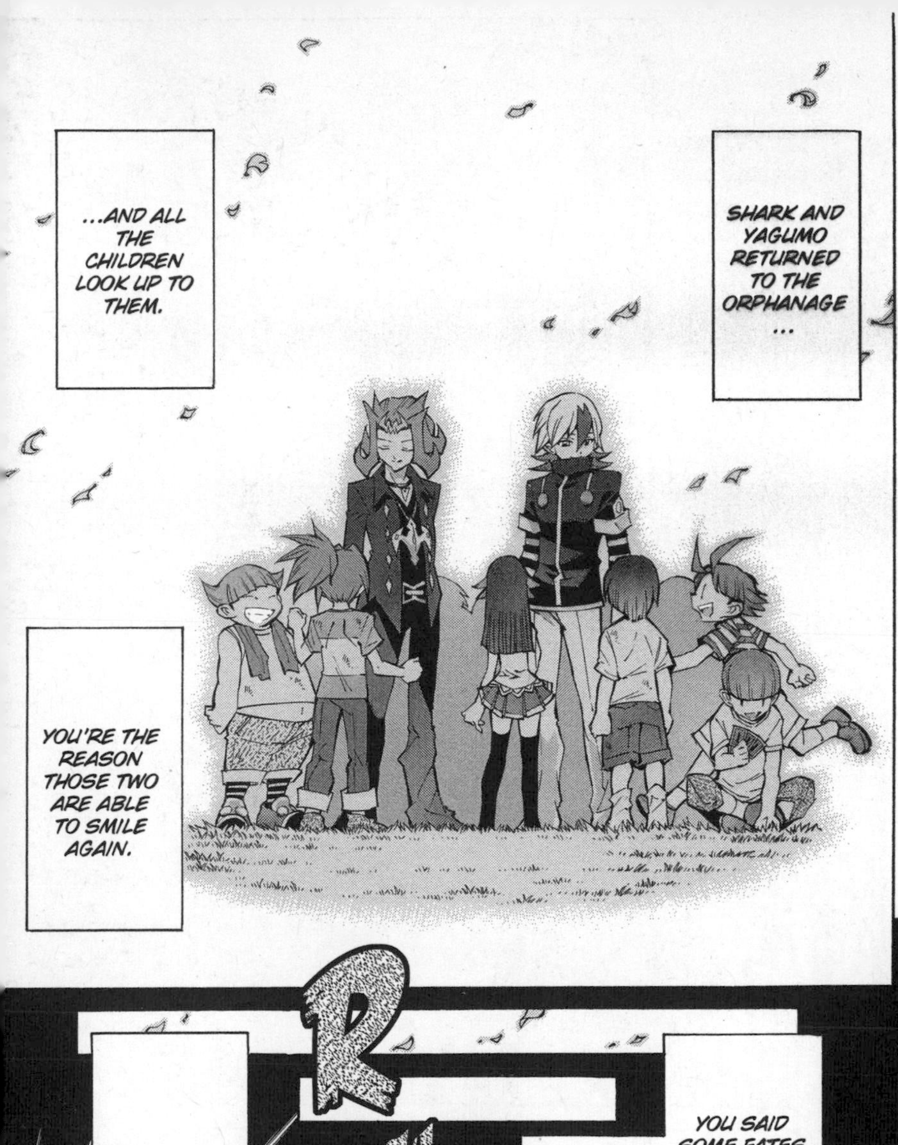
SHARK AND YAGUMO RETURNED TO THE ORPHANAGE ...
...AND ALL THE CHILDREN LOOK UP TO THEM.
YOU'RE THE REASON THOSE TWO ARE ABLE TO SMILE AGAIN.

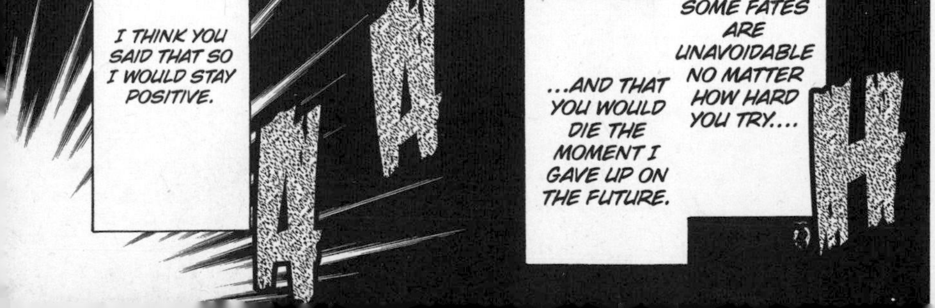
YOU SAID SOME FATES ARE UNAVOIDABLE NO MATTER HOW HARD YOU TRY....
...AND THAT YOU WOULD DIE THE MOMENT I GAVE UP ON THE FUTURE.
I THINK YOU SAID THAT SO I WOULD STAY POSITIVE.

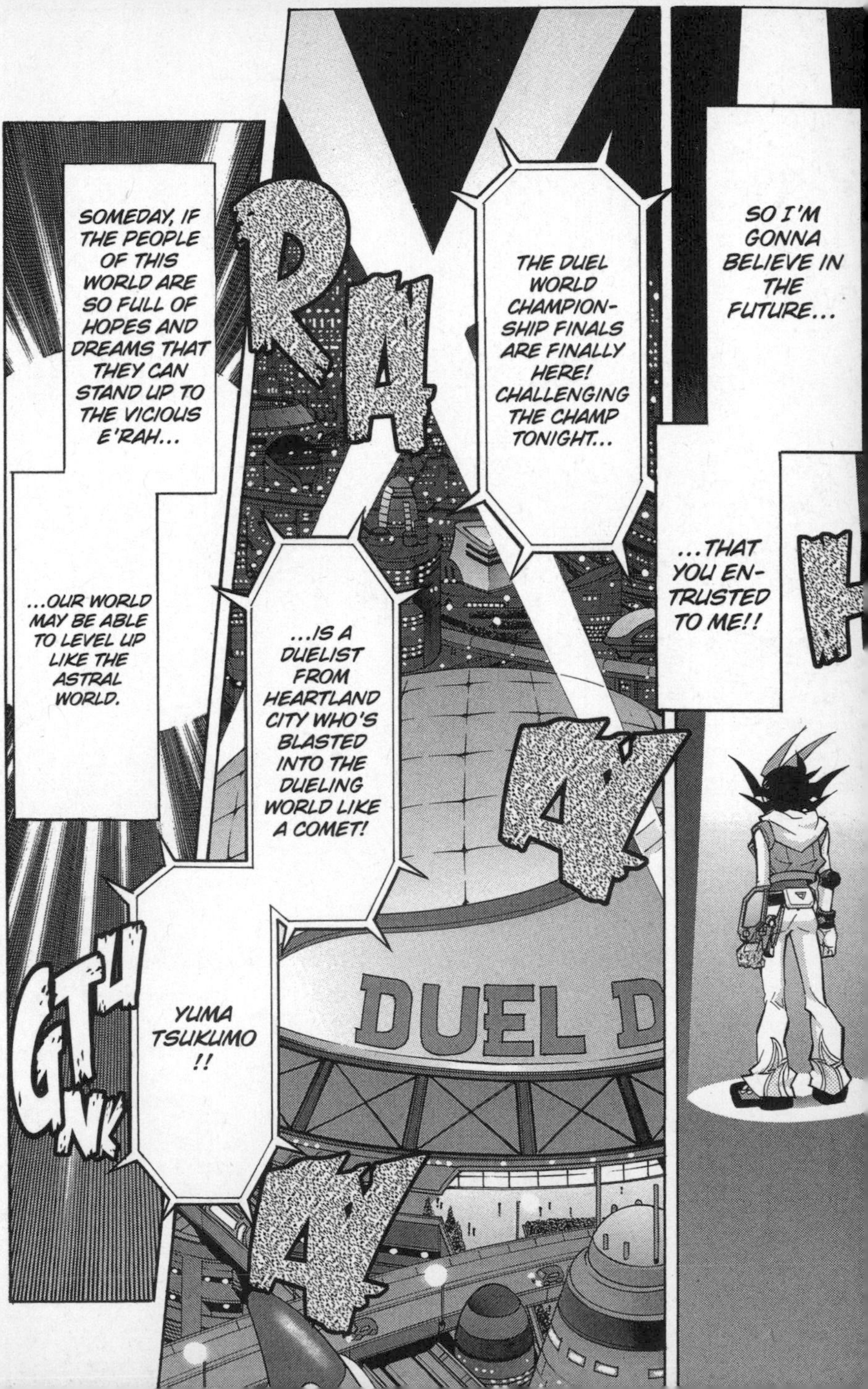
SO I'M GONNA BELIEVE IN THE FUTURE...
...THAT YOU EN-TRUSTED TO ME!!
THE DUEL WORLD CHAMPION-SHIP FINALS ARE FINALLY HERE! CHALLENGING THE CHAMP TONIGHT...
...IS A DUELIST FROM HEARTLAND CITY WHO'S BLASTED INTO THE DUELING WORLD LIKE A COMET!
YUMA TSUKUMO !!
DUEL D
SOMEDAY, IF THE PEOPLE OF THIS WORLD ARE SO FULL OF HOPES AND DREAMS THAT THEY CAN STAND UP TO THE VICIOUS E'RAH...
...OUR WORLD MAY BE ABLE TO LEVEL UP LIKE THE ASTRAL WORLD.

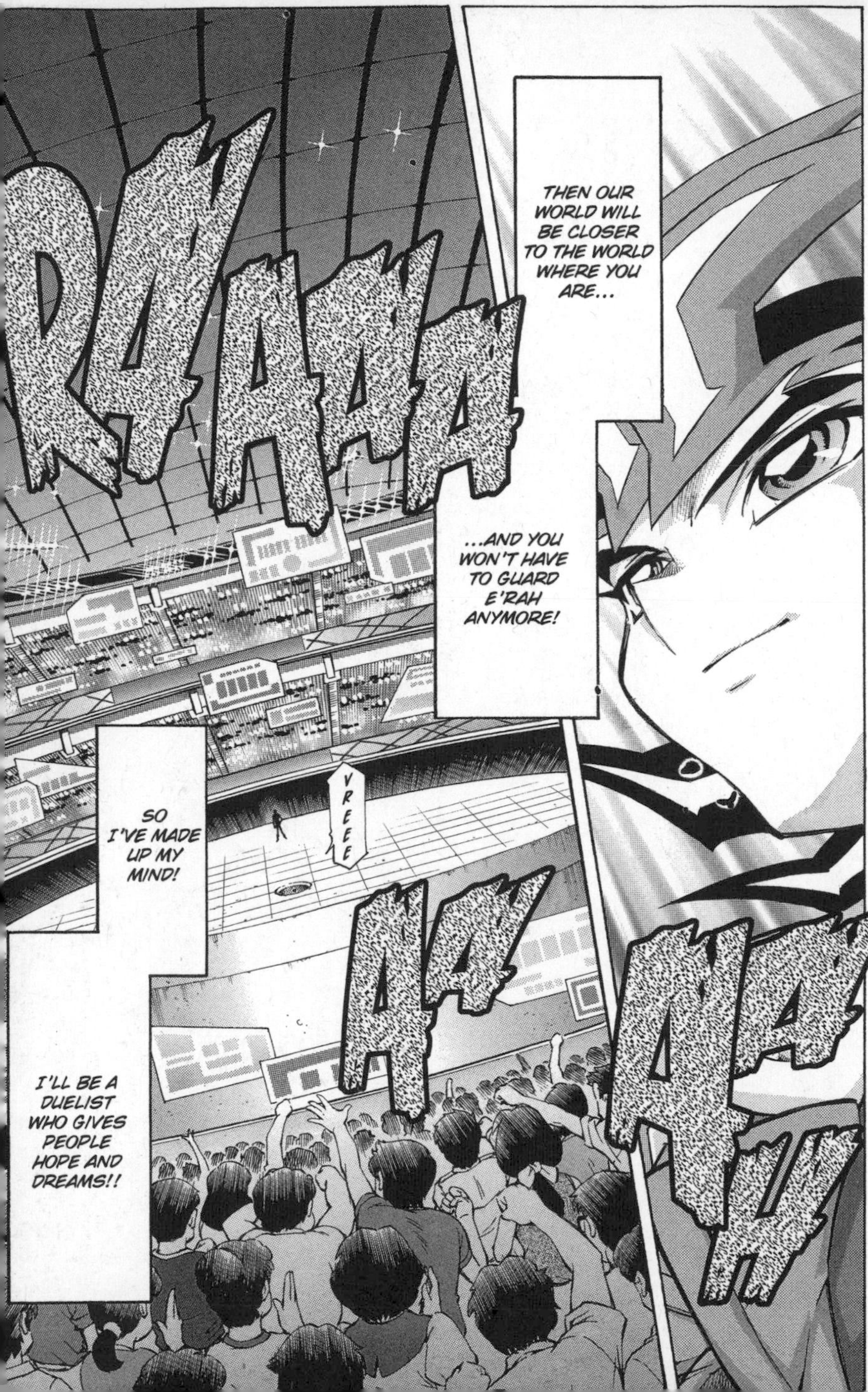
THEN OUR WORLD WILL BE CLOSER TO THE WORLD WHERE YOU ARE...
...AND YOU WON'T HAVE TO GUARD E'RAH ANYMORE!
RAAAAA
SO I'VE MADE UP MY MIND!
VREEE
I'LL BE A DUELIST WHO GIVES PEOPLE HOPE AND DREAMS!!
AAA
AAAH

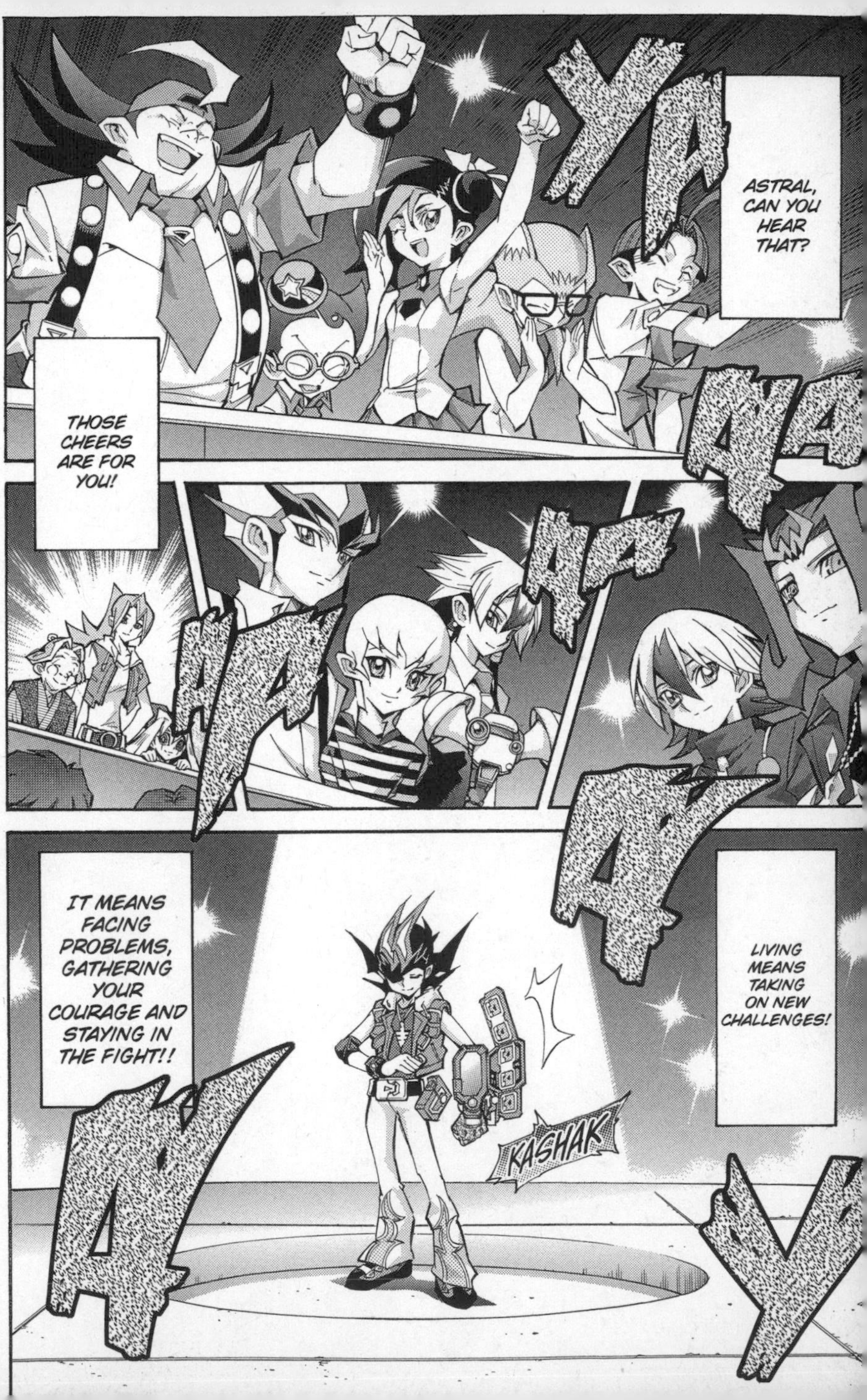
YAAAAAAAAAY
ASTRAL, CAN YOU HEAR THAT?
THOSE CHEERS ARE FOR YOU!
LIVING MEANS TAKING ON NEW CHALLENGES!
IT MEANS FACING PROBLEMS, GATHERING YOUR COURAGE AND STAYING IN THE FIGHT!!
KASHAK

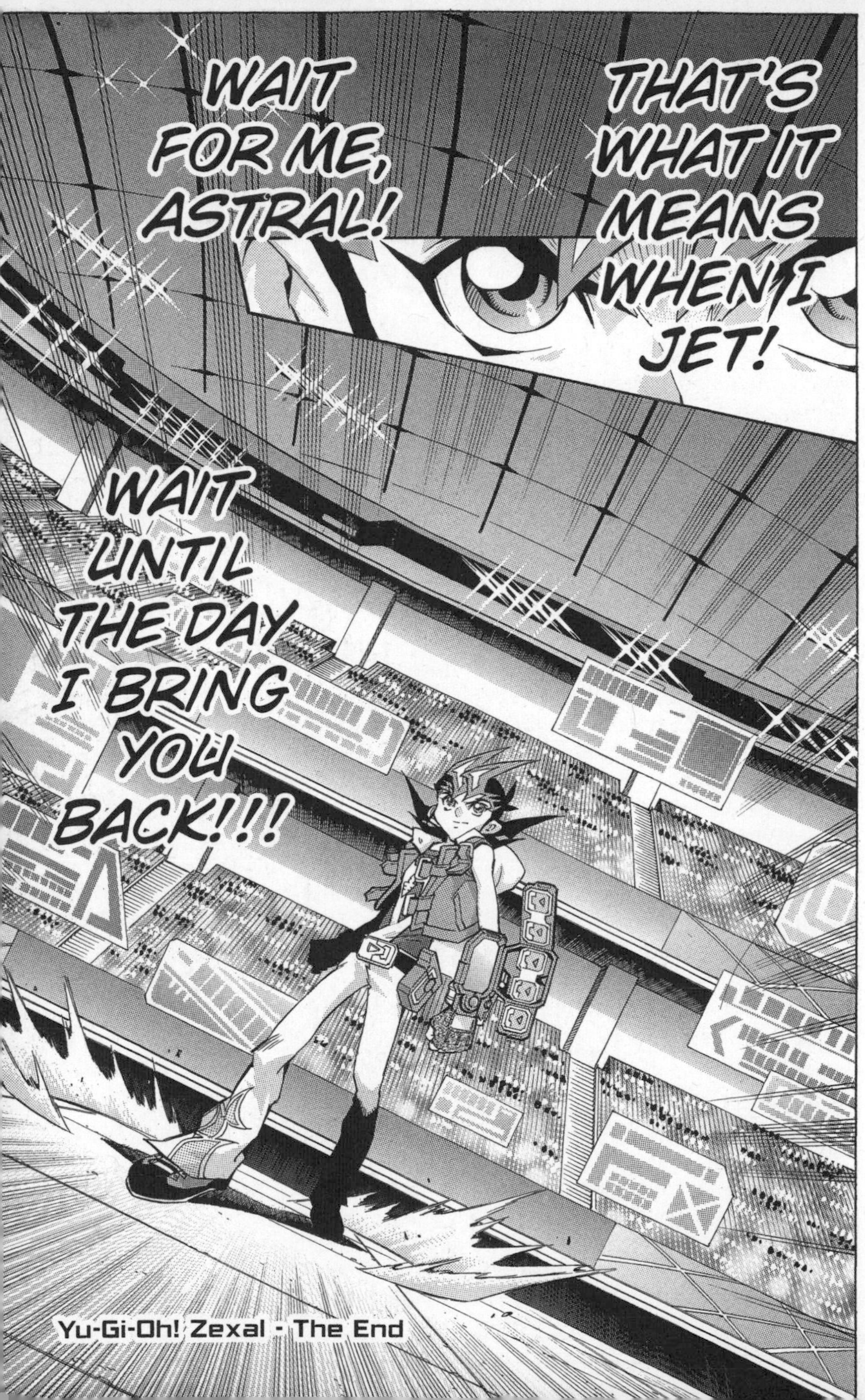
THAT'S WHAT IT MEANS WHEN I JET!
WAIT FOR ME, ASTRAL!
WAIT UNTIL THE DAY I BRING YOU BACK!!!
Yu-Gi-Oh! Zexal - The End

SHIN YOSHIDA SPEAKS:

FINAL

THE SAKE FLOWS... THE STORY PROGRESSES...

* Thoughts on the Final Volume

The *ZEXAL* manga has finally reached the last volume! Here at the end, it seems like it lasted a long time, but it actually wasn't that long. At the start, Takahashi Sensei told me the theme for the new series would be "ascension." I thought, "What's that supposed to mean?!" It feels like that was only yesterday.

I've been involved with *Yu-Gi-Oh!* for over ten years, but *ZEXAL* is actually the first series I've worked on from the beginning. Because of that, I formed an attachment to the characters that wasn't present while working on previous titles.

I had the most trouble with Yuma. I tried to make him an energetic, dumb and clumsy character whose actions would resonate with others. He got further and further into trouble but never wavered. He was really tough to write!

However, the guy writing him was wavering all over the place! (*sweating*)

Day after day, I tossed tough problems into the story and imagined what Yuma would do in those situations. His actions were a challenge for me. It was my first attempt at a manga, but I gave it and the anime everything I had, so it turned out to be a work full of memories for me.

In the end, I'm not sure whether everyone out there was satisfied with *ZEXAL*, but I'm very grateful to the readers who stuck with us all the way.

A MESSAGE FROM MIYOSHI SENSEI!

Yoshida Sensei, you did great! During meetings and things, I really picked up on the depth of your feeling for *Yu-Gi-Oh!* and your respect for Takahashi Sensei. Seeing someone with your record working so hard made me focus my energies too. A lot of talented people are involved with *Yu-Gi-Oh!* When I joined their ranks, I found each day more than challenging (lol), but it was fun! To all the readers, everyone who was involved and Takahashi Sensei...thank you very much!

BEHIND THE SCENES OF ZEXAL

* Thoughts on the Story's Conclusion

For crafting the end of the story, I thought, "What do I want to tell everyone?" And in a word, it's jetting—challenging yourself to stay in the fight! You can't get the wonderful things in life just by being alive. The only ones who get them are the people who've kept on challenging themselves and fighting.

Even then, you don't know whether you'll actually be able to get those things. That's reality, but you should still fight. It hurts and you need courage, but there's no other way if you want to help people or make someone happy. You mustn't run away. That's what I learned through taking on *ZEXAL*.

People will probably ask, "Isn't that kind of painful?" But I'm sure Yuma would keep fighting and wouldn't run away. When things get hard, I hope you remember that Yuma is still fighting even now. That's the message I put into the story.

Finally, to Miyoshi Sensei, Terashi-san, Aikawa-san and Uchida-san, I have to say thank you for all your hard work. And most of all, I want to thank Takahashi Sensei for giving me this opportunity.

Yoshida
Sensei!
Miyoshi
Sensei!
Thank you
for all your
work on this
long series!!

STAFF
Junya Uchino
Kazuo Ochiai
Masahiro Miura

SPECIAL THANKS
Tetsuya Ikeda
Toshiaki Kato
Daiji Fukusawa
Akihiko Miyamoto
Fumitaka Murayama
Atsuyuki Yasutomi!
Naoki Konno

COLORING
Toru Shimizu
Yokooka
(Studio Tac-Takumi)

EDITOR
Takahiko Aikawa

GALLOP
Wedge Holdings

YOU ARE READING IN THE WRONG DIRECTION!!

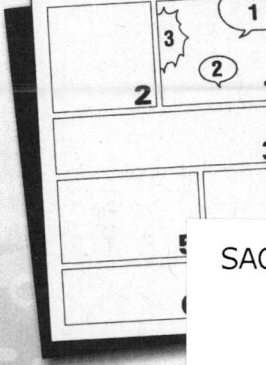

**Whoops!
Guess what?**
You're starting at the wrong end
of the comic!

...It's true! In keeping with the original Japanese format, *Yu-Gi-Oh! ZEXAL* is meant to be read from right to left, starting in the upper-right corner.

Unlike English, which is read from left to right, Japanese is read from right to left, meaning that action, sound effects and word-balloon order are completely reversed... something which can make readers unfamiliar with Japanese feel pretty backwards themselves. For this reason, manga or Japanese comics published in the U.S. in English have sometimes been published "flopped"—that is, printed in exact reverse order, as though seen from the other side of a mirror.

By flopping pages, U.S. publishers can avoid confusing readers, but the compromise is not without its downside. For one thing, a character in a flopped manga series who once wore in the original Japanese version a T-shirt emblazoned with "M A Y" (as in "the merry month of") now wears one which reads "Y A M"! Additionally, many manga creators in Japan are themselves unhappy with the process, as some feel the mirror-imaging of their art alters their original intentions.

We are proud to bring you Shin Yoshida and Naohito Miyoshi's *Yu-Gi-Oh! ZEXAL* in the original unflopped format. For now, though, turn to the other side of the book and let the duel begin...!

—Editor